FOURTH EDITION

Series Director: **Diane Larsen-Freeman**

Grammar Dimensions

Form • Meaning • Use

Jan Frodesen
Janet Eyring

HEINLE
CENGAGE Learning™

Australia • Brazil • Japan • Korea • Mexico • Singapore • Spain • United Kingdom • United States

Series Director: Diane Larsen-Freeman:
Grammar Dimensions 4: Form, Meaning, and
Use, Fourth Edition
Jan Frodesen, Janet Eyring

Publisher: Sherrise Roehr

Consulting Editor: James W. Brown

Acquisitions Editor, Academic ESL:
   Tom Jefferies

Director of Content Development:
   Anita Raducanu

Director of Product Marketing: Amy Mabley

Executive Marketing Manager: Jim McDonough

Senior Field Marketing Manager:
   Donna Lee Kennedy

Development Editor: Michael Ryall

Editorial Assistants: Katherine Reilly,
   Emily Dedinger

Senior Production Editor:
   Maryellen Eschmann-Killeen

Senior Print Buyer: Mary Beth Hennebury

Development Editors:
   Amy Lawler, Sarah Barnicle

Production Project Manager: Chrystie Hopkins

Production Services: Pre-Press PMG

Interior Designer: Lori Stuart

Cover Designer: Studio Montage

Cover Image: ©Ben Hall/
   The Image Bank/Getty

© 2007 Heinle, Cengage Learning

ALL RIGHTS RESERVED. No part of this work covered by the copyright herein may be reproduced, transmitted, stored or used in any form or by any means graphic, electronic, or mechanical, including but not limited to photocopying, recording, scanning, digitizing, taping, Web distribution, information networks, or information storage and retrieval systems, except as permitted under Section 107 or 108 of the 1976 United States Copyright Act, without the prior written permission of the publisher.

For product information and technology assistance, contact us at
Cengage Learning Customer & Sales Support, 1-800-354-9706

For permission to use material from this text or product,
submit all requests online at **www.cengage.com/permissions**
Further permissions questions can be emailed to
permissionrequest@cengage.com

Library of Congress Control Number: 2007924053

ISBN-13: 978-1-4130-2752-5

ISBN-10: 1-4130-2752-0

International Student Edition

ISBN-13: 978-1-4130-2756-3

ISBN-10: 1-4130-2756-3

Heinle
20 Channel Center Street,
Boston, MA 02210
USA

Cengage Learning is a leading provider of customized learning solutions with office locations around the globe, including Singapore, the United Kingdom, Australia, Mexico, Brazil, and Japan. Locate your local office at **international.cengage.com/region**

Cengage Learning products are represented in Canada by Nelson Education, Ltd.

Visit Heinle online at **elt.heinle.com**

Visit our corporate website at **www.cengage.com**

Credits appear on pages C1–C4, which constitutes a continuation of the copyright page.

Printed in China by China Translation & Printing Services Limited
2 3 4 5 6 7 11 10 09

CONTENTS

Unit 14   Discourse Organizers   260

Unit 15   Conditionals
If, Only If, Unless, Even Though, Even If   280

Appendices   A-1

Answer Key   (Puzzles and Problems Only)   A-16

Exercises   (Second Parts)   A-17

Credits   C-1

Index   I-1

A Word from Diane Larsen-Freeman, Series Editor

Before *Grammar Dimensions* was published, teachers would ask me, "What is the role of grammar in a communicative approach?" These teachers recognized the importance of teaching grammar, but they associated grammar with form and communication with meaning, and thus could not see how the two easily fit together. *Grammar Dimensions* was created to help teachers and students appreciate the fact that grammar is not just about form. While grammar does indeed involve form, in order to communicate, language users also need to know the meaning of the forms and when to use them appropriately. In fact, it is sometimes not the form, but the *meaning* or *appropriate use* of a grammatical structure that represents the greatest long-term learning challenge for students. For instance, learning when it is appropriate to use the present perfect tense instead of the past tense, or being able to use two-word or phrasal verbs meaningfully, represent formidable challenges for English language learners.

The three dimensions of *form*, *meaning*, and *use* can be depicted in a pie chart with their interrelationship illustrated by the three arrows:

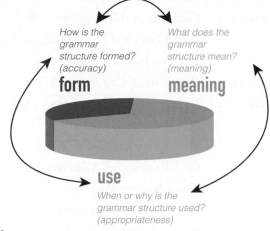

Helping students learn to use grammatical structures accurately, meaningfully, and appropriately is the fundamental goal of *Grammar Dimensions.* It is consistent with the goal of helping students to communicate meaningfully in English, and one that recognizes the undeniable interdependence of grammar and communication.

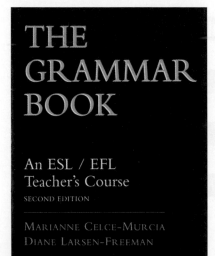

To learn more about form, meaning, and use, read *The Grammar Book: An ESL/EFL Teacher's Course,* Second Edition, by Marianne Celce-Murcia and Diane Larsen-Freeman. ISBN: 0-8384-4725-2.

To understand more about teaching grammar effectively, read *Teaching Language: From Grammar to Grammaring* by Diane Larsen-Freeman. ISBN: 0-8384-6675-3.

Enjoy the Fourth Edition of *Grammar Dimensions*!

Welcome to *Grammar Dimensions*, Fourth Edition!

The **clearest**, most **comprehensive** and **communicative** grammar series available! The fourth edition of *Grammar Dimensions* is more **user-friendly** and makes teaching grammar more **effective** than ever.

 ## *GRAMMAR DIMENSIONS* IS COMPREHENSIVE AND CLEAR.

Grammar Dimensions systematically addresses the three dimensions of language—form, meaning, and use—through clear and comprehensive grammar explanations and extensive practice exercises. Each unit methodically focuses on each student's dimension and then integrates what they have learned in end-of-unit activities. In addition, grammatical structures are recycled throughout the series allowing students to practice and build upon their existing knowledge.

 ## *GRAMMAR DIMENSIONS* IS COMMUNICATIVE.

Grammar Dimensions includes a large variety of lively, communicative, and personalized activities throughout each unit, eliciting self-expression and personalized practice. Interactive activities at the start of each unit serve as diagnostic tools directing student learning towards the most challenging dimensions of language structure. Integrated activities at the end of each unit include reading, writing, listening, and speaking activities allowing students to practice grammar and communication in tandem. New research activities encourage students to use authentic Internet resources and to reflect on their own learning.

 ## *GRAMMAR DIMENSIONS* IS USER-FRIENDLY AND FLEXIBLE.

Grammar Dimensions has been designed to be flexible. Instructors can use the units in order or as set by their curriculum. Exercises can be used in order or as needed by the students. In addition, a tight integration between the Student Book, the Workbook, and the Lesson Planner makes teaching easier and makes the series more user-friendly.

GRAMMAR DIMENSIONS IS EFFECTIVE.

Students who learn the form, meaning, and use of each grammar structure will be able to communicate more accurately, meaningfully, and appropriately.

New to the Fourth Edition

■ **NEW and revised grammar explanations** and examples help students and teachers easily understand and comprehend each language structure.

■ **NEW and revised grammar charts and exercises** provide a wealth of opportunities for students to practice and master their new language.

■ **NEW thematically and grammatically related Internet and *InfoTrac®College Edition*** activities in every unit of books 2, 3, and 4 develop student research using current technologies.

■ **NEW Reflection activities** encourage students to create personal language goals and to develop learning strategies.

■ **NEW design, art, and photos** make each activity and exercise more engaging.

■ **NEW Lesson Planners** assist both beginning and experienced teachers in giving their students the practice and skills they need to communicate accurately, meaningfully, and appropriately. All activities and exercises in the Lesson Planner are organized into step-by-step lessons so that no instructor feels overwhelmed.

SEQUENCING OF *GRAMMAR DIMENSIONS*

In *Grammar Dimensions* students progress from the sentence level to the discourse level, and learn to communicate appropriately at all levels.

Grammar Dimensions Book 1	Grammar Dimensions Book 2	Grammar Dimensions Book 3	Grammar Dimensions Book 4

Sentence level → Discourse level

	Book 1	**Book 2**	**Book 3**	**Book 4**
Level	High-beginning	Intermediate	High-Intermediate	Advanced
Grammar level	Sentence and sub-sentence level	Sentence and sub-sentence level	Discourse level	Discourse level
Primary language and communication focus	Semantic notions such as *time* and *place*	Social functions, such as *making requests* and *seeking* permission	Cohesion and coherence at the discourse level	Academic and technical discourse
Major skill focus	Listening and speaking	Listening and speaking	Reading and writing	Reading and writing

Guided Tour of *Grammar Dimensions* 4

Unit goals **provide a roadmap** for the grammar points students will work on.

"Opening Task" can be used as a **diagnostic warm-up** exercise to explore students' knowledge of each structure.

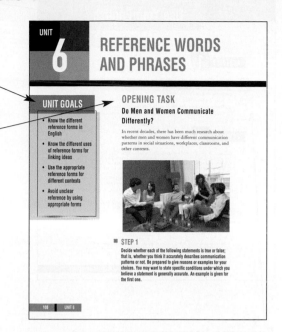

UNIT 6

REFERENCE WORDS AND PHRASES

UNIT GOALS

- Know the different reference forms in English
- Know the different uses of reference forms for linking ideas
- Use the appropriate reference forms for different contexts
- Avoid unclear reference by using appropriate forms

OPENING TASK

Do Men and Women Communicate Differently?

In recent decades, there has been much research about whether men and women have different communication patterns in social situations, workplaces, classrooms, and other contexts.

■ STEP 1

Decide whether each of the following statements is true or false; that is, whether you think it accurately describes communication patterns or not. Be prepared to give reasons or examples for your choices. You may want to state specific conditions under which you believe a statement is generally accurate. An example is given for the first one.

188 UNIT 6

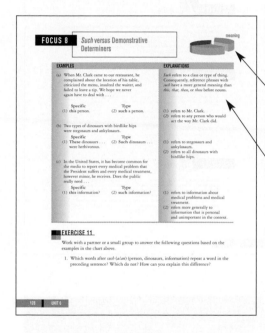

FOCUS 8 *Such* versus Demonstrative Determiners

meaning

EXAMPLES

(a) When Mr. Clark came to our restaurant, he complained about the location of his table, criticized the menu, insulted the waiter, and failed to leave a tip. We hope we never again have to deal with . . .

	Specific	Type
(1) this person.		(2) such a person.

(b) Two types of dinosaurs with birdlike hips were stegosaurs and ankylosaurs.

	Specific	Type
(1) These dinosaurs . . . were herbivorous.		(2) Such dinosaurs . . .

(c) In the United States, it has become common for the media to report every medical problem that the President suffers and every medical treatment, however minor, he receives. Does the public really need . . .

	Specific	Type
(1) this information?		(2) such information?

EXPLANATIONS

Such refers to a class or type of thing. Consequently, reference phrases with *such* have a more general meaning than *this, that, these,* or *those* before nouns.

(1) refers to Mr. Clark.
(2) refers to any person who would act the way Mr. Clark did.

(1) refers to stegosaurs and ankylosaurs.
(2) refers to all dinosaurs with birdlike hips.

(1) refers to information about medical problems and medical treatment.
(2) refers more generally to information that is personal and unimportant in the context.

■ **EXERCISE 11**

Work with a partner or a small group to answer the following questions based on the examples in the chart above.

1. Which words after *such (a/an)* (person, dinosaurs, information) repeat a word in the preceding sentence? Which do not? How can you explain this difference?

128 UNIT 6

"Focus" sections present the **form, meaning,** and/or **use** of a particular structure helping students develop the skill of "**grammaring**"—the ability to use structures accurately, meaningfully, and appropriately.

Clear grammar charts present rules and explanation preceded by examples, so teachers can have students work inductively to try to discover the rule on their own.

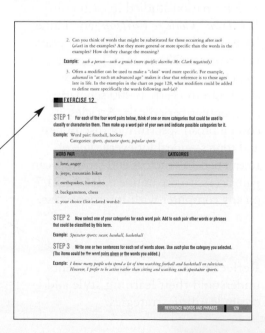

2. Can you think of words that might be substituted for those occurring after *such (a/an)* in the examples? Are they more general or more specific than the words in the examples? How do they change the meaning?

Example: *such a person—such a grouch (more specific; describes Mr. Clark negatively)*

3. Often a modifier can be used to make a "class" word more specific. For example, *advanced* in "at such an advanced age" makes it clear that reference is to those ages late in life. In the examples in the chart on page 128, what modifiers could be added to define more specifically the words following *such (a)*?

■ **EXERCISE 12**

STEP 1   For each of the four word pairs below, think of one or more categories that could be used to classify or characterize them. Then make up a word pair of your own and indicate possible categories for it.

Example: Word pair: football, hockey
Categories: *sports, spectator sports, popular sports*

WORD PAIR	CATEGORIES
a. love, anger	
b. jeeps, mountain bikes	
c. earthquakes, hurricanes	
d. backgammon, chess	
e. your choice (list-related words): ____	

STEP 2   Now select one of your categories for each word pair. Add to each pair other words or phrases that could be classified by this term.

Example: *Spectator sports: soccer, baseball, basketball*

STEP 3   Write one or two sentences for each set of words above. Use *such* plus the category you selected. (The items could be the word pairs given or the words you added.)

Example: *I know many people who spend a lot of time watching football and basketball on television. However, I prefer to be active rather than sitting and watching such spectator sports.*

Purposeful exercises provide a wealth of opportunity for students to practice and personalize the grammar.

REFERENCE WORDS AND PHRASES   129

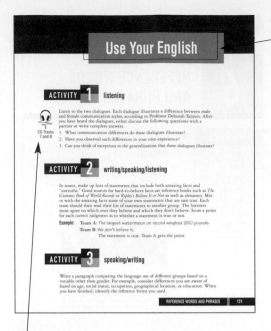

"Use Your English" section offers communicative activities that integrate **grammar with reading, writing, listening, and speaking skills.** Communicative activities consolidate grammar instruction with enjoyable and meaningful tasks.

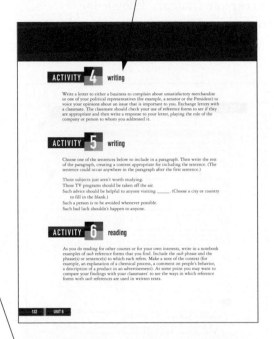

Engaging listening activities on audio cassette and audio CD further reinforce the target structure.

Research activity using *InfoTrac® College Edition* and the Internet encourages students to read articles on carefully selected topics and use this information to reflect on a theme or on information studied in each unit. *InfoTrac® College Edition*, an Online Research and Learning Center, appears in Grammar Dimensions 2, 3, and 4 and offers over 20 million full-text articles from nearly 6,000 scholarly and popular periodicals. Articles cover a broad spectrum of disciplines and topics—ideal for every type of researcher. Instructors and students can gain access to the online database 24/7 on any computer with Internet access.

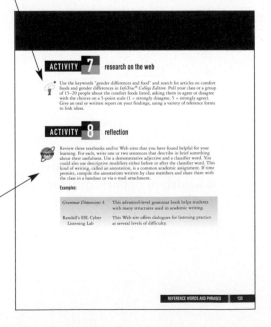

Reflection activities help students understand their learning style and create learning strategies.

Supplements

These additional components help teachers teach and students learn to use English grammar structures accurately.

The Lesson Planner

The lesson planner facilitates teaching by providing detailed lesson plans and examples, answer keys to the Student Book and Workbook, references to all of the components, and the tapescript for the audiocassette activities. The Lesson Planner minimizes teacher preparation time by providing:

- Summary of main grammar points for the teacher
- Information for the teacher on typical student errors
- Step-by-step guidelines for every focus box, exercise, and activity
- Suggested correlations between exercises and activities in the "Use Your English" pages
- Suggested timing for each exercise and each lesson
- Lead-in suggestions and examples for focus boxes
- Suggestions for expansion work follow most exercises
- Balance of cognitive and communicative activities
- Explanation for the teacher of the purpose of each activity, in order to differentiate cognitive from communicative emphasis
- Occasional methodology notes to anticipate possible procedural problems.

 ## Assessment CD-ROM with *ExamView* Test Generator

The Assessment CD-ROM allows instructors to **create customized quizzes and tests** quickly and easily from a test bank of questions. Monitoring student understanding and progress has never been easier! The answer key appears with instructor copies of each quiz or test created.

 ## Audio Program

Audio cassettes and CDs **provide listening activities for** each unit so students can practice listening to **grammar structures.**

Workbook

Workbooks **provide additional exercises** for each grammar point presented in the student text. They also offer editing practice and question types found on many language exams.

 ## Web site

Features additional grammar practice activities: elt.heinle.com/grammardimensions.

Empirical and Experiential Support for the *Grammar Dimensions* Approach

Opening Task Activities

The approach to teaching grammar used in the *Grammar Dimensions* series is well-grounded empirically and experientially. The Opening Task in each unit situates the learning challenge and allows students to participate in and learn from activity right from the beginning (Greeno 2006). In addition, students don't enter the classroom as empty vessels, waiting to be filled (Sawyer 2006). By observing how students perform on the Opening Task, teachers can analyze for themselves what students know and are able to do and what they don't know or are not able to do. Teachers can thus select from each unit what is necessary for students to build on to what they already bring with them.

Consciousness-Raising Exercises and Focus Boxes

Many of the exercises in *Grammar Dimensions* are of the consciousness-raising sort, where students are invited to make observations about some aspect of the target structure. This type of activity promotes students' noticing (Schmidt 1990), an important step in acquiring the grammar structure. The Focus Boxes further encourage this noticing, this time very explicitly. Explicit formulations of the sort found in the Focus Boxes can lead to implicit acquisition with practice (DeKeyser 1998). Moreover, certain learners (those with analytic learning styles) benefit greatly from explicit treatment of grammar structures (Larsen-Freeman and Long 1991).

Productive Practice and Communicative Activities

However, noticing by itself is insufficient. In order to be able to use the grammar structure, students need productive practice (Gatbonton and Segalowitz 1988; Larsen-Freeman 2003). Therefore, many of the exercises in *Grammar Dimensions* are of the output practice sort. Furthermore, each unit ends with communicative activities, where attention to the grammar is once again implicit, but where students can use the grammar structure in "psychologically authentic" or meaningful ways. Psychological authenticity is very important in order for students to be able to transfer what they know to new situations so that they can use it for their own purposes (Blaxton 1989) and so they are not left to contend with the "inert knowledge problem," (Whitehead 1929) where they know about the grammar, but can't use it.

The Three Dimensions of Grammar: Form, Meaning, and Use

Finally, applied linguistics research (Celce-Murcia and Larsen-Freeman 1999) supports the fundamental premise underlying *Grammar Dimensions*: that knowing a grammar structure means being able to use it accurately, meaningfully, and appropriately. Form focus or meaning focus by itself is insufficient (Larsen-Freeman 2001); all three dimensions—form, meaning, and use—need to be learned.

References

Blaxton, T. (1989). Investigating dissociations among memory measures: Support for a transfer-appropriate processing framework. *Journal of Experimental Psychology: Learning, Memory, and Cognition 15 (4): 657–668.*

Celce-Murcia, M. and D. Larsen-Freeman. (1999). *The grammar book: An ESL/EFL teacher's course.* Second Edition. Boston: Heinle & Heinle.

De Keyser, R. (1998). Beyond focus on form: Cognitive perspectives on learning and practicing second language grammar. In C. Doughty and J. Williams (eds.), *Focus on Classroom Second Language Acquisition.* Cambridge: Cambridge University Press, 42–63.

Gatbonton, E. and N. Segalowitz. (1988). Creative automatization: Principles for promoting fluency within a communicative framework. *TESOL Quarterly 22 (3): 473–492.*

Greeno, J. (2006). Learning in activity. In R. K. Sawyer (ed.), *The Cambridge handbook of learning sciences.* Cambridge: Cambridge University Press, 79–96.

Larsen-Freeman, D. (2001). Teaching grammar. In M. Celce-Murcia (ed.), *Teaching English as a Second or Foreign Language.* Third edition. Boston: Heinle & Heinle, 251–266.

Larsen-Freeman, D. (2003). *Teaching language: From grammar to grammaring.* Boston: Heinle & Heinle.

Larsen-Freeman, D. and M. Long. (1991). *An introduction to second language acquisition research.* London: Longman.

Sawyer, R. K. (2006). Introduction: The new science of learning. In R. K. Sawyer (ed.), *The Cambridge handbook of learning sciences.* Cambridge: Cambridge University Press, 1–16.

Schmidt, R. (1990). The role of consciousness in second language learning. *Applied Linguistics 11 (2), 129–158.*

Whitehead, A. N. 1929. *The aims of education.* New York: MacMillan.

Acknowledgments from the Series Director

This fourth edition would not have come about if it had not been for the enthusiastic response of teachers and students using all the previous editions. I am very grateful for the reception *Grammar Dimensions* has been given.

I am also grateful for all the authors' efforts. To be a teacher, and at the same time a writer, is a difficult balance to achieve . . . so is being an innovative creator of materials, and yet, a team player. They have met these challenges exceedingly well in my opinion. Then, too, the Heinle team has been impressive. I am grateful for the leadership exercised by Jim Brown, Sherrise Roehr, and Tom Jefferies. I also appreciate all the support from Anita Raducanu, Amy Mabley, Sarah Barnicle, Laura Needham, Chrystie Hopkins, Mary Beth Hennebury, and Crystal Parenteau of Pre-PressPMG. Deserving special mention are Amy Lawler and Yeny Kim, who never lost the vision while they attended to the detail with good humor and professionalism.

I have also benefited from the counsel of Marianne Celce-Murcia, consultant for the first edition of this project, and my friend. Finally, I wish to thank my family members, Elliott, Brent, and Gavin, for not once asking the (negative yes-no) question that must have occurred to them countless times: "Haven't you finished yet?" As we all have discovered, this project has a life of its own and is never really finished! And, for this, I am exceedingly grateful. Happy Grammaring all!

A Special Thanks

The series director, authors, and publisher would like to thank the following reviewers whose experienced observations and thoughtful suggestions have assisted us in creating and revising *Grammar Dimensions*.

Michelle Alvarez
University of Miami
Coral Gables, Florida

Edina Pingleton Bagley
Nassau Community College
Garden City, New York

Jane Berger
Solano Community College,
California

Mary Bottega
San Jose State University

Mary Brooks
Eastern Washington University

Christina Broucqsault
*California State Polytechnic
    University*

José Carmona
Hudson Community College

Susan Carnell
University of Texas at Arlington

Susana Christie
San Diego State University

Diana Christopher
Georgetown University

Gwendolyn Cooper
Rutgers University

Julia Correia
Henderson State University
Arkadelphia, Arkansas

Sue Cozzarelli
EF International, San Diego

Catherine Crystal
Laney College, California

Kevin Ccross
University of San Francisco

Julie Damron
*Interlink at Valparaiso
    University, Indiana*

Glen Deckert
Eastern Michigan University

Eric Dwyer
University of Texas at Austin

Nikki Ellman
Laney College
Oakland, California

Ann Eubank
Jefferson Community College

Alice Fine
UCLA Extension

Alicia Going
*The English Language Study
    Center, Oregon*

Molly Gould
University of Delaware

Maren M. Hargis
San Diego Mesa College

Penny Harrold
Universidad de Monterrey
Monterrey, Mexico

Robin Hendrickson
Riverside City College
Riverside, California

Mary Herbert
*University of California, Davis
    Extension*

Jane Hilbert
ELS Language Center,
Florida International
University

Eli Hinkel
Xavier University

Kathy Hitchcox
International English
Institute, Fresno

Abeer Hubi
Altarbia Alislamia Schools
Riyadh, Saudi Arabia

Joyce Hutchings
Georgetown University

Heather Jeddy
Northern Virginia
Community College

Judi Keen
University of California,
Davis, and *Sacramento*
City College

Karli Kelber
American Language Institute,
New York University

Anne Kornfield
LaGuardia Community
College

Kay Longmire
Interlink at Valparaiso
University, Indiana

Robin Longshaw
Rhode Island School of Design

Robert Ludwiczak
Texas A&M University
College Station, Texas

Bernadette McGlynn
ELS Language Center, St.
Joseph's University

Billy McGowan
Aspect International, Boston

Margaret Mehran
Queens College

Richard Moore
University of Washington

Karen Moreno
Teikyo Post University,
Connecticut

Gino Muzzetti
Santa Rosa Junior College,
California

Mary Nance-Tager
LaGuardia Community
College, City University of
New York

So Nguyen
Orange Coast College
Costa Mesa, California

Karen O'Neill
San Jose State University

Mary O'Neal
Northern Virginia
Community College

Nancy Pagliara
Northern Virginia
Community College

Keith Pharis
Southern Illinois University

Amy Parker
ELS Language Center, San
Francisco

Margene Petersen
ELS Language Center,
Philadelphia

Nancy Pfingstag
University of North
Carolina, Charlotte

Sally Prieto
Grand Rapids Community
College

India Plough
Michigan State University

Mostafa Rahbar
University of Tennessee at
Knoxville

Dudley Reynolds
Indiana University

Dzidra Rodins
DePaul University
Chicago, Illinois

Ann Salzman
University of Illinois at
Urbana-Champaign

Jennifer Schmidt
San Francisco State
University

Cynthia Schuemann
Miami-Dade Community
College

Jennifer Schultz
Golden Gate University,
California

Mary Beth Selbo
Wright College, City Colleges
of Chicago

Mary Selseleh
American River College
Sacramento, California

Stephen Sheeran
Bishop's University,
Lenoxville, Quebec

Kathy Sherak
San Francisco State
University

Sandra E. Sklarew
Merritt Community College
Oakland, California

Keith Smith
ELS Language Center, San
Francisco

Helen Solorzano
Northeastern University

Jorge Vazquez Solorzano
Bachillerato de la Reina de
Mexico
S. C., Mexico, D. F.,
Mexico

Christina Valdez
Pasadena City College
Pasadena, California

Danielle Valentini
Oakland Community College
Farmington Hills,
Michigan

Amelia Yongue
Howard Community College
Columbia, Maryland

VERB TENSES IN WRITTEN AND SPOKEN COMMUNICATION

UNIT GOALS

- Use verb tenses correctly to describe events and situations

- Use verb tenses consistently

- Understand why tense and time frames may change

OPENING TASK
Describing In-Groups

■ STEP 1

Read the following information about *in-groups* and find the definition of this term.

Gordon Allport, a Harvard psychologist, used the term *in-groups* to describe the groups that individuals are part of at one time or another. We are born into some in-groups, such as our ethnic groups, our hometowns, and our nationalities. We join other in-groups through our activities, such as going to school, making friends, entering a profession, or getting married. Some in-groups, such as ethnic groups, are permanent, but others change as our activities, beliefs, and loyalties change.

STEP 2

Read the list of in-group memberships that Kay, a Thai-American woman in her mid-thirties, currently belongs to or has belonged to In the past.

the family she grew up in

her own family (husband Mark and child Hanna)

Thai people (her ethnic group)

residents of Bangkok (where she was born)

residents of Chicago (where she lived from ages 8 to 18)

residents of Palo Alto, California (the city she lives in now)

her girlhood group of friends

the Girl Scouts (as a child)

students from her elementary and secondary school

Princeton University students

Stanford Medical School students

physicians (her profession)

Buddhists (her religion)

National Organization for Women members

her neighborhood volleyball team

Sierra Club members

residents of the United States

STEP 3

Make a list of some in-groups to which you belonged as a child (pick an age between 5 and 12 years old). Some of these groups might be the same as present ones. Next, make a list of in-groups that you belong to now. Finally, create a third list which consists of your present in-groups that you believe will remain important groups for you ten years from now.

STEP 4

Compare your lists with another class member. Discuss which groups on your childhood lists have changed and which have remained important groups to you at the present time.

STEP 5

As an out-of-class assignment, write three paragraphs. For the first paragraph, describe a childhood in-group that was especially important to you. For the second paragraph, write about your current involvement in an in-group. In the third paragraph, speculate about what might be some new in-groups for you in the future—for example, a new school, a profession, your own family (as contrasted to your family of origin)—and when you think some of them might become a part of your life. Save your paragraphs for Exercise 2.

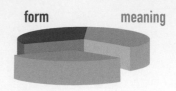

FOCUS 1   The English Verb System: Overview

Verbs in English express how events take place in time. The verb tenses give two main kinds of information:

Time Frame When the event takes place: now, at some time in the past, or at some time in the future.

Aspect The way we look at an action or state: whether it occurs at a certain point in time (for example, *stop*) or lasts for period of time (for example, *study*). (See Unit 2 for more detail on verb aspect.)

Time frame and **aspect** combine in twelve different ways in English.

ASPECT	TIME FRAME		
	PRESENT	**PAST**	**FUTURE***
Simple (at that point in time)	*stop/stops* *study/studies* (simple present)	*stopped* *studied* (simple past)	*will stop* *will study* (simple future)
Progressive (in progress at that point in time)	*am/is/are stopping* *am/is/are studying* (present progressive)	*was/were stopping* *was/were studying* (past progressive)	*will be stopping* *will be studying* (future progressive)
Perfect (before that time)	*has/have stopped* *has/have studied* (present perfect)	*had stopped* *had studied* (past perfect)	*will have stopped* *will have studied* (future perfect)
Perfect Progressive (in progress during and before that time)	*has/have been stopping* *has/have been studying* (present perfect progressive)	*had been stopping* *had been studying* (past perfect progressive)	*will have been stopping* *will have been studying* (future perfect progressive)

*Please note that there are many ways to express the future time frame in English. The chart above gives examples of the future using *will* only. See Focus 7 in Unit 2 for other ways.

EXERCISE 1

In *The Story of My Life,* high school student Farah Ahmedi tells about growing up in Kabul, Afghanistan, during the war between the mujahideen and the Soviets, her life as a refugee in Pakistan, and her immigration to the United States along with her mother, the only other surviving member of her family. The following passages are from her book. Underline the verbs of main clauses in each sentence. Then identify the time frame for each passage: present, past, or future. Circle any words and phrases that help to signal the time frame. The first one has been done as an example.

Example:

1. (a) Our caseworker, Zainab, <u>came</u> from Sudan. (b) (Years ago) she <u>had been</u> a refugee like us. (c) World Relief <u>had brought</u> her to America. (d) She <u>had found</u> her footing here, <u>gone</u> to school, <u>gotten</u> her degree, and now she <u>worked</u> for the organization. Time frame: *past*

2. (a) You have to realize how vastly this world differed from the one we left behind. (b) Everything moves quickly in America. (c) You notice the difference sharply if you have come from a slow-placed land like Pakistan. (d) Here in America events unfold in a flash. (e) Outside your window the traffic never stops zooming. (f) On the street no one has time to answer your questions.

3. (a) Alyce invited us to her house for Thanksgiving that first year. (b) We had never seen a turkey before and didn't know what it was. (c) We never imagined a bird could grow so big. (d) My mother didn't eat any of it.

4. (a) My mother now has a bit of a social life of her own. (b) She has gotten to know some other Afghan women in the neighborhood. (c) On warm days they all walk to the park together with their thermoses. (d) They sit on the grass and chat and have tea. (e) In the last couple of months my mother has even started going to school. (f) She is going to an English-language course three times a week.

5. (a) In my ESL classes I got to know an Indian girl named Apanza. (b) I met two Afghan girls as well. (c) They had come to America one year earlier than I and had therefore gone to American schools one year longer, but we were all in the same class. (d) In any case, I had companions now.

6. (a) Next year I'll be out of ESL altogether. (b) Even my English class will be mainstream. (c) Officially, at least, I'll be caught up.

Exchange the paragraphs you wrote for the Opening Task with those of a classmate. After reading the paragraphs, write one or two questions that you have about your classmate's in-groups and ask him or her to respond to them. Then decide whether there is a consistent time frame used for each paragraph. If so, identify the time frames and underline any time indicators. Check with your classmate to see if he or she agrees with your analysis. Discuss any changes you think should be made.

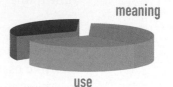

meaning

use

FOCUS 2   Moment of Focus

Verbs can describe events that happen at a point in time (for example, *last night, three weeks ago*) or an event that lasts a period of time (for example, *all night long, three weeks*). We call this the **moment of focus**.

The moment of focus will help you to decide whether to use the verb's present, past, or future tense. Here are examples of moment of focus for each of the three time frames:

	POINT OF TIME	**PERIOD OF TIME**
Present	(a) Her son *is* 4 years old today.	(b) Her son *listens* to music for hours at a time.
Past	(c) The tornado *touched* down just before dawn.	(d) During the early nineteenth century, millions of Italians *immigrated* to the United States.
Future	(e) On Saturday morning, they *will leave* for their trip.	(f) In the decades to come, computer technology *will continue* to change our lives.

The moment of focus may be stated explicitly or it may be implied in the context.

Present	(g) I can't talk now; I'm trying to study.	(h) Her son goes to a private school. (Implied: now)
Past	(i) Until the end of the Cretaceous period, dinosaurs roamed the Earth.	(j) Dinosaurs evolved into two distinct groups. (Implied: during a period of time in the past)
Future	(k) After you finish that chapter, I'll give you a ride to school.	(l) The weather will continue to be warm and sunny. (Implied: for a future period of time)

In written and spoken communication, the moment of focus may be the same for a number of sentences or it may change from sentence to sentence:

SAME POINT OF FOCUS	CHANGING POINT/PERIOD OF FOCUS
(m) When Kay first moved to Chicago from Bangkok, she had a hard time adjusting to her new life. She didn't like the food at school. Other children seldom talked to her and she had no one to play with.	(n) Kay met Mark the summer after she graduated from college. They dated for two years. When they got married, it was on the same date, July 15th, that they had first met. This year they celebrated their fifteenth anniversary.

EXERCISE 3

The following passages are from Studs Terkel's book *The Great Divide*, in which Americans talk about their lives, the lives of their families, and their thoughts on changes in the United States. With a partner or in a small group, do the following: (1) Identify the moment or moments of focus for each passage. (2) State whether the moment of focus is (a) past or (b) present. (3) Determine whether each moment of focus is (a) a point of time or (b) a period of time. (4) State whether the moment of focus is (a) explicitly stated or (b) implied.

1. (a) Right now, he's working the night shift at a twenty-four hour service station, with ten or twelve pumps. (b) He pumps the cash register. (c) His goals are very short-term, to get through the day.

2. (a) I grew up in an environment where my parents sacrificed their lives for their children. (b) They came here as immigrants, circumscribed in opportunity, to a country that allowed freedom. (c) Whether I became a carpenter like my father or a professor was irrelevant as long as I strove and availed myself of what this country offered.

3. (a) In the last five years, there's been much more discussion of ethics on the campuses. (b) Remember, many of the young people of the sixties are the professors of today and they haven't changed their basic beliefs.

4. (a) A friend of mine, who is 40 had been a stock analyst on Wall Street fifteen years ago. (b) She married, had babies, raised her children, and now wanted to go back. (c) They said, "It doesn't matter what you did before."

5. (a) I would like to be chief of police. (b) I'll probably apply for jobs. (c) If nothing happens, I'll go to Cape Cod, build a house, and look at the waves.

6. (a) [My students] have learned how to take college tests. (b) They score high, especially in math. (c) They are quite verbal. (d) They give the impression of being bright. (d) Encouraged by their families, they come with the conviction that education is something they want, something they need. (e) But their definition of education is something else.

use

Being consistent in tense means keeping verbs in the same time frame.

EXAMPLES	EXPLANATIONS
PRESENT TIME FRAME	
(a) Self-help groups have become very common all over America. (b) These groups assist people with everything from weight problems to developing confidence.	The tense may change within a time frame. For example, the tense may change from present perfect to simple present, as in sentences (a) and (b), but the time frame remains in the present.
PAST TIME FRAME	
(c) Vera graduated from college last June.	Sometimes, however, it is necessary to change from one time frame to another, for example from past to present. A time-frame shift is usually signaled by a time marker (for example, *last week, currently, next year.*)
PRESENT TIME FRAME	
(d) She now works for a law firm. (e) She has worked there for a month.	In example (d) *now* signals a shift from past to present time. Example (e) shifts to the present perfect, but remains in the present time frame.
PAST TIME FRAME	
(f) NOT: She had worked there for a month.	If (e) had a past-time reference, as in (f), the verb would be ungrammatical because there is no explicit time marker to signal a time-frame shift. Nor is there any reason to depart from the present time frame, which has been established in (d).

EXERCISE 4

Each of the following passages has one sentence with an inappropriate verb tense. (1) Identify the time frame of the passage. (2) Identify the sentence that has the error and correct it. You may want to consult the time-frame chart in Focus 1 for reference. Correction may involve changing the verb tense or using an explicit time marker to signal the shift in time frame. More than one verb tense can be correct in some cases.

Example: (a) I am taking this coat back to the store. (b) Someone had burned a hole in it. (c) One button is missing too.

Time Frame: *Present*; Error: (*b*)

Possible Corrections: *Someone **has burned** a hole in it.*

OR *Someone **had burned** a hole in it **before I bought it.***

1. (a) My music class is interesting. (b) We have been studying the history of American jazz. (c) I will have been taking this course for six weeks.

2. (a) Sula's in-groups include her softball team. (b) She had belonged to this team for three years. (c) Last year she played second base, but this year she is playing first base.

3. (a) Internet social Web sites are becoming increasingly popular, especially with high school and college students, as ways to meet people. (b) These Web sites offered users their own personalized Web page for posting photos, messages, music and video. (c) Millions of users subscribe to the Web sites to make friends and get information about popular culture.

4. (a) One user of MySpace.com, a social Web site started in 2003, told a reporter he started using MySpace to keep track of his high school classmates. (b) Another user tells the reporter that the site allowed her to get to know people in different ways. (c) But some people expressed negative opinions about Web sites that allow anyone to see your personal information.

FOCUS 4	Time-Frame Shifts in Written and Spoken Communication

use

Time-frame shifts, such as from present to past, can occur in both written and spoken communication. These shifts will often be necessary when you move from statements that introduce a topic to ones that provide further information about the topic. There may or may not be explicit markers to signal time shifts.

Below are some reasons why you might change from one time frame to another, with examples given for each.

EXAMPLES	EXPLANATIONS	
	TYPE OF TIME-FRAME SHIFT	REASON FOR SHIFT
(a) The city of Wichita Falls has an interesting history. It *became* a town over a hundred years ago when the railroad started a route through that area. The land that was to become Wichita Falls *was* a prize in a poker game.	Present → Past	To explain or support a general statement with past description or elaboration on a topic.
(b) Our school is helping to conserve natural resources. We *recycled* tons of aluminum last year. We *started* using paper cups instead of Styrofoam ones.	Present → Past	To support a claim about the present with examples from the past.
(c) The social connections of Americans have changed during the last century. In the past, individuals *depended* on their extended families and neighborhoods for social activities. Today many Americans live far from their extended families and often do not know many of their neighbors.	Present → Past	To support a general statement about change by comparing present and past situations.
(d) Last year our city witnessed an increase in the number of people who volunteered time for organizations helping those in need. Donations to these organizations also increased. We *need* to continue this assistance to others less fortunate than we are.	Past → Present	To express a comment or an opinion about a topic.

NOTE: The simple present and present perfect tenses often "frame" topics. We frequently use them to introduce topics, to make topic shifts, and to end discussion of a topic. These tenses often express general statements that the speaker believes to be true at the present time.

EXERCISE 5

Below are more passages from Farah Ahmedi's *Story of My Life* about her experience as a newcomer to the United States, living in Chicago, Illinois. Discuss the reasons for the verb tense shifts in each passage. Which passages change tenses within a time frame (e.g., two different tenses within the past frame)? Which passages change time frames (e.g., a change from past time to present time)? Which verb tense is used to introduce the topic in each of these passages?

Example: (a) Every time my mother and I left the house, we felt like hares venturing out of our holes. (b) We were panting with nervous dread. (c) Everybody enjoys reading an adventure story or seeing and adventure movie, but a real life adventure is hard to enjoy because you don't know how it will end. (d) I always felt the blood pounding in my wrists when I walked out the doors of our apartment building.

Reason for verb tense shift: The verb tense shifts from past tense to present tense in (c) to add a general comment related to the situation that Farah was describing. This passage changes time frames in (c) but returns to the past time frame in (d).

Introducing the topic: The past tense is used to introduce the topic.

1. World Relief tried to connect us up with other Afghans in the area, but the other Afghans led busy lives of their own. (b) Many of them had to work two jobs just to survive. (c) They had no time for us. (d) Two people don't automatically become friends just because they come from the same country. (e) And we didn't know any Americans, either, so we lived an empty life, homesick by day for a world we never wanted to see again, a world we visited too often in our nightmares.

2. (a) With most people, I have never been much of a talker. (b) Conversation does not come easily to me. (c) In a group I often feel shy and keep my thoughts to myself. (d) But Alyce* brought the stories, questions and confidences pouring out of me! (e) As soon as she walked into our house, her eyes had such a sparkle and her face wore such a flock of smiles that my heart opened wide.

3. (a) When you are trying to master a new language, you learn quicker if you have a chance to speak without hesitation or fear. (b) In class I didn't have the chance to speak much. (c) I had to spend most of my time listening to the teacher. (d) When I was called upon to say something, it was a public situation and a performance. (e) People were looking at me, and even as I tried to shape a thought, I worried that I might make a mistake and that the class might laugh at me. . .

4. (a) When I first came to America, I wanted to forget the past. (b) I wanted to take a big eraser and rub out every memory I had. (c) I wanted to become totally American through and through as quickly as I could. (d) But time passed, and I began to think about it. (e) I realized that it's good to remember my own customs and traditions. (f) Now I don't want to erase, or forget, or destroy any part of myself. (g) I want to love myself and keep adding to who I am.

*Alyce was Farah's English tutor, mentor, and very special friend from the World Relief Organization.

Use Your English

CD Tracks
1, 2

You will hear two passages from the autobiography *I, Rigoberta Menchu*. Rigoberta Menchu is a young Guatemalan peasant woman who won the Nobel Peace Prize in 1992 for her work to ensure human rights and justice for Indian communities in Guatemala. These passages describe her peasant life in Guatemala. In each passage, there is one or more sentences that shift to a different time frame from the main time frame of the passage (for example, from the past to the present).

■ **STEP 1** Listen to each passage once for content and note the main time frame: present, past, or future.

■ **STEP 2** Listen to each passage again and write down the verbs that represent time-frame shifts and as much of the sentences they are in as you can recall.

■ **STEP 3** Explain the reason for each time-frame shift, with reference to Focus 4 for the possible different reasons. Here is some vocabulary from the passage that will be helpful to know while listening:

finca—a Guatemalan farm or plantation where the Indian peasants are contracted to work by the landowners. Crops such as coffee, cotton, and sugar are grown.

lorry—a truck that transports people from their villages to the finca

Altiplano—a high plateau in a mountainous region.

ACTIVITY 2 reading

Scan some comic strips in the newspaper to find ones that use a variety of verb tenses. In groups, discuss what the time frames are for each, and why tense changes occur. As a variation of this activity, cover up or blacken the verbs in comic strips. Then give another classmate the base forms of the verbs (the verb that comes after *to* in *to* + verb) and see if he or she fills in the same tenses as the original. Discuss any differences in choices.

ACTIVITY 3 reading

Select several paragraphs of something you find interesting from a textbook (for example, history, literature, or psychology) or some other book. Analyze the verb tense use in the paragraphs. What types of verb-tense shifts or time-frame shifts occur? Analyze the reasons for tense- or time-frame shifts.

ACTIVITY 4 reading

Look at a piece of writing you or a classmate has done recently, such as an essay or other type of paper. Analyze the types of verb-tense shifts you see, such as shifting from the present tense to the past tense. Describe why the verb tenses shifted. Underline any verb tenses that you think might not be correct and discuss them with your classmates or instructor.

ACTIVITY 5 research on the web

 Millions of young people spend hours every day on social Web sites such as MySpace and Facebook, posting pictures and blogs about themselves and looking at Web pages of others. Although these social Web sites are among the most popular sites on the Internet, the media have warned that there are some problems associated with these sites. Research the topic of problems associated with social Web sites using keywords on a search engine such as Google® or Yahoo®, including the names of the Web sites. Write a summary of what you discovered, using appropriate verb tenses.

ACTIVITY 6 reflection/speaking

Consider an in-group, as defined by Gordon Allport, that has been helpful to your learning of English. The in-group could be friends, relatives, or classmates. Or it could be a particular school or program in which you were a student. Write an essay explaining the ways in which belonging to this group has contributed to your language development in the past and or present. Share with your class.

VERBS
Aspect and Time Frames

UNIT GOALS

- Use simple verb tenses correctly

- Use progressive verb forms correctly

- Use perfect verb forms correctly

- Understand verb-tense meanings and uses in present, past, and future time frames

OPENING TASK
Insiders and Outsiders

In Unit 1, the Opening Task asked you to consider the in-groups to which you belong. At times the process of joining a new group can be uncomfortable. Most of us have experienced the sense of not belonging, of feeling somewhat like an "outsider," when first joining a new group. This often happens when people move to a new place, begin attending a new school, or start a new job.

■ STEP 1

Read the passages below and on the next page about experiences of feeling like an outsider.

In the first passage, Farah Ahmedi, whose life story you read about in Unit 1, describes her difficulties as an Afghan refugee trying to make friends with Americans while attending high school in Chicago, Illinois.

> I have no American friends my age. I guess it's partly because the American kids grew up here and found their friends long ago. They don't need more friends, now, so they ignore anyone they don't already know. If you say hi, they say hi back, but it doesn't lead to conversation.

From Farah Ahmedi with Tamim Ansary (2005). *The Story of My Life: An Afghan Girl on the Other Side of the Sky*. New York: Simon & Schuster.

The next passage describes the sense of not belonging and confusion that many students experience when entering college, especially when they find themselves in large lecture classes, where they do not have much direct contact with a teacher.

People are taking notes and you are taking notes. You are taking notes on a lecture you don't understand. You get a phrase, a sentence, then the next loses you. It's as though you're hearing a conversation in a crowd or from another room—out of phase, muted. The man on the stage concludes his lecture and everyone rustles and you close your notebook and prepare to leave. You feel a little strange. Maybe tomorrow this stuff will clear up. Maybe by tomorrow this will be easier. But by the time you're in the hallway, you don't think it will be easier at all.

From Mike Rose (2005). *Lives on the Boundary*. New York: Penguin Books.

■ STEP 2

For fifteen minutes, write your thoughts in response to the passages. You could discuss one of the passages, or you might want to describe a situation from your own experience, from a movie or TV show you have seen, or from something you have read that relates to the idea of being an outsider in a new place or with a new group. In small groups, take turns reading your responses aloud.

FOCUS 1 Review of Simple Tenses

use

Simple tenses include the simple present, simple past, and simple future. They have the following uses:

TIME FRAME	EXAMPLES	USE
Present	(a) Our in-groups **help** to define our values.	To express general ideas, relationships, and truths.
Past	(b) Immigrants to America in the mid-nineteenth century **included** large numbers of Chinese.	
Future	(c) Families **will** always **be** important to most of us.	
Present	(d) Our family **visits** my grandparents after church every Sunday.	To describe habitual actions.
Past	(e) Almost every year we **celebrated** my great aunt's birthday with a family picnic.	
Future	(f) The club **will collect** dues once a month.	
Present	(g) Kay **thinks** she has chosen the right profession.	To describe mental perceptions or emotions.
Past	(h) People once **believed** the earth was flat.	
Future	(i) You **will love** our new puppy.	
Present	(j) Mark **has** three brothers.	To express possession or personal relationships.
Past	(k) We **owned** an SUV, but we traded it in for a hybrid car.	
Future	(l) By next month, Hannah **will have** a new computer.	
Present	(m) The environmental agency **reports** that new evidence has been gathered about global warming.	To establish the time frame and the moment of focus.
Past	(n) When the United States **passed** the Chinese Exclusion Act in 1882, 100,000 Chinese were living in the United States.	
Future	(o) Phyllis **will call** you Thursday morning; I hope you will not have left for Omaha by then.	

EXERCISE 1

The sentences below tell about James McBride, a writer and jazz musician, and his mother Ruth McBride Jordan, whose life story he describes in *The Color of Water: A Black Man's Tribute to his White Mother*. For each sentence, do the following: (1) Identify the tense of the underlined verb. (2) Decide which of the five uses in Focus 1 (listed below) each verb represents and write the appropriate letter from the list in the blank before the sentence. The first one has been done for you.

a. Expresses a general idea, relationship or truth
b. Describes an habitual action
c. Describes a mental perception or an emotion
d. Expresses possession or a personal relationship
e. Establishes the time frame or a moment of focus

___Past___ ___a___ 1. James McBride <u>grew up</u> in an all-black housing project in Brooklyn, New York.

_____ _____ 2. His father <u>was</u> a black minister, but James was raised by his mother and a stepfather as his father had died before James was born.

_____ _____ 3. James <u>had</u> eleven brothers and sisters, all of whom, like him, went to college, partly as a result of his mother's strong desire for her children to be educated.

_____ _____ 4. As a child, James <u>felt</u> that his mother was strange because she didn't look or act like the other mothers he knew in his neighborhood.

_____ _____ 5. Ruth McBride Jordan, James's mother, always <u>refused</u> to tell her children about her past life before she moved to New York and married James's father.

_____ _____ 6. In *The Color of Water*, James <u>describes</u> a discussion with his mother about God.

_____ _____ 7. When James's mother told him God was a spirit, James <u>asked</u> her what color God's spirit is.

_____ _____ 8. His mother responded that God is the color of water and that water doesn't <u>have</u> a color.

_____ _____ 9. James <u>spent</u> 14 years researching and writing *The Color of Water*.

_____ _____ 10. Through his interviews with his mother and others who knew her, James <u>understood</u> why his mother, the daughter of Jewish immigrants from Poland, left her family and became part of a black community.

_____ _____ 11. In 1986, at the age of 65, Ruth <u>graduated</u> from Temple University with a degree in social work.

_____ _____ 12. Today, Ruth <u>works</u> as a volunteer in a shelter for homeless teenage mothers, <u>runs</u> a reading club, and <u>travels</u> regularly to Europe.

EXERCISE 2

Below are two more passages related to the themes in the Opening Task (pages 12–13): forming friendships and entering college. The first passage, from James McBride's *The Color of Water*, describes an incident from his mother's girlhood, when her Jewish immigrant family was living in rural Virginia in the 1930s. The second passage is from sports journalist Mitch Albom's book *Tuesdays with Morrie*, about Albom's college sociology professor who became his good friend. Identify the tense of each underlined verb. Then choose any five of the underlined verbs from the two passages and state the use or uses of each. The first has been done as an example.

Example: (1) Verb: liked

Tense: *past*

Use: *describes mental perceptions or emotions*

A. (1) Nobody <u>liked</u> me. (2) That's how I <u>felt</u> as a child. (3) I know what it feels like when people <u>laugh</u> at you walking down the street, or snicker when they hear you speaking Yiddish,* or just look at you with hate in their eyes. (4) When I was in the fourth grade, a girl came up to me in the schoolyard during recess and said, "You <u>have</u> the prettiest hair." (5) "Let's be friends." (6) I said, "Okay." (7) Heck, I was glad someone <u>wanted</u> to be my friend. (8) Her name was Frances. (9). I'<u>ll</u> never <u>forget</u> Frances as long as I live. (7) She was thin, with light brown hair and blue eyes. (8) She <u>was</u> a quiet gentle person.

* Yiddish is the language that Jews all over the world speak. It derived from German dialects spoken by Jews in central Europe.
From: James McBride, *The Color of Water: A Black Man's Tribute to His White Mother.* New York: Penguin, 2006, pp. 80–81.

B. (1) It <u>is</u> our first class together, in the spring of 1976. (2) I <u>enter</u> Morrie's large office and notice the seemingly countless books that line the wall, shelf after shelf. (3) There is a large rug on the hardwood floor and a window that <u>looks out</u> on the campus walk. (4) Only a dozen or so students are there, fumbling with notebooks and syllabi. (5) I tell myself it <u>will</u> not <u>be</u> easy to cut a class this small. (6) Maybe I shouldn't take it.

From: Mitch Albom, *Tuesdays with Morrie: An Old Man, A Young Man and Life's Greatest Lesson.* New York: Doubleday, 1997, p. 80.

EXERCISE 3

STEP 1   Write a paragraph summarizing how the experience of James McBride's mother in Passage A of Exercise 2 contrasts with Farah Ahmedi's passage in the Opening Task.

STEP 2   Write a paragraph summarizing how Mitch Albom's experience in Passage B of Exercise 2 contrasts with that described in Mike Rose's passage in the Opening Task.

STEP 3   Go back to the paragraphs you've written and underline the verbs you used. Then state what the verb tenses and uses are.

EXERCISE 4

Underline the verbs in these sentences from Unit 1, Exercise 1 in the first column. Then write the letter for the verb tense and use that matches each one from the second column. The first one has been done as an example.

_b_ 1. Everything <u>moves</u> quickly in America.

_____ 2. Outside your window the traffic never stops zooming.

_____ 3. Alyce invited us to her house for Thanksgiving that first year.

_____ 4. We never imagined a bird could grow so big.

_____ 5. In any case, I had companions now.

_____ 6. Next year I'll be out of ESL altogether.

a. Past: Describes mental perception

b. Present: Expresses general idea or truth

c. Future: Describes general idea of truth

d. Past: Establishes time frame or moment of focus

e. Present: Describes habitual actions

f. Past: Describes possession or personal relationships

FOCUS 2 — Review of Progressive Verbs

Progressive verbs include a form of *be* + a present participle (verb + *-ing*).

EXAMPLES	USES
(a) When Mark gets home from work, Hannah **is** often **studying**. (b) I **was driving** to the restaurant when I saw the meteor shower. (c) Bob **will be working** the night shift when Roberta gets home.	To describe actions already in progress at the moment of focus.
(d) Eric usually goes out to eat on Fridays. This Friday, however, he **is cooking** at home. (e) The robins usually took up residence every spring in our old apple trees. One summer, though, they **were building** nests in some of the taller trees. (f) Most winters we spend our Christmas vacation at home. But this year we **will be going** to Vermont.	To describe actions at the moment of focus in contrast to habitual actions.
(g) She **is** constantly **reminding** me to water the plants. (h) As a young boy, my brother **was** always **getting** into trouble. (i) Our math teacher **will be checking** our assignments each morning when class starts.	To express repeated actions.
(j) Kendra works in the principal's office, but she **is helping** the new school nurse this week. (k) My father lived in Chile most of his life, except for two years when he **was living** in Argentina. (l) We'll live in a new home after the winter. Until then, we'll **be renting** an apartment in the city.	To describe temporary situations in contrast to permanent states.
(m) The final paper is due soon. **I'm finishing** it as fast as I can. (n) Yesterday the students discussed the projects they **were working** on this semester. (o) When they finish their projects, they **will be evaluating** each other's work for several days.	To describe periods of time in contrast to points of time.
(p) Sara **is doing** volunteer work for the homeless this summer. (q) When I last saw Ali, he **was** still **planting** his vegetable garden. (r) I bet the baby **will** still **be sleeping** when we get home.	To express uncompleted actions.

EXERCISE 5

Underline the progressive verbs in the passage below. State what additional information the progressive aspect expresses for each verb. (Refer to the uses presented in Focus 2.)

Example: (a) progressive verb: *am sitting*

additional information expressed: *to describe action in progress at the moment of focus*

(a) I <u>am sitting</u> under a sycamore by Tinker Creek. (b) I am really here, alive on the intricate earth under trees . . . (c) What else is going on right this minute while groundwater creeps under my feet? (d) The galaxy is careening in a slow, muffled widening. (e) If a million solar systems are born every hour, then surely hundreds burst into being as I shift my weight to the other elbow. (f) The sun's surface is now exploding; other stars implode and vanish, heavy and black, out of sight. (g) Meteorites are arcing to earth invisibly all day long. (h) On the planet the winds are blowing: the polar easterlies, the westerlies, the northeast and southeast trades.

From Annie Dillard, *Pilgrim at Tinker Creek*. New York: Bantam, 1974.

EXERCISE 6

Decide whether a simple tense or progressive tense is appropriate for each blank and give the correct form(s) of the verb in parentheses. The first one has been done for you.

1. Andre (a) ___comes___ (come) from Brazil and (b) _____ (be) a native speaker of Portuguese. Currently he (c) _____ (study) English at the University of Colorado. He (d) _____ (take) two courses: composition and American culture.

2. One of my most important in-groups (a) _____ (be) my church group. Right now we (b) _____ (provide) lunches for homeless people in the city park. Also, some of us (c) _____ (tutor) junior high students in math and English for the summer. Others in my group (d) _____ (spend) part of the summer doing volunteer work at senior citizen centers. We all (e) _____ (feel) that we (f) _____ (gain) a great deal ourselves by participating in these activities.

3. Next summer our family (a) _____ (have) a reunion during the July 4th holiday weekend. My uncle from Finland (b) _____ (try) to come, but he (c) _____ (start) a new business this year so it (d) _____ (be) difficult for him to get away. Another uncle (e) _____ (spend) the whole summer with us. He (f) _____ (work) at my mother's travel agency from June through August.

4. For many immigrants to the United States, their ethnic associations (a) _____ (remain) important in-groups long after they have left their home countries. Even while they (b) _____ (learn) a new language, many (c) _____ (look to) speakers of their native language as an in-group that (d) _____ (understand) their struggles to adapt to a new way of life.

EXERCISE 7

Ask another classmate to tell you five things he or she does now as a result of in-group associations. Write a sentence for each, using present-time reference verbs, and report several of the ones you find most interesting to the rest of the class.

Example: *Marco hikes every week with the Sierra Club. As a student at Northwestern, he is majoring in environmental sciences.*

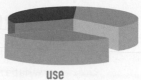

FOCUS 3   Review of Perfect Verbs

Perfect verbs are formed by *have (has, have, had, will have)* + a past participle (verb *-ed* or irregular form).

EXAMPLES		USES
(a) *To date*, Mark **has taken** five days off from work for vacation.		To describe events that happen before the moment of focus.
(b) *When I last spoke to my mother*, she **had sent** me a letter, so she didn't want to repeat her news over the phone.		The time phrases and clauses in italics signal the moment of focus.
(c) *By this time tomorrow*, even more acres of the rain forest **will have been destroyed**.		
Present Perfect (Continuing to present)	**Simple Past (Completed)**	To describe events that started in the past and continue to be true in the present. This contrasts with the use of simple past for completed events.
(d) My parents **have lived** in their house for 40 years; this year they are remodeling the kitchen.	(e) My grandparents **lived** in their house on Tower Avenue until 1996.	
(f) **I have finished** that chapter, so I can help you answer the questions. (My finishing the chapter is relevant to my ability to help now.)		To describe events that the speaker believes are relevant to the moment of focus. In (f), the moment of focus is the present; in (g), it is the past. (f) and (g) contrast with (h), which has a simple past verb. And in (i), it is the future.
(g) **I had finished** the chapter before the soccer match started, so I was able to watch the whole match. (My finishing the chapter is relevant to having watched the match.)	(h) **I finished** the chapter. Then I played video games. (Finishing the chapter and playing games are related only sequentially.)	
(i) **I will have taken** my last exam on the day you arrive here. (My completion of exams is relevant to your arrival date.)		

Underline the present perfect and past perfect verbs in the following passages. Explain what information is expressed by the perfect aspect for these verbs. Decide which of the uses listed in Focus 3 is expressed. (A perfect verb can convey more than one kind of information.) The first has been done as an example.

Example: 1. (d) <u>had seen, heard, learned</u>—past perfect

Information: *describe events that happen before the moment of focus (Fatt Hing at the age of 19) and that are relevant to the moment of focus.*

1. (a) By 1851, in a matter of three years, there were 25,000 Chinese in California. (b) Fatt Hing was one of these 25,000. (c) His story is typical of the pioneer Chinese, many who came with him and many who came after him. (d) As a lad of 19, Fatt Hing had already seen and heard and learned more about the world than most of the men in his village, who had seldom set foot beyond the nearest town square. (e) For Fatt Hing was a fish peddler who went frequently from Toishan to Kwanghai on the coast to buy his fish to sell at the market. (f) Down by the wharves, where the fishing boats came in, Fatt Hing had often seen foreign ships with their sails fluttering in the wind. (g) He had seen hairy white men on the decks, and he had often wondered and dreamed about the land they came from.

2. (a) The dog has got more fun out of Man than Man has got out of the dog, for the clearly demonstrable reason that Man is the more laughable of the two animals. (b) The dog has long been bemused by the singular activities and the curious practices of men, cocking his head inquiringly to one side, intently watching and listening to the strangest goings-on in the world. (c) He has seen men sing together and fight one another in the same evening. (d) He has watched them go to bed when it is time to get up, and get up when it is time to go to bed. (e) He has observed them destroying the soil in vast areas, and nurturing it in small patches. (f) He has stood by while men built strong and solid houses for rest and quiet, and then filled them with lights and bells and machinery.

From James Thurber, *Thurber's Dogs, A Collection of the Master's Dogs, Written and Drawn, Real and Imaginary, Living and Long Ago*. New York: Simon and Schuster, 1955.

EXERCISE 9

Decide whether a simple form (present, past) or present perfect should be used for each verb in parentheses. The first has been done for you.

The Hotter'n Hell Hundred

Near the Texas-Oklahoma border, where the wind never (1) _____seems_____ (seem) to stop, where the sun (2) _____ (broil) the blacktop and (3) _____ (sap) the strength, the cyclists (4) _____ (come) each year. They (5) _____ (come) to Wichita Falls, Texas, by the thousands to ride in what (6) _____ (become) the largest one-hundred-mile bicycle race in the world—the Hotter'n Hell Hundred. The race (7) _____ (take) place on Labor Day weekend at the beginning of September, when temperatures regularly (8) _____ (soar) past 100 degrees.

    The oddity of this race is that, with each passing year, it (9) _____ (become) more and more a symbol of Wichita Falls, a city that, until recently, (10) _____ (be, hardly) a cycling bastion. In days past, the sight of a bicyclist (11) _____ (cause) heads to turn in the pickup truck. Tornadoes (12) _____ (be) once more numerous than bicyclists in Wichita Falls.

    The Hotter'n Hell Hundred (13) _____ (start) in 1982 when a postal worker (14) _____ (suggest) a one-hundred-mile bike ride in 100-degree heat to celebrate Wichita Falls' one-hundredth birthday. Today, the race (15) _____ (command) the attention of almost the whole city as race weekend (16) _____ (approach).

Adapted with permission from J. Michael Kennedy, "It's the Hottest Little Ol' Race in Texas," *Los Angeles Times*, September 2, 1991.

EXERCISE 10

Decide whether a simple future or future perfect verb should be used for each verb in parentheses. The first one has been done for you.

Our class has been discussing which in-groups we think (1) _____will_____ (be) or (2) _____ (be, not) important to us ten years from now. Hua says she knows her family (3) _____ (remain) an important in-group forever. However, she thinks her associations with some campus groups, such as the French Club, (4) _____ (end) by the time she graduates.

    Kazuhiko thinks that he (5) _____ (be) married for several years by that time. He hopes he (6) _____ (have) a few children of his own. He believes his family (7) _____ (represent) his most important in-group in the future. Jose predicts that he (8) _____ (become) a famous physicist by that time and that one of his important in-groups (9) _____ (be) other Nobel Prize winners.

EXERCISE 11

With a partner, take the roles of Person A and Person B below. Each person should write five questions to ask the other person in an interview, based on the information given. In your questions, use present, past, and future perfect verb forms. Use them in your responses when appropriate. Here are some patterns that may be useful for your questions:

Have you ever (done X)?

Had you (done X) before (Y)?

Do you think you will have (done X) before (Y)?

Example: Person A: *So you've taken piano lessons. Have you ever studied any other musical instruments?*

Person B: *Actually, yes. Before I took piano lessons, I had studied the violin for a year, but my playing was terrible!*

Person B: *I see you've lived in two other countries besides the United States. Which one did you live in first, and how long did you live in each one?*

Person A: *Well, I had lived in Peru for 15 years before I moved to Madrid. I lived in Madrid for a little over three years.*

PERSON A	PERSON B
was on the track team in high school	took piano lessons as a child
lived in Peru	grew up in Korea
lived in Madrid	moved to the United States in 1998
traveled in Egypt and Africa	attended the University of Florida
parents live in New Mexico	attended Penn State
enrolled at the University of Texas	currently lives in New York
belongs to a health club	likes to watch basketball
loves old movies	loves to go to music concerts
is a sophomore	works at a television station
will graduate from college in three years	plans to move to Tokyo
plans to do a bicycle tour of Vietnam	will get a degree in broadcast journalism

FOCUS 4 — Review of Perfect Progressive Verbs

use

Perfect progressive verbs include present perfect progressive, past perfect progressive, and future perfect progressive. They are formed by *have (has, have, had, will have)* + *been* + a past participle (verb + *-ing*).

EXAMPLES		USE
Incomplete: Progressive	**Complete: Nonprogressive**	
(a) The jurors **have been discussing** the evidence. They still haven't reported their verdict.	(b) The jurors **have discussed** the evidence for a week. They are ready to report their verdict.	To express actions that have not been completed at the moment of focus, in contrast to actions that have been completed.
(c) Tam **had been listening** to the news when the explosion occurred.	(d) Tam **had listened** to the news before she left for work.	
(e) Jochen **will have been working** on his Master's degree for two years at the end of this month. He expects to finish in six months.	(f) Jochen **will have worked** at the bank for five years when he leaves for his new job in Quebec.	

EXERCISE 12

For each blank below, choose a simple past, present perfect, or present perfect progressive verb. The first one has been done for you.

(1) Alfredo ____joined____ (join) the Friends of the Theater in his community five years ago and _____ (be) an active participant in this group ever since. (2) It _____ (remain) one of his favorite spare time activities even though he _____ (stop) trying out for roles in the plays last year because he _____ (be) too busy. (3) As a member, he _____ (help) promote the plays. (4) At times, he _____ (look for) costumes for the actors. (5) For last month's play, he _____ (work) with the props crew to get furniture and other props for the stage sets. (6) He _____ (find) an antique desk to use for one of the sets, and he also _____ (make) a fireplace facade. (7) Most recently, he _____ (try) to get more businesses to advertise in the playbills.

EXERCISE 13

Write five sentences that express activities you have been doing for six months or more. For each sentence state how long you have been doing the activity and for what purpose.

Examples: *I have been taking yoga classes for two years in order to improve my flexibility.*

I have been working at the bookstore since the beginning of October so that I can pay my tuition.

1. _____

   _____

2. _____

   _____

3. _____

   _____

4. _____

   _____

5. _____

   _____

EXERCISE 14

Write down three things that you are doing right now and plan to continue doing for at least a month. Then, with a classmate, share the information you wrote. For each statement, ask each other how long you will have been doing the activity by the end of a certain time period within the next month (e.g. by a certain date, by the end of the month). Since this is oral English communication, you can use contractions in your responses.

Example: **A:** I've been taking a global studies course.
B: Oh really? How long will you have been taking that course by the end of this week?
A: Let's see . . . by the end of this week, I'll have been taking it for eight weeks.

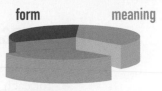

form   meaning

use

FOCUS 5   Summary: Present Time Frame

FORMS	EXAMPLES	USES	MEANINGS
SIMPLE PRESENT base form of verb or base form of verb + -*s*	(a) Children **need** social interaction to develop language.	timeless truths	now
	(b) Kay **plays** on a volleyball team once a week.	habitual actions	
	(c) Kay **considers** her Thai heritage an important in-group.	mental perceptions and emotions	
	(d) Hannah **has** a red bicycle.	possession	
PRESENT PROGRESSIVE *am/is/are* + present participle (verb + -*ing*)	(e) I **am completing** my Bachelor's degree in Spanish.	actions in progress	in progress now
	(f) Hannah **is writing** an essay.	duration	
	(g) Someone **is knocking** at the door.	repetition	
	(h) Kay's brother **is staying** with her this summer.	temporary activities	
	(i) Mark **is making** dinner.	uncompleted actions	
PRESENT PERFECT *have/has* + past participle (verb + -*ed* or irregular form)	(j) Kay **has belonged** to the Sierra Club for four years.	situations that began in the past, continue to the present	in the past but related to now in some way
	(k) Kay **has applied** to several hospitals for positions; she is waiting to hear from them.	actions completed in the past but related to the present	
	(l) Hannah **has** just **finished** junior high school.	actions recently completed	
PRESENT PERFECT PROGRESSIVE *have/has* + present participle (verb + -*ing*)	(m) Both Kay and Mark **have been playing** volleyball since they were teenagers.	continuous or repeated actions that are incomplete	up until and including now
	(n) This weekend Mark **has been competing** in a tournament that ends tomorrow.		

Choose simple present, present progressive, present perfect, or present perfect progressive for each blank. More than one answer could be correct; be prepared to explain your choices. The first one has been done for you.

(1) Ines _____considers_____ (consider) her neighborhood in East Los Angeles to be one of her most important in-groups. (2) She _____ (live) in this neighborhood since birth, and she _____ (know) almost everyone in it. (3) Most of the people in the neighborhood _____ (be) from Mexico, but some _____ (be) from Central American countries. (4) Mr. Hernandez, who _____ (live) next door to Ines, always _____ (insist) that he _____ (live) the longest time in the neighborhood. (5) However, Mrs. Chavez, whom everyone _____ (call) "Tia," usually _____ (tell) him to stop spreading tales. (6) Mrs. Chavez _____ (claim) that *she* _____ (be) around longer than anyone. (7) Ines _____ (watch) many of the children younger than herself grow up, and she often _____ (think) of them as her little brothers and sisters—the ones she _____ (like), that is.

(8) Just as her older neighbors _____ (do) for her, she now _____ (help) her younger neighbors keep out of trouble and _____ (give) them advice.

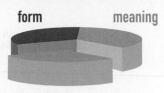
FOCUS 6	Summary: Past Time Frame

FORMS	EXAMPLES	USES	MEANINGS
SIMPLE PRESENT	(a) So on Friday, Terry **calls** Lila and **tells** her to be ready for a surprise.	past event in informal narrative	at a certain time in the past
SIMPLE PAST verb + *-ed* or irregular past form	(b) Kay **joined** the Girl Scouts when she **was** 8.	events that took place at a definite time in the past	at a certain time in the past
	(c) Mark **attended** Columbia University for two years as an undergraduate.	events that lasted for a time in the past	
	(d) Kay **went** to Girl Scout camp every summer until she entered high school.	habitual or repeated actions in the past	
	(e) Kay always **knew** that she wanted to be a doctor.	past mental perceptions and emotions	
	(f) Although she **didn't have** a car in college, Kay **owned** a motorbike.	past possessions	
PAST PROGRESSIVE *was/were* + present participle (verb + *-ing*)	(g) At midnight last night, Kay **was** still **making** her rounds.	events in progress at a specific time in the past	in progress at a time in the past
	(h) Kay **was talking** to one of the nurses when Mark called.	interrupted actions	
	(i) Hannah **was acting** in a community theater play for a month last year.	repeated actions and actions over time	
PAST PERFECT *had* + past participle (verb + *-ed* or irregular form)	(j) Before starting medical school, Kay **had taken** a long vacation.	actions or states that took place before another time in the past	before a certain time in the past
PAST PERFECT PROGRESSIVE *had* + *been* + present participle (verb + *-ing*)	(k) Hannah **had been studying** for two hours when her grandmother arrived to take her to the circus.	incomplete events taking place before other past events	up until a certain time in the past
	(l) Mark **had been working** at his computer when the power went out.	incomplete events interrupted by other past events	

The comic strip below uses the following tenses: simple present, present progressive, simple past, past progressive, and past perfect. Find an example of each of these tenses in the comic strip. Then identify one verb phrase from the strip that expresses each of the following meanings:

1. event in progress
2. present situation
3. event completed in the past before another event
4. action completed at a definite point in the past
5. event in progress at a specific time in the past

Reprinted by permission of the U.F.S. Inc.

EXERCISE 17

The following passage tells the story of the mythological character Dryope. For each blank, choose a simple past, past progressive, past perfect, or past perfect progressive form of the verb in parentheses. More than one choice could be possible. Be prepared to explain your choices. The first one has been done for you.

(1) One day Dryope, with her sister Iole, _____went_____ (go) to a pool in the forest. (2) She _____ (carry) her baby son. (3) She _____ (plan) to make flower garlands near the pool for the nymphs, those female goddesses of the woodlands and waters. (4) When Dryope _____ (see) a lotus tree full of beautiful blossoms near the water, she _____ (pluck) some of them for her baby.

(5) To her horror, drops of blood _____ (flow) from the stem; the tree _____ (be) actually the nymph Lotis. (6) Lotis _____ (flee) from a pursuer and _____ (take) refuge in the form of a tree. (7) When the terrified Dryope _____ (try) to run away, she _____ (find) that her feet would not move; they _____ (root) in the ground. (8) Iole _____ (watch) helplessly as tree bark _____ (grow) upward and _____ (cover) Dryope's body. (9) By the time Dryope's husband _____ (come) to the spot with her father, the bark _____ (reach) Dryope's face. (10) They _____ (rush) to the tree, _____ (embrace) it, and _____ (water) it with their tears. (11) Dryope _____ (have) time only to tell them that she _____ (do) no wrong intentionally. (12) She _____ (beg) them to bring the child often to the tree to play in its shade. (13) She also _____ (tell) them to remind her child never to pluck flowers and to consider that every tree and bush may be a goddess in disguise.

From Edith Hamilton, *Mythology*. Copyright 1942 by Edith Hamilton. Copyright renewed 1969 by Dorian Fielding Reid and Doris Fielding Reid. By permission of Little, Brown and Company.

■ EXERCISE 18

Retell Dryope's story in Exercise 17 in an informal narrative style. Use present tense verbs instead of past tense verbs.

Example: *One day this woman named Dryope and her sister Iole* **go** *to a pool in the woods. Dryope's* **carrying** *her baby son with her. . . .*

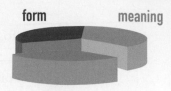

form   meaning

use

FOCUS 7   Summary: Future Time Frame

FORMS	EXAMPLES	USES	MEANINGS
SIMPLE PRESENT	(a) Kay **completes** her residency next May.	definite future plans or schedules	already planned or expected in the future
	(b) After Kay **finishes** her residency, she will take a vacation.	events with future time adverbials in dependent clauses	
PRESENT PROGRESSIVE	(c) I **am leaving** at 7:00 AM tomorrow.	future intentions	already planned or expected in the future
	(d) The family **is spending** the Christmas holidays in Boston.	scheduled events that last for a period of time	
BE GOING TO FUTURE *am/is/are going* *to* + base verb	(e) The movie **is going to start** in a few minutes.	probable and immediate future events	at a certain time in the future
	(f) I **am going to finish** this no matter what!	strong intentions	
	(g) When you get older, you**'re going to wish** that you had saved more money.	predictions about future situations	
	(h) They **are going to travel** in India next summer.	future plans	
SIMPLE FUTURE *will* + base verb	(i) We **will** most likely **stay** at our beach cottage next summer.	probable future events	
	(j) I **will help** you with your homework this evening.	willingness/ promises	
	(k) She**'ll be** very successful.	predictions about future situations	
FUTURE PROGRESSIVE *will* + *be* + present participle (verb + *-ing*)	(l) Kay's parents **will be driving** from Chicago to Palo Alto next week.	events that will be in progress in the near future	in progress at a certain time in the future
	(m) Kay's family **will be living** in Palo Alto until she finishes her residency.	future events that will last for a period of time	

FORMS	EXAMPLES	USES	MEANINGS
FUTURE PERFECT *will* + *have* + past participle (verb + *-ed*)	(n) Kay's parents **will have left** Palo Alto before Hannah starts school.	before a certain time in the future	future events happening before other future events
FUTURE PERFECT PROGRESSIVE *will* + *have* + *been* present participle (verb + *-ing*)	(o) By the end of the year, Kay **will have been living** in California for four years.	up until a certain time in the future	continuous and/or repeated actions continuing into the future

EXERCISE 19

Choose an appropriate future-reference verb tense—simple present, present progressive, *be going to*, simple future, future progressive, or future perfect—to complete the dialogue below between Justin and his friend Patty. More than one verb tense might be appropriate for some blanks. Read the dialogue with a classmate. Discuss any differences in the choices you made. The first exchange has been done for you.

Justin: My brother (1) _____is leaving_____ (leave) tomorrow for his third trip to Europe this year!

Patty: What time (2) _does he go/is he going_ (he, go)?

Justin: His plane (3) _____ (take off) really early—at 6 AM, I think—so he (4) _____ (need) to get out of here by 4 AM or so. I (5) _____ (drive) him to the airport.

Patty: So why (6) _____ (he, go) to Europe again?

Justin: It's for his job. He (7) _____ (meet) his company's executives in Germany and then he (8) _____ (spend) a few days in Denmark. You know something? When I (9) _____(finish) school and (10) _____ (get) a job, I (11) _____ (have) an exciting lifestyle too!

Patty: Oh, really? And what (12) _____ (you, do), if you don't mind my asking.

Justin: Not at all. Next summer, of course, after I (13) _____ (graduate), I (14) _____ (look) for a job for a while. With a little effort, I'm sure I (15) _____ (find) a very challenging and lucrative position in my field. Five years or so from now I (16) _____ (save) enough money to put a down payment on a penthouse condominium. By that time, I (17) _____ (make) enough to buy a flashy little sports car. I (18) _____ (put) away enough money by then to rent a beach vacation home every summer.

Patty: It sounds as if you (19) _____ (live) the good life!

Justin: Well, I just said I (20) _____ (have) enough money to live like that. That doesn't mean I (21) _____ (do) it. Actually, now that I think about it, I (22) _____ (not, get) any of those things. At the end of the five years I (23) _____ (take) all that money I saved and (24) _____ (buy) the largest sailboat I can afford. I (25) _____ (quit) my job and sail around the world! Care to join the crew?

Use Your English

ACTIVITY 1 listening/speaking/writing

In *The Man Who Mistook His Wife for a Hat*, Dr. Oliver Sacks writes about his experiences treating unusual neurological disorders. You will hear a passage summarizing part of Dr. Sacks's true story of Dr. P., the man he refers to in the title.

CD Track 3

STEP 1 Listen to the passage once for overall meaning.

STEP 2 On a separate piece of paper, make a chart like the one below.

STEP 3 Listen to the passage again. In the left-hand column of your chart, write down the past events that occurred before other past events. The first one has been done for you.

EARLIER PAST EVENT	PAST EVENT
1. *He had been a singer.*	1. *Later he became a teacher at the local school of music.*

STEP 4 Listen to the whole passage one more time. In the right-hand column of your chart, write the past event that the earlier past event precedes, as in the example.

STEP 5 Compare your chart with a partner's and discuss the verb forms used in the column.

ACTIVITY 2 writing

Find a place that you think would be interesting to observe nature or people: a quiet place outdoors, a school cafeteria, an airport, or a busy restaurant, for example. Spend 15 or 20 minutes in this place with a notebook to record observations of interesting sights and sounds. You might want to reread Annie Dillard's observations in Exercise 3. Read your observations to the rest of the class or in a small group without telling them where you were. Have your classmates guess the place you are describing.

ACTIVITY 3 writing/speaking

Choose one person in the class. Describe what you think that person will be doing and how he or she will change in the next ten years or so. Read your descriptions to the class or in a small group to see if your classmates can identify the person.

ACTIVITY 4 writing

Reread the passage by James Thurber in Exercise 8. Think of another animal that might have some opinions about the human race that are very different from those humans tend to have about themselves. The animal could be a house pet, such as a canary; another domestic animal, such as a pig; or a wild animal, such as a wolf. Write a description of how this animal has probably regarded the human race.

ACTIVITY 5 speaking/writing

Gordon Allport used concepts of in-groups and out-groups to develop a theory about how prejudices are formed. The very nature of in-groups means that other groups are "out-groups." For example, if someone is Christian, then non-Christians would be "out-groups." Not all "out-groups" are at odds with each other. However, Allport believed that sometimes people treat certain out-groups as "the enemy" or as inferior to their group. As a result, prejudices towards those of other religions, races, or nationalities may form. Do you see evidence, in your school, community, or a larger context, of "out-groups" who are victims of prejudice? Working in groups, list some of the out-groups you think are discriminated against. Then describe the situation affecting one of these out-groups in an essay. State whether the situation has improved or gotten worse over time and whether you think it will have improved by the end of the next decade or so.

ACTIVITY 6 research on the web

Since 2002, Beloit College in Wisconsin has released an annual "Mindset List" for its entering freshmen class. This list is meant to reflect the worldview of its new students. For example, here are a few of the seventy-five "Mindset" items for students in the Class of 2009, most of whom were born around 1987:

- Voicemail has always been available.
- They may have fallen asleep playing their Gameboys in the crib.
- Scientists have always been able to see supernovas.

Look up the Mindset List for one of the Beloit freshman classes (go to www. beloit.edu and use Mindset in your search). Report back on five of the most interesting or humorous items you found. There are many references to American culture (e.g., television personalities and shows) in the lists, so you may need to do more research to learn about the references or ask someone familiar with American culture to explain them to you. As a follow-up, you and your classmates may want to compose your own Mindset List.

ACTIVITY 7 reflection

Learners of a second or foreign language may sometimes feel like outsiders in situations where many people around them are native speakers of that language. For example, they may feel a lack of confidence when they attend social situations such as a party or when they are asked to participate in classroom discussions. Consider strategies you have used in the past to build confidence when communicating in situations with English speakers, strategies you are using now, and strategies that you could use in the future. Here are a few examples:

I have learned some questions that are good to start conversation with people when I go to parties, such as "What did you do over the summer?" or "Do you have any recommendations for places to visit during the spring break?" I am practicing some "starter phrases" to express opinions in class discussions, such as "I agree with what you said, and I also think that . . ." or "That's a good point; however, I feel that . . ." I am going to ask one of my dormitory roommates who is a native speaker of English to explain some of the slang expressions I hear other students using a lot.

Individually or in small groups, write down three to five examples of strategies you have used in the past, are using now, or plan to use, and share your strategies with others in the class.

SUBJECT-VERB AGREEMENT

UNIT GOALS

- Identify the head noun in a subject

- Use correct verb forms for subjects with correlative conjunctions

- Know which kinds of nouns take singular or plural verbs

- Know how subject-verb agreement forms vary in formal and informal English

OPENING TASK
Reading Habits

For over five decades, the Gallup News Service, which examines national trends in the United States, has been surveying Americans' reading habits. They have asked people how often they read, what kinds of reading they do, and how reading compares with other leisure activities, such as going to movies or using the Internet.

■ STEP 1

Read the results on the next page from a 2005 Gallup Poll about reading habits. Then write a paragraph summary of the poll. In your summary, include the following information:

- The number of adults responding to the survey questions
- The percentage of American adults reading books at that time
- What the first question shows about Americans reading in 2005 compared to the poll in 1990
- What the first question shows about which groups are reading more
- What the second question reveals about the number of books that the respondents have read during the year the poll was taken
- What the third question indicates about the effect of the Internet on reading habits

Gallup Poll on Americans' Reading Habits

May, 2005   Based on telephone interviews with 1,006 adults

Question 1. Do you happen to be reading any books or novels at the present?

	YES %
2005 May 20–22	47
1990 Dec 13–16	37
1957 Mar 15–20	23

WHO IS READING A BOOK?		YES %
Overall		47
Gender		
	Male	42
	Female	53
Age		
	18–29	40
	30–49	47
	50–64	51
	65+	47
Education		
	High school or less	33
	Some college	46
	College grad	63
	Postgraduate	74

Question 2. During the past year, about how many books, either hardcover or paperback, did you read either all or part of the way through?

NONE	1 to 5	6 to 10	11 to 50	51+	NO ANSWER
16%	38%	14%	25%	6%	1%

Question 3. What best describes the effect that the Internet has had on the amount of time that you, personally, spend reading books?

READING MORE BOOKS	NOT AFFECTED	READING FEWER BOOKS	NO OPINION
6%	73%	16%	5%

From *Gallup New Service* June 3, 2005.

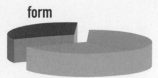

FOCUS 1 — Overview of Subject-Verb Agreement

EXAMPLES	EXPLANATIONS
	In English, all verbs in the present tense must agree in number with the subjects of sentences.
(a) I **am** you/we/they **are** he/she/it **is**	• Present tense *be* has three forms.
(b) I/you/we/they **have** he/she/it **has**	• Present tense *have* changes to *has* with third-person singular subjects.
(c) I/you/we/they **work** He/she/it **works**	• Other present tense verbs add an *–s* or *–es* at the end for third-person singular subjects.
(d) I/you/we/they **pass** He/she it **passes**	
(e) I/he/she/it **was** we/you/they **were**	• Past tense *be* has two forms.
(f) This book **has** been a bestseller for a year.	If the verb is complex, the first part or auxiliary agrees with the subject.
(g) **Science fiction** and **mysteries** **are** two of my favorite kinds of summer reading.	If the subject has more than one part (two or more noun phases), the verb is plural.
(h) There **is one book** I especially like. (i) There **are two books** I need to buy.	In formal English, when the grammatical subject is *there*, the verb agrees with the logical subject, the noun phrase that follows the verb. Choosing the correct verb form is not always easy, even for native speakers of English. Some reasons for difficulties are the following:
Head Noun (j) (The main **reason** we decided to take a trip to the Rocky Mountains) **is** to learn geological history. (k) (That **novel** about alien invasions in several South American countries) **has** been made into a TV film.	• subjects with long modifying phrases following the main noun requiring agreement, as in (j) and (k). This noun is often called the **head noun**.
(l) The **pair of scissors** you bought **is** really dull now. (m) **Every book** in the library **has** been entered in the new computer system.	• nouns and pronoun phrases whose number (singular/plural) may be confusing, as in (l) and (m).
Plural Noun (n) Those comic **books** make me laugh. **Singular Verb** (o) That comic book **makes** me laugh.	• the *–s* ending in English as both a plural marker for nouns and a singular marker for third-person present-tense verbs, as in (n), which has a plural noun, and (o), which has a 3rd person singular verb.

EXERCISE 1

To check for subject-verb agreement, (1) identify the subject of the sentence and then (2) find the noun that is the head of the subject. In each of the following sentences, underline the head noun of the subject. Then circle the correct form of the verb in parentheses.

Example: _Book clubs_ (is/(are)) _very popular social activities._

1. The popularity of book clubs (seem/seems) to be increasing throughout the world.

2. Organizing a successful book club (involve/involves) a number of considerations.

3. Some of the many considerations (is/are) are how often to meet and whether the members (want/wants) to conduct serious discussions or just have social chats about books.

4. A book club organizer also (has/have) to think about how large the group should be.

5. Other questions to consider (concern/concerns) where the book club will meet, such as in the members' homes or in a public place like a bookstore, and who will be responsible for structuring each meeting.

6. Once the book club (is/are) formed, the members (need/needs) to agree on how they will select the books; sometimes, each member (suggest/suggests) a number of books and then the members (vote/votes) on them.

7. During the book club discussions, an individual who (is/are) critical of a book that other members (like/likes) (has/have) to be careful not to hurt anyone's feelings.

8. There (is/are) now hundreds of virtual book clubs online.

9. These online book clubs, which (connect/connects) readers around the world, (has/have) helped to promote interesting discussions about books from multicultural perspectives.

10. Another advantage of online book clubs (is/are) that they can link groups of friends who (want/wants) to discuss books but who (do/does) not live near each other.

EXERCISE 2

Write three questions about the Gallup reading habits poll results shown in the Opening Task. Check to make sure that your verbs agree with their subject. With a classmate, take turns asking and responding to the questions.

Examples: _What percentage of Americans say they have not read any books during the past year?_
Which group has more people reading a book: males or females?

Identifying Head Nouns in Long Subjects

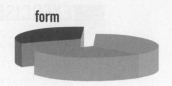

form

EXAMPLES	EXPLANATIONS
(a) That **novel** about alien invasions in several southwestern states **has** recently been made into a TV movie. (b) All of the **characters** in that story written by our teacher **were** very believable. (c) One **poll** of Americans' reading and attitudes **was taken** in 2004.	When the subject head noun and the verb are separated from each other, it is harder to check for agreement. It can be especially troublesome when the head noun is singular but nouns in a modifying phrase are plural or vice versa. Here are strategies to find the head nouns: • First, find the verb for the clause or sentence. This will help you determine what the subject is.
Head Noun before Prepositional Phrase (d) Another **poll** of Americans' reading and attitudes **was taken** in 2005.	• If the subject has a prepositional phrase, locate the head noun to the left of the first preposition (for example, *of*).
Head Noun before Compound Preposition (e) The **library,** $\left\{\begin{array}{l}\text{together with}\\\text{along with}\\\text{as well as}\end{array}\right\}$ bookstores, **provides** reading materials.	• Use the same strategy with subjects followed by compound prepositions, such as *together with, along with,* and *as well as.* Look for the head noun to the left of these phrases.
Head Noun with *Not* + Noun Phrase (f) The **child,** not her parents, **was** an avid reader.	• Locate the head noun before *not* + a noun phrase.
Relative Clause (g) A **child** who likes to read **books** and whose parents encourage reading **does** better in school.	• Similarly, look to the left of relative clauses (*who, which, that, whose* clauses) to identify the head noun.

EXERCISE 3

For each of the following sentences, put brackets {} around any modifying phrases or clauses following the head noun of the main clause. Underline the head nouns of main clauses and subordinate clauses. Then circle the appropriate verb from the choices given in parentheses.

Example: *The library, {along with bookstores}, (provides/provide) reading materials.*

1. About one in every two Americans (was/were) reading some type of book, according to a recent Gallup poll.

2. People who usually (follow/follows) current events (is/are) also likely to read books.

3. A high frequency of movie attendance (do/does) not seem to decrease book reading.

4. Tom Clancy, along with John Grisham and Louis L'Amour, (rank/ranks) very high in popularity among contemporary authors.

5. Horror story writer Stephen King, as well as romance novelist Danielle Steele, (remain/remains) extremely popular with readers.

6. A person who (belong/belongs) to one of the higher income groups (tends/tend) to read more.

7. While the leisure activity of reading books (seem/seems) to be thriving, as indicated by polls and other sources, some researchers in universities and public agencies (express/expresses) concern about the kinds of material that people (report/reports) reading.

8. In Great Britain, a study of people's diaries about reading habits (reveal/reveals) that although most people reported they (was/were) reading a book at some point during a three-month period, many of them only consulted a reference book on gardening or cooking.

9. In other words, a reference book, and not literature or serious nonfiction, (was/were) the only kind of book read.

10. A recent survey of literary reading in America by the National Endowment for the Arts (conclude/concludes) that literary reading among almost all groups of Americans (is/are) declining.

Information from: *Gallup News Service* June 3, 2005 and July 21, 1999 www.gallup.com; *The Bookseller,* April 11, 2003 p27(3). Source: *InfoTrac® College Edition.*

EXERCISE 4

Edit the following paragraph to correct errors in subject-verb agreement.

(1) Comics and comic books are very popular kinds of reading for young people throughout the world. (2) Some of the most well-known characters from American comics is Charlie Brown and Snoopy, his beagle dog, from the comic *Peanuts*. (3) The comic book super heroes, such as Superman, has also been very popular. (4) Of course some of these heroes are also featured in movies as well as reading

materials. (5) In Korea and Japan, students like to read comic books called *manga* to pass the time. (6) The United States are now publishing manga for American readers. (7) Meanwhile, in Japan, two American English teachers has conducted a study on reading of manga. (8) They found that many of the most popular manga for college students is about school life. (9) Although many young people enjoy comic books as an escape from everyday life, parents and teachers often disapprove of this kind of reading. (10) They believe that such reading are not productive and that students may become lazy readers.

Information adapted from "Manga Literacy: Popular Culture and the Reading Habits of Japanese College Students," Kate Allen and John Ingulsrud, *Journal of Adolescent & Adult Literacy*, May 2003, v46, i8 p674 (10). *InfoTrac College Edition®*.

| FOCUS 3 | Agreement in Sentences with Correlative Conjunctions: *Both . . . and; Either . . . or; Neither . . . nor* |

form

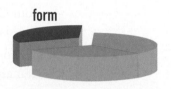

EXAMPLES	EXPLANATIONS
(a) Both J. K. Rowling and J. R. R. Tolkien were named as favorite authors by Britons in recent polls.	**Both . . . and** When two subjects are connected by *both . . . and*, use a plural verb.
(b) Either the library or **bookstores have** current magazines. (c) Either bookstores or the **library has** current magazines. (d) Neither the book nor the **magazines discuss** this issue. (e) Neither the magazines nor the **book discusses** this issue.	**Either . . . or; Neither . . . nor** The traditional rule is that the verb should agree with the head noun after *or* or *nor*.
(f) Either Kay or **I am** going to the library this afternoon. (g) Neither the twins nor **he is** planning to go to the library. (h) Obviously, neither she nor **they are** interested in that topic.	This agreement rule also determines verb form when one or more of the subjects is a pronoun.

EXERCISE 5

Select the appropriate verb form and, in some cases, the correct noun phrase after the verb, for each sentence. In cases of *either . . . or* or *neither . . . nor*, use the rule in Focus 3 to select the verb.

Example: *Neither the books nor the bookshelf ((is)/are) mine.*

1. Either books or a magazine subscription (makes a nice gift/make nice gifts) for someone.

2. For a less expensive gift, both bookplates and a bookmark (is a good choice/are good choices).

3. Neither the Russian novelist Leo Tolstoy nor the Irish writer James Joyce (was/were) known to more than 50 percent of American respondents in one Gallup Poll.

4. She said that either the reserved book librarian or the librarians at the main checkout desk (has/have) the information you need.

5. Both reading and writing (is/are) what we consider literacy skills.

6. Either you or I (am/are) going to present the first report.

7. In my opinion, neither the front page of the newspaper nor the sports pages (is/are) as much fun to read as the comics.

8. (Does/do) either the lifestyle section of the newspaper or the business section interest you?

9. I can see that neither you nor he (is/are) finished with your sections yet.

10. Both my brother and my parents (is/are) reading that new book about Bill Gates. Neither he nor they (has/have) read more than a few chapters, though.

EXERCISE 6

In groups of three, ask and answer questions about the kinds of reading you like to do. Make up five statements summarizing the responses of your group using *both . . . and* or *neither . . . nor*. Report your findings to another group.

Examples: ***Neither*** *Mohammed* ***nor*** *Juanita likes to read novels.*

Both *Tomoyo* ***and*** *Wanbo enjoy reading sports magazines.*

FOCUS 4 — Agreement with Noncount Nouns, Collective Nouns, and Nouns Derived from Adjectives

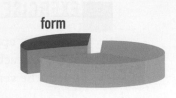

form

EXAMPLES	EXPLANATIONS
	Noncount Nouns
(a) The new gym **equipment has** just been delivered.	Noncount nouns in English include mass nouns and abstract nouns. These nouns take a singular verb.
(b) That **information is** very helpful.	
(c) My English **vocabulary has** increased.	**Mass Nouns** / **Abstract Nouns**
(d) Your **advice is** always appreciated.	equipment — advice furniture — behavior grass — education homework — information machinery — knowledge money — research traffic — transportation vocabulary — violence
	Collective Nouns
(e) The **audience is** waiting patiently for the performance to begin.	Some collective nouns define groups of people, animals, or things:
(f) A **flock** of geese **is** flying overhead.	audience — group class — herd committee — the public family — swarm flock — team
(g) The **class is** going on a field trip.	If the group is considered as a whole, use a singular verb. In most cases, collective nouns take singular verbs.
(h) The **team has** been practicing all week.	Note: In American English, a later pronoun reference to a collective noun can use a plural pronoun and plural verb, as in (i).
(i) The **committee** is meeting tomorrow. **They** will choose a new Chairperson.	
(j) A **variety** of art books **has** been added to the library.	Some collective nouns also can refer to things as well as to people and animals. These include *assortment, collection, variety.*
(k) A **collection** of old coins **remains** one of my grandfather's most cherished possessions.	
(l) **The young want** to grow up fast and **the old wish** to be younger.	**Nouns Derived from Adjectives**
(m) Is it true that **the rich are** getting richer and **the poor are** getting poorer?	Noun phrases derived from adjectives that describe people, such as *the young, the rich,* and *the homeless,* take plural verbs.

EXERCISE 7

Take turns giving oral responses (between one and five sentences) to the following questions. Use the noun or nouns in bold print as the subject in at least one sentence for each response. The first one is done as an example.

1. What kind of **transportation** do you prefer for getting to school?

   *Well, the **transportation** I prefer is driving my own car. But finding a parking space is difficult, so I take the bus most of the time. Once in a while my friend gives me a ride.*

2. What is some good **advice** you've gotten during the past year from a friend, a relative, or something you read?

3. What is some useful **information** you've learned in your English class?

4. What computer **equipment** do you think is the most helpful for you as a student?

5. Do you think **violence** is ever justified? Explain your opinion.

6. How would you describe your **knowledge** of sports? (Good? Fair? Poor? Does it vary according to particular sports?)

7. Do you think **the homeless** are being neglected in our society? What evidence do you have for your opinion?

8. Do you believe that **a college education** is necessary for everyone in our society? Who might not need a college education?

EXERCISE 8

Write an answer for each question using the noun phrase in parentheses as the subject of your sentence.

Example: What is going on outside the courthouse? (group of protesters)

   A group of protesters seems to be gathering on the street.

1. Were there a lot of people at the political rally? (the audience)

2. What did that restaurant offer for dessert? (an assortment of sweets)

3. How do you celebrate birthdays in your family? (my family)

4. What did the city government decide to do about the rise in crime? (the government)

5. What is that nest-like thing under the roof of the house? (a swarm of bees)

6. Do you think the city you live in getting bigger or smaller? (the population of [CITY'S NAME])

7. What do you like best about shopping in that store? (the variety of [PRODUCT NAME])

8. Do young people have much influence on fashion trends? (the young)

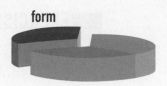

FOCUS 5   Subjects Requiring Singular Verbs

Some types of subjects always take singular verbs.

EXAMPLES	EXPLANATIONS
	Some common or proper singular nouns that end in -*s*:
(a) **Mathematics is** my favorite subject. Others: *physics, economics*	• courses
(b) **Measles is** no fun to have! Others: *mumps, arthritis*	• diseases
(c) **Leeds is** where my aunt was born.	• place names
(d) **The news** from home **was** very encouraging.	• news
(e) *Tracks* **was** written by Louise Erdrich.	• book and film titles
(f) *Dances with Wolves* **was** awarded an Oscar for the best movie.	
	Plural unit words of distance, time, and money:
(g) **Six hundred miles is** too far to drive in one day.	• distance
(h) **Two weeks goes** fast when you're on vacation.	• time
(i) **Fifty dollars is** a good price for that painting.	• money
	Arithmetical operations (addition, subtraction, multiplication, division):
(j) **Seven plus three equals** ten; **seven minus three equals** four.	• addition, subtraction
(k) **Four times two equals** eight; **four divided by two equals** two.	• multiplication, division

EXAMPLES	EXPLANATIONS
	Items that have two parts when you use the noun _pair_
(l) My **pair** of scissors **is** lost. BUT (m) My **scissors are** lost. (n) A **pair** of plaid shorts **was** on the dresser. BUT (o) Those plaid **shorts were** on the dresser.	In (l) and (n), the head noun _pair_ takes a singular subject. Note, however, that you would use the plural verb as in (m) and (o) if the noun _pair_ is absent.
Subject (p) [**What we need**] **is** more reference books.	**Clause subjects:** Clause subjects have a subject and a verb embedded within them. These subjects may begin with noun clause markers such as _what_ or _that._ The verb is singular even when the nouns referred to are plural.
(q) [**That languages have many differences**] is obvious.	
(r) [**Reading books and magazines**] is one of my favorite ways to spend free time.	Gerund (verb + _-ing_) and infinitive (_to_ + verb) clauses also take singular verbs.
(s) [**To pass all my exams**] is my next goal.	

EXERCISE 9

Imagine that you are competing on a quiz show. For each definition below, you will be given three words, phrases, or numbers. You must choose the correct match and state the answer in a complete sentence.

Example: a film set in California (_Badlands, Down and Out in Beverly Hills, Star Wars_)

Answer: **_Down and Out in Beverly Hills_** _is a film set in California._

1. the number of days in a leap year (364, 365, 366)

2. a disease that makes you look like a chipmunk (shingles, mumps, warts)

3. four (54 divided by 9, 100 divided by 20, 200 divided by 50)

4. a poem written by Geoffrey Chaucer (_The Canterbury Tales, Great Expectations, Guys and Dolls_)

(_Continued on next page_)

5. a common plumber's tool (a pair of scissors, a pair of pliers, a pair of flamingoes)

6. a city in Venezuela (Buenos Aires, Caracas, Athens)

7. what you most often find on the front page of a newspaper (sports news, political news, entertainment news)

8. the study of moral principles (ethics, physics, stylistics)

9. the number of years in a score (ten, twenty, thirty)

10. a course that would discuss supply and demand (mathematics, economics, physics)

EXERCISE 10

What are your opinions and attitudes about each of the following topics? State at least two things that could complete each of the sentences below. Share some of your answers with the class. The first one has been done as an example.

1. What my country needs _is health insurance for everyone and better jobs_____.

2. What my country needs _____.

3. What I would like to have in five years _____.

4. Having a job while going to school _____.

5. That energy costs are rising _____.

6. What really irritates me _____.

7. What I find most enjoyable about being in school _____.

8. Learning the rules of subject-verb agreement in English _____.

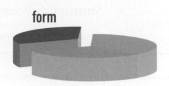

FOCUS 6 Agreement with Fractions, Percentages, and Quantifiers

With fractions, percentages, and quantifiers *all (of)* and *a lot of*, agreement depends on the noun or clause after these phrases.

EXAMPLES	EXPLANATIONS
(a) Fifty percent of the **book is** about poetry.	Use a singular verb when the subject is: • a singular noun
(b) Half of **what he says is** not true.	• a noun clause
(c) All (of) our **information is** up-to-date.	• a noncount noun
(d) One-fourth of the **students have** computers.	With plural nouns, use a plural verb.
(e) All (of) the **computers need** to be checked.	
(f) One-sixth of our **Spanish club has** relatives in Mexico.	With collective nouns after percentages and fractions, the singular verb is usually used
(g) A lot of my **family live** in Pennsylvania.	in American English. However, a plural verb is used when the collective noun follows quantifiers such as *a lot of* or *many*
(h) Each **book has** a code number.	With quantifiers *each, every*, and *every one*, use a singular verb, whether the noun is singular or plural.
(i) Every one of the **students is** on time.	
(j) A number of **students are** taking the TOEFL® Test today.	With *a number of*, use a plural verb since the noun it modifies is always plural.
(k) The number of **students** taking the exam **is** 175.	*The number of*, however, takes a singular verb.
(l) None of the **advice was** very helpful.	With *none of*, use a singular verb in formal written English.
(m) None of the **magazines** I wanted **is** here.	

*TOEFL is a registered trademark of the Educational Testing Service (ETS). This publication is not endorsed or approved by ETS.

Summary: Form of the Verb Following Traditional Agreement Rules

	SINGULAR NOUN	NONCOUNT NOUN	PLURAL NOUN	COLLECTIVE NOUN
percentages	singular	singular	plural	singular/plural
fractions	singular	singular	plural	singular/plural
all (of)	singular	singular	plural	singular/plural
a lot of	singular	singular	plural	singular/plural
each, every	singular	singular	singular	
a number of			plural	
the number of			singular	
none of	singular	singular	singular	singular

EXERCISE 11

Circle the correct verb in parentheses, using the traditional agreement rules presented in Focus 6.

Example: *Almost three-fourths of the respondents (believe/believes) they spend too little time reading books for pleasure.*

1. Forty-two percent of Americans (claim/claims) they have a favorite author.

2. Forty-nine percent of the population surveyed in a recent poll (consider/considers) Ernest Hemingway to be the greatest author of all time.

3. However, almost none of the respondents (mention/mentions) Hemingway as their favorite author.

4. Although half of Americans polled (say/says) that they have read a book by Ernest Hemingway, less than a third of the respondents (was/were) able to recognize him as the author of one of his most famous novels, *The Old Man and the Sea*.

5. All of the information for the Gallup Poll (was/were) obtained through telephone interviews.

6. A number of Gallup Polls (is/are) now being conducted in countries other than the United States, such as China and India.

Information from *Gallup News Service* June 3, 2005 and July 21, 1999 www.gallup.com.

EXERCISE 12

The National Endowment of the Arts conducted a survey to see how literary reading compared to other leisure activities. Summarize the information below from the survey by writing five sentences about some of the findings, using present tense verbs. To refer to the participants in this study, you could use any of the following or others: U.S. adults, the population, the respondents. Use a variety of phrases to refer to the participants.

Examples: *Almost half of the population does some kind of gardening.*

The majority of the respondents do some kind of exercise.

U.S. Adults' Participation in Cultural, Sports, and Leisure Activities in a 12-Month Period

	% OF POPULATION
Watch at least one hour of TV per day (on average)	95.7
Go out to movies	60.0
Jog, lift weights, walk or follow other exercise program	55.1
Work with indoor plants or do any gardening	47.2
Read literature	46.7
Watch three or more hours of TV per day (on average)	46.2
Go to amusement/theme park or carnival	35.0
Visit historic park or monument	31.6
Do outdoor activities such as camping, hiking, or canoeing	30.9
Visit art museum or gallery	26.5

Adapted from *Reading At Risk: A Survey of Literary Reading in America June.* 2004, National Endowment of the Arts.

Write three sentences that are true and three that are false about the members of your class, using the words in parentheses as the subjects. Read your sentences aloud to a classmate. Your classmate should decide which are true and which are false and should orally correct each false statement.

Example: *The number of female students in our class is 12.*

Response: *False. The number of female students in our class is 14.*

1. (The number of) _____.

2. (Each) _____.

3. (None) _____.

4. (All) _____.

5. (A lot of) _____.

6. (A number of) _____.

Fill in each blank of the following radio news report with a *be* verb form that would be appropriate for formal English use.

Example: *A number of reporters from other states __are__ in town to cover news about the earthquake.*

Here is the latest report on the aftermath of the earthquake. As most of you know, the earthquake has caused a great deal of damage and disruption to our area. A lot of the houses near the epicenter of the quake (1) _____ badly damaged. A number of trees (2) _____ uprooted in that area also, so be careful if you are driving. All the electricity (3) _____ shut off for the time being. Water (4) _____ turned off also. None of the freeways in the vicinity (5) _____ currently open to traffic. Almost every side street (6) _____ jammed with drivers trying to get back home. The police (7) _____ directing traffic at major intersections. To date, the number of deaths resulting from the earthquake (8) _____ two. All people (9) _____ urged to stay at home if at all possible.

Exceptions to Traditional Agreement Rules

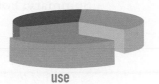

use

Some of the agreement rules presented in this unit are observed mainly in formal English contexts, especially in formal written English. The following are cases where native speakers of English frequently do not follow the formal (traditional) rules, especially in spoken and less formal written English:

EXAMPLES	EXPLANATIONS
	Either/Neither of the + **Noun Phrase**
	Formal rule: use a singular verb with *either* or *neither*.
(a) Either of the outfits **is** appropriate.	Formal
(b) Either of the outfits **are** appropriate.	Informal
(c) Neither of the choices **is** desirable.	Formal
(d) Neither of the choices **are** desirable.	Informal
	Either . . . or / Neither . . . nor
	Formal rule: the verb agrees with the closest subject noun.
(e) Either my parents or John **has** the car.	Formal
(f) Either my parents or John **have** the car.	Informal
(g) Neither you nor I **am** convinced.	Formal
(h) Neither you nor I **are** convinced.	Informal
	None + **Prepositional Phrase**
	Formal rule: use a singular verb.
(i) None of the magazines **is** here.	Formal
(j) None of the magazines **are** here.	Informal
	There + **Be (present tense)** + **Plural Noun**
	Formal rule: use *are* with plural nouns.
(k) There **are** three books here you might like.	Formal
(l) There**'s** three books here you might like.	Informal

Note: Many informal forms are becoming more common in all but the most formal written English contexts. *There are* is usually used with plural noun phrases in written English, however.

Summary: Form of the Verb in Formal versus Informal Usage

	FORMAL	INFORMAL
Either of the + (plural noun)	singular verb	singular or plural verb
Neither of the + (plural noun)	singular verb	singular or plural verb
Neither (noun) *nor* (singular noun)	singular verb	singular or plural verb
None of the + (plural noun)	singular verb	singular or plural verb
There + singular logical subject	singular verb	singular verb
There + plural logical subject	plural verb	singular or plural verb

EXERCISE 15

Decide which of the underlined verbs would be appropriate for formal written contexts and which would be acceptable in spoken English. Write "formal" or "informal" to indicate the usage.

Examples: *Either of these economics courses <u>are</u> useful for my major.*

         Informal

1. Neither of those political surveys <u>are</u> valid because the population sample was not random.

2. I am sure that either Professor Tori or Professor Kline <u>have</u> already addressed the issues you mention.

3. As far as we know, none of the experiment's results <u>has</u> been duplicated to date.

4. There <u>are</u> some results that will surprise you.

5. Neither Dr. Gonzalez nor Dr. Vuong <u>are</u> presenting the findings of their studies until the results are checked again.

6. In conclusion, either of the textbooks I have reviewed <u>is</u> an excellent choice for an introductory chemistry course.

7. We have reviewed the report. None of the figures <u>seem</u> correct; they should be checked again.

8. Either of the reports submitted <u>are</u> useful for further study of this environmental problem.

9. Neither the campus medical center nor the library <u>is</u> safe should a strong earthquake occur.

10. Either you or I <u>are</u> responsible for this month's financial report; please let me know if I should submit it.

11. Neither of the claims Senator Holmes presented <u>is</u> justified.

12. There<u>'s</u> a number of errors in this report.

Use Your English

ACTIVITY 1 listening

You will hear a summary of information from another Gallup survey. This one asked people questions about raising children.

■ STEP 1 As you listen to the summary, take notes on the information you hear.

■ STEP 2 At the end of the summary, you will hear eight statements based on the information in the survey. Listen to all the statements and decide whether each statement is true or false.

■ STEP 3 Listen to the statements again, pausing after each one. On a separate piece of paper, write T or F after you hear each statement. If a statement is false, write a correction using a complete sentence.

■ STEP 4 Listen to the summary again to check your answers and corrections.

ACTIVITY 2 speaking

Below are some examples of spoken and written English that were found in a newspaper. Discuss the traditional rules of subject-verb agreement that have not been observed. How do they illustrate some of the troublesome cases of subject-verb agreement? (Why do you think the speaker or writer used a singular or plural verb in each situation?)

1. "I have decided that everyone in these type of stories are rich." (Quoted statement by an actress in reference to a TV movie she appeared in)

2. "Her expertise in the water as a lifeguard and her understanding of ocean currents, coupled with the fact that she is a strong swimmer, makes her a strong competitor." (Quoted comment about a champion swimmer)

3. "I know there is going to be a major hassle with certain smokers, plus there is going to be a lot of attempts to bypass the regulation." (From a letter to the editor about no-smoking regulations)

4. ". . . the chances of him coming back in the next eight years was very unlikely." (Quoted comment about a politician who ran for President)

5. "In the Jewelry Center, All That Glitter Sure Is Gold" (Headline for a feature article)

ACTIVITY 3 research/speaking/writing

Conduct a poll within your class using the three questions in the reading habits survey from the Opening Task on page 39. Tally the results and write a survey report comparing them to the Gallup Poll results.

ACTIVITY 4 research/speaking/writing

Usage surveys have suggested that native speakers of English often use plural verbs with *either of* + plural noun, such as in sentences like this: "*Either of those times are okay with me for a meeting.*" Which verb do you think native speakers would use in the following question form: "*Are / Is either of those times okay with you?*"

■ **STEP 1**   In groups or with a partner, create a set of five questions with *either + of + plural noun* to test what verbs native speakers would choose. Here are some examples:

Examples: 1. *Do/does either of you boys have a match?*

2. *Is/are either of you going to come with us to the movies?*

3. *Has/have either of your parents ever worked in a restaurant?*

■ **STEP 2**   Conduct a survey by giving your set of questions to at least ten native speakers of English. Ask them to choose the verb they would use.

■ **STEP 3**   Write a report of your results or give an oral report to the class.

ACTIVITY 5 research on the web

Using *InfoTrac® College Edition*, research the topic of reading surveys. The survey could be one conducted anywhere in the world. Write a summary of your results using the present tense and, if possible, compare some of the findings to the Gallup Poll survey in the Opening Task.

ACTIVITY 6 reflection

Most students have to do a great deal of reading for their academic courses. What are some of the skills and strategies that a good reader uses? With a partner, brainstorm a list of all the things you can think of that a good reader does.

Example: *A good reader previews a textbook or chapter before starting to read.*

PASSIVE VERBS

UNIT GOALS

- Know when to use passive verbs rather than active verbs

- Use correct forms of *be* and *get* passives

- Know the correct form and use of passives in descriptions

- Use passives correctly after *that* clauses and infinitive clauses

- Use passives to create connections in discourse

OPENING TASK
A Short-Term Memory Experiment

Short-term memory describes the brain function in which information is retained temporarily, somewhere between 30 seconds and a few minutes. Numerous experiments have been conducted to test the recall of information stored in short-term memory, resulting in various theories about memory. One phenomenon believed to characterize short-term memory is called the *serial position effect*. In this task, you will be testing this effect. (You will find out later exactly what it means.)

STEP 1

Work with a partner. One person will be the researcher; the other will be the subject. Have a blank piece of paper and a pen ready. The subject's book should be closed.

STEP 2

Researcher: Show the list of words on page A-17 to your partner. Ask your partner to study the list of words for one minute. After one minute has passed, close the book.

STEP 3

Subject: Immediately write down on the blank sheet of paper as many words as you can recall for one minute. You can write the words in any order. Then give the list to the researcher. Note: It is important that you start writing immediately after the study time is up.

STEP 4

Read the explanation of the serial position effect on page A-17. Do the results of your experiment support or contradict this belief about short-term memory?

STEP 5

Write a brief report of the experiment, using the written list of words as your data. Assume that your reader has no previous information about your experiment. Describe the procedures and summarize the results. Use the model below to start the report. Save the report for exercises later in the unit.

Memory Experiment

This experiment was conducted to test the serial position effect on recalling information. One subject participated in the experiment. The subject was shown a list of 30 common words . . .

Overview of Passive versus Active Verb Use

use

EXAMPLES		EXPLANATIONS
ACTIVE VERBS	**PASSIVE VERBS**	We often use passive instead of active in the following contexts:
(Agent) (a) The brain **retains** (Recipient) information temporarily in short-term memory.	(Recipient) (b) Information **is retained** (Agent) temporarily by the brain in short-term memory.	• when we want to focus on the receiver of an action (recipient) rather than the performer (agent) of the action. We do this by making the recipient the grammatical subject. We may express the agent in a *by*-phrase following the verb.
(c) I **asked** the subject to look at the word list for one minute.	(d) The subject **was asked** to look at the word list for one minute.	• when the agent is less important than the recipient of an action. In reporting research procedures, for example, we do not need to refer to the researcher.
(e) The subject wrote down all the words she could remember. She **recalled** a total of 13 words.	(f) The subject wrote down all the words she could remember. A total of thirteen words **were recalled.**	• when the agent is obvious from the context.
(g) It appears that something **is altering** the rats' brain cells.	(h) It appears that the rats' brain cells **are being altered.**	• when the agent is unknown.
(i) The researchers who did this study **have made several major** errors in analyzing the data.	(j) Several major errors **have been made** in analyzing the data.	• when we want to avoid mentioning the agent. For example, we may not want to say who is responsible for some wrongdoing or mistake.

EXERCISE 1

Provide a likely reason for each of the italicized passive verbs in the sentences below. Refer to the explanations in Focus 1.

Example: Two masterpieces of sixteenth-century painting *were taken* from the museum. *The agent is unknown.*

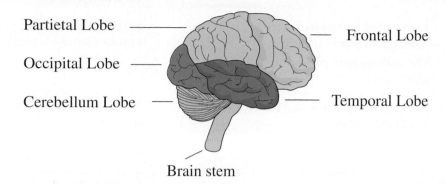

Partietal Lobe ——— ——— Frontal Lobe

Occipital Lobe ———

Cerebellum Lobe ——— ——— Temporal Lobe

Brain stem

1. One method that is *used by* psychologists in research on memory is the relearning method.

2. In the relearning method, people have to relearn information that *was learned* earlier.

3. Sometimes when you *are introduced* to another person, you forget the person's name a few minutes later.

4. It seems that some misleading statements *were made* in advertising your auto repair services.

5. We have just received reports that a bomb *was set off* in the airport terminal shortly before midnight.

6. Construction of the Leaning Tower of Pisa *was begun* by Bonanno Pisano in 1173.

7. Small bits of information *are* often *remembered* by grouping the information into larger units, known as chunks.

8. Short-term memory *has been called* "a leaky bucket."

EXERCISE 2

Reread the first paragraph of the Opening Task on pages 60–61. Identify the passive verbs and state why they are used.

EXERCISE 3

With your partner for the Opening Task, identify any passive verbs you used in your report, and state why they are used. If you didn't use any passive verbs, find one or two sentences that you might change from active to passive based on the information in Focus 1. State what use each would reflect.

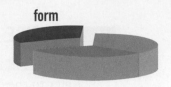
form

FOCUS 2   Review of Passive Verb Forms

All passive verbs are formed with *be* or *get* + past participle.

EXAMPLES	EXPLANATIONS
(a) I **am called** by telemarketers more than I would like. (b) The garbage **gets picked up** once a week.	**SIMPLE PRESENT** *am/is/are* (or *get*) + past participle
(c) The possibility of life on Mars **is being explored.** (d) We **are getting asked** to do too much!	**PRESENT PROGRESSIVE** *am/is/are* + *being* (or *getting*) + past participle
(e) The butterflies **were observed** for five days. (f) Many homes **got destroyed** during the fire.	**SIMPLE PAST** *was/were* (or *got*) + past participle
(g) The Olympics **were being broadcast** worldwide. (h) She **was getting beaten** in the final trials.	**PAST PROGRESSIVE** *was/were* + *being* (or *getting*) + past participle
(i) Short-term memory also holds information that **has been retrieved** from long-term memory. (j) Did you hear he's **gotten fired** from his job?	**PRESENT PERFECT** *has/have* + *been* (or *gotten*) + past participle The passive with a form of GET instead of BE is common in spoken English.
(k) This store **has been being remodeled** for six months now! I wonder if they'll ever finish. (l) Our computer system **has been getting threatened** by viruses a lot this year.	**PRESENT PERFECT PROGRESSIVE*** *has* + *been* + *being* (or *getting*) + past participle
(m) The National Anthem **had** already **been sung** when we entered the baseball stadium. (n) He was disappointed to learn that the project **hadn't gotten completed** in his absence.	**PAST PERFECT** *had* + *been* (or *gotten*) + past participle
(o) The horse races **will be finished** in an hour. (p) The rest of the corn **will get harvested** this week.	**SIMPLE FUTURE** *will* + *be* (or *get*) + past participle

EXAMPLES	EXPLANATIONS
(q) I bet most of the food **will have been eaten** by the time we get to the party. (r) The unsold books **will have gotten sent back** to the publishers by now.	**FUTURE PERFECT** *will* + *have* + *been* (or *gotten*) + past participle
(s) The election results **will have been getting tallied** by the time we reach the headquarters	**FUTURE PERFECT PROGRESSIVE**[*] *will* + *have* + *been* + *being* (or *getting*) + past participle
(t) A different chemical **could be substituted** in this experiment. (u) Don't stay outside too long. You **may get burned** by the blazing afternoon sun	**MODAL VERBS (Present Time Frame)** modal (*can, may, should,* etc.) + *be* (or *get*) + past participle
(v) All of our rock specimens **should have been identified**, since the lab report is due. (w) The file **might have gotten erased** through a computer error.	**MODAL VERBS (Past Time Frame)** modal (*can, may, should,* etc.) + *have* + *been* (or *gotten*) + past participle

[*]Note: The *be* form of these passive tenses is quite rare. Even the *get* form is not very common.

EXERCISE 4

Rewrite each sentence below to put focus on the recipients of action rather than on the performers (agents) of the action. Delete the agent if you do not think it needs to be mentioned. In some cases, you may want to restate the agent in a prepositional phrase beginning with *in* rather than with *by*.

Example: The brain stores information.

Information is stored in the brain.

1. A bundle of millions of fibers connects the brain cells.

2. In visual processing, the right hemisphere of the brain registers unfamiliar faces; the left hemisphere registers familiar ones.

3. The memory does not store an exact replica of experience.

4. The brain alters, organizes, and transfers information into one or more memory stores.

5. The multistore model of memory cannot explain some facts about processing information.

(*Continued on next page*)

6. Researchers are now investigating other ways in which we organize information in long-term memory.

7. Scientists have demonstrated the difference between recognition and recall in numerous experiments.

8. The researchers used case studies of stroke victims to learn more about information storage.

EXERCISE 5

Rewrite the underlined sentences or clauses in the following research report, changing the verbs to passives. Delete the agent if it is not needed.

Example: Researchers gave students a questionnaire about food likes and dislikes.

Students were given a questionnaire about food likes and dislikes.

(1) Psychologist Elizabeth Loftus and a team of researchers have been exploring a new method of weight control that involves manipulating subjects' memories about certain kinds of food. (2) <u>In a series of experiments, the research team convinced university students</u> that certain foods made them sick when they were children. (3) The scientists said they also successfully implanted positive memories about nutritious fruits and vegetables. (4) In one experiment involving attitudes toward strawberry ice cream, <u>the researchers asked 131 students to complete forms in which they described food experiences, likes and dislikes.</u> (5) <u>The researchers then gave the subjects a computer analysis of their responses.</u> (6) <u>The analysis inaccurately told some students</u> that strawberry ice cream had made them sick as children. (7) Later, almost 20 percent of these students agreed on a questionnaire that <u>this kind of ice cream had sickened them</u> and that they planned not to eat it in the future. (8) In a second experiment, <u>the researchers encouraged students to detail the imaginary ice cream episode.</u> (9) At the end of this experiment, an even greater percentage of the students believed the false information. (10) Although the scientists have been able to plant false memories about strawberry ice cream,

they have not been able to implant false memories about two popular snack foods: chocolate chip cookies and potato chips. (11) Loftus believes that <u>researchers could resolve this problem of limited influence</u> by additional feedback and drills. (12) Meanwhile, Stephen Behnke, ethics director of the American Psychological Association is concerned about the ethics of such research. (13) He comments that <u>the deliberate implanting of false memories raises serious ethical questions.</u> (14) Loftus acknowledges that <u>scientists need to discuss ethical issues,</u> but she notes that <u>parents often tell their children things that aren't true.</u>

Information summarized and adapted from "Swallowing a Lie May Aid in Weight Loss, Research Suggests," Rosie Mestel, *Los Angeles Times*, August 2, 2005.

FOCUS 3   Stative Passives in Contrast to Dynamic Passives

use

EXAMPLES		EXPLANATIONS
DYNAMIC PASSIVES	**STATIVE PASSIVES**	
(a) The missing library book **was found** in the parking lot by a custodian.	(b) A map of Miami **can be found** on the Internet.	Many verbs can be either dynamic or stative depending on their meaning. *Dynamic* passive verbs describe activities. *Stative* passive verbs do not report activities; they express states or conditions. Stative passive verbs do not have agents. (More about stative verbs in Focus 4.)
(c) Our telephone line **is** finally **being connected** tomorrow.	(d) The transmission of a car **is connected** to the gearshift.	
(e) Stella **was called** for a job interview yesterday.	(f) The biological rhythm with a period of about 24 hours **is called** a circadian rhythm.	

EXERCISE 6

Each of the famous monuments or group of buildings below can be matched to two descriptions in a–j. (1) Match each landmark to the appropriate descriptions. (2) Rewrite each description as a sentence with a passive verb (or verbs) to put focus on the monuments and buildings as the main topics. (3) Delete the agents if they do not add much to the meaning or if they can be inferred from the context. (4) Make any other necessary changes.

Example: *The Parthenon is considered to represent the peak of Greek architectural achievement.*

MONUMENTS AND BUILDINGS

1. The Parthenon

2. Osaka Castle

3. Machu Picchu

4. Ankor Thom

5. The Pyramids of Giza

DESCRIPTIONS

a. Some call this Peruvian ruin the "Lost City of the Incas."

b. The Cambodian god-king Suryavarman II intended it to be a funerary monument for himself.

c. Unlike in Europe, where builders used stone for castles, builders made this of wood.

d. People believe that workers constructed them using mounds or ramps to position the stone blocks.

e. Many consider it the peak of Greek architectural achievement.

f. In ancient times, a large complex of buildings surrounded them.

g. Located south of the Cambodian capital of Ankor Thom, people built it in the twelfth century.

h. Pericles had it built to celebrate Athens' victory over the Persians.

i. You can find this fifteenth-century ruin on a high mountain ridge above the Urubama Valley in Peru.

j. Historians regard it as the most formidable stronghold in Japan before people destroyed it in the early seventeenth century.

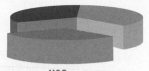

use

FOCUS 4   Uses of Stative Passive Verbs

Stative passive verbs have a number of descriptive uses in discourse. Note that many of the stative passives in the examples below are followed by prepositions such as *in, with, by,* or *for.*

EXAMPLES	USES
(a) The Amazon River **is located** in Brazil. (b) The ratel, a fearless animal, **is found** in Africa and India. (c) The Secret Service agents **were positioned** near the President.	• To describe location or position *Located* is often used in geographical description. *Found* typically describes plant and animal habitats. *Positioned* often suggests placement Other verbs: *placed, situated, bordered (by), surrounded (by)*
(d) *The Daily Scandal* **is filled** with untrue stories. (e) The sea horse's body **is covered** with small bony plates.	• To describe characteristics or qualities This type of description is common in science.
(f) Temperature **is measured** in degrees. (g) The elements **are listed** according to weight.	• To describe manner or method This use is common in science and mathematics.
(h) France **is divided** into regions. (i) Geology **is made up** of many subfields, such as seismology and petrology.	• To describe part-whole relationships Other verbs: *composed (of), organized into*
(j) The Geiger counter **is used** for detecting radiation. (k) Greetings such as "How are you?" **are intended** to promote communication, not to get information.	• To describe purpose These verbs may be followed by *for* + gerund (verb + *-ing*) or an infinitive (*to* + verb). Other verbs: *designed, meant*

EXAMPLES	USES
(l) Do you know the old song that begins: "The knee bone's **connected** to the thigh bone"? (m) The two buildings **are joined** by an elevated walkway.	• To describe physical connection Other verbs: *attached (to), accompanied (by), separated (by, from)*
(n) El Greco **is** best **known** for his religious paintings. (o) Nagoya Castle **is considered** one of the greatest fortresses in the history of Japan.	• To describe reputation or association Other verbs: *regarded (as), thought to be, viewed (as); linked to; associated with*
(p) The ratel **is** also **known** as "the honey badger." (q) Pants having legs that flare out at the bottom **are called** bellbottoms.	• To define or name Other verbs: *labeled, named, termed*

EXERCISE 7

Identify the stative passive verbs in the following passage and state the use of each, based on the categories in Focus 4.

Example: The answer can be found deep inside the brain.

Stative passive: *can be found*   Use: *to describe location*

(1) What makes people engage in the activities they do, whether running marathons, solving crossword puzzles, or playing a musical instrument? (2) Gregory Burns, a neuroscientist and psychiatrist, says that the answer can be found deep inside the brain. (3) In his book, *Satisfaction: The Science of Finding True Fulfillment*, Burns claims that explanations for the activities people pursue are connected not with pleasure and happiness but rather with satisfaction. (4) While pleasure and happiness may be regarded as passive emotions, satisfaction, according to Burns, is a much more active component. (5) Satisfaction, in turn, is made up of two essential ingredients that humans, by nature, desire: novelty and challenge. (6) Burns has identified the neurotransmitter dopamine, a structure that has long been associated with happiness and well-being, as a key element in the biology of satisfaction. (7) In adolescence, a time of life that is known for impulsive behavior and great enthusiasm, our brains are rich with dopamine. (8) As people grow older, they need a greater stimulus to trigger the flow of dopamine. (9) The hormone cortisol has also been linked to feelings of satisfaction. (10) Although cortisol is known mainly as a stress hormone, the level of this hormone rises during vigorous exercise and thus can elevate mood and even help to improve memory. (11) According to Burns, this is why even physical activities that cause pain can be regarded as satisfying. (12) This area of psychology has been called "positive psychology" because it focuses on positive emotions rather than psychological problems.

Information from "For True Fulfillment, Seek Satisfaction, Not Happiness," Marianne Szedgedy-Maszak, *Los Angeles Times*, September 5, 2005.

EXERCISE 8

1. Match each numbered word or phrase in column A to the appropriate phrase in column B.
2. Write a sentence for each, using a stative passive.
3. Add other words or change word forms as necessary.

Examples: 1, c. *Language **may be defined** as the spoken or written means by which people express themselves and communicate with others. The spoken or written means by which people express themselves and communicate with others **is called** language.*

A	B
1. language	a. the part of consciousness that involves feeling or sentiment
2. challenge	b. usually a negative condition to be avoided
3. emotions	c. the spoken or written means by which people express themselves and communicate with others
4. stress	d. a key component of human satisfaction

EXERCISE 9

With a partner, take turns asking and responding to the questions below. Use a stative verb in your responses.

Example: **Question:** Where is the city or town in which you were born?

Answer: *It's located in the southern part of China.*

1. Where is the city or town in which you were born?
2. What is your hometown (or the place you live now) best known for?
3. How is the country you were either born in or live in now divided geographically (such as states, provinces etc.) and how many divisions are there?
4. Do your friends or family call you by any special nicknames?
5. What are you considered good at doing?
6. What do you think the following cities in the United States are often associated with?
   a. Las Vegas, Nevada
   b. New York, New York
   c. Los Angeles, California
   d. Orlando, Florida

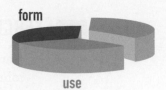

FOCUS 5 Complex Passives

Complex passives are passive constructions followed by *that* clauses or infinitive clauses (*to* + verb).

EXAMPLES	EXPLANATIONS
(a) It **is believed** that primates first appeared on the earth about sixty-nine million years ago. (b) It **is said** that the number 13 is bad luck. (c) It **was reported** that a man suspected of burning an abandoned building was arrested this morning.	**Form:** Introductory *it* + passive verb + *that* clause **Use:** This form often serves to introduce a topic, since the new information comes at the end of the sentence.
(d) The topic of today's lecture is early primates. Primates **are believed** to have appeared on the earth about sixty-nine million years ago. (e) Many numbers are associated with superstitious beliefs. For example, thirteen **is said** to be an unlucky number. (f) Police arrested a man suspected of burning an old factory building The suspect **was reported to have been** near the building when the fire started.	**Form:** Subject (other than introductory *it*) + passive verb + *to* infinitive The infinitive may often be a perfect form: *to* + *have* + past participle as in (d) and (f) **Use:** This form could also be used to introduce topics, but it is especially appropriate after a topic has been introduced because the topic can then be put in the subject position.

◼ EXERCISE 10

For each of the following numbered sentence groups, choose the wording or sentence that best fits the context, using the principles of introducing or continuing topics as discussed in Focus 5. Consider each numbered group to be the beginning of a written article or spoken announcement.

1. Some people believe that opening an umbrella in the house will bring bad luck. In parts of Asia, as early as the eleventh century,
   a. it was considered to be an insult to open an umbrella inside a building.
   b. opening an umbrella inside a building was considered to be an insult.

2. a. It has been alleged that an employee of the museum is responsible for the theft of dozens of paintings.

    b. An employee of the museum is alleged to be responsible for the theft of dozens of paintings. Police are currently investigating the claim.

3. a. It was reported this morning that a Pacific blacktip shark gave birth to three healthy pups at Sea World.

    b. A Pacific blacktip shark was reported to have given birth to three healthy pups at Sea World this morning. Officials commented that this marks the first documented birth of the species in captivity.

4. Of the comets that have been recorded, the least frequently returning one is Delavan's Comet, which appeared in 1914.

    a. This comet is not expected to return for twenty-four million years.

    b. It is not expected that this comet will return for twenty-four million years.

EXERCISE 11

What will happen if you step on a spider? Walk under a ladder? Every culture has superstitions describing good or bad things that may result from something else happening. In small groups, discuss some of the superstitions that you have heard or read about. Write down four or five of the superstitions, using a complex passive structure.

Example: *It is said that if you break a mirror, you will have seven years of bad luck.*

   OR *Breaking a mirror is believed to result in seven years of bad luck.*

use

FOCUS 6 — Contexts for the Use of Complex Passives

Complex passives are often used in journalism, in business, and in academic writing. Although not commonly used in informal spoken English, complex passives are frequent in formal spoken English (for example, news reports, speeches). Some of the most common uses follow.

EXAMPLES	USES
	To achieve an impersonal tone, avoiding the use of *I* or *we:*
(a) It **should be noted** that the results of our experiment cannot be generalized.	• in explanations and observations.
(b) This product **is known** to be inferior.	
(c) It **is assumed** that all employees have completed the necessary hiring papers.	• in statements of desired or expected behavior.
(d) All homework **is expected** to be turned in on time.	
(e) It **has been ruled** that the prisoner was unfairly convicted.	• in evaluations or judgments.
(f) The house **was considered** to be vastly overpriced.	
(g) It **is believed** that baseball was being played in England in the early eighteenth century.	To express information that has not been verified as factual or true.
(h) Mr. Blau **is alleged** to have stolen several car stereos.	
(i) In the nineteenth century, it **was thought** that personality traits and mental abilities could be detected by bumps on the head.	To describe past beliefs that are no longer regarded as true.
(j) In ancient Greece, lightning bolts **were believed** to be weapons used by Zeus, the king of gods.	
(k) It **is assumed** that more and more species will become extinct if we continue to destroy the world's rain forests.	To express a general expectation about some future event.
(l) The weather **is expected** to be warm and sunny all weekend.	

EXERCISE 12

The *Guinness Book of World Records* presents hundreds of fascinating facts about the natural world, human feats, and other topics. Rewrite the following facts in complete sentences. Use the passive form of the verb given in parentheses. Change the phrasing of information and add words as needed. The first has been done as an example. Note that if an activity happened in the past (as in 1b), an infinitive verb expressing it must be perfective: *to + have* + past participle.

1. a. longest living individual fish: European eel (think)
       The longest living fish is thought to be the European eel.
       OR *It is thought that the longest living fish is the European eel.*

   b. life span of one specimen of European eel: 88 years (report)
       It was reported that one specimen lived for 88 years.
       OR *One specimen was reported to have lived for 88 years.*

2. animal with the highest frequency hearing: the bat (believe)

3. longest sneezing bout of a human: 978 days (record)

4. the deepest and oldest freshwater lake in the world: Lake Baikal in Siberia, Russia (know)

5. the greediest living animal: larva of the polyphemus moth, which consumes an amount equal to 86,000 times its own body weight (consider)

6. coldest place in the universe: The Boomerang Nebula, 5,000 light years from earth (think)

7. Sirius A, the Dog Star: brightest of the 5776 stars we are able to see (presume)

8. fastest text message typed on a cell phone: 43.2 seconds for a 160-character text by a Korean woman (allege) (Hint: use *a Korean woman* for the subject.)

Using the Passive to Create Cohesion in Discourse

use

EXAMPLES	EXPLANATIONS
(a) For the first time, researchers have found **the remains of a mammal that has been entombed in amber. The remains,** including a backbone and ribs, **are estimated** to be eighteen million to twenty-nine million years old. Discovered in the West Indies, **these remains are believed** to be those of a tiny insect-eating mammal.	As explained in Focus 1, we put focus on a topic in English by making it the grammatical subject. Often a new topic is introduced at the end of a sentence. This topic then becomes the subject of the next sentence. As a result, a passive verb may be needed. Putting the topic in the subject position helps to create cohesion, making it easier for the reader or listener to understand the main ideas.
(b) Biologists have recently determined that **even the tiny brains of bees can recognize and interpret patterns. This feat was** once **thought** possible only through reason. In an experiment, bees learned to look for food only near **certain symmetrical or asymmetrical patterns. These patterns are reflected** in nature, such as blossoms of plants.	Often a synonym for the topic or a shortened form of the topic is used as the subject with a passive verb. (See Unit 6, Focus 2 for more information about these forms of reference.) This also helps to create cohesion. In some cases, it allows the writer or speaker to avoid using a subject with a long modifying phrase.
(c) Most theories of long-term memory **distinguish** skills or habits ("knowing how") from abstract or representational knowledge ("knowing that"). **This distinction is supported** by recent evidence that skill learning and the acquisition of knowledge are handled by different areas of the brain.	The subject of a passive verb may also be derived from the verb of a previous sentence.

EXERCISE 13

Circle the passive verbs in the following passages. Then explain why each passive verb is used.

Example: One of the world's largest pharmaceutical companies has recently fired its chairperson. The chairperson (was suspected) of unethical accounting practices. Explanation: *The passive verb "was suspected" is used in the second sentence to put focus on the topic, "the chairperson."*

1. Researchers in Hungary have been studying the cognitive and communication skills of dogs. In numerous experiments, dogs were found to be very sensitive to cues produced by humans and performed some tasks better than humans' closest relative, the chimpanzee.

2. The ability of electric currents to float through certain materials completely untouched, without energy loss, is called superconductivity. This phenomenon was explained in a theory developed in 1972, an accomplishment that won the Nobel Prize. Superconductivity was thought to exist only at extremely cold temperatures, but in 1986 a scientist in Germany discovered a high-temperature superconductor.

3. The repeated eruptions of Mexico's Popocatepetl volcano have resulted in the growth of a lava dome to within 50 feet of the rim of the volcano. The dome is being fed by 20,000 cubic feet of fresh lava daily. If the lava overtops the rim, it could melt glaciers on the side of the mountain and create life-threatening mudflows.

4. In experiments to examine the ways in which infants form attachments to mothers or other caretakers, researchers separated infant chimpanzees from their mothers. Extended separations were found to result in abnormal social development.

5. A team of scientists have decoded the 1700 genes of a microbe living on the ocean floor. This microbe belongs to a class called arachae, a different class from the two most common branches of life—bacteria and eukaryotes, which include plants, animals, and humans. The existence of archaea was first proposed by Carl Woese and Ralph Wolfe at the University of Illinois. Archaea has some characteristics of other life forms but functions differently. About five hundred species of archaea have been identified. The life form is thought to produce about 30 percent of the biomass on earth.

Adapted from "Decoding of Microbe's Genes Sheds Light on Odd Form of Life," *Los Angeles Times*, August 8, 1996.

EXERCISE 14

After each sentence or group of sentences, add a sentence with a passive verb to create cohesion, using the information given in parentheses.

Example: Any substance that is toxic to insects is known as an insecticide. (We use insecticides to control insects in situations where they cause economic damage or endanger health.)

Insecticides are used to control insects in situations where they cause economic damage or endanger health.

1. The ancient city of Troy was the setting of the legendary Greek siege described in *The Iliad*. (An earthquake destroyed the city around 1300 BCE)

2. There are three types of muscle in humans and other vertebrates. One type is skeletal muscle. (Under a microscope, we see that this muscle is striped or striated.)

3. Most people associate the phrase "Survival of the fittest" with Darwin's Theory of Evolution. (However, a British philosopher, Herbert Spencer, first used the phrase, and Darwin later adopted it.)

4. The Great Wall of China served as a defensive wall between the old Chinese border with Manchuria and Mongolia. The first section was completed in the third century BCE. (The Chinese later extended it until it was 1400 miles long.)

5. Although the idea of submarines is an old one, the first submarine, made of wood and covered with greased leather, was not built until 1620. David Bushnell invented the first submarine used in warfare in 1776.

Use Your English

ACTIVITY 1 listening/writing/speaking

CD Track 5

A famous psychology laboratory experiment conducted by Stanley Milgram tested subjects' willingness to obey authority even when they believed they would be required to administer painful electric shocks to other subjects. Listen to the audio recording, in which you will hear a description of the procedures and the results of this experiment. Take notes on the information you hear. With a partner, compare notes to get information you may have missed. Then write a summary of the experiment, using passive verbs where appropriate to put focus on recipients of action and to achieve coherence.

ACTIVITY 2 reading

Find a text that has a number of passive verbs. (Science texts, instruction manuals, and texts that define or classify are good sources). Analyze ten passives that you find. Are they dynamic passives or stative passives? Why do you think the writer used them?

ACTIVITY 3 writing/speaking

In small groups, make up five sentences describing people, places, or things, but don't reveal who/what they are. In each sentence, use a stative passive verb. See if other groups can guess who or what you are describing. Here are some examples. Can you guess the answers?

Examples:
1. *It is divided into nine innings.*
2. *It can be found in tacos, spaghetti sauce, and ceviche.*
3. *This famous British dramatist is known as the Bard of Avon.*
4. *They are also called twisters.*
5. *This country is bordered by Italy, Austria, Germany, and France.*

ACTIVITY 4 writing

Draw a diagram or map of one of the following:

- an area (your room, apartment or house, a neighborhood, or commercial district, for example)
- a machine or device
- an invention of your own creation (a machine that writes your papers for you? a device that gets you out of bed in the morning?)

In your diagram/map, label at least four or five objects, parts, buildings, or whatever would be found there. Then write a paragraph describing the locations of objects or the ways in which you have divided your diagram/map into parts. Use stative passives in your descriptions. (As reviewed in Focus 4 on page 69.)

ACTIVITY 5 writing

As the manager of a large office-supply store, you have observed repeated inappropriate behavior among some of the employees. This behavior includes the following:

- showing up late for work and leaving early
- taking breaks longer than the 15 minutes allowed
- eating snacks at the service counter
- talking to other employees while customers are waiting for service.

Write a memo to the employees to let them know what kind of behavior is expected of them while they are at work. Since you want to assume an impersonal tone, use complex passives.

ACTIVITY 6 speaking/listening/writing

Interview a classmate about family or hometown history. Ask him or her to tell you about some events that are thought to be true but are not documented. The events might concern some long-ago period (for example, "Juan's great-grandfather was believed to have been born in Guatemala. The family is thought to have moved to Mexico in the early 1900s."). They could also include information about your classmate's youth as reported by his or her parents (for example, "Sonia is said to have been very good-natured as a baby."). Take notes during the interview. Then write up a report from your notes, using complex passives where appropriate to express some of the information. If time permits, present your report orally to the class.

ACTIVITY 7 research on the web

 Read more interesting facts and world records on the Guinness Book of World Records Web site: www.guinnessworldrecords.com. Divide the class into groups, with each group finding five interesting facts from one of the following categories: Human Body, Amazing Feats, Natural World, Science and Technology, Arts & Media, Sports and Games. Write down the facts using complex passives as was done in Exercise 12.

ACTIVITY 8 reflection

How can good language learners be described by the kinds of activities they engage in and strategies they practice? Make a list of qualities by completing the statement "A good language learner can be defined as someone who . . ." in five ways on a piece of paper. Then compare your definitions with a partner to see if you had any in common.

Example: *A good language learner can be defined as someone who is willing to make mistakes.*

ARTICLE USAGE

UNIT GOALS

- Distinguish classification from identification meaning in articles

- Use definite, indefinite, and zero articles appropriately

- Distinguish particular from general (generic) reference in articles

- Distinguish abstract generic from concrete generic meaning in articles

- Use the article in definitions of generic nouns

- Use the appropriate articles to correspond to body parts and illnesses

OPENING TASK

■ STEP 1

Read the list of current or possible practices in the medical profession on the next page. Check whether you believe they are ethical or not ethical.

ETHICAL?

Yes	No	
❏	❏	a. Researchers using animals (mice, cats, cows, etc.) to test the poison level of drugs or the effect of artificial organs that might be implanted into a human being.
❏	❏	b. Doctors refusing to accept calls from patients who do not have medical insurance.
❏	❏	c. Drug companies bribing doctors with vacations and other perquisites ("perks") to prescribe new but less well-known drugs to their patients.
❏	❏	d. Using doctors to torture accused terrorists in prison.
❏	❏	e. Machines keeping alive severely injured people who are in a vegetative state.
❏	❏	f. Childless couples using surrogate (substitute) mothers to bear children.
❏	❏	g. Engineering genetic changes in embryos to prevent birth defects or diseases.
❏	❏	h. Medical students practicing techniques on patients who are technically still alive but beyond the help of extraordinary life-saving measures.
❏	❏	i. Forcing birth control on a population that for religious or cultural reasons does not desire it.
❏	❏	j. Parents conceiving a child in order to obtain a matching organ or tissue to save the life of another one of their children.
❏	❏	k. Poor people selling their own organs in order to make a living.
❏	❏	l. Requiring doctors to reveal the results if they have a positive AIDS test and to quit their active medical practices.

■ STEP 2

In small groups, discuss the pros and cons of several of these practices based on information you have heard or read about. Choose one member of your group (the Recorder) to take notes on the discussion.

■ STEP 3

(Recorder) Summarize your group's discussion for the rest of the class. Which topics were the most controversial? Which opinions did your group agree on?

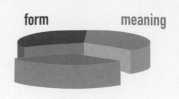

FOCUS 1   Classification versus Identification*
Meaning of Articles

EXAMPLES	EXPLANATIONS
	An indefinite article (*a/an* or Ø) classifies a noun and shows that it represents or reflects a type, group, or a class distinct from some other type, group or class.
(a) What did you see yesterday? I saw a horror movie last week.	• singular nouns (*a/an*)
(b) An earthquake (a natural disaster) struck at 7:10 AM.	
(c) A gas (a type of gas) that can be deadly is carbon monoxide.	
(d) Ø Stars (celestial bodies) shine brightly.	• plural nouns (Ø)
(e) We expect Ø complications (additional problematic conditions) while she is sick.	
(f) Have you ever seen Ø traffic (passage of vehicles) like this?	• noncount nouns (Ø)
(g) Ø Mango juice (tropical fruit juice) can be made from Ø syrup (thick sweet liquid).	
	The definite article (*the*) can *identify* a noun and show that it has been singled out in some way. Generally, the speaker or writer knows the listener or reader is aware of the noun because it was previously mentioned or he or she can see it, has heard of it, has experienced it, has read about it, etc.
(h) **The** movie (you heard about it) featured Dracula.	• singular nouns (*the*)
(i) **The** earthquake (you know about it) destroyed many buildings.	
(j) **The** gas (you smell it) can be harmful.	
(k) **The** stars (we read about them) were discovered in 1952.	• plural nouns (*the*)
(l) **The** medical complications (you experienced them) were unexpected.	

*Adapted from P. Master, *Systems in English Grammar*. Englewood Cliffs, New Jersey: Prentice-Hall Regents, 1996.

EXAMPLES	EXPLANATIONS
(m) **The** traffic (we are riding in it) is dangerous. (n) Could you pass the maple syrup (you are near it)?	• noncount nouns (*the*)

EXERCISE 1

Look at the use of *a, an,* or *the* in each of the following cartoons.

STEP 1   Describe what is happening in each cartoon.

STEP 2   Discuss how the article classifies or identifies its corresponding noun.

Example: *Two children are pretending to be a doctor and a nurse to a teddy bear mother. The doctor is announcing the gender of a stuffed animal.*

• *"A" is used to classify the newborn as a male.*

It's a boy!

1.

Do you think Bob minds sitting in the back row?

2.

A bone doesn't seem to satisfy his appetite anymore!

3.

I beat the eggs. Now what?

Answer the following questions with noun phrases. Use *a/an, the*, or Ø to show that the noun is classified (shows kind, type, class, etc.) or identified (shows specific feature, aspect, characteristic, etc.).

Examples: What part of a holiday dinner do you enjoy the most? *The stuffed turkey (identified)*

What kind of meat do you like the most? *Beef, a hot dog (classified)*

1. What kind of movie is most exciting?

2. What feature of your classroom is unusual?

3. What kind of person would make a good roommate?

4. What type of vegetables do you dislike the most?

5. What aspect of your English class was most interesting this week?

6. What type of clothing is usually made of wool?

7. What characteristic of the weather is most frustrating where you live?

8. What class of animal gives birth to live young?

9. What part of the day is your most effective work time?

10. What aspect of your home or your friend's home is unusual?

EXERCISE 3

Fill in the following blanks with *a/an, the*, or Ø. In which blanks did you use *the* to refer to identifiable nouns?

On (1) ___the___ night of January 11, 1983, Nancy Cruzan, (2) _____ healthy, 25-year-old woman, lost control of her car while driving in Jasper County, Missouri. As (3) _____ car overturned, Nancy was thrown into (4) _____ ditch. When the ambulance reached (5) _____ ditch, (6) _____ paramedics found her with no (7) _____ detectable breathing or (8) _____ heartbeat. For seven years, Nancy lay in (9) _____ Missouri state hospital, in what was described all too neatly as (10) _____ "persistent vegetative state." In reality, she lay in (11) _____ bed in (12) _____ hospital, horribly contorted with (13) _____ irreversible muscular and (14) _____ tendon damage. She was fed through (15) _____ tube in her side. (16) _____ Cruzan family were hopeful that Nancy would recover. However, after five years they fought and lost (17) _____ battle in court to euthanize her. This case brought (18) _____ question of the morality of an individual's right to die to (19) _____ national attention.

Fill in the following blanks with *the* or Ø. In which blanks, did you use the Ø to refer to classifiable nouns?

(1) _The_ students entering our medical schools have (2) _____ outstanding grade-point averages, and (3) _____ impressive scores on (4) _____ Medical College Admissions Test, and (5) _____ glowing recommendations. There's no doubt that they have (6) _____ capability to become (7) _____ good scientists and (8) _____ good science doctors. But do they have (9) _____ makings of humanists with (10) _____ commitment to treat everything from (11) _____ broken bones to (12) _____ broken hearts? It is this delicate balance between (13) _____ science and (14) _____ wisdom that makes (15) _____ great physicians— (16) _____ ability to know what to do with what has been learned.

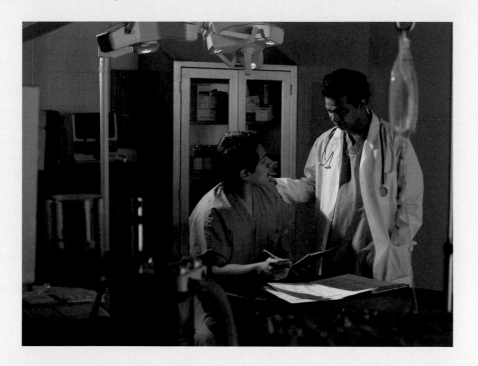

FOCUS 2 · Special Uses of the Definite Article

EXAMPLES	EXPLANATIONS
	Use *the*:
(a) **The sun** is very bright.	• with unique nouns
(b) **The most significant effect** occurred in June.	• before superlatives
(c) **The third component** was missing.	• before ordinals (*first, second, third*, etc.)
(d) **The main operator** was not on duty.	• before modifiers that make the noun that follows specific (*same, sole, chief, only, single, solitary, main*, etc.)
(e) Each **of the experiments** was successful.	• in phrases that refer to a specific part of a whole group
(f) Half of **the population** suffered greatly.	
(g) **The effect** of an earthquake can be felt for miles.	• with identifiable nouns that are followed by a modifying *of*-phrase
(h) We were uncertain about **the cause** of the fire.	
(i) **The beginning** of the movie was frightening.	
(j) A major urban problem is caring for **the poor** (people).	• before adjectives that represent groups of people
(k) "Heartbreak" is a song on **the radio**.	• with certain nouns, such as mechanical inventions and devices, to refer to a general example of something rather than a specific object the speaker/writer has in mind
(l) She got here fast because she took **the train**.	
(m) I went to **the barber** after classes.	• before locations associated with certain typical or habitual activities. The listener/reader may have no idea of the exact location to which the speaker/writer is referring.
(n) Have you been to **the beach** this summer?	
(o) She needs to pick up a few things at **the store**.	

For each of the following sentences, circle the correct article in parentheses. Explain your choices to a partner.

Example: (A/(The)) sun is very bright today. I need to buy ((a)/the) cap at (a/(the)) store.

The sun is very bright today. I need to buy a cap at the store.

Sun *is a unique noun; therefore,* ***the*** *is used.* ***A cap*** *is used because it refers to a type of hat, not to a particular one.* ***The store*** *is used because a location referring to a specific habitual activity (shopping) is being referred to.*

1. All civilizations of (a/the) world are enriched by trade and (a/the) stimulating impact of other cultures.

2. There are two main precursors to skin cancer. (A/the) first indication is spontaneous bleeding on some part of (a/the) skin. (A/the) second is the enlargement of a freckle or mole.

3. I'll be late for (a/the) meeting because I have to make (a/the) deposit at (a/the) bank.

4. (A/the) most significant effect of (an/the) earthquake was (a/the) destruction of many homes.

5. I read (a/the) wonderful story yesterday. (A/the) beginning of the story takes place in Vienna about (a/the) turn of (a/the) century.

6. In (a/the) past, (a/the) most important factor determining world power was (a/the) navy that could navigate (a/the) Mediterranean.

7. There were many reasons for (a/the) success of (a/the) project. (A/the) main reason was that at least half of (a/the) workgroup had PhDs from around (a/the) globe.

8. (A/the) radio described several ways in which (an/the) elderly could obtain (a/the) best medical help.

9. In (a/the) next year, (an/the) exact mechanism by which cell receptors work will be better understood.

10. (A/the) last decade has been marked by (a/the) large increase in violence.

Review and Special Uses of Ø (Zero Article)

use

EXAMPLES	EXPLANATIONS
	Ø is used when the following noun is nonspecific. Use Ø with:
(a) Ø Flowers should be watered regularly.	• nouns that have general or generic reference (see Focus 4)
(b) I need to get Ø gas before we start for Seattle.	• nonspecific nouns that do not refer to a specific quantity or amount
	Also use Ø with:
(c) The children ran directly Ø home.	• certain nouns associated with familiar destinations
(d) They went Ø downtown after supper.	
(e) My grandmother walked to Ø school everyday.	
(f) He worked until Ø midnight.	• certain nouns of time (*night, dusk, noon, midday, midnight,* etc.)
(g) Ø Spring is a wonderful time of year.	• names of seasons (*spring, summer, fall, winter*)
(h) We had Ø lunch at a very good restaurant.	• names of meals (*breakfast, brunch, lunch, dinner,* etc.)
(i) The group arrived by Ø car.	• means of transportation (*by boat, by plane, on foot,* etc.)
(j) They came on Ø foot from the meeting.	
(k) We were informed by Ø mail that our subscription had been canceled.	• means of communication (*by phone, by mail, by telegram,* etc.)
	Certain idioms use Ø:
(l) They walked Ø arm in Ø arm down the aisle.	• phrases joined with *by, in,* or *and* (*day by day, week by week, side by side, arm in arm, neck and neck,* etc.)
(m) The ship was lost at Ø sea.	• participle + preposition + noncount noun (*wounded in action, lost at sea, missing in action, cash on delivery,* etc.)
(n) He put his heart and Ø soul into the project.	• phrases joined by *and* (*heart and soul, bread and butter, husband and wife,* etc.)
(o) Peter took Ø care of the details.	• verb + objects + preposition (*shake hands with, take care of, take advantage of, take part in, take notice of, take pride in,* etc.)

Fill in the following blanks with *a/an, the,* or Ø. More than one answer may be appropriate depending on the meaning you want to convey.

It was (1) _____Ø_____ spring and (2) _____ young GI, returning (3) _____ home from (4) _____ war, called his parents from (5) _____ phone booth in (6) _____ bus station. His parents had waited for a message by (7) _____ mail or (8) _____ telegram, but he had not gotten around to writing. On (9) _____ phone, he told his parents that he would be coming by (10) _____ bus and that he would be (11) _____ home by 5:00 that evening. But he hesitated (12) _____ moment and then added that he was bringing (13) _____ home (14) _____ friend, and he hoped that it would be okay with them because his friend was handicapped. He had been wounded in (15) _____ action and had no legs. He asked his parents' permission. They told him that they felt very sorry for (16) _____ friend but they were not really set up to cook (17) _____ breakfast, (18) _____ lunch, and (19) _____ dinner for him—this was not (20) _____ good time for him to come. The mother worked; there were two floors in (21) _____ house; she would have to run up and down; (22) _____ money was tight, etc., etc. As it turned out, (23) _____ young man did not get off (24) _____ bus that night, because he was (25) _____ handicapped soldier. It was their son who had been wounded in (26) _____ action. The parents never saw him again.

FOCUS 4 | Particular versus Generic Reference of Articles

Generic reference relates to the general rather than the particular nature of something. Particular reference indicates one member of a class; generic reference indicates all or representative members of a class. Note in the following examples the particular and generalized meanings of *laser* in different contexts.

EXAMPLES	EXPLANATIONS
(a) Her doctor used a laser to treat her varicose veins.	• particular reference
(b) The laser cured Paul's cataract problem.	• particular reference
(c) The laser has been used in medicine since the 1960s.	• generic reference
(d) A laser can cut through soft tissue with a searing light.	• generic reference
(e) Lasers reduce the recovery period needed for ordinary operations.	• generic reference

EXERCISE 7

For each of the following pairs of sentences, circle the option that makes a general rather than a particular reference about the italicized noun phrase. Note that different references are not always marked by different articles.

Example: (a.) An *immunity* is a resistance to infection.

         b. I have an *immunity* to small pox.

1. a. You should take *the vitamins* on the counter.
   b. You should take *vitamins* in order to stay healthy.

2. a. A *cholera epidemic* was started by contaminated food and water.
   b. *Cholera epidemics* kill many people every year.

3. a. A *doctor* claimed to have discovered a miracle burn ointment.
   b. A *doctor* is trained to treat burns.

4. a. *The motion picture industry* has created many movie idols.
   b. She is working for *the motion picture industry* in Los Angeles.

5. a. There is no cure for *a cold*.
   b. I have had *a cold* for four weeks.

6. a. *The mouse* used in the experiment was injected with morphine.
   b. *The mouse* is an excellent research animal.

7. a. The patient will sit in *the wheelchair* until her daughter arrives.
   b. *The wheelchair* has improved the lives of the handicapped.

8. a. Angela has been playing *the saxophone* for three years.
   b. Angela has been playing *the saxophone* that was in the corner.

9. a. *Some people* have been sitting in the waiting room since 11:00 AM.
   b. *People* kept alive only by machines should be allowed to die.

10. a. *Water* from springs contains minerals.
    b. *The water* from the spring cured my illness.

<table>
<tr><td>FOCUS 5</td><td>The + Plural Nouns for
General Reference</td></tr>
</table>

use

EXAMPLES	EXPLANATIONS
	Sometimes, *the* may be combined with plural nouns when referring generally to:
(a) The Sierra Club is intent on saving **the redwoods**. (b) We went to a fund-raising benefit for **the whales**.	• plant and animal groups that are the target of special attention.
(c) **(The) Neo-Nazis** propagate discrimination and hate. (d) **(The) Republicans** have conservative values. (e) **(The) Jews** celebrate Passover. (f) **The Dutch** are very good at learning languages.	• social, political, religious, and national groups. (Note that *the* is optional here.) The names of some nationalities do not allow plural endings and require *the*: *the Swedish, the Danish, the Finnish, the Polish, the Swiss, the English, the French, the Dutch, the Irish, the Welsh, the British, the Chinese, the Japanese,* etc.).

Match up the following associations with the corresponding types of people. (Some associations may apply to more than one group.) Select five of them and write about them in complete sentences below.

Example: *(The) Italians eat a lot of pasta.*
Criminals commit serious crimes.

Association	People
1. face racial discrimination	a. Swiss
2. want equality in marriage	b. Muslim
3. know many languages	c. professor
4. like to dance	d. racist
5. eat a lot of pasta	e. politician
6. like to loan money at high interest	f. Brazilian
7. discriminate against different races	g. criminal
8. must "publish or perish"	h. feminist
9. forget campaign promises	i. laborer
10. pray to Allah	j. African American
11. want more than the minimum wage	k. Italian
12. commit serious crimes	l. banker

1. _____

_____

2. _____

_____

3. _____

_____

4. _____

_____

5. _____

_____

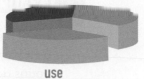

use

EXAMPLES	EXPLANATIONS

definite article = the laser indefinite article = a laser zero article = Ø lasers = Ø blood	The most common way to signal general reference in English is: • *the* + singular count nouns • *a/an* + singular count nouns • Ø + plural count nouns • Ø + noncount nouns

(a) **The dermatologist** specializes in skin care. (b) **The platypus** is an unusual creature. (c) The heaviest organ is **the skin.** (d) **The eucalyptus** is native to Australia. (e) What has revolutionized the workplace is **the computer.** (f) It is difficult to play **the harp.** (g) NOT: The towel absorbs water. (h) **The/A dermatologist** uses a **special solution** to remove warts. (i) **The/A kangaroo** carries **its young** in a pouch. (j) NOT: An elephant is in danger of becoming extinct.	There are two types of generic reference[*]: • *Abstract* generic reference uses *the* with singular countable nouns and noncount nouns to refer to certain well-defined, entire classes of entities. These entities are humans, animals, organs of the body, plants, complex inventions, and devices that can often serve as agents of change. They are not simple inanimate objects. • Abstract generic nouns can also be preceded by *a(n)* if there are subsequent references which relate to the human, animal, organ of the body, etc. noun one member at a time.
(l) **An operation** is stressful to one's body. (m) **Ø Carriers** may pass infections on to others. (n) **Ø Ultrasound** can detect the sex of an unborn baby.	• *Concrete* generic reference pertains to each or all of the representatives of a class rather than to the whole class. It uses a greater variety of forms than abstract generic reference does. *a(n)* + singular count noun Ø + plural noun Ø + noncount noun

(o) **A police officer carries a gun.** (p) **A laser** directs **a beam of light** to make an incision.	*Singular concrete* generic nouns with *a(n)* describe generalized instances of something. This means that the noun class is being referred to one member at a time and there may be references to other singular count nouns in the sentence.

[*]P. Master, "Teaching the English Article System, Part II: Generic versus Specific." *English Teaching Forum.* July 1988.

In each set, select one noun phrase that we can refer to with abstract generic *the*. Then, use that noun phrase in a general sentence. Note that descriptive words before and after nouns do not affect the use of generic *the*.

Example: tattered flag/California redwood/stepbrother
The California redwood is older than other trees.
Correct answer: The redwood is a well-defined class of plants and can be preceded by abstract generic "the". "Tattered flag" and "stepbrother" do not refer to well-defined classes of entities.

1. lining of the coat/apartment made of brick/African elephant
2. dust on the moon/illustration of the month/telephone for emergency communication
3. barbecue/artificial heart/Persian rug
4. free love/fin of a fish/French marigold
5. Hungarian embroidery/American automobile/Spanish tile
6. locksmith/key/door
7. accurate diagnosis/radiation/family-practice physician
8. bottom layer/Golden Delicious apple/proteins
9. automatic dishwasher/detergent/waste paper
10. bold pattern/air bag/lunch menu

EXERCISE 10

Check the sentences in which *the* could be substituted for *a(n)* to make a generic reference. Then explain why.

Example: A transistor is used in computers.
*Because the transistor is a complex device, the use of **the** is possible.*

_____ 1. An X-ray machine is used in radiotherapy.
_____ 2. A solar eclipse lasts about 7.5 minutes.
_____ 3. An octopus has eight legs.
_____ 4. A sprain is suffered when an ankle is wrenched.
_____ 5. A piano has 52 white keys.
_____ 6. A road is wider than an alley.
_____ 7. A human brain is larger than a bird brain.
_____ 8. A governor of a state (in the United States) has limited power.
_____ 9. A headache is a common physical complaint.
_____ 10. A polygraph detects if a person is telling a lie.
_____ 11. A deodorant can help eliminate odor.
_____ 12. A kangaroo guards its young within a frontal pouch.

EXERCISE 11

Read the following sentences that use *the* for abstract generic reference of a noun. Replace *the* with *a/an* and add singular noun phrases within a new sentence to show that you are talking about generalized instances of something.

Example: <u>The dog</u> is man's best friend. *A dog needs its owner's attention every day.*

1. <u>The store manager</u> needs good organizational skills.

   _____

2. One of the slowest animals is <u>the snail</u>.

   _____

3. <u>The cactus</u> grows in warm climates.

   _____

4. <u>The piano</u> is commonly found in American homes.

   _____

5. <u>The stomach</u> is essential for digestion.

   _____

6. <u>The ophthalmologist</u> examines eyes.

   _____

7. <u>The printing press</u> was essential to mass communication.

   _____

EXERCISE 12

Describe a usual or general tendency by completing the sentences below.

Example: A chocolate chip cookie is made of <u>sugar, flour, butter, and chocolate chips.</u>

1. A good party consists of _____
2. The Internet has changed _____
3. A healthy life includes _____
4. Builders name streets after _____
5. The police are needed for _____
6. Amnesia causes _____
7. Skillful architects create _____
8. A valuable education includes _____
9. Ladies' shoes come in all varieties including _____
10. The digital camera allows _____

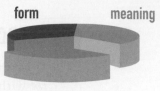

FOCUS 7 — Definitions of Common Nouns

Standard definitions of generic nouns follow the pattern below. Generic nouns appear in the subject position of these definitions.

GENERIC NOUN	+ *BE*	+ CLASSIFYING NOUN*	+ RELATIVE PRONOUN	+ VERB PHRASE
(a) The dinosaur	is	a prehistoric animal	that	scientists discovered through excavations.
(b) A dinosaur	is	a prehistoric animal	that	is now extinct.
(c) Dinosaurs	are	prehistoric animals	that	roamed the earth during the Mesozoic Age.

(d) **The chicken** is an animal that lays eggs.

(e) **A chicken** is an animal that lays eggs.
(f) **Chickens** are animals that lay eggs.
(g) **Chicken** is a meat that is very moist.

(h) **The platypus** is a mammal that lays eggs.
(i) **A duck** is a bird that has webbed feet.
(j) **Vultures** are birds that are larger than rats.

*See Focus 1.

Abstract generic nouns emphasize:
- a class

Concrete generic nouns emphasize:
- an example, any members
- a group, all members
- all/any of something

Definitions can include:
- classifications
- attributes
- comparisons

EXERCISE 13

Write incorrect definitions for the words provided below. Then, in pairs, take turns reading and correcting each other's definitions.

Examples: bicycle
A bicycle is a four-wheeled vehicle that you can sit on.
No, a bicycle is a two-wheeled vehicle that you can sit on.

1. stethoscope
2. koala bears
3. liver
4. spatula
5. palm tree
6. eye
7. nail
8. movie stars
9. honey
10. violin
11. patient
12. straw

EXERCISE 14

Find the incorrect article (*a/an, the*, Ø) in the following definitions. Then, correct the error.

Example: ^The Universe is a system of galaxies that was created 10,000 million years ago.

1. The fashion design is a major that requires artistic talent.
2. A radio telescope is telescope that collects long-wavelength radiation.
3. Astronaut is a person who travels in space.
4. A neurosis is mental disorder that is relatively minor.
5. Dirge is a musical piece played at a funeral.
6. In many homes, prayers are said before meal.
7. The somnambulism is a word for a condition called sleepwalking.
8. The mercury is a white metallic element, which is liquid at atmospheric temperature.
9. Vaporization is the conversion of liquid into a vapor.
10. The blackboard is a surface that is used for writing.

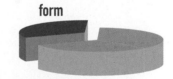
form

FOCUS 8	Articles with Names of Body Parts

EXAMPLES	EXPLANATIONS
	When generally referring to names of organs, parts of the body, or body fluids, we can use *the* for:
(a) **The heart** can be transplanted.	• singular body parts (*the* + noun)
(b) Cancer of **the bladder** has been linked to cigarette smoking.	
(c) **(The) blood** carries nutrients to body tissues.	• massive areas or fluids of the body (*the* + noncount noun)
(d) **(The) skin** is sensitive to ultra-violet rays.	
(e) Excessive smoke inhalation damages **the lungs.**	• plural or paired body parts (*the* + noun + plural)
(f) Regular exams of **the teeth** will prevent serious dental problems.	
(g) **The veins** carry blood throughout the body.	

EXERCISE 15

Study the following diagram and write sentences describing the location or function of at least eight of the following body parts.

Examples: *The diaphragm is below the lungs.*

The brain controls all muscular movements of the body.

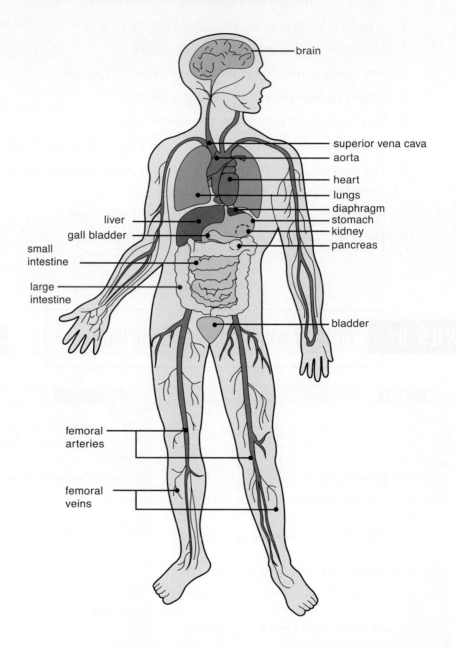

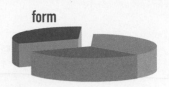

FOCUS 9   Articles with Names of Illnesses

The names of illnesses follow a range of noun patterns:

THE + NOUN	*A/AN* + NOUN		*(THE)* + NOUN + PLURAL
the flu	a cold	an ulcer	(the) mumps
the gout	a hernia	a stroke	(the) measles
the plague	a headache	an earache	(the) hiccups
	a heart attack	a sore throat	

Ø + NONCOUNT NOUN		*Ø* + NOUN (WITH FINAL *-S*)
influenza	leukemia	diabetes
pneumonia	diarrhea	rabies
malaria	mononucleosis	herpes
arthritis	cardiovascular disease	AIDS
cancer	tuberculosis	

EXERCISE 16

Work with a partner. Fill in a correct disease/illness that matches the information in the following blanks.

Example: _AIDS_ is caused by a blood-borne virus (HIV, Human Immunodeficiency Virus).

1. _____ is a disease that ravaged Europe between 1347 and 1351.

2. _____ is the bulging out of a part of any of the internal organs through a muscular wall.

3. _____ is a contagious disease that causes red spots to appear on the skin.

4. _____ is caused by a parasite, which is transmitted by a female mosquito.

5. _____ is a form of cancer that is marked by an increase in white blood cells.

6. _____ is an inflammation of the lungs caused by bacteria or viruses.

7. _____ is a decompression sickness experienced in the air or the water.

8. _____ consists of sores on the skin or internal parts of the body and is often caused by stress.

9. _____ is a common name for a cerebral hemorrhage.

10. _____ is a sound caused by contractions of the diaphragm.

EXERCISE 17

Make a "Health Log" which lists the illnesses that you (or other family members) have had as far back as you can remember. Indicate the name of the disease, the kind of doctor that cared for you, and the remedies or medicines that helped you get better. Then, share some or all of this information with a partner. If you are not comfortable sharing this information, make up fictional information to discuss with your partner.

Example: *A general practitioner recommended aspirin, tea with lemon, and bed rest for my cold.*

FAMILY MEMBER	DISEASE	DOCTOR (IF ANY)	REMEDY OR MEDICINE
Self	a cold	general practitioner	an aspirin, tea with lemon, bed rest
Mother	tonsillitis	an ear, nose, and throat doctor	tonsil surgery
Brother	cancer	oncologist	radiation, chemotherapy

EXERCISE 18

Review all of the rules in this unit. Locate ten article errors with *a/an, the*, or Ø in the following paragraph. The first one has been done for you.

(1) The gap between ^{the}∧ rich and the poor, among countries and within countries, is widening. (2) Most of world's AIDS cases and HIV-infected people are in the developing countries. (3) Yet drug and hospitalization costs mean that "early intervention" is still meaningless concept in these countries. (4) Drug AZT remains too expensive for most of people who need it. (5) The industrialized world's total annual contributions to the AIDS in the developing world is estimated at $200 million or less. (6) The last year, the total expenditure for AIDS prevention and care in New York state alone was five times greater. (7) Total budget of the average national AIDS program in the developing world today is less than medical cost of caring for only fifteen people with AIDS in United States.

Adapted from J. Mann, "Global AIDS: Revolution, Paradigm, Solidarity." In O. Peterson, ed., *Representative American Speeches*, New York: The H.W. Wilson Co., 1991.

EXERCISE 19

Review all of the rules in Unit 5. Locate ten article errors with *a/an, the*, or Ø in each of the following blanks. Explain your choices to a partner.

(1) _____Ø_____ insulin functions as (2) _____ indispensable middleman in (3) _____ metabolism. When we eat (4) _____ carbohydrate foods such as (5) _____ bread, (6) _____ vegetables, or (7) _____ fruit, (8) _____ simple sugar called (9) _____ glucose is usually (10) _____ end product of (11) _____ digestion, and this sugar provides (12) _____ energy to each living cell; (13) _____ insulin, in its turn, functions as (14) _____ doorman to these cells, controlling (15) _____ access of (16) _____ glucose molecules and other food sources such as (17) _____ protein and (18) _____ fat across (19) _____ cell membrane and into each cell's interior. With (20) _____ insulin, (21) _____ metabolism is (22) _____ finely tuned feedback mechanism. Without it, only (23) _____ trickle of (24) _____ fuel leaks into (25) _____ cells, hardly enough to stoke (26) _____ great human metabolic furnace.

Adapted from S. Hall, *Invisible Frontiers*, New York: The Atlantic Monthly Press, 1987.

EXERCISE 20

Look at the underlined articles and nouns in the following paragraph. Explain the choice of article in each case. Refer to rules throughout this unit.

Example: the Monterey pine *abstract generic noun requires "the"*

(1) The Monterey pine may bring tidings of (2) Ø joy to many a household during (3) the holiday season, but its own fate is less cheery. Although (4) Ø researchers are cautiously optimistic that (5) the species may survive in (6) the wild, it faces (7) an uphill battle in its native habitat as a result of (8) Ø human interference.

(9) Ø Monterey pine (Pinus radiata) has various personalities—that of (10) a Christmas tree and (11) Ø landscaping enhancement, especially on (12) the West Coast, and that of (13) a hard-working timber producer in plantations in (14) the southern hemisphere.

(15) Ø Refinements of (16) the original California stock have enabled (17) Ø forestry experts in (18) Ø Australia, (19) Ø Chile, (20) Ø New Zealand, and (21) Ø Spain to produce (22) Ø straight-trunked "workhorse" trees much sought after by (23) the lumber industry. More than 10 million acres of domesticated Monterey pine are grown in (24) plantations worldwide.

Adapted from "Monterey Pine Struggles to Survive." In *UC MexUS News*, University of California Institute for Mexico and the United States (UC MEXUS), UC Riverside, Number 43, Spring 2006, p. 19.

EXERCISE 21

Imagine that you have just taken notes on a lecture about the medical field. Rewrite your notes (given below) in a paragraph, inserting articles where necessary.

Example: medical field changed rapidly last century
The medical field has changed rapidly in the last century . . .

1. in past, family practitioner responded to all of family's medical needs (childbirths, surgeries, diseases, etc.)

2. doctor relied on natural remedies to alleviate pain

3. doctor's role was more of onlooker as "nature took its course"

4. today, doctors play more active role in healing

5. with their more specialized training, they are able to prescribe wonder drugs and perform surgeries on patients

6. prolonging life has always been ideal goal

7. sometimes lifesaving/enhancing procedures come in conflict with well-established social, religious, and moral values

8. thus, there is need for medical ethics

9. this is field that considers ethical implications of medical procedures and argues reasonable rights and limits doctors should have in making decisions about improving, prolonging, or saving lives

Use Your English

CD Track 6

ACTIVITY 1 listening/writing

Listen to the mini-lecture about computers.

■ **STEP 1** Take notes about the following items in the grid below.

■ **STEP 2** Extend your notes to make as many sentences as you can, using the principles about article selection that you have learned in this unit.

Example: abacus

An abacus was the earliest computing device used by the ancient Greeks and Romans.

1. use of the slide rule	
2. type of machine Gottfried Liebniz built	
3. invention of Charles Babbage	
4. mathematical theory of Alan Turing	
5. CPU	
6. memory	
7. VDU	
8. four ways computers can function	

ACTIVITY 2 reading/speaking

Select an 800 to 1000- word article from your local newspaper. Underline all instances of nouns preceded by *the*. With a partner, discuss why *the* was chosen instead of *a/an* or Ø articles.

Example: *Ernesto Sanchez grabbed his wife's hand when <u>the ground</u> reared up beneath them, cracking roads and collapsing nearby buildings in seconds.*

The is chosen in this example because it describes a location associated with typical, daily activities but no specific idea of the exact location is provided.

ACTIVITY 3 reading/writing

Locate one chapter in an introductory science textbook (physics, chemistry, biology, etc.) that talks about general principles in that field. With a partner, read the first five paragraphs of the chapter. Make a list of abstract generic and concrete generic articles. Which type seems to be more frequent in this type of writing?

ACTIVITY 4 speaking

Discuss which types of political, social, or religious groups would disagree most with each of the medical practices mentioned in the Opening Task on page 83. For example, would (the) Catholics be in favor of birth control? Would doctors be in favor of declaring positive AIDS tests results for themselves?

ACTIVITY 5 research on the web/writing

 The field of medicine can vary in different cultures. Do research on the Internet and conduct interviews with other students to learn about the practice of medicine in a place you are not familiar with. What are the medical training, medicine, and techniques associated with synthetic drugs, surgical technology, CAT scans, natural herbal drugs, acupuncture, homeopathy, massage, osteopathy, etc.? From your Web research and interviewing, select one aspect of medical practice that interests you and write a short paper, incorporating correct use of the generic article.

ACTIVITY 6 reflection

Think of a difficult school-based problem you would like to solve.

■ **STEP 1**   Try to state the problem in the form of a question.

Example: *How can I write a research paper on a current events topic?*

■ **STEP 2**   List the steps you will need to follow to complete your goal.

Example: 1. Develop a working hypothesis.
2. Conduct interviews with experts and take notes.
3. Find sources in the library or on the Internet.
4. Read sources and take notes.
5. Create an outline.
6. Write a rough draft.
7. Obtain peer and teacher feedback.
8. Revise and edit the final paper.

■ **STEP 3**   Discuss your plan with a classmate, elaborating on each step.

Example: *First, I plan to develop a working hypothesis like "Genetic engineering can alleviate many serious illnesses today." Then, I plan to interview one or two professors in the Biology Department to try to refine my hypothesis. Next . . .*

REFERENCE WORDS AND PHRASES

UNIT GOALS

- Know the different reference forms in English

- Know the different uses of reference forms for linking ideas

- Use the appropriate reference forms for different contexts

- Avoid unclear reference by using appropriate forms

OPENING TASK

Do Men and Women Communicate Differently?

In recent decades, there has been much research about whether men and women have different communication patterns in social situations, workplaces, classrooms, and other contexts.

■ STEP 1

Decide whether each of the following statements is true or false; that is, whether you think it accurately describes communication patterns or not. Be prepared to give reasons or examples for your choices. You may want to state specific conditions under which you believe a statement is generally accurate. An example is given for the first one.

1. Women talk more than men.

   This statement may be true if we compare two women talking together with two men talking together. But I don't think it's the case when women and men are together at a social event or in classroom discussions. In those situations, I think men do more of the talking. So overall, I'd say the statement is false.

2. Men are more likely to interrupt women than to interrupt other men.

3. Female speakers are more animated in their communication style than are males; for example, they gesture more than men do.

4. In business situations, female managers communicate with more emotional openness than male managers do.

5. During conversations, women spend more time looking at their partner than men do.

6. Women are more likely to answer questions that are not addressed to them.

7. In general, men smile more often than women.

8. Women are more likely to disclose information about intimate personal concerns than men are.

■ **STEP 2**

Discuss your answers and explanations with a partner.

■ **STEP 3**

Turn to page A-16 to see answers and explanations based on research about the ways in which American men and women communicate. Match each with one of the eight statements above. Check your answers with classmates.

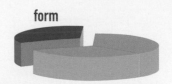
form

FOCUS 1 — Review of Reference Forms

EXAMPLES	EXPLANATIONS
Referent (a) Ruth enjoys talking about [gender-based language differences]. She finds **the topic** an interesting one.	Words and phrases that refer to information previously stated are called *reference forms*. The information that you are referring to is called a *referent*. The referents are here indicated by brackets
(b) Alma agrees that [men and women communicate differently in our society]. She believes **the observation** is true based on her personal experience.	**Reference Forms** • *the* + noun phrase
(c) **Lin:** Do you know much about [language variation]? **Yumi:** Not a lot, but I did read a little about **it** in my introductory linguistics course.	• Pronouns: *it*
(d) [Phonology and semantics] are areas of linguistics. **They** are concerned with language sounds and meanings, respectively. I studied **them** a few years ago.	*they, them*
(e) Our sociology professor says that [male students tend to be criticized more than female students in classroom situations]. My experience supports { **this.** **this claim.**	• Demonstrative pronouns and determiners: *this; this* + singular/noncount noun
(f) **Fred:** Do you think [men tend to interrupt more than women do]? **Yani:** I would agree with { **that.** **that generalization.**	• *that; that* + singular/noncount noun
(g) [Two of the gender differences] seem especially true to me. **These** **These differences** } will be the topic of my paper.	*these; these* + plural noun
(h) **George:** I know [people who constantly interrupt other people]. **Lily:** **Those** **Those people** } are the ones that I avoid!	*those; those* + plural noun
(i) I read several studies about how [young boys are often encouraged to be aggressive and competitive]. I think **such an upbringing** would influence a boy's behavior when he gets older.	• Reference forms with *such a/an* + singular noun. The reference form *such* will be covered in greater detail in Focus 7 of this unit.
(j) I've never thought much about how [age, social status, and gender] influence the way we use language. However, I agree that **such factors** probably do affect greatly the ways in which we communicate.	• *such* + plural or noncount noun

EXERCISE 1

Find five different types of reference forms in the sentences giving answers for the quiz in the Opening Task on pages 108–109. In the first column write the number of the item and the reference form. In the second column, write what the form refers to (the referent). You can paraphrase the referent. An example is given to start you off.

Example: **Reference Form:** this

Referent: that women look at their partners more than men do

REFERENCE FORM	REFERENT
1.	
2.	
3.	
4.	
5.	

EXERCISE 2

Underline the reference forms (*the* + noun, *it, this*, etc.) in the second sentence of each problem that refer to information in the previous sentence. Put brackets around the referents. There may be more than one reference form in a sentence.

Example: Our group discussed [the responses to Situation 1].
We didn't always agree that such responses were typical.

1. According to our psychology professor, for women, talk is important for creating connections between people. For men these connections tend to be formed more through activities than talk.

2. Men and women sometimes experience frustration with each other because of their different communication styles. The frustration may be especially great between men and women who spend a great deal of time together.

3. Our professor notes that women have a tendency to make suggestions rather than give commands when they want something done. She thinks this tendency may reflect women's sense that they lack authority in certain situations.

4. Speakers use language differently depending on differences in age, education, social status, and gender. Such differences are of interest to linguists.

5. Pitch and volume are two aspects of speech. The way we use them in speech may affect how we are perceived by others in communication situations.

6. Women have higher-pitched voices than men do. This can be a disadvantage when they are trying to assert authority.

(Continued)

7. In some business contexts, women may regard personal questions, such as how a fellow worker spent the weekend, as a way of showing friendliness. Men may consider the questions inappropriate in these contexts.

8. Some studies show that men tend to dominate conversation in groups including males and females. Based on your experience, do you agree with that?

9. I agree with the idea that men and women should try to understand each other's different communication styles. It makes sense to me.

10. We could accept the communication differences we have with the "other gender," or we could try to negotiate different ways of communicating that would be more productive and less frustrating. These are two possible approaches to our differences in communication styles.

EXERCISE 3

In the book *You Just Don't Understand: Women and Men in Conversation*, sociolinguistics professor Deborah Tannen describes a number of situations in which men and women have different communication styles. Choose one of the two situations summarized below and write a paragraph in response to two questions that follow. Exchange your paragraph with a classmate. Underline the reference forms in your classmate's paragraph.

Situation 1: Talking About Troubles

Someone (male or female) has a personal problem. He or she is very upset and tells a friend about the problem.

If the friend is female: She empathizes by telling the person that she knows how it feels to have the problem. She may provide an example of the same problem or a similar one from her own experience (e.g.,"I know what you mean. Something like that happened to me too!")

If the friend is male: He offers advice about how to solve the problem (e.g., "Well, why don't you stop seeing your friend if her behavior bothers you?")

Situation 2: Expressing Troubles

Someone expresses an opinion about a topic or presents his or her ideas on a topic.

If the listener is female: She expresses agreement with the speaker or, if she disagrees, asks for clarification or further explanation.

If the listener is male: He challenges the speaker's views and explores possible flaws in the argument or idea.

Questions

1. Do you agree that such responses are typical of men and women in the situations described? Why or why not?

2. Do you think the gender-based communication differences described are common in cultures other than American culture?

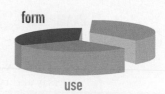

form

use

FOCUS 2 — Reference Forms with *the* and Demonstrative Determiners

EXAMPLES	EXPLANATIONS
(a) I liked [the novels] very much. I might even reread some of them. I would recommend **the novels** to anyone who wants to know more about Chinese history.	**Complete Repetition** Reference forms may repeat all of the referent. We use this form more often as a later mention than as a second mention.
(b) Oh, look at [this book] in the children's section! My sisters and I must have read **it** a hundred times when we were young. (c) I read [two interesting studies about language variation between different age groups]. I have summarized { **the two studies** / **these two studies** } in the introduction of my paper.	**Partial Repetition** Some reference forms repeat only part of the referent. We do not usually repeat a demonstrative determiner (*this, that, those, those*) + noun. Instead, we tend to us *it, them* or *the* + (noun phrase). We do not usually repeat descriptive modifiers. In (c), only *two* and *studies* have been repeated for both example reference forms.
(d) I read [one study about language differences based on educational levels]. I did not, however, use { **the article** / **that article** } in my paper.	**Synonym** A reference form can be a synonym of the referent. In (d), *article* is used as a synonym for *study* and the modifiers are not repeated.
(e) We went to see [*Hamlet*]. **The play** was performed outdoors at the city center. (f) I would like to take [South American literature and the history of jazz] next quarter. Several of my friends recommended **those courses**.	**Classifier** A reference form can also be a classifier of the referent. A classifier word or phrase describes a class or group that could include the referent. In (e), *Hamlet* can be classified as a play. In (f), *courses* classifies the two courses mentioned.

EXAMPLES	EXPLANATIONS

EXAMPLES

(g) Over the weekend [you should revise your essay and type it]. **The revised paper** should be turned in on Monday.

(h) [The aerosol is sprayed into the chamber where the water vaporizes.] **This vaporization process** is repeated.

EXPLANATIONS

Paraphrase
A reference form can also paraphrase a clause or sentence. We commonly use this form to refer to activities and the results of them:

Activity: You revise an essay.
Result: The revised paper

Paraphrases also refer to processes, as in (h). The reference form may repeat part of the referent as in (g) (*revise*), or it may include a word that classifies or describes, such as process, effects, or *results* as in (h).

■ EXERCISE 4

STEP 1 Underline reference forms with *the* and demonstrative adjectives in the second sentence of each sentence pair.

STEP 2 Bracket the referents in the first sentence.

STEP 3 State what type of reference is used: (1) complete repetition of the referent, (2) partial repetition, (3) synonym, (4) classifier, or (5) paraphrase.

As a class, you may want to discuss why the various forms are used.

Example: Psychologists have distinguished [three dimensions of emotions]. These dimensions can be used to characterize differences in the ways cultures recognize and express emotions.

partial repetition: It is not necessary to repeat the entire referent. We do not usually use complete repetition when there are modifiers.

1. One dimension distinguishes between what are called the primary emotions and what are termed the secondary emotions. The primary emotions are considered universal by some psychologists.

2. The primary emotions are also considered to be biologically based. These feelings include anger, grief, joy, and disgust.

3. The secondary emotions are blends of the primary emotions. These emotions, such as contempt (a blend of anger and disgust), are not universal.

4. Another dimension of emotions distinguishes pleasant feelings from unpleasant ones. The positive emotions are ones such as love and joy, whereas the negative emotions are ones such as sorrow and shame.

5. The last dimension classifies emotions based on intensity. This classification of feelings can distinguish worry from terror and sadness from depression.

6. All societies have what are called display rules regarding emotions. These rules dictate how and when people may express certain emotions.

7. For example, in some cultures, people would express grief by crying. In other cultures, this emotion might be expressed by silence.

EXERCISE 5

Make up a sentence using *the* reference or demonstrative reference to elaborate on ideas in each of the sentences below. The referent is underlined. Try to use a variety of the reference types discussed in the chart on pages 113–114.

Example: <u>Anger</u> is a primary emotion.
This emotion is biologically based.

1. Everyone has <u>negative feelings</u>.
2. Psychologists note that <u>the smile</u> does not have universal meaning.
3. <u>Facial expressions</u> are important signals of emotion.
4. <u>Fury</u> is a very intense emotion.
5. <u>Nonverbal signals such as posture, gestures, and eye contact</u> also express emotions.

use

EXAMPLES	EXPLANATIONS
(a) I like [that book] a lot. I read **it** last year. (b) Kip is taking [math and English]. **They** are his most challenging subjects, and he has homework for both of **them** almost every day.	Use the personal pronouns *it*, *they*, *them* when there is only one possible referent.
(c) **Toni:** There is some evidence that [women are likely to worry more than men.] **Ricardo:** I believe it. (d) **Rita:** [Men tend to apologize less than women do.] **Lee:** I don't doubt **it**.	Use *it*: • when the one possible referent is a clause. • when the one possible referent is a sentence.
(e) I read [the book *The Bee Season*] before I saw the movie. I thought **the book** was very interesting. (f) To Whom It May Concern: I am returning [the enclosed MP3 player]. The volume control does not work. Also, the sound quality does not seem very good. **The player** came with a one-year warranty. (g) [Violence] is increasing in our society. **The problem** cannot be ignored. (h) This medicine should not be taken when you are driving because [it can make you sleepy or it may affect your vision]. **The adverse effects** are only temporary, but nevertheless, you need to be cautious.	Use *the* + noun phrase: • when there is more than one possible referent. In (e), *the book* and *the movie* would be possible referents if you used it. • when the referent might not be clear unless a noun phrase rather than a pronoun is used. In written English, this is often the case when the referent is more than one sentence before the reference form. • when you want to replace the referent with a classifier, a synonym, or a paraphrase. Sometimes you may want to replace a referent with a paraphrase because you cannot repeat the whole referent, and a pronoun reference would not be clear. In (h), the referent is an entire clause. Using *they* for reference would be too vague.

EXERCISE 6

Decide whether *it, they, them*, or *the* + noun phrase is appropriate for each item below.

1. Identify the referent and bracket it.

2. If *the* + noun phrase should be used, choose a noun phrase that fits the context.

Example: Have you read [the book *Men Are from Mars, Women Are from Venus*]? <u>It</u> also discusses communication differences between men and women.
(Only one possible referent, so it is appropriate.)

1. I have to write a paper for my sociology class about the 1960s. I can't decide whether to write my paper about the Civil Rights marches in the early '60s or about the women's movement in the late '60s. (a) _____ appeals to me because I'd like to find out more about the history of segregation in the South. (b) _____ are both interesting topics, however.

2. **Felix:** Do you think it's true that men tend to be more direct about what they want than women do?
   Alicia: Oh yes, I'm convinced of _____.

3. I am not surprised by the research finding that boys get reprimanded in school more than girls. _____ corresponds with my own experience.

4. Neurologists at Stanford University have been studying differences in how men and women react to humor. In their experiments, they studied brain responses when men and women looked at a series of cartoons. They discovered that women and men used different parts of their brains in reacting. They also found that women reacted more intensely when they viewed _____ .

5. Scientists believe that there are more than five senses. The organ for the sense of hearing is, of course, the ear. However, in addition, _____ has receptors that help us to create a sense of balance.

FOCUS 4 — Demonstrative Determiners and Pronouns

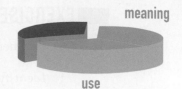

meaning

use

The forms of demonstrative pronouns and determiners *this, that, these,* and *those* tell the reader/listener whether a referent is singular or plural and whether the speaker/writer regards the referent as near or far.

	SINGULAR	PLURAL
Near	this	these
Far	that	those

EXAMPLES	EXPLANATIONS
	The concept of distance (near or far) may involve the following:
	Space
(a) Take **this chair** right here.	• Near: The speaker regards something as physically nearby.
(b) I'll get two of **these**, please. And one melon.	
(c) Can you see **that** tall **tower** in the distance?	• Far: The speaker regards something as physically distant.
(d) **Those buildings** next to the tower are part of the new arts center.	
(e) Let's finish watching **this movie**. It's almost over.	**Time**
	• Near: There is a link to present time.
(f) **These** are difficult times because of the economy.	
(g) I'd like to see **that** again. It was one of my favorite musicals.	• Far: Reference is to a time in the past not regarded as close to the present.
(h) **Those** were called the golden years because prosperity was widespread.	
	Discourse Distance
(i) [Age] is another factor affecting language use. **This influence** can be seen in the use of slang.	• Near: The referent is close to the reference form in the text.
(j) [The introduction to my thesis] provided background on my topic. It offered several hypotheses about language differences. **That section** also presented an outline of my thesis.	• Far: The speaker or writer views the referent as distant. In (j), the writer regards the introduction as distant from the part being written.

EXAMPLES	EXPLANATIONS
(k) I believe [gun control laws are needed]. I feel very strongly about **this**.	**Psychological Distance** • Near: The referent is mentioned by the speaker herself or himself; and is something she believes.
(l) **Hal:** I think [gun control laws are needed]. **Tori:** I don't agree with **that**.	• Far: The referent is mentioned by another speaker. Tori disagrees with Hal's position.
(m) When Wilhelm Roentgen discovered the X-ray in 1895, he did not completely understand the nature of these new rays. He called them X-rays because the letter x stands for an unknown quantity in mathematics. **That** is how the X-ray came to be named.	Finally, we often use the demonstrative pronoun *that* in concluding statements to refer to an explanation or description we have given.

EXERCISE 7

Put an appropriate demonstrative form (*this, that, these*, or *those*) in each blank. If you think more than one might be appropriate, discuss the contexts (including speaker attitude) in which each might be used.

Example: In ancient Greece, the great classical philosophers, such as Aristotle and Plato, developed theories about emotions. At ____that____ time, they were especially interested in the effect of poetry and drama on the emotions. (In referring to ancient Greece, *that* indicates distance in terms of time.)

1. The ancient philosopher Aristotle wrote that it was easy to become angry; however, to become angry with the right person to the right degree at the right time and for the right purpose was not so easy. I think _____ was a very wise reflection about the emotion of anger.

2. New theories about intelligence include emotional intelligence. As defined by psychologist Daniel Goleman, (a) _____ type of intelligence refers to the capacity to recognize our own feelings and (b) _____ of others.

3. **Erin:** Did you know that scientists are using neuroimaging to see how the human brain responds to emotions such as fear?
   Victor: No, I hadn't heard about _____.

4. Have you ever wondered how the brain processes fear? (a) _____ emotion relies on pathways deep in a part of the brain called the amygdala. Research shows that (b) _____ pathways will be activated by frightening stimuli such as loud buzzing or fearful faces. The brain can also store information about signals that suggest danger. (c) _____ is, in brief, what happens.

5. **Eduardo:** I think I'm going to watch a program about emotional intelligence on the science channel tonight. Do you want to come over?

   Soo: Do you really like (a) _____ science shows? I think I'd rather stay home and watch some videos. Take a look at (b) _____ movies I just picked up. Maybe you'll change your mind.

6. Dear Senator Gilman: I am writing (a) _____ letter to urge you to do something about improving services for our homeless people who have severe emotional problems. (b) Right now _____ situation is disgraceful; some people in our community have suggested asking the homeless people to move to a larger city where there are more services, but (c) _____ is certainly not the answer to (d) _____ problem.

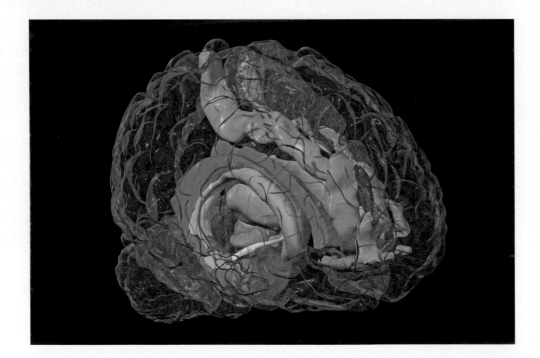

| FOCUS 5 | Using Demonstrative Determiner +
Noun Phrase for Clear Reference |

EXAMPLES	EXPLANATIONS
(a) When you do strenuous exercise, you should wear proper clothing and [you should warm up first]. **This warm-up** will help prevent injuries.	Sometimes we need to use a demonstrative determiner + a noun phrase for clear reference.
(b) NOT: **This** will help prevent injuries.	In (b), *this* does not clearly signal the referent. *This* could be interpreted as both wearing proper clothing and warming up.
(c) Before writing your essay, you should try to [brainstorm some ideas and then put your ideas into categories]. **These prewriting techniques** can help you get started on your paper.	Like *the* + noun phrase reference, demonstrative determiner + noun phrase reference can help to describe or classify the referent.

EXERCISE 8

Use a demonstrative determiner and a classifying or descriptive noun from the list below to complete each of the blanks. Change the noun to plural where needed. The reference forms should refer to the words that are in brackets, [. . .]. There may be more than one possible answer.

Example: [Research indicates that men tend to tell jokes more than women do]. <u>This tendency</u> has been observed among Americans.

difference	idea	response	trait
expression	issue	result	
factor	pattern	tendency	

1. Psychology researchers at the University of Wisconsin examined differences between men and women based on [120 different aspects of human behavior], including personality, communication skills, and leadership potential. They found significant differences in only 22 percent of _____.

(Continued)

2. In Canada and the United States, brain research has indicated that [men and women appear to use different parts of the brain for different purposes, such as storing memories, solving problems and sensing emotions; some research shows that men's and women's brains are constructed differently]. The implications of _____ have been hotly debated by other researchers and scholars.

3. Some scholars argue that [brain research showing male and female differences could lead to discrimination]; others point out that [physical differences in men's and women's brains may be the results of conditioning that starts in infancy and lifelong mental processes]. _____ and others will be debated for years to come.

4. [Smiles, frowns, raised eyebrows, and shrugs of the shoulder] all convey emotions. _____ may have different meanings in different cultures, though.

5. [Women] sometimes [think men are being unsympathetic] when they give advice about a problem rather than share troubles. _____ stems from a difference between men and women in what they think is an appropriate reaction to such a situation.

use

FOCUS 6 — Demonstrative Forms versus *The* and *It/Them* References

EXAMPLES	EXPLANATIONS
(a) Oh, I've heard { that joke. / the joke before. / it. } (b) Norm told us { the jokes. / those jokes. / them. }	In many contexts, you can use demonstrative, *the*, or *pronoun* reference forms. All would be acceptable. The choice often depends on (1) the speaker's or writer's intentions, or (2) what the speaker/writer thinks the listener/reader knows.
(c) More emphasis: I heard [a speaker] on campus this afternoon. **This speaker** was the best I've heard on the topic of workplace communication. (d) Less emphasis: I heard [a speaker] on campus this afternoon. **The speaker/she** was talking about communicating effectively in the workplace. (e) Less emphasis: I'm not sure if I'll [type my paper myself]. If I do, **it** will probably take me all day! (f) More emphasis: I'm not sure if I'll [type my paper myself]. I have more important things to do than **that!**	**Emphasizing the Referent** Use demonstrative determiners or pronouns when you want to emphasize the referent. Demonstrative adjective *this* in the second sentence of (c) emphasizes the referent "a speaker" more. The reference forms in the second sentence of (d) do not emphasize the referent "a speaker." In (e), *it* puts less emphasis on the referent, focusing on new information (the result of having to type without help). In example (f) placing *that* at the end of the sentence puts more emphasis on the referent *type my paper*.
(g) I asked my instructor if I needed [to include a bibliography with my draft]. She told me **that** would not be necessary. (h) Repetitious: She told me [**including the bibliography**] would not be necessary. (i) [This paper] is one of the best I've written. I'm sure my classmates will enjoy **it.** (j) NOT: I'm sure my classmates will enjoy **this paper**.	**Avoiding Unnecessary Repetition** Use a demonstrative pronoun to avoid unnecessary repetition. In example (h), the paraphrase with *the* + noun phrase gives too much information. We often use demonstrative pronouns when the referent is a clause or a sentence. As mentioned in Focus 2, we do not usually repeat demonstrative phrases in second mention. We use some other reference form such as *it* or *the*.

EXERCISE 9

Put an appropriate reference form in each blank. The referent is in brackets. Use one of the following forms: (1) *it*, (2) *the* + noun phrase, (3) demonstrative determiner (*this, that, these,* or *those*) + noun phrase, (4) demonstrative pronoun (*this, that, these,* or *those*). Use the notes in parentheses to guide your choice. For some blanks, more than one choice might be possible.

Example: An article I read claims that [hot water freezes faster than cold water]. Were you aware of _____that_____? (Also possible: *that fact*)

1. I read [an article reporting on a survey about Americans' ideas of comfort foods]. _____ discusses how women tend to prefer snack-related comfort food like candy and chocolates while men prefer meal-related comfort foods such as pasta or casseroles. (Put focus on the new information in the second sentence, not the referent.)

2. The article stated that men may be conditioned from upbringing to prefer hot, labor-intensive meals, while women like comfort foods that require less preparation. _____ was an interesting explanation of the survey results. (Put focus on the subject of the second sentence.)

3. I just found out that [Einstein's brain actually weighed less than the average man's brain]. I didn't know _____ before.

4. The ancient Egyptians believed that the heart, rather than the brain, was the source of all human wisdom. In fact, they believed the brain's only function was to pass fluids to the nose. _____ and other beliefs were, of course, discarded as science developed.

5. One theory of the origin of language is closely related to emotions. _____ maintains that speech started when people made instinctive sounds caused by emotions.

6. Some studies have suggested that women tend to speak less assertively than men. [When they do so], _____ may cause others to doubt their authority or credibility. (Emphasize the result.)

7. Whether true or not, it is commonly believed that [men will not ask for directions when they are lost]. _____ has been a topic of many jokes and cartoons in American culture. (Emphasize the referent.)

"WE'RE NOT *LOST*, AND I'M **NOT** STOPPING TO ASK FOR DIRECTIONS!"

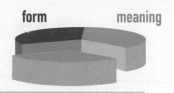

FOCUS 7   Reference Forms with *Such*

EXAMPLES

(a) We need [a strong and honest leader]. **Such a person** is Mario Baretta.

(b) Men and women often have [different responses to the same situations]. **Such responses** may result from the ways they have been brought up.

(c) You should try to eat more [fruits, vegetables, and whole grains]. **Such foods** are important for good health.

(d) The police thoroughly investigated [the burglary]. They concluded that only experienced thieves could have accomplished **such a crime.**

(e) Did you hear [what he said]? I've never heard of **such an idea** before.

(f) [Impatiens and fuchsia plants] need little sun. **Such plants** are good for shady areas of your garden.

(g) I can't believe [the things] they told us about their neighbors. In my opinion, they shouldn't repeat **such personal information**.

(h) [Several students] have demonstrated superior performance in the field of mathematics. **One such student** is Ruby Pereda.

(i) Now more than ever we need reform-minded candidates for our city council. **Two such candidates** are Ben Ho and Ulla Teppo.

(j) I admire **your attitude.** Such an attitude shows great respect for others.

(k) They said that **women should stay at home.** Such an attitude does not reflect the feelings of most Americans.

EXPLANATIONS

The meaning of *such*, when referring to previous information, is similar to "like that" or "of that type of thing." In (a) *such a person* refers to a person belonging to the type "a strong and honest leader." In (b), *such responses* refer to responses that can be classified as "different for the same situation." With plural nouns, *such* phrases often follow a list or series of things as in (c).

Structure forms with *such*:
- *Such* + singular noun
  Use *a* or *an* after *such*.

- *Such* + Plural Noun

- *Such* + Noncount Noun
  No article is used after *such* before a noncount noun.
- (Number) + *Such* + Singular or Plural Noun
  Note that no article is used before *student* in (h).

Referents of *such* phrases
The information that references with *such* refer to may be:
- a phrase

- a clause

EXAMPLES	EXPLANATIONS
(l) "The world owes me a living." Such an attitude will not get you very far, my father always tells me.	• a sentence
(m) **Girls should do all the housework. Women should serve the men in the family.** Such an attitude about the role of women is common in some cultures, but it seems to be changing.	• more than one sentence

EXERCISE 10

Underline the *such* reference in each of the following groups of sentences or dialogues. Then state what the referent is. If you wish, you may paraphrase the referent.

Example: Men tend to view conversation as a way to assert status and to impart information. <u>Such attitudes</u> are not as common with women.
Referent: <u>Men's attitudes that conversation is for asserting status and imparting information.</u>

1. The Italian composer Guiseppe Verdi wrote one of his greatest operas, *Falstaff*, when he was 80. To have created this brilliant musical work at such an advanced age is truly remarkable.

   Referent: _____

   _____

   _____

2. In the early decades of American filmmaking, Asians were often portrayed as servants, launderers, cooks, gardeners, and waiters. Such stereotypes denied the many achievements of Asian-Americans at that time.

   Referent: _____

   _____

   _____

3. Lightning never strikes in the same place twice. Rattlesnakes intentionally give warnings to their victims by rattling their tails. The sap of a tree rises in the spring. Such beliefs, although common, are not supported by scientific evidence.

Referent: _____

_____

_____

4. Some people who pursue physical fitness with a passion fill up their homes with stationary bicycles, rowing machines, and stair climbers. Each time a new exercise machine appears on the market, they rush to their local sporting goods stores. However, such equipment is not needed to become physically fit.

Referent: _____

_____

_____

5. We are now faced with a number of serious problems in our metropolitan areas. One such problem is how to best help the thousands of homeless people.

Referent: _____

_____

_____

6. When you have just met someone, what types of personal questions should you avoid asking? The answer depends on what culture you are in. For example, in some cultures it might be acceptable to ask a woman how old she is, how much money she makes, or even how much she weighs, but in many cultures such questions are considered impolite.

Referent: _____

_____

_____

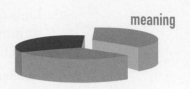

FOCUS 8 — *Such* versus Demonstrative Determiners

EXAMPLES	EXPLANATIONS
(a) When Mr. Clark came to our restaurant, he complained about the location of his table, criticized the menu, insulted the waiter, and failed to leave a tip. We hope we never again have to deal with . . .	*Such* refers to a class or type of thing. Consequently, reference phrases with *such* have a more general meaning than *this, that, these*, or *those* before nouns.

Specific	Type
(1) **this** person.	(2) **such** a person.

(1) refers to Mr. Clark.
(2) refers to any person who would act the way Mr. Clark did.

(b) Two types of dinosaurs with birdlike hips were stegosaurs and ankylosaurs.

Specific	Type
(1) **These** dinosaurs . . . were herbivorous.	(2) **Such** dinosaurs . . .

(1) refers to stegosaurs and ankylosaurs.
(2) refers to all dinosaurs with birdlike hips.

(c) In the United States, it has become common for the media to report every medical problem that the President suffers and every medical treatment, however minor, he receives. Does the public really need . . .

Specific	Type
(1) **this** information?	(2) **such** information?

(1) refers to information about medical problems and medical treatment.
(2) refers more generally to information that is personal and unimportant in the context.

EXERCISE 11

Work with a partner or a small group to answer the following questions based on the examples in the chart above.

1. Which words after *such* (*a/an*) (person, dinosaurs, information) repeat a word in the preceding sentence? Which do not? How can you explain this difference?

2. Can you think of words that might be substituted for those occurring after *such* (*a/an*) in the examples? Are they more general or more specific than the words in the examples? How do they change the meaning?

Example: *such a person—such a grouch (more specific; describes Mr. Clark negatively)*

3. Often a modifier can be used to make a "class" word more specific. For example, *advanced* in "at such an advanced age" makes it clear that reference is to those ages late in life. In the examples in the chart on page 128, what modifiers could be added to define more specifically the words following *such* (*a*)?

EXERCISE 12

STEP 1 For each of the four word pairs below, think of one or more categories that could be used to classify or characterize them. Then make up a word pair of your own and indicate possible categories for it.

Example: Word pair: football, hockey
Categories: *sports, spectator sports, popular sports*

WORD PAIR	CATEGORIES
a. love, anger	_____
b. jeeps, mountain bikes	_____
c. earthquakes, hurricanes	_____
d. backgammon, chess	_____
e. your choice (list-related words): _____	_____

STEP 2 Now select one of your categories for each word pair. Add to each pair other words or phrases that could be classified by this term.

Example: *Spectator sports: soccer, baseball, basketball*

STEP 3 Write one or two sentences for each set of words above. Use *such* plus the category you selected. (The items could be the word pairs given or the words you added.)

Example: *I know many people who spend a lot of time watching football and basketball on television. However, I prefer to be active rather than sitting and watching such spectator sports.*

STEP 4 Discuss the difference in meaning that would result if you replaced *such* in each statement with a demonstrative determiner (*this, that, these, those*).

Example: *However, I don't enjoy **those** spectator sports.*
"**Such** spectator sports" refers to any sports that people watch; "**those** spectator sports" refers only to football and baseball.

EXERCISE 13

Correct the inappropriate or repetitive reference forms in each of the following sentences. There may be more than one way to correct errors.

Examples: My friend suggested that I drop out of school and work for a while. I'm not sure what I think about such an advice.
Correction: *I'm not sure what I think about **such advice**.* (*Advice* is a noncount noun, so no article is used.)

1. In my paper, I plan to discuss two emotions that all cultures share. The two emotions that all cultures share are joy and grief.

2. In ancient times, people thought that fear was a result of the brain overheating and that anxiety arose from the brain cooling off. I may use those information in the introduction to my paper.

3. This year I took both an English course and a Spanish course. It was quite easy for me because French is my native language and the two languages are similar.

4. Our math teacher gave us a surprise quiz. Can you believe he would be this unkind man?

5. I have a friend who likes to wear only two colors of clothing: blue and purple. She dresses in such colors every day.

6. One study says that male children do not pay as much attention to female children as they do to other males. What do you think about it?

7. Some people insist on giving advice even when it's not requested. Such an advice is generally not appreciated.

8. I am keeping the blue shirt I ordered from your catalog. This shirt fits fine. However, I am returning the sweater because this was much too small.

9. Did you hear her boast that she never has to study for her courses? The student misses the point of what an education means.

10. What do you think about the claim that teachers are more likely to give praise to female students? I disagree with the claim that teachers are more likely to give praise to female students.

Use Your English

ACTIVITY 1 listening

CD Tracks
7, 8

Listen to the two dialogues. Each dialogue illustrates a difference between male and female communication styles, according to Professor Deborah Tannen. After you have heard the dialogues, either discuss the following questions with a partner or write complete answers.

1. What communication differences do these dialogues illustrate?

2. Have you observed such differences in your own experience?

3. Can you think of exceptions to the generalizations that these dialogues illustrate?

ACTIVITY 2 writing/speaking/listening

In teams, make up lists of statements that include both amazing facts and "untruths." Good sources for hard-to-believe facts are reference books such as *The Guinness Book of World Records* or *Ripley's Believe It or Not* as well as almanacs. Mix in with the amazing facts some of your own statements that are **not** true. Each team should then read their list of statements to another group. The listeners must agree on which ones they believe and which they don't believe. Score a point for each correct judgment as to whether a statement is true or not.

Example: **Team A:** The largest watermelon on record weighed 260 pounds.

Team B: We don't believe it.

The statement is true. Team A gets the point.

ACTIVITY 3 speaking/writing

Write a paragraph comparing the language use of different groups based on a variable other than gender. For example, consider differences you are aware of based on age, social status, occupation, geographical location, or education. When you have finished, identify the reference forms you used.

ACTIVITY 4 writing

Write a letter to either a business to complain about unsatisfactory merchandise or one of your political representatives (for example, a senator or the President) to voice your opinions about an issue that is important to you. Exchange letters with a classmate. The classmate should check your use of reference forms to see if they are appropriate and then write a response to your letter, playing the role of the company or person to whom you addressed it.

ACTIVITY 5 writing

Choose one of the sentences below to include in a paragraph. Then write the rest of the paragraph, creating a context appropriate for including the sentence. (The sentence could occur anywhere in the paragraph after the first sentence.)

Those subjects just aren't worth studying.

Those TV programs should be taken off the air.

Such advice should be helpful to anyone visiting _____. (Choose a city or country to fill in the blank.)

Such a person is to be avoided whenever possible.

Such bad luck shouldn't happen to anyone.

ACTIVITY 6 reading

As you do reading for other courses or for your own interests, write in a notebook examples of *such* reference forms that you find. Include the *such* phrase and the phrase(s) or sentence(s) to which each refers. Make a note of the context (for example, an explanation of a chemical process, a comment on people's behavior, a description of a product in an advertisement). At some point you may want to compare your findings with your classmates' to see the ways in which reference forms with *such* references are used in written texts.

ACTIVITY 7   research on the web

Use the keywords "gender differences and food" and search for articles on comfort foods and gender differences in *InfoTrac® College Edition*. Poll your class or a group of 15–20 people about the comfort foods listed, asking them to agree or disagree with the choices on a 5-point scale (1 = strongly disagree, 5 = strongly agree). Give an oral or written report on your findings, using a variety of reference forms to link ideas.

ACTIVITY 8   reflection

Review three textbooks and/or Web sites that you have found helpful for your learning. For each, write one or two sentences that describe in brief something about their usefulness. Use a demonstrative adjective and a classifier word. You could also use descriptive modifiers either before or after the classifier word. This kind of writing, called an annotation, is a common academic assignment. If time permits, compile the annotations written by class members and share them with the class in a handout or via e-mail attachment.

Examples:

Grammar Dimensions 4	This advanced-level grammar book helps students with many structures used in academic writing.
Randall's ESL Cyber Listening Lab	This Web site offers dialogues for listening practice at several levels of difficulty.

RELATIVE CLAUSES MODIFYING SUBJECTS

UNIT GOALS

- Use restrictive relative clauses to modify subjects

- Use restrictive relative clauses to make nouns more specific

- Know how to reduce restrictive relative clauses

OPENING TASK

Trivia Challenge

■ **STEP 1**

The object of this game is to get the most answers right in a trivia game. Student A looks at page 135. Student B looks at page A-17.

■ **STEP 2**

To begin, Student A will create definitions or descriptions of a person or thing, offering three options. Student B will listen and repeat the definition, completing the sentence with the correct word or phrase. If correct, he or she will receive one point.

■ **STEP 3**

Student B will now create definitions or descriptions in the same way. The partner with the most points wins the game.

Example: a person
explores and studies caves
Options: (a) transducer,
*(b) spelunker, (c) coanchor
Student A creates a definition: *A person who explores and studies caves is called a (a) transducer, *(b) spelunker, or (c) coanchor*
(The correct answer is asterisked (*).)

Student B makes a guess: *A person who explores and studies caves is called a spelunker*.
Congratulations to Student B. He or she will be awarded one point for the correct answer.

TRIVIA CHALLENGE

Create a Definition or Description:

1. an animal

   It mates for life.

   (a) seahorse, (b) boa constrictor, *(c) Canada goose

2. a book

   Its original title was changed six times.

   (a) *War and Peace* by Leo Tolstoy, *(b) *The Great Gatsby* by F. Scott Fitzgerald,

   (c) *Pride and Prejudice* by Jane Austen

3. an inventor

   Teachers gave him poor report cards.

   *(a) Thomas Edison, (b) Alexander Graham Bell, (c) Robert Fulton

4. a person

   He or she fits the interior parts of pianos.

   (a) mucker, (b) hooker inspector, *(c) belly builder

Guess the Correct Answer:

5. (a) dragonfly, (b) flycatcher, (c) firefly

6. (a) cornball, (b) impostor, (c) daytripper

7. (a) amphora, (b) amulet, (c) aspartame

8. (a) bodice, (b) causerie, (c) bloomers

Overview of Restrictive Relative Clauses

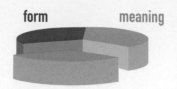

form   meaning

A restrictive relative clause modifies a noun phrase in a main clause. It is placed as close to the noun phrase as possible and is used to identify the noun. A relative pronoun (*that* in this sentence) is used to replace the noun being identified.

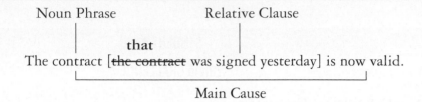

Noun Phrase   Relative Clause

that

The contract [~~the contract~~ was signed yesterday] is now valid.

Main Cause

There are four general types of restrictive relative clauses. They may modify main clause subjects or objects. Relative pronouns may be subjects or objects in their own clauses. Note the function of the labeled nouns in each clause:

Main clause: The contract is now valid ("contract" is the **subject**).

Relative clause: that was signed yesterday ("that" is the **object**)

TYPES OF RELATIVE CLAUSES	NOUN PHRASE IN MAIN CLAUSE	RELATIVE PRONOUN IN RELATIVE CLAUSE
S S (a) *The contract* **that was signed yesterday** is now valid.	Subject	Subject
S O (b) *The contract* **that he signed yesterday** is now valid.	Subject	Object
O S (c) I have not read *the contract* **that was signed** yesterday.	Object	Subject
O O (d) I have not read *the contract* **that** he signed yesterday.	Object	Object

This unit will focus on restrictive relative clauses that modify subjects in main clauses (like (a) and (b) on page 136). These clauses can have various relative pronouns, and the relative pronouns can fulfill various grammatical functions. *Whose* can function as a relative determiner. This unit will also deal with *whose* as a relative determiner.

EXAMPLES	SUBJECT BEING MODIFIED	RELATIVE DETERMINER	FUNCTION OF RELATIVE DETERMINER
(e) A person **who/that** sells houses is a realtor.	person	*who/that*	subject
(f) The secretary **whom/that** she hired is very experienced.		*whom/that*	direct object
(g) The employees **to whom** she denied a pay raise have gone on strike.		*whom*	indirect object
(h) The mansions **that/which** were sold last week were expensive.*	thing or animal	*that/which*	subject
(i) The computer **that/which** they purchased operated very efficiently.*		*that/which*	direct object
(j) The place **that/which** you spoke about is Denver.*		*that/which*	object of a preposition
(k) Clerks **whose** paychecks were withheld are in trouble.	person, thing, or animal	*whose*	possessive determiner
(l) The division **whose** sales have reached a million dollars will go to Hawaii.		*whose*	possessive determiner

* In many formal contexts, *that* is considered the only correct choice of relative determiner when a thing or animal is modified.

EXERCISE 1

STEP 1   Here is a picture of a rather complex invention created by the artist Rube Goldberg. What do you think this device is used for?

From Charles Keller, *The Best of Rube Goldberg*, 1979. RUBE GOLDBERG™ and © of Rube Goldberg Inc. Distributed by United Media.

STEP 2   Read the passage and underline all of the relative pronouns/determiners. Then, with your partner, identify and write down the function of the relative pronouns/determiners in each relative clause (subject, direct object, etc.). There may be more than one relative clause in a sentence. The first one has been done for you.

Example: Sentence (1) *that* —*subject function in relative clause*

(1) A kerosene lamp that is set near the window has a high flame that catches on to the curtain. (2) A fire officer whom a neighbor calls puts out the flame with a stream of water that the officer shoots from outside the window. (3) The water hits a short man who is seated below the window. (4) He thinks it is raining and reaches for an umbrella which is attached to a string above him. (5) The upward pull of the string on one side of a platform causes an iron ball that is resting on the other side of the platform to fall down. (6) The ball is attached to a second string that wraps around a pulley and connects to a hammer. (7) The downward pull of the ball on the second string causes a hammer to hit a plate of glass. (8) The crashing sound of the glass causes a baby pup that is in a cradle to wake up. (9) In order to soothe the pup, its mother rocks the cradle in which the pup was sleeping. (10) The cradle, to which a wooden hand is attached, is on a high shelf above a stool. (11) A man who is sitting on the stool below the shelf and whose back is positioned in front of the wooden hand smiles as the wooden hand moves up and down his back.

STEP 3   Without looking at the sample passage, summarize the process shown in the picture.

EXERCISE 2

For each of the phrases below, write two sentences describing a person who will do the following things. Use a *who* relative clause for one and a *whose* relative clause for another.

Example: will not get a job
   A person who is not skilled will not get a job.
   A person whose interview skills are poor will not get a job.

1. will not pass the course
2. will be a good leader
3. will make a lot of friends
4. can never take a vacation
5. is prepared to take a test
6. should not drive a car

meaning

FOCUS 2   Making Noun Phrases More Specific with Relative Clauses

LESS SPECIFIC	MORE SPECIFIC	EXPLANATION
(a) A man walked into the office.	(b) A man **who was wearing a pinstriped suit** walked into the office.	A relative clause makes the meaning of the noun it modifies more specific.
(c) The secretary can type 70 words per minute.	(d) The secretary **whom Dolores hired yesterday** can type 70 words per minute.	
(e) A computer is sitting on the desk.	(f) A computer **that has a high-speed Internet connection** is sitting on the desk.	

EXERCISE 3

Imagine that you are a new employee for a company. One of your co-workers has agreed to orient you to the new office. Ask a question about the objects in each of the pictures in the left column while covering up the right column. Have your partner distinguish these objects or persons, explaining what he or she knows by looking at the pictures in the right column.

Example:

New Employee:
Ask about what you see
(cover up the right column)

Experienced Employee:
Tell about what you know
(cover up the left column)

box/contains file folders

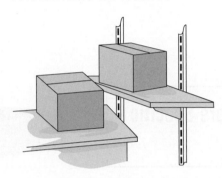 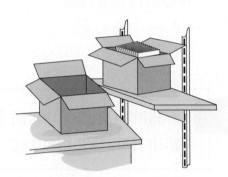

New Employee: *Which box contains the file folders?*

Experienced Employee: *The box that is sitting on the shelf.*

1. project/I should work on first

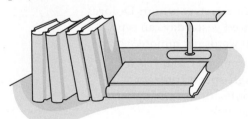 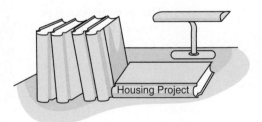

2. door/leads to the restroom

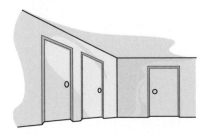 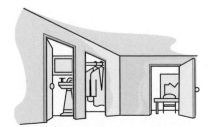

3. telephone number/belongs to the Moesler Corporation

Now switch roles with your partner.

4. computer/has the Internet connection

5. light switch/illuminates the front of the conference room

REAR   FRONT

6. book/our boss, Mr. Blake, wrote

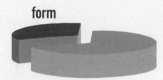

FOCUS 3 Review of Reduced Relative Clauses

EXAMPLES	EXPLANATIONS
(a) The letter ~~that~~ he sent was never received. (b) The accountant ~~whom~~ he corresponded with was well qualified. (c) NOT: The accountant with ~~whom~~ he corresponded was well qualified.	We can delete relative pronouns if they function as objects in relative clauses. In examples (a) and (b), *that* and *whom* can be deleted. Relative pronouns cannot be deleted if they follow prepositions such as *with* or *to*.
(d) The conference room ~~that is~~ situated at the end of the hall is closed. (e) The water ~~that was~~ left in the pitcher evaporated. (f) The customer ~~who is~~ complaining to the manager is my aunt. (g) A child ~~who had been~~ playing on the equipment was asked to leave.	We can delete relative pronouns in relative clauses with auxiliary *be* in progressive or passive constructions. Both the relative pronoun and *be* are deleted.
(h) Chairs ~~that are~~ in the conference room cannot be moved. (i) A board member ~~who was~~ at the meeting decided to resign.	We can delete relative pronouns in relative clauses with *be* + preposition phrases. Both the relative pronoun and *be* are deleted.
(j) People ~~who have~~ credentials can be hired. _{with} ^ (k) The workers ~~who did not have~~ identification were asked to leave. _{without} ^	In relative clauses with *have* or *have not* (= possession or lack of possession), we can delete the relative pronoun and paraphrase *have* or *have not* with *with* or *without*.

EXERCISE 4

Look again at the stages of the drawing in Exercise 1 and analyze the operation of the backscratcher. Look particularly at how the objects listed below were affected during each stage in the process. Then, write a sentence containing a relative clause with an object relative pronoun. Put parentheses around the words that can be deleted.

Example: (Stage B) The curtain _(that) the flame touched caught on fire._

1. (Stage C) The water ————————————————————————
2. (Stage E) The umbrella ————————————————————
3. (Stage J) The hammer ——————————————————————
4. (Stage K) The plate of glass ————————————————
5. (Stage N) The cradle ——————————————————————
6. (Stage O) The wooden hand ———   ————————————————

EXERCISE 5

Read the following sentences. Identify relative clauses that can be reduced. Mark your suggested revisions directly on the text. Then explain your revisions to your classmates.

Example: A person ~~who is~~ in a new job should act confidently.
I changed the sentence to "A person in a new job should act confidently" because the relative clause contains "be" + preposition.

1. The decision maker in an American business meeting is usually a person who is leaning toward the other members of the group and who is giving direct eye contact.

2. Body language that is composed of many gestures can communicate 80 percent of a message.

3. Anyone who has been working in the same position for a while will receive criticism at one time or another.

4. A person who is dressing for success in an American business setting should worry about the material, color, and style of his or her clothing.

5. Generally, a suit that is made of an expensive wool appears authoritative.

6. If you are someone who is feeling unsatisfied with your personality, do not be discouraged.

7. Anyone who has the determination to keep a mental picture of what he or she wants to be in mind can make his or her new image a positive reality.

EXERCISE 6

Look at the pictures in Exercise 3 and write six sentences with reduced relative clauses that distinguish the objects. Share your sentences with your classmates.

Example: *The box sitting on the top shelf has file folders.*

EXERCISE 7

Below you will find information about four homes that celebrities sold for various reasons. Write sentences about this information using as many relative clauses modifying subjects as you can. Put parentheses around words that can be deleted.

Example: *The mansion (that) the oil tycoon sold for $2,000,000 has three fireplaces.*
The penthouse whose owner was a world-renowned physician sold for $4,000,000.

VILLA

Owner: country western singer

Reason for sale: divorce

Price: $3,000,000

Enter through walled gates and find sophisticated hacienda. 2-acre home with horse corral. 6 bedrooms/ 8 baths. Pool, tennis, jacuzzi, spa.

MANSION

Owner: oil tycoon

Reason for sale: bankruptcy

Price: $2,000,000

European chateau with hardwood floors, 50 miles from the coast. 4 bedrooms/4 bathrooms. 3 fireplaces. View of lake. Very private acre far from crowds.

PENTHOUSE

Owner: world-renowned physician

Reason for sale: death

Price: $4,000,000

Towering 20 stories above downtown. 3 bedrooms/4 bathrooms. Close to Music and Performing Arts Center. Modern design. 20 minutes from beach.

BEACHHOUSE

Owner: corporate executive

Reason for sale: job move

Price: $5,000,000

On the beach. 3 acres + private 120 ft. of beachfront. Bright and spacious. Pool room. 3 stories. State-of-the-art sound/ video system. 5 bedrooms/ 4 bathrooms. Greenhouse.

Use Your English

ACTIVITY 1 listening

STEP 1   Listen to the audio of a lecture that explains various important business terms. On a separate piece of paper take notes about the terms introduced.

CD Track 9

STEP 2   Use your notes to fill in the blanks of the following quiz.

1. The process in which someone decides how their property will be distributed after their death is called _____.

2. A term which means to substitute an inoffensive term for an offensive one is a/an _____.

3. A person who has died is referred to as a/an _____.

4. A term which means to die leaving a will is _____.

5. The action which describes someone dying without a will is _____.

6. The land and property which someone owns is called _____.

7. _____ is called "personal property."

8. _____ is called "a gift."

ACTIVITY 2 writing

Write a letter of complaint to a store or company about a defective item that you bought recently. Try to include at least two sentences with relative clauses modifying main clause subjects.

Example: *Dear Sir:*

The toaster that I bought in your store last week is defective. The selector lever that determines how dark the toast will be is stuck.

ACTIVITY 3 speaking

Exercise 1 described an unusual invention—a backscratcher. Working with a partner, try to draw a similar diagram for another device. Then describe the various features of the device, following the format of Exercise 1. Choose one of the following ideas or one of your own. Explain to the class how your invention works.

fly swatter   cheese cutter   door opener

window washer   pencil sharpener   adjustable chair

ACTIVITY 4 writing

Find an outline, chart, or flow diagram that has various levels or interdependent steps in one of your textbooks or a magazine or newspaper. Describe the diagram using at least three sentences with relative clauses.

Example:

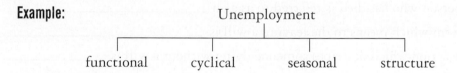

Unemployment

functional   cyclical   seasonal   structure

There are several types of unemployment. A person who is functionally unemployed has lost his or her job and is looking for another. A person who is a victim of a temporary downswing in the trade cycle is cyclically unemployed. A person who is seasonally unemployed means that he or she is not working during a particular season. . . .

After you have written your description, reduce all of the relative clauses that can be reduced according to the rules discussed in this unit.

ACTIVITY 5 speaking/writing

Discuss the following business-related terms with a partner. Then write a definition for each term. Use a relative clause in each of your definitions. For example, term: per capita income; definition: *The average annual income that a particular population earns is called "per capita income."*

bankruptcy   gross national product   exchange rate
sales commission   prime rate   mortgage

ACTIVITY 6 writing/speaking

Create your own "Trivia Challenge" game, like the one you played in the Opening Task on pages 134–135.

Example: an animal

It doesn't carry its young in a pouch.

(a) seahorse, (b) kangaroo, *(c) ostrich

■ **STEP 1** Work with a partner. Think of five items and definitions/descriptions (you may use your dictionary for ideas).

■ **STEP 2** Get together with another pair. See if they can guess the correct option. The team with the most correct guesses wins the game.

ACTIVITY 7 research on the web

With a partner, go to *InfoTrac® College Edition* and locate and print out four articles on *inventions*. Underline all examples of relative clauses. Then, place a check next to relative clauses in which the relative pronoun is a subject. What generalization can you make about the frequency of relative clauses in which the relative pronoun is a subject versus the frequency of relative clauses in which the relative pronoun is an object in formal written discourse?

ACTIVITY 8 reflection

Review Focus 3 and create a mnemonic device to remember the four ways that relative clauses may be reduced. A mnemonic device is a strategy for remembering a set or sequence of ideas using word or sound associations. For example, one way to remember the three branches of government in the United States is to remember the word "jel." The word "jel" sounds like "gel," as in gelatin, a substance that combines everything together. The Judicial, Executive, and Legislative branches help gel or "jel" the nation together. Note that these letters begin each of the key terms that you want to remember. Try to create a similar mnemonic strategy to remember ways that you can reduce relative clauses.

RELATIVE CLAUSES MODIFYING OBJECTS

UNIT GOALS

- **Use restrictive relative clauses to modify objects**

- **Use multiple restrictive relative clauses in a sentence**

- **Reduce relative clauses by deleting relative pronouns**

- **Choose appropriate relative clause forms for formal and informal communication**

OPENING TASK
Describing Inventions

Work on this task with a partner. Student A should look at the inventions and the invention dates on page 149, and Student B should look at the pictures and dates on page A-18. Take turns describing one of the inventions on your page without actually naming it. Your partner will guess what you have described.

Example: Student A: *I'm thinking of something that was invented in 1593 and that you use to measure the temperature.*
Student B: *Is it a thermometer?*
Student A: *Good guess!*

Thermometer
1593

Example: Student B: *I'm thinking of something that was invented about 1590 and that you can look through.*
Student A: *Is it glasses?*
Student B: *No, but it has a lens that you can look through to make small substances appear large.*
Student A: *Oh, it's a microscope.*
Student B: *That's right!*

Compound Microscope
about 1590

Student A

Jet Engine Aircraft 1939

Polaroid Land Camera
1947

Telescope 1608

Zipper 1893

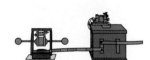
Radio 1895

X-ray Machine 1895

Safety Razor 1901

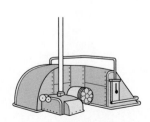
Air Conditioning 1902

Skyscraper 1885

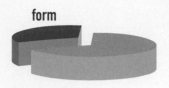

FOCUS 1 — Types of Relative Clauses Modifying Objects

Relative clauses that modify objects can have various relative pronouns/determiners and different functions:

EXAMPLES	OBJECT BEING MODIFIED	RELATIVE PRONOUN	FUNCTION OF RELATIVE PRONOUN
(a) She knows a girl **who/that** can dance very well.	person	*who/that*	subject
(b) He looked for the banker **whom/that** he had met at the party.		*whom/that*	direct object
(c) He was angry at the person **whom/that** he had written a letter to.		*whom/that*	indirect object
(d) She talked to the students **whom/that** she was best acquainted with.		*whom/that*	object of a preposition
(e) OR She talked to the students with **whom** she was best acquainted.		*whom*	object of a preposition (directly following preposition)
(f) I have noticed the trash **that/which** is piled on the street.*	thing or animal	*that/which*	subject
(g) Did you see the apartment **that/which** he furnished himself?*		*that/which*	direct object
(h) He patted the dog **that/which** he had given a bone to.*		*that/which*	indirect object
(i) Toronto has a tall tower **that/which** you can get a great view from.*		*that/which*	object of a preposition
(j) Toronto has a tall tower from **which** you can get a great view.		*which*	object of a preposition (directly following preposition)

EXAMPLES	OBJECT BEING MODIFIED	RELATIVE PRONOUN	FUNCTION OF RELATIVE PRONOUN
(k) I need to find the man **whose** credit card has expired.	person	*whose*	possessive determiner
(l) I was impressed by the trees **whose** branches seemed to touch the sky.	thing or animal	*whose*	possessive determiner

* In many formal contexts, *that* is considered the only correct choice of relative determiner when a thing or animal is modified.

■ EXERCISE 1

Read the following story. Underline all relative clauses that modify objects. Circle the noun that is modified by each relative clause.

(1) When my mother and I came to the United States, I experienced (a move) from which I felt that I would never recover. (2) My mother and I never got along very well. (3) She was a glamorous fashion model, but I looked like "a plain Jane" who was clumsy and overweight.

(4) I was often left alone as my mother left for fancy parties at which she mingled with famous actors, artists, and musicians. (5) I desperately wanted to return to the country from which we had fled in Eastern Europe.

(6) My mother was fortunate when she first arrived, for she got her first job through friends of a fellow countryperson who had married an American millionaire. (7) These friends immediately introduced her to everyone that they knew. (8) However, most of these friends were childless, and I had no one with whom I could share my loneliness and misery.

(9) Not knowing where I could find happiness, I decided to begin copying the standards of style for which my mother was famous. (10) It had worked for her; perhaps it could work for me. (11) I followed numerous diets that would help me resemble a starved model. (12) Nothing delighted my mother more than the attempts that I made to become more like her. (13) I did not really believe in my new preoccupation with fashion. (14) It actually sent me into deep depressions which lasted weeks.

(15) As the years went by, I went away to a prestigious college which provided me with many opportunities to travel abroad and meet famous people. (16) I always seemed to be looking for something that I had not obtained in my youth. (17) Finally, I met someone who could liberate me from all of the fashion nonsense. (18) The love of my life turned out to be a scientist who liked to climb mountains and build things. (19) In fact, he built the first home that we lived in. (20) Believe it or not, this country cottage made possible the quiet life that I had always dreamed of as a teenager.

EXERCISE 2

Take turns asking and answering questions about the story in Exercise 1. In each response, use a relative clause that modifies an object.

Examples: **Student A:** *What kind of move did the author experience?*

Student B: *She said that it was a move from which she would never recover.*

Student A: *What did the young girl look like?*

Student B: *She looked like "a plain Jane" who was clumsy and overweight.*

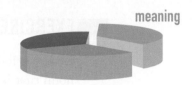
meaning

FOCUS 2	**Using Relative Clauses to Modify Nouns**

EXAMPLES	EXPLANATION
(a) The police caught a criminal who **had robbed three banks.** (b) He applied for work at companies **that his father recommended.**	A relative clause provides information that is necessary to identify or limit the noun it modifies. The clause specifies what type of thing(s) or person(s) is being described.

EXERCISE 3

STEP 1   A crime was committed at the Royal Restaurant. In pairs, take the roles of a criminal investigator and a witness. The investigator demands that the witness give certain information from the left column below. The witness provides a response with a relative clause modifying an object using events, people, conditions, etc. in the right column.

Example: **Investigator:** *Tell me the name of the man whom you saw at the Royal Restaurant.*

Witness: *I don't remember the name of the man that I saw.*

INVESTIGATOR INFORMATION REQUIRED	WITNESS EXPERIENCES/OBSERVATIONS
1. Name of the man the witness saw at the Royal Restaurant.	You don't remember the name.
2. Name of a woman the man was with.	Nobody told you the name, but you think the name is Jones or Johnson.
3. Type of car the witness saw parked near the Billings Bank.	You saw a blue compact car. It had a scratch on the right side.
4. Type of tip the suspect left at the last meal.	He left a large tip. You found it under the salt and pepper shakers.
5. Name of the company. Its truck was seen across the street from the Royal Restaurant.	You forgot the name of the company.
6. Type of sound the witness heard near the restaurant.	You heard a scream. The scream startled you.
7. Type of button the witness picked up at the scene of the crime.	You picked up a gold button. You think it fell from the robber's jacket.
8. Sequence of events following the robbery.	You saw the man run down the stairs to a car. Its license plate was XXX 123.
9. Type of dog in the car.	You saw a small, black dog. It had blue eyes.
10. Name of a relative close to the female suspect.	You know she had a son. His name was Biffo.

STEP 2   Using some of the information obtained at the interview, write one paragraph about the Royal Restaurant crime. Include at least five relative clauses in your narrative.

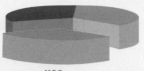
FOCUS 3 — Multiple Relative Clauses

EXAMPLES	EXPLANATIONS
(a) **Do you need a sleeping bag** which resists rain **and** which you can stuff into a pouch?	It is possible to use more than one relative clause in a sentence. These relative clauses may modify the same or different nouns.
(b) **She was wearing a hat** that my friend designed for a woman who had a funeral to attend.	
(c) AWKWARD: Marissa wrote a letter. The letter complained about cosmetics. She had ordered cosmetics last week.	Multiple relative clauses are used in formal writing to be specific and concise.
(d) BETTER: **Marissa wrote a letter** that complained about cosmetics that she had ordered last week.	With multiple relative clauses, we can communicate more information using fewer words and/or sentences.

EXERCISE 4

The following patented inventions were never sold on a wide-scale basis. Write sentences for each one, describing for whom the inventions were probably made. Use two relative clauses modifying objects in each sentence. Then, share your responses with a partner.

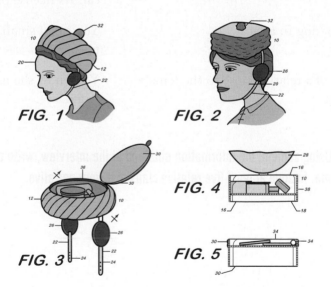

FIG. 1 FIG. 2 FIG. 3 FIG. 4 FIG. 5

Example: carry-all hat

The carry-all hat was probably invented for someone who does not want to carry a purse and who always needs her cosmetics nearby.

1. combination deer carcass sled and chaise lounge

2. eyeglass frame with adjustable rearview mirrors

3. power-operated pool cue stick

4. toilet-lid lock

5. baby-patting machine

6. alarm fork

7. car bib

8. motorized picnic table

EXERCISE 5

Combine the following groups of sentences into one sentence that contains two relative clauses modifying objects.

Example: Molly purchased a house. The house's former owner had made movies. The movies were box-office successes.

Molly purchased a house whose former owner had made movies which were box-office successes.

1. Students should be given scholarships. Scholarships cover all college expenses. College expenses include tuition and living expenses.

   _____

2. I am amazed at the invention. The man created the invention for some people. These people are disabled.

   _____

3. Most people did not buy chocolates. The youths were selling chocolates at a booth. The booth was located outside a supermarket.

   _____

4. Salespeople require an official contract. Clients have provided their signatures on the official contract. Their signatures are legible.

   _____

5. She admires one teacher. The teacher knew her subject area. The teacher was fair in grading.

   _____

6. A man was held hostage by thugs. Their main interest was obtaining money for drugs. The drugs could be sold for thousands of dollars on the black market.

   _____

7. The women applauded the policy. The company instituted the policy for pregnant employees. The pregnant employees needed a three-month leave after their children were born.

   _____

8. The woman tightly clasped a locket. Her son had given her the locket before he left for an assignment. The assignment was in Saudi Arabia.

   _____

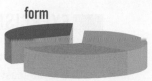

FOCUS 4 Deleting Relative Pronouns

EXAMPLES	EXPLANATIONS
(a) I sent a letter ~~which~~ he never received.	You can delete relative pronouns with the following functions: • direct object
(b) The faculty admired the student ~~whom~~ they gave the award to.	• indirect object
(c) Tom saw the movie ~~which~~ Sahib talked about.	• object of preposition
(d) They hope to find an apartment ~~which is~~ in a quiet area of town.	You can also delete relative pronouns that serve as subjects when the subject is followed by the *be*-verb. When you delete the relative pronoun, the *be*-verb must be deleted as well. The resulting sentences can have:
(e) NOT: They hope to find an apartment is in a quiet area of town.	
(f) I met the athlete ~~who was~~ **chosen** as "Player of the Year."	• passive and progressive participles
(g) The child is delighted with the puppy ~~that is~~ **licking** her face.	
(h) The realtor sold the home ~~which is~~ located **on Elm Street**.	• prepositional phrases
(i) She doesn't know anyone ~~that is~~ **smart enough** to pass the test.	• adjective phrases
(j) I do not want to be around a person **who has** the flu.	When the subject is followed by *have (not)* to indicate possession, you can paraphrase with *with (without)* for the relative pronoun + *have (not)*.
(k) I do not want to be around a person **with** the flu.	
(l) Have you ever considered a job **that doesn't have** benefits?	
(m) Have you ever considered a job **without** benefits?	
(n) Could you recommend a book that appeals to all ages?	You cannot delete relative pronouns if they are subjects of a relative clause that uses a verb other than *be* or *have*.
(o) NOT: Could you recommend a book appeals to all ages?	

With a partner, write descriptions of one or more sentences for the following pictures. Use at least one relative clause in each description. Then revise each description, deleting as many relative pronouns as possible. (Follow the rules in Focus 4.)

Example: A man brought flowers to a woman whom he admires.

Revision: *A man brought flowers to a woman he admires.*

1. _____

3. _____

2. _____

4. _____

FOCUS 5	Relative Clauses in Formal and Informal Communication

use

EXAMPLES	EXPLANATIONS
Formal (a) I know the person **whom** he hired. (b) I know the person **who** he hired. (c) I know the person **that** he hired. (d) I know the person he hired. *Informal*	The use or omission of object relative pronouns may vary according to formality. *Whom* is used in formal writing but is often reduced to *who* or *that* in speaking. It can be omitted altogether in informal speech.
Formal (e) He met the person **to whom** she had written. (f) He met the person **whom** she had written **to**. (g) He met the person **who** she had written **to**. (h) He met the person she had written **to**. *Informal*	In formal written English, the preposition should always precede the object relative pronoun.

EXERCISE 7

Reread the story in Exercise 1. Mark word-order changes and cross out relative pronouns that will make the story less formal.

Example: When my mother and I came to the United States, I experienced a move ~~from which~~ I felt that I would never recover. *from* I was often left alone as my mother left for fancy parties ~~at~~ which she mingled with famous actors, artists, and musicians. *at*

In pairs, read the following dialogue aloud. Then, edit the dialogue to create a less formal style. The first line has been done for you as an example. (Be sure to focus on relative clauses modifying objects and contractions.) Finally, reread the dialogue aloud, including the revisions that you have made.

Luca: *Did you hear from the accountant ~~to whom~~ we talked* ^to *last month?*

Maya: No, I did not. Is he concerned about the bank account which we closed in January?

Luca: No, he is calling about personal taxes that *you* have not paid yet.

Maya: That makes another item that I do not need now—a reminder that I owe money.

Luca: I know what you mean. The accountant with whom I deal is always asking me if I have any earnings that I neglected to mention.

Maya: Well, this year has been especially bad for me. I bought a car for one of my daughters who has very expensive tastes. I came up short at the end of the year, and I still owe taxes on the book royalties that I earned in April and the horse race that I won in September.

Luca: Sometimes I wish the United States collected a tax which is a strict percentage of a person's salary. A lot of other countries collect this type of "flat" tax.

Maya: Well, until that happens, I guess I will have to deal with the accountant after all. Let me know if he calls again.

Use Your English

CD Track 10

■ **STEP 1** Listen to the audio and take notes on descriptive information about the following items. You may want to listen a second time to check your notes.

Example: *an apartment building* <u>near downtown</u>

1. braids —————————————————————————
2. a joke —————————————————————————
3. excuses —————————————————————————
4. a ring —————————————————————————
5. a model car —————————————————————————
6. a writer —————————————————————————
7. an engineer —————————————————————————
8. colleges —————————————————————————
9. a nurse —————————————————————————
10. an artist —————————————————————————
11. the hotel —————————————————————————
12. a carnation —————————————————————————
13. unattractive man —————————————————————————
14. a phone booth —————————————————————————

■ **STEP 2** Now describe how each item fits into the story. Create sentences using relative clauses modifying objects.

Example: *Kimi and Fred lived in the same apartment building which was located near the downtown of Los Angeles.*

■ **STEP 3** What do you think will happen next? Write a short paragraph that describes your thoughts. Use at least one relative clause modifying an object in your paragraph.

■ **STEP 1**   In pairs, look at the following picture and describe what you see.

Eviction by Dierdre Luzwick

■ **STEP 2**   Write a paragraph using at least five relative clauses modifying objects.

Example: *This picture depicts the dangers of pollution on the environment. Animals are standing in line on a beach which is littered with boxes and cans . . .*

ACTIVITY 3 research on the web

Using an Internet search engine such as Google® or Yahoo®, search for information on inventions, inventors, inventors' groups, or the Yankee Invention Exposition, then answer the questions below using reduced relative clauses.

Example: *Who do inventors look for at the Yankee Invention Exposition?*

Inventors look for anyone ~~that has~~ with the ability to inspect their widgets.

1. What inventions have a greater chance of being successful?
2. Why do inventors like to join clubs?
3. Who leads inventors' groups?
4. Where can inventors go to display or market their inventions?

ACTIVITY 4 reflection

Imagine that you are setting up the perfect study session. How do you normally organize your time? What kinds of materials, writing implements, locations do you prefer? Do you ever study with other students? What tasks or subjects do you study first? Write a short paragraph answering these questions about arranging and planning your time. Use at least five relative clauses that modify objects in your paragraph. When possible, try to reduce the relative clauses for greater conciseness.

Example: *I like to choose a desk (which is) near a well-lit window to begin my study session. I always use a pencil (~~that has~~) with a brand-new eraser. . . .*

NONRESTRICTIVE RELATIVE CLAUSES

UNIT GOALS

- **Distinguish restrictive from nonrestrictive relative clauses**

- **Use nonrestrictive relative clauses in definitions**

- **Use relative clauses to comment upon an entire idea**

- **Use nonrestrictive relative clauses with quantifying expressions**

OPENING TASK

The travel section of the newspaper is often filled with descriptive stories about interesting and exotic travel ideas. What kind of trip would you like to go on? What types of activities would you prefer? How could you persuade someone to take a similar tour?

◼ STEP 1

With a classmate, select one of the following types of tours in which you would like to participate.

☐ Take a safari or other wildlife trek
☐ Go backpacking or hiking in the mountains
☐ Take a guided expedition
☐ Take a cross-country bike trip
☐ Take a cruise to one or more destinations
☐ Explore ancient ruins

☐ Take a wine-tasting tour
☐ Travel the route of a famous explorer
☐ Visit historic battlegrounds
☐ Tour one or more great castles
☐ Take a wellness vacation
☐ Visit one or more amusement parks
☐ Go camping
☐ Visit a ranch

STEP 2

With a partner, jot down notes to answer these questions about the tour you have selected.

- Where will you go? (*Go to a coast and swim with dolphins*) Where exactly is this located? (*Maui; one of the Hawaiian Islands in the U.S.A.*)

- What will you do? (*Swim with dolphins; intelligent mammals*) What equipment or skills are necessary for this activity? (*Snorkel; masks, snorkels, and fins*) What more can you say about this?

- In the evenings, what kind of cuisine will you eat? (*Luau*) What are the specific foods of this type of cuisine? (*roast pig, salmon, long rice, Haupia*)

STEP 3

Write a short paragraph for the travel section of the newspaper, convincing your reader to take this tour. Explain locations of special places and details about special equipment so that your reader will understand.

Example:

Anyone who is planning a trip should not forget the idea of going to Maui, which is the closest island to the big island of Hawaii in the Hawaiian Islands. Dolphins will be your morning swim companions. In the afternoon, you can rent masks, snorkels, and fins to snorkel around the beautiful coral reefs, which ring the island. In the evening, you can enjoy a traditional Hawaiian luau with roast pig, salmon, long rice, and Haupia, which is a traditional coconut pudding.

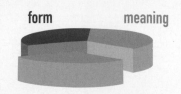

FOCUS 1

Restrictive versus Nonrestrictive Relative Clauses

EXAMPLES	EXPLANATIONS	
Meaning	A restrictive clause . . .	A nonrestrictive clause . . .
(a) I tip tour guides **who provide good tours.**	• is necessary to identify the head noun it describes (not all tour guides, only the ones who give good tours).	
(b) I tipped my tour guide, **who provided a splendid tour.**		• adds additional information; it does not help identify the tour guide in (b).
Form		
(c) I prefer to fly on airlines **that have direct routes to major cities.**	• is not set off by commas.	
(d) When I return home to Chicago, I will telephone my mother, **who lives in Joliet.**		• is set off by one or more commas; it adds additional information to an already identified noun preceded by possessive adjective (*my mother*).
(e) Joliet, **which is a suburb of Chicago,** was a wonderful place to grow up.		• adds additional information to an already identified proper noun (*Joliet*).
(f) My mother will pick me up at O'Hare **(which is the international airport near Chicago).**		• is sometimes set off by parentheses.
(g) She usually meets me at the baggage claim, **which exits onto the street,** rather than at the gate inside the building.		• uses *which* (not *that*) to describe places or things; it adds additional information to a noun preceded by a definite article which is identifiable by inference (*the baggage claim (at the airport)*).
(h) NOT: She usually meets me at the baggage claim, that exits onto the street, rather than at the gate inside the building.		
(i) I always take the midnight flight, [*pause*] **which is never crowded.**		• is set off by a pause and a drop in intonation in speech.

STEP 1 With a partner, underline the relative clauses in the following sentences and double underline the corresponding head nouns they refer to.

STEP 2 Determine if the clause carries essential information needed to identify the head noun or additional information by writing E (essential) or A (additional) next to each sentence.

STEP 3 Punctuate the relative clauses which carry additional information with commas.

STEP 4 Discuss why the information in the restrictive relative clause is essential and the information in the nonrestrictive relative clause with commas is additional and not necessary.

Example:

a. *The smog that covers Mexico City has become a serious health hazard.*

b. *Smog, which is a fog that has become polluted with smoke, is a pervasive problem in many large cities.*

a. <u>The smog <u>that covers Mexico City</u> has become a serious health hazard.</u> ___E___

The smog is specific smog in Mexico City that has become a serious health hazard. Therefore, the relative clause contains essential information and should not be separated from the head noun by commas.

b. <u>Smog, <u>which is a fog that has become polluted with smoke</u>, is a pervasive problem in many large cities.</u> ___A___

This nonrestrictive relative clause between commas adds additional information that is not essential to identifying which smog since the sentence is referring to all smog as a problem in many large cities.

1. a. The son who lives in New York will visit his mother in California.
    b. Her only son who lives in New York will visit her in California.
2. a. The teacher who got married last year will not be returning this year.
    b. Your English teacher who has a thorough knowledge of English grammar can help you with your grammar problems.
3. a. I studied at the University of Illinois which has a very good undergraduate program.
    b. I studied at a university in Illinois which has a very good undergraduate program.
4. a. People who drink should not drive.
    b. People who require water to survive may someday run out of pure water.

5. a. When I get to New York, I'm going shopping at a store which I heard about from a friend.

    b. When I get to New York, I'm going shopping at Saks Fifth Avenue which is located in downtown Manhattan.

6. a. We have spent a great deal of time refining a document which will be sent to the Grants and Contracts Office.

    b. We have spent a great deal of time refining this document which will be sent on to the Grants and Contracts Office.

7. a. The world which is actually pear-shaped was once thought to be flat.

    b. The world which we live in today is very different from the world a century ago.

8. a. He took an IQ test which refers to "intelligent-quotient" test before he moved to a different school.

    b. He took an IQ test which measured verbal and math ability before he moved to a different school.

9. a. Have you heard about the Fulbright Scholars who receive scholarships to work and study in other countries?

    b. Have you heard about the Fulbright Scholars who received scholarships to work and study in Hungary?

10. a. I would like to introduce the Professor Smith who chaired the task force report.

    b. I would like to introduce Professor Smith who chaired the task force report.

11. a. We praise the university community which came forward and volunteered in a time of need.

    b. We praise a university community which can come forward and volunteer in a time of need.

12. a. Internet addiction which has become more common today has many harmful effects.

    b. Internet addiction which affects one's sense of self control is a harmful effect of computer use.

EXERCISE 2

Reread your notes from the Opening Task on pages 164–165. Write sentences from your notes with restrictive and nonrestrictive relative clauses. Write N next to the nonrestrictive relative clauses and R next to the restrictive relative clauses. Then, read your sentences aloud, inserting pauses with your nonrestrictive clauses.

Example: *Why not take an expedition to Macchu Picchu, which is the old capital of the Inca empire?* N

You can explore the ruins which the ancient Peruvians built on steep mountainsides. R

EXERCISE 3

For each numbered sentence, put brackets around the nonrestrictive relative clauses and circle the noun phrases they modify.

(1) *The Specialty Travel Index*, which was founded in 1980 by C. Steen Hansen and Andy Alpine, is an excellent source of information for travel agents as well as the average person interested in travel. (2) More than 400 tour operators advertise in this index, which is available in paper and online versions (www.specialtytravel.com) (3) The paper version, which is published twice a year, offers alphabetical listings of tour operators with accompanying websites, e-mails, addresses, and telephone numbers. (4) Entries are organized by subject matter and geographical emphasis and are cross-indexed for convenience. (5) In the online version, if travelers want to visit Aruba, which is an island in the Caribbean, they only need to search under "A" in the geographical location index. (6) If they would like a tour which specializes in "ranching," "river rafting," "rock climbing," or "romance," they only need to look under "R" in the "interest/activity" index. (7) "Cooking classes," "walrus-watching tours," "astrology tours," and "film festival tours" are some of the other special interest tours listed in the index.

(8) *The Specialty Travel Index*, which is considered the "bible" of the special interest and adventure tour industry, includes many interesting and experienced advertisers. (9) Expo Garden Tours, which was established in 1988, provides an opportunity for individual gardeners to explore some of the most beautiful gardens in the world. (10) Travelers can see tulip blooms in Holland, which are most exquisite in the spring. (11) Another "must-do" tour is the fourteen-day tour to gardens in Japan, which features spectacular views of cherry blossoms and kurume azaleas as well as visits to cultural sites. (12) Margaret Sanko and Heidi Beaumont, who are co-founders of International Ventures, Ltd., specialize in trips to Eastern and Southern Africa. (13) They feature several types of safaris which would delight any traveler. (14) They have "highlight safaris," which are for those who want to see the animals in premier game parks. (15) They have "ventures," which involve travel by road (often dusty and bumpy) with experienced guides from start to finish. (16) They also have "wing safaris," for travelers who would like to see the animals and landscape by air. Finally, Jay and Annette Ciccarelli, a husband-wife team, sponsor culinary tours in Mallorca, where they lead morning tours through food markets, wineries, cultural sites, and restaurants and spend the afternoons and evenings doing hands-on cooking workshops and serving travelers the creations which they have made.

(17) Anyone planning a trip should not forget to consult *The Specialty Travel Index*, which describes tours that fit any interest!

Imagine you are a tourist visiting Vancouver, British Columbia, on your own. To entertain yourself, you took several tours of the city, which are listed below. Describe three tours you took in a letter to a friend. Use at least one nonrestrictive relative clause in each tour description.

Example:

Dear Owen,

I've really been enjoying myself in Vancouver. I've already spent a lot of money on tours, but it has been worth it. First, I took the City of Vancouver Tour, which was a five-hour tour of important sights around the city . . .

Regards,

Your Name

Name: City of Vancouver Tour
Price: $35.00
Description: five-hour bus tour of important points of interest: Stanley Park, Queen Elizabeth Park, Capilano Suspension Bridge

---

Name: Dinner Theatre Evening
Price: $70.00
Description: bus transportation, six-course dinner, tip, and ticket to theatre to see *A Streetcar Named Desire*

Name: Victoria City Tour
Price: $75.00
Description: 12-hour bus ride to the capital of British Columbia, ferry toll included, world famous Butchart Gardens

---

Name: Whistler Resort
Price: $100.00
Description: one day of skiing at world-class resort, lunch, ski rentals not included

---

Name: Fishing Trip
Price: $175.00
Description: half-day of fishing on Pacific Coast, private boat, guide, tackle, bait, license, lunch

Nonrestrictive Relative Clauses in Definitions

use

EXAMPLES	EXPLANATION
(a) Gastroenteritis, **which is an inflammation of the stomach and the large intestines,** is on the rise because of passengers eating contaminated food or drinking tainted water on some cruise ships.	Nonrestrictive relative clauses are often used for defining terms in sentences.
(b) When a higher than normal number of passengers or crew become sick on a cruise, ships implement the "vessel sanitation program," **which requires additional cleaning procedures and restriction of sick passengers to their cabins.**	

 ## EXERCISE 5

Review your answers to Exercise 3 and identify which nonrestrictive relative clauses are used for describing terms. Rewrite these sentences on a separate sheet of paper.

 ## EXERCISE 6

Imagine you are a world traveler describing to an inexperienced traveler what you bring on a trip. Look at the list below, and add one more item of your own. Then, write sentences describing the items you always take with you and why. Use a nonrestrictive relative clause to define each item.

Example: laptop
I always bring a laptop, which is a portable computer, so that I can work on the plane and in my hotel room. OR
To assure that I can do my work while I am away, the first thing I pack is a laptop, which is a portable computer.

1. luggage cart
2. money belt
3. travel iron
4. adapter
5. travel calculator
6. Swiss army knife
7. book light
8. _____

use

FOCUS 3 — Using a Relative Clause to Comment on an Entire Idea

EXAMPLES	EXPLANATION
(a) Last week I returned from a three-week cruise, **which was a relief.** (b) I had eaten too much food, **which was a big mistake.**	Some nonrestrictive relative clauses comment on a whole idea in the main clause. These are used most often in informal conversation and always begin with *which*.

 EXERCISE 7

STEP 1 Below are excerpts from letters you have written to friends and family about your travel mishaps. How would you characterize these mishaps to your next-door neighbor in conversation? Use one of the following adjectives in your comments or one of your own:

disappointing	frightening	painful
exasperating	tiring	embarrassing
expensive	stressful	upsetting

Example: My brother and I were traveling in Mexico City. We got stuck in a horrible traffic jam in our taxi.

When my brother and I were traveling in Mexico City, we got stuck in a horrible traffic jam, which was very exasperating.

1. My friend and I wanted to save money in Venice. We walked from the train station all the way to our hotel.

2. I went hiking in the Sierra Nevada Mountains. I almost fell off a mountain trail.

3. I went on a bike tour of Canada. I fell down and broke my leg.

4. I left my traveler's checks in my hotel room. I did not have any way to pay my bill at an expensive Tokyo restaurant.

5. Last year I flew to Paris. I had to wait three extra hours to catch my return flight home.

6. I went on a ski trip and broke my wrist. I did not have health insurance so I had to pay for the X-ray myself.

7. I almost missed my flight to London. I had to run to the check-in counter with my suitcase and only had two minutes to spare.

8. I ate something in a restaurant that I had never tasted before. I got sick and could not sleep the entire night.

STEP 2 In groups of three, talk about a travel mishap similar to the ones in Step 1. Student A tells about a mishap. Student B comments on Student A's travel mishap. Student C summarizes the mishap and comments on it using a relative clause.

Example: Student A: *When I was in San Francisco, I took the wrong bus to Fisherman's Wharf.*

Student B: *That must have been frustrating.*

Student C: *When Kathy (Student A) was in San Francisco, she took the wrong bus to Fisherman's Wharf, which was really frustrating.*

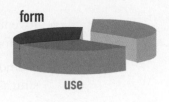

form

use

FOCUS 4 — Using Nonrestrictive Relative Clauses to Quantify and Comment about Features

EXAMPLES	EXPLANATIONS
(a) There are many benefits to the new plan, **many of which** are not quantifiable.	Some nonrestrictive relative clauses comment on all of or some portion of a group of persons or things. To form this type of clause, combine a quantifier or number (such as *all of, the rest of, none of, many of, each of, two of, one-hundred of*) with a relative pronoun.
(b) I need three volunteers, **one of whom** must be strong.	
(c) Dr. Tom is the President of the Pharmaceutical League, **the title of which** is less important than the responsibility.	Other nonrestrictive relative clauses comment upon some features or aspects of persons, things, or ideas by combining a noun phrase (such as *purpose, title, design, sense, appearance, result, news*) with a relative pronoun *which*. Note that the relative pronoun is an object of a preposition in (c) and (d).
(d) **They could not agree on anything,** the result of which **was a divorce.**	

■ EXERCISE 8

A group of teachers are traveling to Vietnam this summer; however, because of different travel interests, they will be arriving and departing at different times from the same three cities: Ho Chi Minh City (HCMC), Hue, and Hanoi.

Study the following schedule with the dates and times (morning or afternoon) of arrival. Then, write a fax to a travel service in Vietnam that will arrange to pick up the teachers from the airport and deliver them to their hotels. The beginning of the letter appears on the next page.

NAME	CITY	ARRIVE	DEPART	CITY	ARRIVE	DEPART	CITY	ARRIVE	DEPART
Peterson	HCMC	6:15 AM	6:20 AM	Hue	6:20 AM	6:21 PM	Hanoi	6:21 PM	7:30 PM
McGill	HCMC	6:18 AM	6:20 AM	Hue	6:20 AM	6:27 AM	Hanoi	6:27 AM	7:30 PM
Orselli	HCMC	6:15 AM	6:20 AM	Hue	6:20 AM	6:27 AM	Hanoi	6:27 AM	7:30 AM
Hopf	HCMC	6:18 PM	6:22 AM	Hue	6:22 AM	6:27 AM	Hanoi	6:27 AM	7:30 AM
Nguyen	HCMC	6:18 PM	6:22 AM	Hue	6:22 AM	6:27 PM	Hanoi	6:27 PM	7:30 AM

```
Date: _____          Time: _____

To: Vietnam Travel Service    Phone: _____    Fax: _____

From: _____          Phone: _____    Fax: _____

Number of Pages:  __1__

Comments:

To Whom It May Concern:
A group of teachers will be coming to Vietnam for a visit. I would very much
appreciate it if you could arrange airport transportation for the teachers, all
of whom have slightly different schedules. Peterson and Orselli, both of whom
will arrive at Ho Chi Minh City on June 15, must be picked up in the morning...
```

▮ EXERCISE 9

Create sentences using nonrestrictive relative clauses containing the following
nouns/clauses and noun phrases followed by *of-which* clauses.

Example: the city hall (the design of which)

Mapleton built a new city hall, the design of which was meant to inspire its citizens.

1. a mining accident (the news of which)

2. A man leaped out from behind the bushes (the appearance of which)

3. a civil war (an event of which)

4. They opened some new nursery schools (the result of which)

5. poverty (circumstances of which)

6. two papers (the purpose of which)

7. His children were all failures in the business world (an observation of which)

8. the robbery (the circumstances of which)

Use Your English

ACTIVITY 1 listening/writing

CD Tracks
11, 12, 13

Listen to the audio, which gives excerpts from tour guides of three different places. Take notes about the famous sights. Afterwards, summarize the tour or portions of the tour using nonrestrictive relative clauses.

	Sights	Characteristics
Example:	Lafayette Park	one of the best groomed parks in Washington, D.C.
	The White House	construction began in 1792
	Treasury Building	Andrew Jackson wanted to keep his eye on people handling cash.

First, they saw Lafayette Park, which is one of the best-groomed parks in Washington, D.C. Then, they saw the White House, whose construction began in 1792. Finally, they saw the Treasury Building, which Andrew Jackson wanted to watch carefully because it housed the money.

ACTIVITY 2 writing/speaking

■ **STEP 1** In groups of three, name two facts that are common knowledge about the following people. Then, create one or more sentences that contain relative clauses about these individuals.

John Lennon	Princess Diana	Winston Churchill	Mother Teresa
Abraham Lincoln	Joan of Arc	Mahatma Gandhi	Fidel Castro

Example: *John Lennon (lead singer of the Beatles, born in Liverpool, England, was killed in New York) John Lennon, who was the lead singer of the Beatles, was born in Liverpool, England.*

■ **STEP 2** Now think of another famous person you are familiar with. Present facts about this person to your classmates.

ACTIVITY 3 writing

You are preparing to be a tour guide of your hometown or the city you are presently living in. Think of 5 sights that are in a two-mile radius and write the script you would use, incorporating as many details as possible about the sights, such as historical origin, age, and unique aspects.

Example: *At the beginning of the tour, we will start with the most important place in my town, which is the Plaza Leon. The Plaza Leon, which is more than one hundred years old, is the gathering place for young people on Friday and Saturday nights and for parents and children on Sunday afternoons. Four streets extend out from the Plaza, which have wide sidewalks and are tree-lined. Hernandez Street, which was named after the first mayor of the city, contains all of the food stores—bakeries, fish markets, vegetable stands, etc. Fernando Street, which the first mayor named after his only son, is where all of the professional offices are housed. Via del Mar Street, whose pavement is made of cobblestone, is the only street which still has its original surface. Finally, two universities, one of which is the most famous university in my home country, are located on Horatio Street, which is my favorite street of all.*

Interview several members of your class about various aspects of their native countries. Record that information below. Then, write several sentences on a separate sheet of paper, summarizing what you have learned using nonrestrictive relative clauses

Example: *María, who is from Mexico, likes mariachi music. She also likes horchata, which is a popular white milky drink.*

1. Name _____ Native Country _____

   National Foods, Sports, Dances, etc. _____

   _____

   _____

2. Name _____ Native Country _____

   National Foods, Sports, Dances, etc. _____

   _____

   _____

3. Name _____ Native Country _____

   National Foods, Sports, Dances, etc. _____

   _____

   _____

4. Name _____ Native Country _____

   National Foods, Sports, Dances, etc. _____

   _____

   _____

5. Name _____ Native Country _____

   National Foods, Sports, Dances, etc. _____

   _____

   _____

ACTIVITY 5 research/speaking

Visit a travel agency and bring in various travel brochures for places you would like to visit. In small groups, compare different destinations and places to stay.

Example: *I want to go to Hong Kong, which has many four-star hotels.*

ACTIVITY 6 research on the web

With a partner, go to *InfoTrac® College Edition* and locate four scientific articles on any topic of your choice. Then, locate examples of nonrestrictive relative clauses in each one. Identify whether each nonrestrictive relative clause is used to provide a definition or to comment upon an entire idea or some portion of a group of persons, animals, or things.

ACTIVITY 7 reflection

Select one of your textbooks which contains some subject matter which is new to you. Skim through the pages to identify at least five words you do not know. If the words are not described, try looking them up in a dictionary or by referring back to your textbook. Then, write five sentences describing these words. Be sure to use nonrestrictive relative clauses.

Example: *A debit card, which looks like a credit card, is used to obtain instant cash from an automatic teller.*

UNIT GOALS

- Know when relative adverbs can be used in place of relative pronouns

- Know the different patterns for using relative adverb clauses and use them correctly

- Know when to use the different patterns in speaking versus writing

OPENING TASK

What Do You Do to Stay Healthy?

As we all know, just as important as work are the activities that help us to maintain physical and mental health. Such activities could include working out in a health club, playing individual sports or team sports, dancing, gardening, playing chess, or meditation as just a few examples.

STEP 1

Pair up with a classmate. Take turns interviewing each other to find out two things that each of you do to promote your physical or mental health. For each activity, ask and respond to the following information.

1. the date or time period when you started this activity (for example, when you were a certain age or a certain number of months or years ago)
2. the main reasons why you engage in the activity (for example, to enjoy the out of doors, to get aerobic exercise)
3. the place or places where you do the activity
4. your favorite times for doing the activity (for example, a certain time of day or a certain day or days of the week)

STEP 2

Share some of the information that you have gathered about each other with your classmates.

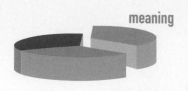

FOCUS 1 Relative Adverbs versus Relative Pronouns

Relative adverbs *where, when, why,* and *how* can replace prepositions + the relative pronoun *which* when these prepositions refer to place, time, reason, or manner.

RELATIVE ADVERB	MEANING
where	place
when	time
why	reason
how	manner

RELATIVE ADVERB	REPLACES PREPOSITION + *WHICH*
(to which) (a) A spa is a place **where** you go either to exercise or relax.	*to* *at* *from* } *which* *in*
(during which) (b) Summer is the time **when** many people take vacations.	*during* *at* *in* } *which* *on*
(for which) (c) One reason **why** people join health clubs is to take a variety of group exercise classes.	*for which*
(the way in which) (d) I'd like to find out **how** the game of soccer originated.	*(the way) in which*
(e) I admire **how** you dance.	Note that when *how* replaces *in which* you must also delete the noun phrase *the way* before it.
(f) NOT: I admire the way how you dance.	

Substitute relative adverbs for preposition + *which* whenever possible. Make necessary deletions. In one sentence you cannot replace *which* with a relative adverb; explain why.

Example: The beginning of a new year is a time ~~during which~~ *when* many Americans decide to make changes in their lifestyles.

1. On January 1, the day on which resolutions for the new year are often made, we hear people vowing to lose weight, quit smoking, or perhaps change the way in which they behave toward family or friends.

2. Those who want to shed pounds may go to weight loss centers; these are places which offer counseling and diet plans.

3. Others may join a health club at which they can lose weight by exercising.

4. Still others choose a less expensive way to lose weight: They just avoid situations in which they might snack or overeat.

5. People who want to quit smoking may contact organizations that can help them to analyze the times at which they have the greatest urge to smoke and to develop strategies to break the habit.

6. Those who decide to change their behavior toward others may also seek professional help, to find out the reasons for which they act in certain ways.

7. Most people are sincere about their promises on the day on which they are made; however, by February, many New Year's resolutions are just a memory!

JANUARY						
Sun.	Mon.	Tue.	Wed.	Thur.	Fri.	Sat.
			1	2	3	4
5	6	7	8	9	10	11
12	13	14	15	16	17	18
19	20	21	22	23	24	25
26	27	28	29	30	31	

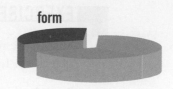

| FOCUS 2 | Pattern 1: Relative Adverb Clauses that Modify Nouns | form |

EXAMPLES	EXPLANATIONS

Head Noun	+	Relative Adverb	+	Clause
a place		where		you can relax
a time		when		I can call you
a reason		why		you should attend

Relative adverb clauses often modify nouns. The modified noun is called a head noun because it is the head of the clause that follows.

Place

(a) A hardware store **where** we can get gardening tools is just around the corner.

Place

(b) Hilton Head, South Carolina, is an island **where** many people go to play golf.

Time

(c) I'll always remember the day **when** I ran in my first marathon.

Time

(d) We read about the period **when** the Olympics were first developed in Greece.

The head noun is often a general word such as *place, time,* or *reason*, but it can also be a more specific word, especially for places and times.

Definite Noun	Indefinite Noun
the day when	**a day** when
the reason why	**one reason** why
	some reasons why
the place where	**places** where

(e) The nutritionist explained to us
the way ⎤
how ⎦ to balance carbohydrates and proteins in our meals.

(f) NOT: The nutritionist explained to us **the way how** to balance carbohydrates and proteins in our meals.

The head noun can be definite (*the* + noun) or indefinite (*a, an, one, some,* or Ø modifier + noun). The head noun can also be singular or plural.

When you use *how*, you must delete the head noun. *How* adverb clauses have only two patterns: (1) *the way*; (2) *how.*

EXERCISE 2

Identify each of the head nouns in the Focus 1 chart on page 182. What other phrases could you substitute for these head nouns? Are your substitutions more general or more specific in meaning than the original ones?

Example: A spa is a place where . . .

Head noun: a place

Substitution: A spa is *a kind of health club* where . . .

(More specific than *place*)

EXERCISE 3

STEP 1 Match each of the times in the first column with an event in the second column. Then make sentences using an appropriate head noun + a relative adverb.

Example: 1897 the first Boston Marathon held

1897 *was* **the year when** *the first Boston Marathon was held.*

1. 1958	a. one of the earliest forms of soccer played in Japan
2. February 24	b. most health clubs are not very crowded
3. 5 A.M.	c. many people in the United States take skiing vacations
4. Mesozoic Era	d. Brazil won the World Cup in soccer for the first time
5. 1004 BCE	e. Mexicans celebrate Flag Day
6. December	f. dinosaurs roamed the earth

STEP 2   Now match places with events. Again, make sentences using an adverb clause with an appropriate head noun. Try to use nouns other than *place* if possible.

Example: Shanghai, China Basketball star Yao Ming was born here.

*Shanghai, China is **the city where** basketball star Yao Ming was born.* (Note that *here* is deleted.)

1. Beijing	a. you can get a sandwich here
2. the kidneys	b. you can hike underground here
3. Uruguay	c. site for the 2008 Olympics
4. basement	d. the first World Cup soccer competition held here
5. deli	e. sports equipment often stored here
6. caves	f. the water in your body gets regulated here

STEP 3   Match the following reasons to the statements in the second column. Again, give a sentence for each match.

Example: reduce stress people try meditation because of this

Reducing stress *is one reason why* people try meditation.

1. improve heart health	a. some people look forward to the new year for this reason
2. fear of sharks	b. some people eat frozen yogurt instead of ice cream because of this
3. the chance to "turn over a new leaf"	c. many people love autumn hikes for this reason
4. lack of sleep	d. people sometimes avoid swimming in the ocean because of this
5. beautiful foliage	e. people take up jogging or bicycling for this purpose
6. low fat content	f. students sometimes don't perform well in class for this reason

STEP 4 Finally, match processes or methods in the first column to statements in the second. Make sentences for your matches using either the head noun *way* or the relative adverb *how*.

Example: Practicing swings you do this to improve your tennis game

*Practicing swings is **the way** you improve your tennis game.*

*Practicing swings is **how** you improve your tennis game.*

1. studying kinesiology

2. trimming dead flowers and fertilizing plants

3. conducting an opinion poll

4. repeating commands and giving rewards

5. eating healthy food and not smoking

6. reducing his head movements

a. you do this to teach a dog to walk by your side

b. you can do this to help prevent heart disease

c. you can promote new growth of flowers in your garden

d. the championship golfer Tiger Woods did this to improve his golf shots

e. people do this to survey the attitudes of large populations

f. someone does this to prepare for a career as a chiropractor

EXERCISE 4

Complete each of the blanks with appropriate words or phrases about yourself.

Example: <u>The shoreline</u> is a place where I <u>go to watch the birds.</u>

<u>Starting with my conclusion</u> is the way I <u>often begin to write a draft for a paper.</u>

1. _____ was the year when I _____.

2. _____ is the place where I _____.

3. The reason why I don't like _____ is _____.

4. The way I get to school/work is _____.

5. _____ is a/the day when I _____.

6. _____ is a reason why I _____.

7. A _____ where I _____ is _____.

8. _____ is how I _____.

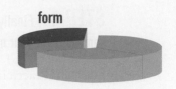

FOCUS 3 — Pattern 2: Relative Adverbs without Head Nouns

EXAMPLES

Relative Adverb	+	Clause
where		he lives
when		the term starts
why		I called
how		she knows

(a) This is **where** we will meet tomorrow.

(b) That was **when** I decided to go to work.

(c) **Why** she left is a mystery.

(d) She explained **how** to change a tire.

EXPLANATIONS

A second pattern with relative adverbs has no head noun. As with Pattern 1, this pattern can express:

• place

• time

• reason

• manner

EXERCISE 5

Restate each of the sentences you made in Exercise 3 without the head nouns (except for the ones in Step 4 for which you used *how*).

Example: *1897 was **when** the first Boston Marathon was held.*

EXERCISE 6

Working with a partner or in a small group, decide whether each statement is true or false. If a statement is false, replace the phrase in italics with something that will make the statement true.

Example: *Spring is* when birds in the northern hemisphere begin their migration south.

Answer: *False. **Autumn** is when they migrate south.*

1. *New York* is where you can see the Lincoln Memorial.

2. *Late November* is when we celebrate the winter solstice.

3. *Religious persecution* is why many Europeans first settled in what became the United States of America.

4. *Majoring in mathematics* is how most undergraduate students prepare for a career in medicine.

5. *The 1970s* was the decade when Ronald Reagan was president.

6. *The drugstore* is where a bibliophile would go to add to her collection.

7. *Either July or August* is when a person born under the zodiac sign of Leo will celebrate his or her birthday.

8. *Using a meat barometer* is how you check to make sure meat is cooked well enough in the oven.

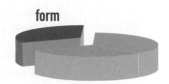

form

| FOCUS 4 | Pattern 3: Head Nouns without Relative Adverbs |

EXAMPLES

Head Noun	+	Clause
the place		we moved to
the time		I start school
the reason		they left
the way		you do this

(a) Sports Galore is **a store** I go to for exercise equipment.

(b) August 10th is **the day** Ecuadorians celebrate Independence Day.

(c) **The reason** spiders can spin perfect webs is that they have an innate ability to do so rather than having learned it.

(d) Public transportation is **the way** many city dwellers get to work.

(e) Dominic's is the restaurant I go **to** for pizza.

(f) NOT: Dominic's is the restaurant I go for pizza.

(g) Denver is the city I live **in**.

(h) NOT: Denver is the city I live.

(i) Dominic's is the place I $\left\{ \begin{matrix} \textbf{go} \\ \textbf{go to} \end{matrix} \right\}$ for pizza.

EXPLANATIONS

A third pattern uses only the head noun and its modifying clause.

This pattern can also express:

• place

• time

• reason

• manner

With specific head nouns that express place, you must often include a preposition of direction or position.

The preposition is often optional in informal English when *place* is the head noun.

Make sentences using Pattern 3 (head nouns without relative adverbs) to provide information about yourself.

Example: where you live

Winnipeg, Manitoba, Canada, is the city I live in.

1. where you were born
2. the date (month, day) when you were born
3. the way you make a certain food you like
4. the reason you are taking a specific course
5. a place you like to go to relax or have fun
6. a reason you like or dislike a course you are taking
7. the way people say "good luck" in your native language

FOCUS 5	Contexts for Relative Adverb Patterns

use

Here are some general guidelines for using the three patterns.

EXAMPLES	EXPLANATIONS
	Pattern 1: Head Noun + Relative Adverb + Clause
	We tend to use this pattern:
(a) Today is **a day when** all nations will want to join in prayers for peace in the world.	• to focus on or emphasize the time, place, reason, or manner.
(b) This is **the field where** we used to play softball every summer as kids.	
(c) I know **a nursery where** you can get beautiful orchids.	• when the meaning of the head noun is specific.

EXAMPLES	EXPLANATIONS
(d) Barton's is **a store where** one can find ski equipment discounted. (Less formal: Barton's is **where** you can get a fantastic deal!)	• when the context is more formal (such as written versus spoken English).
(e) **A place where** you can take dance lessons is at the corner of Hammond and Belknap.	• when the head noun is the subject of a sentence rather than the predicate. In example (e), **a place** helps to introduce new information.
(f) The corner of Hammond and Belknap **Predicate** is **where** we usually meet.	
	Pattern 2: Relative Adverb + Clause We often omit the head noun:
(g) I know **where** you can find tomato sauce in this market.	• when the head noun has a general meaning (the time, the place) rather than a specific one.
(h) She told us **when** to show up.	
(i) Greece is **where** the Olympics started. (inferred: the country)	• when you can infer the head noun from the context or from general knowledge.
(j) 1901 was **when** ping pong became a trademark name for table tennis.	
Less formal	
(k) **Why** she did that is a mystery to me!	• when the context of speech or writing is informal.
	Pattern 3: Head Noun + Clause This pattern tends to be used in contexts similar to ones for Pattern 1:
(l) Let us know **the day** you will arrive.	• when the head noun has a more specific meaning.
(m) Please state **the reason** you are seeking this position.	• when the context is more formal.

Decide whether the form given in (a) or (b) would be more typical or appropriate for each context. Use the guidelines given in Focus 5. Explain your choices.

1. **Ethel:** Max! What did you just turn off that light for?

   Max: Dear, if you'll wait just a minute, you'll find out . . .
   a. the reason why I did it.
   b. why I did it.

2. a. The day I got married
   b. When I got married

   . . . was one of the happiest days of my life.

3. a. A place where you can get a great cup of coffee
   b. Where you get a great cup of coffee

   . . . is right across the street.

4. Oh no! Can you believe it? I forgot . . .
   a. the place where I put my keys again.
   b. where I put my keys again.

5. a. One reason many people feel stress
   b. Why many people feel stress

   . . . is that they don't have enough spare time.

6. I would now like all of you in this audience to consider . . .
   a. the many times your families offered you emotional support.
   b. when your families offered you emotional support. It's hard to count them all, isn't it?

7. Let me show you . . .
   a. the way this MP3 player works.
   b. how this MP3 player works.

8. Ms. Cordero just told us . . .
   a. the time when we should turn in our papers.
   b. when we should turn in our papers.

9. Last year my family took a trip to see . . .
   a. the house where my great-grandfather grew up.
   b. where my great-grandfather grew up.

Use Your English

ACTIVITY 1 listening

CD Track 14

Form groups of three or four and compete in teams. The audio you'll hear will consist of 20 phrases that need to be identified with a place, time, reason, or manner. The phrases will use preposition + *which* clauses. Your instructor will pause the audio after each phrase. Taking turns, each team needs to identify the phrase by using a sentence with a relative adverb clause. You may use any of the patterns discussed in this unit. If a team gives the wrong answer, the next team will have a chance to correct it. Award points for each correct answer.

Examples: Audio: The continent on which the country of Rwanda is located.

Answer: *Africa is the continent where Rwanda is located.*

Audio: The month in which we celebrate both Lincoln's and Washington's birthdays.

Answer: *February is the month when we celebrate both birthdays.*

Audio: The way in which you say "Thank you" in French.

Answer: *"Merci" is how you say "Thank you."*

ACTIVITY 2 writing/speaking

How would you complete statements that begin as follows?

- I'd like to know the date (day, year, century, etc.) when . . .
- I'd like to find out the place (country, city, etc.) where . . .
- I wish I knew the reason(s) why . . .
- I am interested in finding out how . . .

Write a list of statements using each of the relative adverbs above (with or without head nouns) to express things you'd like to know. Use the patterns given in the list above to begin your sentences. Share your statements with others in your class to see if anyone can provide the answers.

ACTIVITY 3 writing/speaking

Make a new list of places and times/dates such as are shown in Exercise 3 on page 185, either individually or in teams. Then present the items on your list one by one to others who must define or identify the word or phrase in some way with a relative adverb clause. (If you prefer to do this as a competitive game, you could set time limits for responses and award points.) The following are a few examples of items and responses.

PLACE/DATE/TIME	POSSIBLE RESPONSE
February 14	*That's a day when people exchange valentines.*
Switzerland	*It's a country in Europe where skiers like to go because of the Alps.*
Trattoria	*It's a restaurant where you can get Italian food.*

ACTIVITY 4 speaking/writing

With a classmate, take turns telling each other about dates and places that have been important or memorable in your lives. These could be times and locations of milestone events such as birth and graduation, but they could also include a few humorous incidents or dates/places that may not seem so important now but were when you were younger.

Examples: *1990 was the year when I broke my leg playing Frisbee.*
I'll never forget a trip to Florida, the place where I first saw the ocean.

Take notes on your partner's events. Then report some of them orally to the class, using relative adverb clauses in some sentences. (In addition to *when* and *where*, you might also use the relative adverb *why* in giving reasons why a date or place was important.)

ACTIVITY 5 writing

Create a booklet providing information for tourists or new students about the city where you now live. The following are some ideas for possible categories; you may come up with additional ones.

- the places where you think visitors would most like to go
- the reasons why you think visitors would enjoy spending time in this city
- the places where it's fun to go shopping or to get the best food

You could divide the project so that individuals or small groups would each be responsible for a section or two of the guide.

ACTIVITY 6 research on the web

What were some of the interesting and important events that happened during the year when you were born? Using the date of your birth as the topic of a search, find four or five things on the Internet that took place during that year. Write down your findings, using relative adverbs clauses.

Example: *October 17, 1989 was the day when a 7.1 magnitude earthquake struck San Francisco.*

ACTIVITY 7 reflection

In developing good academic study skills, it is helpful to reflect on your goals as well as the optimal conditions you might create for various kinds of learning, whether it's reading, writing, thinking, or a combination of different skills. Write responses to the following questions using relative adverb clauses.

1. Consider one of your courses or a major/program of study you are pursuing right now. What is one of the reasons why you are taking the course or program?
2. What are the times of the day when you can generally study the best? Why?
3. What are the times of the day when you are least able to study well? Why?
4. What are the places where it is easiest for you to study?
5. What are the places where it is difficult for you to get studying done?
6. What are the places where you can write most comfortably?

CORRELATIVE CONJUNCTIONS

UNIT GOALS

- Use correlative conjunctions for emphasis

- Join phrases and clauses with correlative conjunctions

- Write sentences with parallel correlative constructions

OPENING TASK

Planning a Course Schedule

Imagine that you would like to enter the New World Alternative College in order to earn an Associate's degree. The following list contains the classes that are offered and the number of courses and electives required in each category to obtain a degree.

NEW WORLD ALTERNATIVE COLLEGE
Course Offerings, Requirements, and Electives

English Composition
  (1 course)
  Expository Writing
  Technical Writing
Humanities (2 courses)
  Linguistics
  Philosophy
  Religious Studies
Social Sciences
  (2 courses)
  Anthropology
  Communication Studies
  Economics
  Geography
Physical Sciences
  (2 courses)
  Geology
  Astronomy
  Physics
Mathematics (1 course)
  General Mathematics
  Computer Science

Life Sciences
  (2 courses)
  Psychology
  Biology
  Microbiology
**Environmental
  Sciences (4 courses)**
  The Greenhouse
    Effect
  Air Pollution
  Garbage Disposal
  Hazardous Waste
  Acid Rain
  Endangered Wildlife
History (1 elective)
  U.S. History
  World History
Foreign Language
  (1 elective)
  Chinese
  French

STEP 1

In the following table, write in two courses from each category that you would be interested in taking. In some cases, there are only two courses to choose from. These are written in for you.

COURSES I WOULD LIKE TO TAKE	CHOICE 1	CHOICE 2
English Composition	Expository Writing	Technical Writing
Humanities	_____	_____
Social Sciences	_____	_____
Physical Sciences	_____	_____
Mathematics	General Mathematics	Computer Science
Life Sciences	_____	_____
Environmental Sciences	_____	_____
History	U.S. History	World History
Foreign Language	Chinese or French	_____

STEP 2

Discuss your choices in groups of four. Are there any courses you would *not* like to take?

STEP 3

Summarize the results of your discussion.

Examples: *All of us must take either expository writing or technical writing.*

Maria is interested not only in Geology but also in Astronomy.

Neither Tom nor Gustaf would like to take Garbage Disposal.

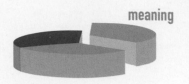

FOCUS 1 — Correlative Conjunctions for Emphasis

EXAMPLES		EXPLANATIONS
Coordinating Conjunctions	**Correlative Conjunctions**	Coordinating conjunctions and correlative conjunctions can be used to show different types of relationships:
and	*both . . . and* *not only . . . but also*	• additive
or	*either . . . or*	• alternative
nor	*neither . . . nor*	• negative In general, the correlative conjunctions are more emphatic.

	Additive Relationships
(a) **A:** I hope Pablo **and** Karl come to the debate next Saturday.	• less emphasis
B: You're in luck! **Both** Karl **and** Pablo are coming.	• more emphasis
(b) **C:** I hope Pablo is coming to the debate next Saturday. **D:** Guess what? **Not only** is Pablo coming, **but** Karl is **also**.	• even greater emphasis (*not only* usually comes before already known information, and *but* introduces new or surprising information)
	Alternative Relationships
(c) **A:** Can you come on Wednesday **or** Thursday?	• less emphasis
B: Yes, I can come on **either** Wednesday **or** Thursday	• more emphasis
	Negative Additive Relationships
(d) **A:** Milly doesn't want to take calculus or trigonometry, **nor** do I.	• less emphasis
B: You mean **neither** you **nor** Milly likes mathematics?	• more emphasis

EXERCISE 1

Answer the following questions with correlative conjunctions for emphasis. Write your answers in complete sentences.

Example: Spain doesn't border on Portugal or France, does it?

Yes, it borders on both Portugal and France.

1. President's Day and Valentine's Day aren't in February, are they?
2. Cameroon and Algeria are in South America, aren't they?
3. Honey or sugar can be used to sweeten lemonade, can't it?
4. Whales and dolphins are members of the fish family, aren't they?
5. Niagara Falls is situated in Brazil and Uruguay, isn't it?
6. Martin Luther King Jr. and Jesse Jackson were prominent black lawyers, weren't they?
7. You can travel from California to Hawaii by boat or airplane, can't you?
8. Ho Chi Minh City and Saigon refer to different places in Vietnam, don't they?

EXERCISE 2

Using the information in parentheses, respond to the following statements with *not only . . . but also*.

Example: I heard that Samuel has to work on Saturdays. (Sundays)

*Samuel has to work **not only** on Saturdays **but also** on Sundays.*

1. Shirley Temple could dance very well. (sing)
2. The language laboratory is great for improving pronunciation. (listening comprehension)
3. Nola should exercise twice a week. (go on a diet)
4. Becky has to take a test on Friday. (finish a project)
5. Thomas Jefferson was a great politician. (inventor)
6. The dictionary shows the pronunciation of a word. (part of speech)
7. The International Student Office will help you to locate an apartment. (get a part-time job)
8. It rained all day last Tuesday. (last Wednesday)

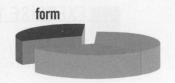

FOCUS 2 | Joining Phrases and Clauses with Correlative Conjunctions

EXAMPLES	EXPLANATIONS
(a) **Neither** the pedestrian **nor** the bicyclist saw the car approaching.	All four correlative conjunction pairs can join phrases.
(b) Mary will **not only** complete her coursework **but also** write her Master's thesis by June.	
(c) Mrs. Thomas was **both** surprised **and** jubilant that her daughter was awarded a scholarship.	
(d) Mark usually eats **either** at home **or** on campus.	
(e) **Either** the teacher has to slow down the lecture pace **or** the students need to take notes faster.	Only two of the correlative conjunction pairs can join clauses.
(f) **Not only** was Mr. Jones strict **but** he was **also** unfair.	
(g) **Not only is she** taking physics **but** she is also taking biology.	In combinations with *not only . . . but also*, the position of the subject following *not only* is inverted with the first auxiliary verb, *be,* or *do.*
(h) NOT: Not only she is taking physics but she is also taking biology.	

EXERCISE 3

Underline the correlative conjunction pairs in the sentences and identify what type of structure is being conjoined: adjective phrase, adverb phrase, noun phrase, prepositional phrase, verb phrase, or clause.

1. The improvement of education has to do not only with content knowledge but also with higher-order thinking skills.

2. We think it is both appropriate and important to restate our position on the new performing arts center.

3. Not only is this an issue for students to discuss at school but also for their parents to discuss at home.

4. I appreciate both the progress that has been made and the planning that went into the business school.

5. Either they will use the laboratory equipment now or they will use it later.

6. We tried to calculate what it will take not only to attract new students into the engineering program but also to keep them there.

7. They can shop for supplies either by phone or on the web.

8. We commend you both in terms of how the advertising was done and in terms of how the ticket sales were made.

9. He is active in the club as not only the vice-president but also the activities chair.

10. We can use the achievement test as a measure of not only how well a student is doing but also how effective the new program is.

11. They can either demonstrate the problem experimentally or describe the problem conceptually.

12. Not only do I have to provide the question but I also have to provide the answer.

13. Both students and faculty have spoken out against the war.

14. They have been unsuccessful either because they do not try or because they do not care.

15. We need to approach the athletics problem both quickly and efficiently.

EXERCISE 4

Write a few of your own sentences using correlative conjunction pairs and the words provided.

1. urgent . . . important

2. silently . . . slowly

3. required courses . . . electives

4. in the cafeteria . . . at the snack bar

5. to construct . . . to remodel

6. they will succeed in their mission . . . they will die trying to achieve their dream

7. to suggest an alternative . . . to solve the problem

8. before the play begins . . . at the intermission

EXERCISE 5

Using the information you obtained in the Opening Task on pages 196–197, write sentences about your classmates' preferences.

Examples: *Natasha may take either U.S. History or World History.*

She wants to enroll in microbiology and either psychology or biology.

EXERCISE 6

Think of a couple you know who have lived together for a long time. Fill out the grid with information about the couple (putting each name at the top of a column). Then, with a partner, discuss the couple's appearance, preferences, habits, or other features of their lives together. Use as many correlative conjunctions as you can.

Examples: Appearance: *Both Chau and George have black hair.*

Preferences: *On weekends Chau and George like to go either out to eat or to the movies.*

Habits: *Chau and George neither smoke nor drink.*

	NAME 1:	NAME 2:
Appearance:		
Preferences:		
Habits:		

Correlative Conjunctions: Parallelism; Being Concise

use

NOT PARALLEL	PARALLEL	USES
clause/noun phrase (a) Not only was he an honors student but also a scholarship recipient.	**noun phrase/noun phrase** (b) He was not only an honors student but also a scholarship recipient.	In formal usage, the two phrases that correlative conjunctions join must have the same grammatical structures. If they do not, the sentence will not be parallel and should be rephrased.
gerund/infinitive (c) Both **gaining work experience** and **to earn academic credit** are important benefits of an internship.	**gerund/gerund** (d) Both **gaining work experience** and **earning academic credit** are important benefits of an internship.	

NOT CONCISE	CONCISE	USES
(e) She knew either **that she needed an A** or **that she needed a B** to pass the course. (g) Not only was **John disqualified because of poor attendance** but **Betty was also disqualified for poor attendance.**	(f) She knew that she needed **an A** or **a B** to pass the course. (h) Not only **John** but also **Betty** was disqualified because of poor attendance.	In addition, parallel structures should be concise, without unnecessary repetition.

Read each sentence. Write OK next to sentences that are well-formed, parallel, and not repetitious. Rephrase the rest for concise, formal style. The first two have been done as examples.

1. I cannot stand to eat either liver or raw fish. OK

2. Not only is Maria tired but also sick. Maria is not only tired but also sick.

3. Not only *The New York Times* carried but also *The Los Angeles Times* carried the story of the train disaster in Algeria.

4. Juanita will both major in English and in sociology.

5. The Boston Red Sox either made the finals in the baseball competition or the Detroit Tigers did.

6. Suzuki neither found her watch nor her wallet where she had left them.

7. The Smith family loves both cats and dogs.

8. Mr. Humphrey thinks either that I should cancel or postpone the meeting with my advisor.

9. Not only am I going to the dentist but also the barber tomorrow.

10. Mary is going to either quit her job or is rearranging her work schedule to take astronomy.

11. I hope that the musicians are both well-rehearsed and that they are calm before the concert.

12. Todd neither saw or talked to his roommate, Bill.

13. Both bringing a bank card and cash is necessary for any trip.

14. Nor my two daughters nor my son wants to take an aisle seat on the airplane.

EXERCISE 8

The following paragraphs have some nonparallel, inconcise structures with correlative conjunctions. Identify and rephrase them for formal usage.

(1) In the last 40 years, family life trends have changed dramatically in the United States. (2) In the past, it was expected that everyone would get married in their early twenties. (3) Now having to choose either between a family or a career, many are opting for the career and remaining single. (4) Others are postponing first marriages until their thirties or forties.

(5) If and when couples decide to marry, many are deciding to limit their family size. (6) Not only couples are having fewer children but they are also deciding to have no children at all. (7) On the other hand, some singles are either deciding to raise their own or adopt children by themselves. (8) In addition, many same-sex partners are not only choosing to form binding relationships but also to become parents.

(9) In the past, women worked either for personal satisfaction or to earn extra money for luxuries. (10) Today both husband and the wife must work in order to survive. (11) Because of this, husbands and wives do not always adhere to traditional sex roles. (12) Now either the husband might do the cooking and cleaning or the wife might do the cooking and cleaning.

(13) Both because of the greater stress of modern life and the greater freedom that each partner feels, divorce is becoming more and more common. (14) Neither the rich are immune nor the poor. (15) In some states, the divorce rate approaches fifty percent. (16) Marriage cannot be all bad, though. (17) Not only many people get divorced but these same people also get remarried one or more times throughout their lifetimes.

Use Your English

ACTIVITY 1 listening

CD Track 15

Listen to the audio of a dialogue between a college advisor and a student. As you listen to the conversation, fill in the grid as the student responds to the advisor's questions.

NEW WORLD ALTERNATIVE COLLEGE STUDY PLAN		
	Fall	Spring
Year 1		
Year 2		

ACTIVITY 2 writing

Imagine that you are a supervisor for a company that allows fairly flexible hours for its part-time employees. Your boss recently called you to find out which day and time would be most convenient for each employee's evaluation conference. In order to help you in your decision, you asked the four workers you are supervising to indicate which hours they are available on the following blank schedule forms. An "A" indicates that a worker is available during a particular hour.

Conference Availability Charts

Pepita

	M	T	W	Th	F
9–10	A		A		A
10–11	A	A			
11–12		A	A	A	
12–1					
1–2		A	A		A

Tuan

	M	T	W	Th	F
9–10					
10–11					
11–12			A	A	A
12–1	A	A	A	A	A
1–2			A		A

Tom

	M	T	W	Th	F
9–10					
10–11	A	A			
11–12			A		
12–1	A	A	A	A	A
1–2		A		A	

Laleh

	M	T	W	Th	F
9–10	A		A		A
10–11					
11–12			A		
12–1					
1–2		A		A	

Now write a memo to your boss, detailing who is and who is not available at various times for their evaluation conferences. Try to use the words *both, either*, or *neither* in your writing.

Example:

Memo

Dear Mr. Masters,
Both Pepita and Laleh are available from 9 to 10 on Monday, but neither Tuan nor Tom can come at that time . . .

ACTIVITY 3 speaking

Imagine that you have two children and both you and your spouse have to work outside the home, which leaves little time for running a household. In the chart below, choose which chores you would like to do and which chores you would like your spouse to do by marking an "X" under the appropriate column. If you feel that any of the tasks should be shared, write "B" (for both) under each column. Discuss your choice of respective duties with a classmate, using as many of the expressions you have learned in this unit as possible.

Example: *Both my spouse and I should share cooking meals because we both work.*

CHORES	MY CHORE	MY SPOUSE'S CHORE
cook meals	B	B
wash dishes		
vacuum floors and dust		
care for the yard		
shop for food		
shop for clothes		
pay bills		
clean toilets and fixtures		
do laundry		
take out garbage		
get the children dressed		
give the dog a bath		
take care of a child who is sick		

ACTIVITY 4 listening/writing/speaking

Listen carefully to a television program and jot down the statements you hear that contain *both/and, not only/but also, either/or*, or *neither/nor*. Share your notes and discuss which types of correlatives were used often and if they were used to show emphasis or not.

Example: *You can use either butter or margarine in the recipe. (cooking program)*
Not only did he strike out but he also got hit by a flying bat. (sports program)

ACTIVITY 5 research on the web

Search the Web using a search engine such as Yahoo® or Google® to compare course offerings in the same major at one or more different universities, colleges, or vocational schools. You may compare your present school with another school or compare two entirely new schools to each other. Using correlative conjunctions, make several comparisons about course requirements.

Example: Dance Division at the Juilliard School and Dance/Theatre Department at California State University, Fullerton

Both Juilliard and CSU Fullerton require dance majors to take ballet and modern dance.
Neither Juilliard nor CSU Fullerton requires courses in piano.
Not only does Juilliard require courses in acting but it also requires courses in anatomy.

ACTIVITY 7 reflection

Some researchers feel that the following strategies contribute to more effective language learning:

- Arranging and planning your learning
- Evaluating your learning after a period of study
- Lowering your anxiety levels by eliminating stressful events in your environment
- Encouraging yourself
- Evaluating your emotional state after a period of study
- Asking questions of peers or others more knowledgeable about new material
- Creating mental images when learning sets of ideas or sequences of terms
- Reviewing what you have learned
- Analyzing and reasoning through new material
- Making intelligent guesses about new material

Write a short composition about which activities are most beneficial to you during your learning sessions. Use several examples with *either/or*, *neither/nor*, or *not only/but also* structures in your response to explain what you do, what you would like to do, and what you do not find beneficial during your study sessions.

Example: I have found my own set of learning strategies that work during my learning sessions. Although some people find studying with others useful, I neither study in groups nor ask questions of peers or others when learning new material. Instead, I . . .

UNIT GOALS

- Understand the differences between conjunctions and sentence connectors

- Use appropriate sentence connectors to express various logical meanings

- Choose appropriate sentence connectors for formal and informal contexts

- Use correct punctuation for sentence connectors in writing

OPENING TASK

How Things Came to Be

Cultures all over the world have creation myths, which explain how life on earth came to be.

■ STEP 1

Read the two creation myths from Finland and Polynesia that are summarized on the next page. They describe how the earth, the sky, and the first people on earth came to exist.

■ STEP 2

Write a paragraph describing the similarities and differences between the two creation myths. In comparing the stories, consider the following questions:

1. What existed at the beginning of creation?
2. In what order were things created?
3. How were the earth and sky created?
4. Who was responsible for creating the first people and how were they created?

From Finland:

In the beginning there was only Water, Air, and Air's daughter, Ilamatar. Ilamatar spent her time wandering around the world. One day Ilamatar sank down to rest upon the ocean's face as she was very tired. When she lay down, the seas rolled over her, the waves tossed her, and the wind blew over her. For seven hundred years, Ilamatar swam and floated in the sea. Then one day while she lay floating with one knee up out of the water, a beautiful duck swooped down and landed on her knee. There it laid seven eggs. As the days went by, the eggs grew hotter and hotter until Ilamatar could no longer endure the heat and pulled her knee into the water. Because of this, the eggs rolled into the ocean and sank to its bottom. Eventually, one of the eggs cracked. From the lower half of its shell, the earth was formed. From the egg's upper shell, the sky formed over the land and sea. From the yolk of the egg, the sun rose into the sky. From the white of the egg, the moon and stars were created and took their place in the heavens. Later, Ilamatar gave birth to the sea's child, whom she called Vainamoinen. For seven years Vainamoinen swam the seas. Then he went ashore and became the first person on earth.

From Polynesia:

In the beginning there was Darkness and the Sea. While soaring over the Sea, Old Spider discovered a large clam shell and climbed inside it. It was very dark inside the clam shell, and Old Spider was feeling cramped. Then she found a snail inside and asked the snail to open the shell a little. After the snail opened the shell, Old Spider took the snail, put it in the West and made it into the Moon. Old Spider, however, felt the space was still too tight and wanted to raise the shell higher. It turned out there was another snail around to help the Old Spider raise it. In this way, the sky, called Rangi, was created. After the sky had been created, Old Spider pushed down hard on the lower part of the shell, and it became the earth, called Papa. Together Rangi, God of the Sky, and Papa, Goddess of the Earth, created all of the plants and animals. Finally they produced the first people. Everyone lived together in the clam shell. Because of the crowded conditions, the many children begged Kane, the god of the forests, to separate Rangi and Papa to create more space. Kane obliged; as a result, Rangi and Papa were no longer together.

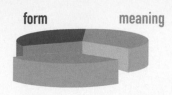

FOCUS 1   Connectors

Connector Relationships

Many types of meaning relationships can exist within one sentence or from one sentence to another. Words or phrases that express these relationships are called **connectors**. The chart below shows some of these relationships.

EXAMPLES	TYPES OF RELATIONSHIPS	EXAMPLES WITH CONNECTORS
(a) Old Spider climbed inside the clam shell. She discovered a snail there.	time sequence	**After** Old Spider climbed inside the clam shell, she found a snail there.
(b) Old Spider lived in a clam shell. Two snails lived there.	added idea	Old Spider lived in a clam shell. Two snails lived there **as well.**
(c) In the Finnish myth, the heavens were created from an egg. The sun was formed from the yolk of the egg.	example	In the Finnish myth, the heavens were created from an egg. The sun, **for example**, was formed from the yolk of the egg.
(d) In the Finnish myth, the earth did not exist in the beginning. In the Polynesian myth, at first there was only darkness and the sea.	similarity	In the Finnish myth, the earth did not exist in the beginning. **Similarly,** in the Polynesian myth, at first there was only darkness and the sea.
(e) In the Polynesian myth, the moon was a snail. In the Finnish myth, the moon came from an egg white.	contrast	In the Polynesian myth, the moon was a snail, **whereas** in the Finnish myth the moon came from an egg white.
(f) Ilamatar was very tired. She lay down on the ocean's face.	result	Ilamatar was very tired, **so** she lay down on the ocean's face.
(g) Creation myths are universal. They are found throughout the world.	clarification	Creation myths are universal. **That is,** they are found throughout the world.

Note: Refer to Appendix 3, page A-6, for a complete chart of sentence connectors.

Types of Connectors

There are three main types of connectors: coordinating conjunctions, subordinating conjunctions, and sentence connectors.

EXAMPLES	EXPLANATIONS
Independent Clause (h) Ilamatar kept the eggs on her knee, **Independent Clause** **but** eventually they got too hot.	• **Coordinating conjunctions** connect the ideas in two independent clauses. The coordinating conjunctions are *and, but, for, or, nor, so,* and *yet*. In written English, we usually write these clauses as one sentence, separated by a comma.
Dependent Clause (i) **After** Old Spider made the sky, **Independent Clause** she created the earth. **Independent Clause** (j) Old Spider made the sky **Dependent Clause** **before** she created the earth.	• **Subordinating conjunctions** connect ideas within sentences. They show the relationship between an idea in a dependent clause and an idea in an independent clause. Common subordinating conjunctions include **Time** *after, before, once, since, until, when, whenever, while* **Reason** *as, because, since* **Result** *in order that, so that, that* **Contrast** *although, even though, though, whereas* **Condition** *if, even if, provided that, unless* **Location** *where, wherever*
Independent Clause (k) Rangi and Papa created the plants and animals. **Independent Clause** **In addition,** they produced the first people. **Independent Clause** (l) Ilamatar could not endure the heat from the eggs; **consequently,** **Independent Clause** she put her knee back into the water.	• **Sentence connectors** usually express relationships between two or more independent clauses. The independent clauses may be separate sentences, as in (k). They may also be in the same sentence, separated by a semicolon, as in (1). The remainder of this unit is concerned with the third type of logical connector, sentence connectors.

Note: Refer to Appendix 3, page A-6, for a complete chart of sentence connectors.

For each of the sentence pairs below, state what the relationship of the second sentence is to the first: *time sequence, added idea, example, similarity, contrast, result,* or *clarification.*

Example: Ilamatar's child swam the seas for seven years. He went ashore.
Relationship: *time sequence*

1. The myths of many cultures include a god of thunder. The Mayan god of thunder was Chac. _____

2. In Greek mythology, Ares, the god of war, was often violent and belligerent. The goddess Athena was a peacemaker. _____

3. Myths help us to understand human behavior. They also entertain us.
_____

4. Ancient civilizations did not know the scientific explanations for natural phenomena such as storms. They made up stories to explain these events. _____

5. In North American Indian cultures, cosmogony is a major theme in myths. These myths explain how the universe was created. _____

6. In a Chinese creation myth, a man named Pan Gu lived in an egg for eighteen thousand years. He woke up and chopped the egg in two with an ax. _____

7. The village represents a place of order in African folktales. The bush, or jungle, represents a place of mystery and destructive forces. _____

8. Jason, the leader of the Argonauts in Greek mythology, went on a long sea voyage to get the Golden Fleece. The Greek hero Odysseus embarked on a long voyage. _____

9. In an Indonesian myth, the first woman in the world caused a great flood that washed away her garden. She was punished with a malformed child who had only one eye, one arm, and one leg. _____

10. A common animal in many myths and folktales is the trickster. In Asia, the trickster is often a rabbit or a monkey. _____

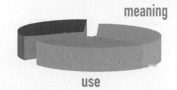

meaning

use

Simple Addition

CONNECTORS	EXAMPLES	MEANINGS
also	(a) Myths often tell stories about how things originated. They **also** attempt to explain why things occur in nature.	These connectors express simple addition. They have the meaning of *too* or *and*.
in addition	(b) In oral traditions, cultures passed myths down to later generations. **In addition,** many cultures told historical stories, known as legends.	
furthermore	(c) Many creation myths begin with a formless universe, or chaos. **Furthermore,** they often explain how the earth and sky are formed by separating the matter of the universe.	
moreover	(d) In many creation myths, the world is first covered by a great sea. **Moreover,** the sea is often the origin of the first animals.	

Emphatic Addition

CONNECTORS	EXAMPLES	MEANINGS
what is more (informal: *what's more*)	(e) Some African myths emphasize the need for individuals to help the community. **What is more,** even the animals are expected to help out.	Emphatic connectors signal an idea that stresses some aspect of what has been previously stated. Their meaning is similar to "Not only *that* (what I just said), but also *this* (what I am saying now)."
as well	(f) The Polynesian sea-god Tangaroa sometimes appeared as a huge fish. He could take on the form of a green lizard **as well.**	
besides (*this*)*	(g) Myths may represent cultural values. **Besides this,** they can reflect fears about forces beyond control.	

* In this example and others in the unit, the word ***this*** refers to the idea that has been previously mentioned. The word THIS will often be a demonstrative pronoun (*this, that, these,* or *those*) or a demonstrative determiner + noun phrase (for example: as well as *this fact*).

Note: Refer to Appendix 3, page A-6, for a complete chart of sentence connectors.

Simple Addition versus Emphatic Addition

EXAMPLES	MEANINGS
(h) Urban legends, a kind of contemporary folktale, have been written about in a number of recent books. **Simple Addition** (i) They are **also** the topics of a recent television series and a horror film. **Emphatic Addition** (j) A number of Web sites dedicated to discussing urban legends have been developed **as well.**	We often use simple addition and emphatic addition in the same contexts. The emphatic connector simply stresses the added information more than the simple connector does.

Intensifying Addition

CONNECTORS	EXAMPLES	MEANINGS
in fact	(k) Some myths tell stories of terrible destruction. **In fact,** in many stories the entire world is destroyed.	Intensifying connectors show that an idea will strongly support another one.
as a matter of fact	(l) Urban legends are often communicated in writing rather than orally. **As a matter of fact,** e-mail has become the source of many urban legends.	
actually	(m) In one well-known urban legend, a woman with an elaborate hairdo was killed by spiders nesting in it. **Actually,** this never happened.	

Intensifying Addition versus Emphatic Addition

EXAMPLES	EXPLANATIONS
(n) Urban legends, despite the name, do not always take place in an urban setting.	(Introductory sentence)
Emphatic Addition (o) **Besides that,** urban legends are not historical tales as were the ancient legends such as "King Arthur" or "Saint George and the Dragon."	We use emphatic connectors when we add a related idea. (o) adds another fact that makes the term "urban legend" rather inaccurate.
Intensifying Addition (p) **In fact,** many urban legends are more like a folktale or a joke with a dark theme.	We use intensifying connectors to elaborate an idea. (p) supports the idea of urban legends not being historical tales as many ancient legends were.

Note: Refer to Appendix 3, page A-6, for a complete chart of sentence connectors.

EXERCISE 2

Use an appropriate sentence connector from the list below to show the kind of addition relationship expressed in the last sentence of each pair or group of sentences. More than one connector could be appropriate for most contexts. Try to use each connector in the list once.

also	moreover	besides
in addition	what is more	in fact
furthermore	as well	as a matter of fact
		actually

Example: The study of folklore includes legends. It includes proverbs.

   The study of folklore includes legends and proverbs as well.

1. In ancient myths, the possession of fire is a common theme. It is often a source of conflict between gods and humans.

   _____

2. The Greek hero Prometheus stole fire from the king of gods, Zeus, and was seriously punished. He was chained to a rock.

   _____

3. Our teacher asked us if we had ever read the myth of Prometheus. I hadn't. I had never even heard of it. (Connect ideas in the second and third sentences.)

   _____

4. The Aztec deity Quetzalcoatl was the god of the sun and the air. He was the god of wisdom and a teacher of the arts of peace.

   _____

5. The primordial sea is present in many creation myths. It is one of the most common elements in these stories.

   _____

6. Many of the gods in ancient myths acted very much like the humans they created. They fall in love with each other and fight with each other. They make mistakes and regret their actions. (Connect ideas in the second and third sentences.)

   _____

7. I read about some of the most well-known urban legends on a Web site. I can't believe that people think some of those stories are true. I can't believe that they would tell them to others.

   _____

8. Humankind has always tried to explain questions about the origins of the universe. We are still trying to answer some of these questions today.

   _____

EXERCISE 3

Make up two sentences for each of the following instructions. Use an addition connector to link ideas between sentences. An example has been given for the first one.

1. Give two reasons why you enjoy something you often do in your spare time.

Example: *I enjoy volunteer work with children at the hospital because I like children. Besides that, it gives me work experience for my future career in medicine.*

2. Give two reasons why you like one movie or television show you've seen more than another.

_____

_____

3. State two advantages of flying over driving when a person goes on a long trip.

_____

_____

4. State two uses for computers.

_____

_____

5. Give two reasons why people tell stories about themselves.

_____

_____

6. Give two reasons why you would want to improve your English grammar skills.

_____

_____

7. State two differences between English and your native language.

_____

_____

8. Give two reasons why someone should visit a particular city or country.

_____

_____

9. Give two reasons why someone should get to know you.

_____

_____

10. State two things that you are very good at doing.

_____

_____

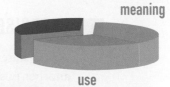

FOCUS 3 Alternative Connectors

CONNECTORS	EXAMPLES	MEANINGS
on the other hand *alternatively*	(a) We can read myths simply as stories. **On the other hand,** we can see them as reflections of cultural values and ideas. (b) You could take the history course you eventually need this semester. **Alternatively,** you could complete your schedule with a science course.	These connectors indicate a possibility in addition to the one just mentioned. *On the other hand* and *alternatively* have similar meanings. *Alternatively* is a more formal connector. It is used mainly in written English.
	(c) Washington, D.C. might be fun to visit this summer.	The "other possibility" could be various parts of a previously mentioned idea. (d) through (f) are some alternative statements that might follow example (c).

	Other possibility	Part changed in (c)
	(d) **On the other hand,** it might be too crowded.	fun
	(e) **On the other hand,** Minneapolis might be a better city to visit in the summer.	Washington, D.C.
	(f) **On the other hand,** it might be better to go there in the fall.	this summer

Note: Refer to Appendix 3, page A-6 for a complete chart of sentence connectors.

EXERCISE 4

Add a statement after each sentence below and on the next page that would express another possibility. Use *on the other hand* or *alternatively* to signal the connection.

Example: I could get a job this summer.
On the other hand, I could take a few courses in summer school.

1. I could stay home this weekend.

   _____

2. The theory of the Big Bang, explaining the origins of the universe, could be correct.

   _____

3. If you're looking for a used car to buy, you could check the classified ads in the newspaper.

   _____

4. Legalizing heroin in the United States could help decrease crime.

   _____

5. Parents who are upset with the violence that their children see every day on television could write letters to the television stations.

   _____

EXERCISE 5

Form small groups. Read each of the statements below. Then take turns forming alternative statements for each one. Each person must focus on a different part of the statement. Use *on the other hand* or *alternatively*.

Example: It could be fun to get a job making pizzas this summer.
On the other hand, it could get boring after awhile.
(focus: fun)
It might be more interesting to get work at a television studio.
(focus: a job making pizzas)
It would probably be more fun to eat the pizzas!
(focus: making)

1. Chile might be a good place to go for our winter vacation.
2. Advanced Composition could be a good course for me to take next quarter.
3. It might be fun to go to the art museum on Saturday.
4. You could call your family this weekend.

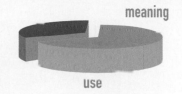

FOCUS 4   Exemplifying, Identifying, and Clarifying Connectors

EXEMPLIFYING CONNECTORS	EXAMPLES	MEANINGS
for example	(a) The struggle between gods and their offspring is a frequent theme in ancient myths. The Greek god Zeus, **for example,** fought with the Titans.	These connectors introduce examples of what has been mentioned.
e.g.	(b) Mythic stories about floods are told in many cultures (e.g., Scandinavian, Celtic and Turkish mythology all have such stories).	The abbreviation *e.g.* (from Latin *exempli gratia*) is sometimes used as an abbreviation for *for example.* In professional writing, the sentence beginning with *e.g.* is put in parentheses, Note that a comma follows *e.g.*
for instance	(c) Some urban legends involve food contamination. Take, **for instance,** the story about the mouse in the fried chicken.	*For example* and *for instance* introduce a typical member of a group or a typical instance.
especially	(d) Violence in movies seems to be increasing. Action films **especially** are getting more violent.	*Especially* and *in particular* introduce an important member of a group or an important instance.
in particular	(e) Learning the rules for article usage in English is a challenge. **In particular,** the use of articles with generic nouns may be confusing.	
to illustrate	(f) The steps for saving your computer files are quite simple. **To illustrate,** we will save the file you have just created.	*To illustrate* and *as an example* often introduce a lengthy example such as a process or narrative.
as an example	(g) Many great composers have had their share of misery. **As an example,** consider the life of Mozart.	

IDENTIFYING CONNECTORS	EXAMPLES	MEANINGS
namely	(h) Many fairy tales have common features; **namely,** they often involve magical events and royalty, such as kings or princesses.	These connectors identify something either previously mentioned or implied. They introduce a more specific or detailed elaboration.
specifically	(i) I have a question about connectors. **Specifically,** when do you use *in fact*?	

CLARIFYING CONNECTORS	EXAMPLES	MEANINGS
that is	(j) Some fairy tales are morality tales in disguise; **that is,** they were created to teach a lesson about how people should or should not behave.	These connectors signal that something will be rephrased or clarified.
i.e.	(k) Fairy tales are part of an oral tradition (**i.e.,** the stories were first told orally rather than being written down).	In written English, we sometimes use *i.e.* (from Latin *id est*) as an abbreviation for *that is*. In professional writing, the sentence beginning with *i.e.,* is put in parentheses. Note that a comma follows the abbreviation.
in other words	(l) Fairy tales are not usually historical. **In other words,** they are not set in a particular time or place.	We use *that is* and *in other words* in both spoken and written English.
I mean	(m) I don't quite understand the difference between legends and epics. **I mean,** they seem very similar to me.	*I mean* is less formal; we generally do not use it in formal academic English to clarify a statement.

Note: Refer to Appendix 3, page A-6, for a complete chart of sentence connectors.

EXERCISE 6

Use an exemplifying, identifying, or clarifying connector from the list below that would be appropriate for each blank. The first has been done as an example.

for example	especially	to illustrate	that is
for instance	in particular	as an example	in other words

1. Many words in English have origins in Greek myths. *Chaos*, <u>for example</u>, is a word the Greeks used to describe the unordered matter that existed before creation.

2. Some natural objects have English names that derive from Roman words for mythological characters. Planets, _____, have been given such names. _____, here are a few of them. Jupiter is named after the god of the sky. Neptune, in Roman mythology, was the god of springs and rivers. And Saturn was one of the gods of agriculture.

3. Some English names for metals also derive from myths. The metal uranium, _____, comes from the Latin *Uranus* (the god of the sky). The metal tellurium comes from the Latin *Tellus* (the goddess of the earth).

4. Sometimes we may refer to an idea as *chimerical*; _____, it is unrealistic or fanciful. This word comes from the name for a Greek monster, the Chimaera, which had a lion's head, a goat's body, and a dragon's tail.

5. Some English names for bodies of water also derive from Greek words. This is true _____ in the case of oceans. The name for the Arctic Ocean, _____, comes from the Greek word for *bear: arkto*. The name for the Atlantic Ocean derives from *Atlantides*, who were sea nymphs. And the word ocean itself comes from *Oceanus*, the oldest member of the mythological race, the Titans.

6. Some governments are known as *plutocracies*; _____, they are governments run by the wealthy. The word *plutocracy* comes from *Plutus*, the god of wealth.

EXERCISE 7

For each sentence below, fill in the correct abbreviation, *e.g.* or *i.e.* Then explain your choice.

Example: There are many kinds of fruit trees that grow in our state (e.g., there are orange, pear, and peach trees).
The second sentence gives examples of fruit trees, so e.g. is the correct connector.

1. The caterpillar underwent a metamorphosis (_____, it became a butterfly).

2. Cows are herbivores (_____, they do not eat meat).

3. American folktales often use exaggeration for humor (_____, in the tale of the giant lumberjack Paul Bunyan, his pancake griddle was so big that to grease it, men had to skate across it with bacon on their skates).

4. Many fairy tales have a heroine who is treated very badly (_____, in the story of Cinderella, her stepmother and stepsisters are very unkind to her).

5. *Young* and *old* are antonyms (_____, they are opposite in meaning).

6. Some words in English can be spelled several ways (_____, *theater* can also be spelled *theatre*).

7. Ancient stories were sometimes recited as epic poems (_____, long poems about a heroic mythological person or group of persons).

8. Some of the epic poems were sung (_____, in Ukraine during the sixteenth and seventeenth centuries, epic poems called *dumy* were performed by traveling musicians).

EXERCISE 8

Add an identification statement after each of the following sentences to further specify information conveyed. Use *namely* or *specifically* to indicate its relationship to the sentence before it.

Example: There is one thing I really like about you.
<u>Namely, you never blame other people when something is your fault.</u>

1. I'd like to know a few things about you.

   _____

2. I have one bad habit I wish I could break.

   _____

3. There are several things you might do to improve your financial situation.

   _____

4. There are two movies I'd like to see.

   _____

5. There are a few things about my future I often wonder about.

   _____

6. There is one thing I would like to have accomplished by this time next year.

   _____

EXERCISE 9

Following is a list of words along with their definitions. Make up one sentence using each word. Then for each, add an independent clause that explains the word. Use *in other words, that is,* or *I mean* to signal the relationship between the clauses. Use a semicolon to punctuate them.

Example: intractable, difficult to manage or get to behave
   Our new Labrador puppy is intractable; in other words, it is hard to make him behave.

1. digress   (verb)   to stray from the main topic in speech or writing

2. equivocate   (verb)   to avoid making a direct statement about something

3. incessant   (adj.)   continuing without interruption

4. polychromatic (adj.)   having many colors

5. xenophobic   (adj.)   having a fear or dislike of strangers or foreigners

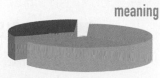

meaning

use

FOCUS 5 Similarity Connectors

CONNECTORS	EXAMPLES	MEANING
similarly	(a) Mythological stories were often handed down orally from generation to generation. **Similarly,** folk tales were part of the oral traditions of many cultures throughout the world.	These connectors signal that two or more ideas or situations are alike.
likewise	(b) If you practice speaking a second language everyday, you will most likely improve your fluency. **Likewise,** if you write in a journal every day, you will probably become a better writer.	
in the same way	(c) Learning to play a musical instrument well requires practice. **In the same way,** developing athletic abilities cannot be accomplished without practice.	

Using Similarity Connectors

EXAMPLES	EXPLANATIONS
(d) Blake likes to read folk tales. **Likewise,** this has been one of Karen's favorite leisure reading activities. (e) NOT: Blake likes to read folk tales. **Likewise,** Karen likes to read folk tales.	Paraphrase the information after the connector. Don't just repeat the previous information word for word.
(f) Football players try to carry a football across their goal line. **Similarly,** soccer players try to kick a soccer ball into a goal.	The comparison can involve differences in several terms: FOOTBALL SOCCER *players* ⟷ *players* *carry* ⟷ *kick* *football* ⟷ *soccer ball*
(g) Patrice bought some new clothes when we went shopping. **Likewise,** Mara purchased a few new outfits. (h) The spots on leopards help to camouflage them in the jungle. **Similarly,** colorations on deer help to hide them in the woods.	*Likewise* and *in the same way* often suggest greater similarity, or sameness, than *similarly* does.
(i) Dogs may get disturbed during an electrical storm. Cats may react **in the same way.** (j) A man in the audience started to heckle the speaker. Others behaved **similarly.**	You can use similarity connectors at the end of sentences when you are expressing the point of similarity in a verb phrase.

Note: Refer to Appendix 3, page A-6, for a complete chart of sentence connectors.

EXERCISE 10

The chart below gives information about myth and folklore spirits in Western Europe. Imagine that you are a folklorist, and that you have been asked to write a summary of the ways in which these spirits are similar. As preparation for your summary, use the information in the chart to make at least five pairs of sentences expressing similarity. Use a similarity connector with the second sentence of each pair.

Example: *Pixies enjoy playing tricks on humans; elves, **likewise**, enjoy fooling people.*

Name of Spirit	fairy	pixie	brownie	elf
Where found	Ireland, England, Scotland	England	Scotland	Scandinavian countries
Typical residence	forests, underground	forests, under a rock	humans' houses, farms	forests
Appearance	fair, attractive, varied size	handsome, small	brown or tawny, small, wrinkled faces	varied: some fair and some dark
Visibility to humans	usually invisible; visible by use of a magic ointment	usually invisible	usually invisible	usually invisible; visible at midnight within their dancing circle
Clothing color	green, brown, yellow favorite: green	always green	brown	varied
Favorite pastime(s)	dancing at night	dancing at night; playing tricks on humans	playing tricks on humans	dancing at night; playing tricks on humans
Rulers	fairy king and queen	pixie king	none	elf-king

FOCUS 6 Contrast and Concession Connectors

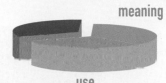

CONTRAST CONNECTORS	EXAMPLES	MEANINGS
however	(a) In some creation myths, the sun exists before people do. In others, **however,** people create the sun.	These connectors show that two ideas contrast.
in contrast	(b) The characters in legends may be based on people who actually lived. **In contrast,** the characters in fables, often animals, are fictional.	
on the other hand	(c) The proposed new hotel complex will benefit our city. **On the other hand,** it will create serious problems with increased traffic.	
though	(d) This lake is not very good for fishing. It's great for swimming and water skiing, **though.**	
in fact	(e) Early civilizations thought *the earth was the center of the universe.* **In fact,** *the earth revolves around the sun.*	These connectors signal that the following statement is contrary to something previously stated. The contrary parts are shown in italics.
however	(f) Some people think that *whales are fish.* **However,** *these animals are actually mammals.*	

CONCESSION CONNECTORS	EXAMPLES	MEANINGS
even so	(g) The heroes in myths often had superhuman powers such as great strength. **Even so,** they also had weaknesses that could lead to their downfall.	These connectors signal a reservation about something. The first statement is true, but the second statement is also true or needs to be considered.
however	(h) Both parables and allegories are stories that have moral lessons; parables, **however,** are much briefer and usually convey a single principle or moral.	
nevertheless	(i) Native Americans have often had difficulty preserving their traditions in modern society. **Nevertheless,** they have been able to pass down old stories about their culture to the new generations.	The second statement may also express surprising or unexpected information.
nonetheless	(j) I know mountain climbing can be dangerous. I'd like to try it **nonetheless.**	
despite (this)	(k) Chifumi has to get up at 5 A.M. to get to school on time. **Despite this,** she has never missed a class.	
in spite of (this)	(l) The day was cold and rainy. **In spite of the inclement weather,** we decided to take a hike.	
on the other hand	(m) Learning a new language can be frustrating sometimes. **On the other hand,** it can be a lot of fun.	

Note: Refer to Appendix 3, page A-6, for a complete chart of sentence connectors.

EXERCISE 11

Use the information in the chart from Exercise 10 to make up five sentence pairs expressing differences between the various European folklore spirits.

Example: *The favorite pastime of fairies is dancing at night. Brownies, in contrast, enjoy playing tricks.*

EXERCISE 12

The chart below gives information about people who made and have made remarkable achievements in the face of adversity. Use the information to make up sentence pairs linked by a concession connector.

Example: *Helen Keller was deaf and blind. In spite of these difficulties, she became an eloquent communicator.*

Person	Difficulty	Achievement
Helen Keller	was deaf and blind	became an eloquent communicator
Martin Luther King, Jr.	encountered racial prejudice	preached nonviolence toward adversaries
Beethoven	became deaf	continued to write symphonies
Charles Dickens	grew up in poverty	became a famous novelist
Stephen Hawking	is confined to a wheelchair by Lou Gehrig's disease	became an internationally acclaimed physicist
Jim Abbott	had only one hand	played professional baseball as a pitcher

EXERCISE 13

As you have seen in this unit, some sentence connectors may signal more than one meaning relationship. These include *on the other hand* (alternative, contrast, concession), *in fact* (intensifying addition, contrast), and *however* (contrast, concession). Review these connector meanings in Focus 2, Focus 3, and Focus 6. Then write down which relationship each signals in the sentences below. You may also want to refer to Appendix 3 on pages A-6 and A-7.

Example: You could drive to Denver if you have time. <u>On the other hand</u>, you could consider flying there.

Relationship: *alternative*

1. The mechanic told me the fuel pump in my car needed to be replaced. In fact, the fuel pump was fine.
   Relationship: _____

2. Your research paper on Hindu epic poems is very good. It could use some more variety in vocabulary, however.
   Relationship: _____

3. I might take biology next quarter. On the other hand, I may take geology if it fits my schedule better.
   Relationship: _____

4. In the distance, the next city looked fairly close. However, as it turned out, it wasn't very close at all.
   Relationship: _____

5. That plasma television set is expensive. In fact, it costs triple what my old one cost.
   Relationship: _____

6. The weather forecast predicted heavy rain all weekend. On Saturday, however, there was not a cloud to be seen anywhere.
   Relationship: _____

7. This soup has a really good flavor. On the other hand, it could use a little salt.
   Relationship: _____

8. Nylon is a very light material. It is, however, very strong.
   Relationship: _____

9. I'm having a hard time following these cell phone directions for creating an address book. In fact, it seems impossible to figure them out.
   Relationship: _____

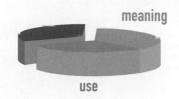
FOCUS 7 — Connectors Expressing Effects/Results and Purposes

EFFECT/RESULT CONNECTORS	EXAMPLES	MEANINGS
accordingly	(a) Rain is an important theme in many African religions. **Accordingly,** their rituals often focus on rain-making and rain-stopping.	These connectors signal that a statement is an effect or result of something. They differ mainly in their degrees of formality. We use *as a result (of), because of,* and *due to* in both spoken and written English. We use *therefore, consequently, thus,* and *hence* more in written English. *Thus* and *hence* are the most formal connectors.
as a result	(b) English spelling rules can be confusing. **As a result,** some have proposed simplified spelling.	
as a result of (this)	(c) Some people suffer from acrophobia. **As a result of this phobia,** they avoid heights.	
because of (this)	(d) Rainbows look like bridges in the sky. **Because of this image,** in many cultures rainbows were thought to be gateways to the heavens.	
due to (this)	(e) A megaphone is a hollow cone. **Due to its shape,** it can amplify sound.	To express cause-effect or reason-result relationships in conversation, speakers tend to use subordinating conjunctions like *because* and *since* as in (j), more than sentence connectors.
consequently	(f) Some of the older fairy tales were thought to have too much violence for children. **Consequently,** later versions of these stories removed the violence.	
therefore	(g) The plot of this book is not very original. The ending, **therefore,** is easy to predict.	
thus	(h) In myths, fire was considered the property of the gods. **Thus,** anyone caught stealing it was usually punished severely.	
hence	(i) With the invention of print, long stories could be published in books; **hence,** epic poems are no longer recited orally.	
because	(j) The ending of this book is very easy to predict **because** the plot isn't very original.	

PURPOSE CONNECTORS	EXAMPLES	MEANINGS
in order to (do this)	(k) You should check your computer for possible viruses. **In order to check it,** you'll need to close all programs.	Purpose connectors also express causal relationships.
with this in mind	(l) In rewriting fairy tales for children, authors wanted to make the stories more pleasant. **With this in mind,** they sometimes changed unhappy endings to happy ones.	
for this purpose	(m) Throughout human history, people have wanted to convey moral lessons in a way that would interest their audiences. **For this purpose,** they created fables, parables, and other kinds of moralistic stories.	Of the connectors shown here, *for this purpose* is the most formal.

Note: Refer to Appendix 3, page A-6, for a complete chart of sentence connectors.

■ EXERCISE 14

The two charts on the next page give information about various characters from myths and legends. Use the information from Chart A to make sentence pairs expressing reason-result relationships. Use Chart B to make sentence pairs expressing purpose relationships. For all sentence pairs, use an appropriate sentence connector.

Examples: *The Norse gods believed nothing could harm Balder, the sun god. Consequently, they thought it fun to hurl weapons at him.*

Robin Hood wanted to help the poor. For this purpose, he robbed the rich.

Chart A

Character(s)	Event/Situation	Result
1. Norse gods	believed nothing could harm Balder, the sun god	thought it fun to hurl weapons at him
2. Con, relative of Pachacamac, Incan god of fertility	was defeated in battle by Pachacamac	left Peru and took the rain with him
3. Gonggong, Chinese god of the waters	had his army destroyed by Zhurong, god of fire	fled in disgrace to the west and smashed into a mountain pillar holding up the sky
4. Paris, Trojan hero	wanted the beautiful Helen of Troy for his wife	gave the goddess Aphrodite a golden apple to win her favor

Chart B

Character(s)	Action/Event	Purpose
1. Robin Hood	robbed the rich	help the poor
2. Haokah, Sioux god of thunder	used the wind as a drumstick	create thunder
3. The Pied Piper of Hamlin	played his musical pipe so the rats would follow him out of town	rid Hamlin Town of rats
4. Momotaro	left his Japanese village and made the dangerous journey to Oni Island	conquer the horrible Oni ogres and bring back the priceless treasures they had stolen

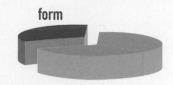

FOCUS 8   Punctuation of Sentence Connectors

Many sentence connectors can be used at the beginning, the middle, or the end of a sentence or independent clause. The punctuation surrounding a sentence connector depends on where it appears in a sentence.

EXAMPLES	EXPLANATIONS
(a) Apollo is the god of the sun in Greek mythology. **Similarly,** Balder is the sun god in Norse myths.	If the connector begins a sentence, use a period before it (ending the previous sentence) and a comma after it.
(b) Balder was much loved by the other gods; **however,** he was accidentally killed with a mistletoe dart by one of them.	If the connector begins an independent clause after another independent clause in the same sentence, use a semicolon before it and a comma after it.
(c) Many mythological characters have more than one name. Some, **in fact,** have several name variations.	If the connector is in the middle of a sentence or an independent clause, we usually separate it from the rest of the clause with commas.
(d) Aphrodite is the Greek goddess of love. She is **also** the goddess of beauty.	We do not usually use commas with *also* when it is in the middle of a sentence.
(e) Balder died from his dart wound. His wife Nanna died **as well,** having suffered a broken heart.	We do not use commas before *as well* when it follows a verb.
(f) The gods were grief-stricken when Balder died. The mortals reacted **in the same way.** (g) Tu, known in Polynesian myths as the angry god, was quite belligerent. He could sometimes be very kind, **however.**	If the connector comes at the end of the sentence, punctuation is usually not necessary except for two connectors: *however* and *though.*

Add, delete, or change punctuation in the following sentences to make them correct.

1. The rainbow plays a role in the myths and religious stories of cultures throughout the world, in fact, most cultures hold symbolic beliefs about what rainbows consist of and what they represent.

2. In some Native American myths, the rainbow is thought to be a bridge or ladder to other worlds likewise in Norse myths the rainbow Asbru is a bridge connecting heaven and earth.

3. The rainbow has also been perceived as an object similar to manmade ones, for example in a German creation myth it is a bowl holding the paint God used to color the birds.

4. The Mojave Tribe of Arizona sees the rainbow as a manmade object also unlike the German myth however they believe it is a toy used by the creator to stop rain storms.

5. Some Native Americans say that the rainbow was created from the souls of wildflowers that once lived in the forest. They believe that lilies from the prairies were used to complete it, as well.

6. In Islam four colors of the rainbow are thought to correspond to the four elements, some Buddhists on the other hand believe there are seven colors of the rainbow which relate to the seven planets and the seven regions of the earth.

7. In some cultures the rainbow represents reconciliation between God and humanity e.g. in Mayan mythology the rainbow stands as a promise that God will not destroy the world again after devastating rains, similarly in the Old Testament of the Bible a rainbow appears to Noah after the great flood.

EXERCISE 16

As a review of the connectors in this unit, go back to Exercise 1 on page 214. Rewrite the second sentence in each numbered pair, adding an appropriate sentence connector and punctuation where needed.

Use Your English

ACTIVITY 1 listening/writing

CD Tracks
16, 17

There are a number of Greek myths that explain how certain flowers came to be. Like many myths, different versions exist of these stories; they usually have common elements but vary in some details of the story. Listen to the audio for two versions of the Greek myth of Echo and Narcissus, which tell how the Narcissus flower came to be. Listen once to both versions to get a general idea of how they are similar and how they differ. Listen a second time and take notes on each version. When you have finished, briefly collaborate with two or three classmates to fill in any details you might have missed. From your notes, write a description of the similarities and differences of the two versions. Use a variety of contrast and similarity sentence connectors.

ACTIVITY 2 writing

In groups, create a list of ten facts or opinions on different topics. Below each fact, leave several spaces. Then pass the list to another group. The members of that group have to add another fact to each statement, using an addition sentence connector to signal the relationship. When they are finished, they should pass the list to another group who will do the same thing until several groups have added sentences to each list.

Examples: Group 1: *Tomatoes are very good for you.*

Group 2: *In fact, they are a good source of vitamins.*

Group 3: *In addition, they taste good.*

Group 4: *Furthermore, you can use them in a lot of different ways, such as in making sauces or salads.*

Group 1: *San Francisco is a beautiful city.*

Group 2: *It also has great restaurants.*

Group 3: *It's a book lover's city as well.*

Group 4: *What's more, you can go sailing in the bay.*

ACTIVITY 3 writing/research

■ **STEP 1**   Make a list of five words that you think others in the class might not be very familiar with. Use a dictionary if necessary. Try to find words that could be useful additions to someone's vocabulary.

■ **STEP 2**   Exchange lists with one of your classmates. Each of you should look up the words you have been given in the dictionary to see its range of meanings. Then write one sentence using the word in a context and add a statement defining the word, using one of the clarification sentence connectors (*that is* or *in other words*) as was done in Exercise 9. If you wish, you can connect the sentences with a semicolon to show their close relationship.

Example: *Some folktales are moralistic; in other words, these stories instruct people on how to behave.*

■ **STEP 3**   Give your sentences to your partner; check each other's sentences for correctness.

ACTIVITY 4 writing

"Turning point" is a term we sometimes use to describe an event that has changed or influenced someone in an important way. Consider three turning points in your life. Write an essay in which you explain how each turning point has changed your life. Use reason-result sentence connectors in your explanations.

Example: *One of the major turning points in my life was when my family left Bosnia for the United States. Because of this, we had to start a new life and adjust to an entirely different culture. . . .*

ACTIVITY 5 speaking/listening/writing

■ **STEP 1**   Pair up with another classmate. Your task is to find out six things that you have in common and six things that are different about you. The similarities and differences should not be things that are apparent (for example, do not use similarities or differences in physical appearance or the similarity of both being in the same class). Consider topics such as goals, hobbies, travels, language learning, families, and various likes and dislikes (foods, sports, courses, books, movies, etc.).

■ **STEP 2**   As you discover the similarities and differences, make a list of them. Then, each of you should write six sentence pairs expressing your discoveries, using similarity and contrast connectors. Divide the task equally so that each of you states three similarities and three differences. Share some of your findings with your classmates.

Examples: *Sven started learning English when he was 12.* **Similarly,** *I first started taking English courses when I was 13.*

Wenxia loves to read science fiction. **In contrast,** *I read mostly nonfiction books.*

I love math. Tina, **on the other hand,** *hopes she never has to take another math course in her life.*

ACTIVITY 6 research on the web

Creation myths from around the world often have similarities; for example, in many myths, the earth and sky are formed by dividing an egg. Using Internet search engines such as Google® or Yahoo®, find two more creation myths from different cultures. Prepare a report in which you summarize each myth and describe similarities and differences between the two myths.

To make progress in your language learning at advanced levels, it is sometimes useful to focus on a few areas at a time in which you would especially like to improve.

■ **STEP 1**   Identify one area of language proficiency that you would especially like to improve (e.g., academic writing, reading, listening comprehension, vocabulary, pronunciation, oral presentation skills) in English or another language.

■ **STEP 2**   Think of three specific things you could do within the next few months to develop this area, and write a sentence for each.

■ **STEP 3**   Finally, state what you hope will be the result of your efforts.

Example:

Language area: *Improve oral skills for seminar presentations*

Specific activities: *To improve my oral presentation skills, I will pay close attention to the talks that will be given for the next six weeks in my engineering seminar class, and I will make notes on both the positive and negative features. Besides that, I plan to watch a videotape at the skills center that shows how to use transitional expressions for introducing and changing topics. I'll also prepare a short talk using a slideshow program on my laptop and ask a few friends in my department to be my audience and give me feedback. As a result of these activities, I expect to learn more about what makes a good research presentation in my field. In addition, I hope to make the ideas in my presentation easier for the audience to follow. Finally, I'd like to become more aware of what I most need to work on.*

MODAL PERFECT VERBS

UNIT GOALS

- Use the correct forms of modal perfect verbs

- Choose correct modals to express judgments, obligations, and expectations

- Choose correct modals to make deductions and guesses

- Choose correct modals to express results of past conditions and to make predictions

OPENING TASK

Mr. Retrospect's Hindsight and Sage Advice

Mr. Retrospect is an advice columnist who specializes in telling people what they should have done—after the fact.

■ **STEP 1**

Read the following letter sent to Mr. Retrospect and his reply.

Dear Mr. Retrospect:

Like many people my age, I joined a social Web site to make new friends. After corresponding on this site for several weeks with a young woman in my area—I'll call her Annie—I arranged to contact her by telephone. We had a very nice conversation during which we found out that we both love out-of-doors activities. Annie then asked me if I liked to shop. That seemed like a rather abrupt topic change, but I said "Oh, sure," thinking that going shopping together might be a good way to get to know more about her. We made plans to meet the next weekend. When I arrived at her house, Annie came to the door with a big smile and, then after chatting just a few minutes, ushered me out into her backyard . . . to chop wood for her fireplace! I suddenly realized what she had asked me on the phone had nothing to do with shopping! I didn't know what to say, so I grabbed the axe and went to work, but I felt I had been taken advantage of. What do you think I should have done?

Henry

Dear Henry:

Sorry, but from what you have written, it's clear that you misheard Annie's question, so you can hardly fault her. I don't think you could have done anything much differently at the time, but perhaps you should have just laughed at yourself for the amusing misunderstanding and made the most of the outdoor activity. Besides, it must have been great exercise for your biceps! You might have thought of some way that she could have returned the favor—maybe chopping vegetables for a dinner at your place. Better luck next time!

Mr. Retrospect

STEP 2

Write responses to the following letters.

Dear Mr. Retrospect:

On a recent trip, I visited a relative I don't know very well, one of my great-aunts. She lives in a remote rural area; the nearest large city is three hundred miles away. I'm her only nephew, so she was really looking forward to my visit. Everything was fine until we sat down to eat. When I asked her what was in the stew she had just served, she announced, "Possum and squirrel, dear." I was so shocked that I refused to eat anything and had to leave the table. I'm afraid that I hurt my great-aunt's feelings even though later I said I was sorry. Now I am wondering what I could have said to be more polite.

Wild animal lover (well, squirrels anyway)

Dear Mr. Retrospect:

My hairdresser recently talked me into a new hairstyle that makes me look like a porcupine! I hated it! Unfortunately, he thought it was the perfect style for me. After he finished styling my hair he proclaimed "Oh Sally, it's *so you*!" I was speechless. How do you think I should have responded?

Sally

STEP 3

In small groups, share the responses you wrote.

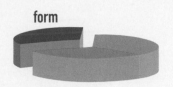

FOCUS 1   Review of Modal Perfect Verbs

Although modal perfect verbs have a number of meanings, the forms are fairly simple.

EXAMPLES	EXPLANATIONS
(a) Henry **should have listened** more carefully to Annie. (b) They **must have come** from miles away.	**Active voice:** modal + *have* + past participle
(c) That concerto **should have been played** slowly. (d) Her house **must have been built** during the last century.	**Passive voice:** modal + *have* + *been* + past participle
(e) I **must have been dreaming**! (f) They **could have been waiting** for us somewhere else.	**Progressive:** modal + *have* + *been* + present (-*ing*) participle
(g) The game **might not have ended** yet. (h) You **may not have read** the instructions correctly.	**Negative:** In negative forms, *not* comes after the modal.
(i) That **must've** (/must əv/) been Ted on the phone. (j) NOT: That **must of** been Ted. (k) You **should've** (šud ə/) told me sooner! (l) Oh, I **could've** (/kud ə/) done that.	**Pronunciation in Contractions and Fast Speech** Speakers often contract *have* when using perfect modals in informal speech, pronouncing *have* as /əv/. This often leads writers to use *of* instead of *have* in modal perfect verbs, but this is not correct for written English. In fast speech, /əv/ may be further reduced to /ə/ as shown in (k) and (l).

Summary of Modal Perfect Forms

	SUBJECT + MODAL (NOT) + HAVE BEEN				PAST PARTICIPLE	PRESENT PARTICIPLE	
ACTIVE	He	could (not)	have —		eaten	—	all that food.
PROGRESSIVE	He	could (not)	have been		—	eating	all day.
PASSIVE	It	could (not)	have been		eaten	—	so quickly.

Note: There is also a passive progressive form for perfect modals: modal + *have* + *been* + *being* + past participle: *The food* **could have been being eaten** *during the week that we were gone.* This verb form, however, is not very common in either spoken or written English.

Complete each blank with a modal perfect verb, using the cues in parentheses. The first one has been done as an example.

My friends and I discussed the letters Mr. Retrospect received and the responses we would make to them. Andrew thought that Henry (should/listen) (1) <u>should have listened OR should have been listening</u> more carefully during the phone conversation. Celeste added that Henry's new friend Annie (must/think) (2) _____ he was a pretty nice guy to be so willing to chop wood. Takiko agreed with Mr. Retrospect that Henry (might/ask) (3) _____ Annie to help him with something later if he felt taken advantage of. For a response to his letter, we (would/inform) (4) _____ Henry that in the future, he should repeat what he thinks he heard if something sounds a little strange in the context. As for the Wild Animal Lover's dining experience, we all agreed that we (not/could/eat) (5) _____ that dinner either, but we (not/would/want) (6) _____ to hurt the great-aunt's feelings. I suggested that he (might/say) (7) _____ he was allergic to squirrel or possum. That excuse (not/would/stray) (8) _____ too far from the truth since he probably (would/get) (9) _____ sick from eating it. Finally, concerning the last letter, we disagreed about how Sally (should/respond) (10) _____ to her hairdresser. Rosa thought Sally (could/ask) (11) _____ that the hairdresser to restyle her hair. Marty said she (might/suggest) (12) _____ to him that her spiked hair could hurt someone. We all concurred that Sally (should/find out) (13) _____ what her hairdresser planned to do before he styled her hair. We also agreed that the hairdresser (must/think) (14) _____ only of his own preferences at the time and that Sally should look for a new stylist.

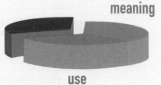

meaning

use

FOCUS 2	Expressing Judgments about Past Situations: *Should Have, Could Have, Would Have, Might Have*

EXAMPLES	EXPLANATIONS
(a) You **should have gone** to bed earlier. (But you didn't.) (b) They **shouldn't have spent** so much money. (But they did.) (c) The teacher **could have warned** us that we would have to know all the math formulas for the test. (But she didn't.) (d) Robert **might have written** us that he was coming. (But he didn't.)	The modal forms *should have* (and negative *should not have*), *could have*, and *might have* express judgments about something that did not happen.
(e) You **shouldn't have taken** the day off from work. It created a burden for everyone else. (f) Carmelita **should have treated** her sister better. (g) I **shouldn't have taken** the day off from work. Now I'm even more behind. (h) We **should have treated** our sister better. Now she won't even talk to us, and it's all our fault. (i) If I had known years ago what I know now, I **would have made** much better use of my time in school. (j) You ${\text{could} \atop \text{might}}$ **have called** us when you were in town. We didn't even know you were here. (k) You **might have asked** me if I wanted some dessert before you told the waiter to bring the bill. (l) Ian **could have offered** to contribute to the cab fare. He certainly had the money to do so.	These modals can express a variety of attitudes: • *Should have* and *should not have* with second- or third-person subjects often imply criticism. • With *I* or *we* as the subject, *should have* and *should not have* may express regret. • *Would have* may also express regret when used in the result clause of a conditional sentence. • *Should have*, *could have*, and *might have* can all express irritation, anger, or reproach. In certain contexts, they may express the speaker's judgment that someone has shown a lack of thoughtfulness or courtesy. • *Could have* also expresses capability more directly than *should have* and *might have* do.

244   UNIT 13

EXERCISE 2

English speakers sometimes use the expression *coulda woulda shoulda** informally to refer to past opportunities that went unfulfilled: things they could have done or should have done, for example, but didn't do.

STEP 1 In the following passage, the writer discusses some regrets about college years. Underline each modal perfect verb. Which sentence explicitly states the *if*-clause that is implied for the modal perfect verbs with *would have*?

Coulda, Woulda, Shoulda!

(1) At some point in life, most people wish they had done something they instead passed up. (2) There are very few times in my life that I would go back and redo. (3) But I do have several regrets when I look back at my time at college. (4) What would I have done differently? (5) What are my coulda, woulda, shouldas?

(6) Well, I would have looked more carefully into the courses I selected, especially those in my majors, art and history. (7) I also should have picked up my education courses. (8) Even though I wasn't interested in teaching at that time, trying to pick up those courses later is a struggle. (9) I could have picked up my teaching credentials or another backup plan while I was already in school.

(10) Take advantage of all the opportunities available to you in college. (11) I should have gone to more plays, attended more sports events, gone to more concerts and art exhibits, and joined more groups. (12) After college, those opportunities are never as available as when you are right there on campus. (13) I would have done more if I knew what I know now.

(14) I would have gotten to know more people, different kinds of people. (15) I would have gone up to more people to say hello. (16) I would have asked more questions. (17) I wouldn't have waited for others to notice me first. (18) I would have taken the initiative to meet new friends and acquaintances.

From John Naisbitt and Patricia Aburdene. Megatrends 2000. Copyright © 1990 by Megatrends LTD.

STEP 2 Next write down three things that you could have, should have or, given what you now know, would have done during this past year. Share your responses with classmates.

EXERCISE 3

Make a statement expressing a judgment about each of the following situations. Use *should have, could have,* or *might have* + verb in your response.

Example: A friend failed a test yesterday.
  *She **could have spent** more time studying.*
  *She **might have asked** her teacher for help before the test.*

1. One of your classmates returned a paperback book to you with the cover torn. When you gave it to him, the book was new.

2. Someone you know said she found a pair of sunglasses lying on the ground near a classroom building on her school campus and kept them since she didn't know who they belonged to.

3. You were stopped by the police while driving your car. Your license plates had expired.

4. A neighbor locked herself out of her apartment and didn't know what to do. So she just sat down on the front steps and waited for someone to notice her.

5. A friend wanted to get a pet but her roommates didn't like cats or dogs. So she moved out of the house she shared with them.

EXERCISE 4

The following story describes the unfortunate experiences of the Park family—Seung, Eun Joo, and their daughter Sophie—at a hotel where they recently spent a vacation. For each situation, state what you think the hotel staff or the Parks should have, could have, or might have done.

Examples: When the Parks arrived at the hotel, the front desk clerk was talking on the phone to her boyfriend and ignored them.
  The clerk could have at least acknowledged their presence.
  The Parks should have looked for another hotel!

1. When the clerk got off the phone, she told the Parks that their rooms had been given to someone else. However, other rooms would be available in four hours.

2. The Parks decided to have lunch in the hotel restaurant. Their waiter, who had a bad cold, kept coughing on their table as he took their orders.

3. When the food arrived, Eun Joo's soup was so salty she could feel her blood pressure rising by the second. Seung's pork chop was about as edible as a leather glove. Sophie's spaghetti looked like last week's leftovers and it tasted worse.

4. When the Parks were finally able to check into their rooms, the bellman forgot one of their bags in the lobby. Instead of getting it, he rushed off, explaining that he had to catch a train. Mr. Park ended up bringing the bag up by himself, which made him quite angry.

5. When Sophie tried to take a shower, she discovered there was no hot water.

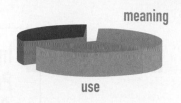
meaning

use

Be supposed to have and *be to have* are perfect forms of phrasal modal verbs. Their meanings depend somewhat on the tense of the *be* verb.

EXAMPLES	EXPLANATIONS
(a) We **were supposed to have taken** our exam on Friday, but our teacher was sick.	We use the past tense of *be supposed to have* + past participle to refer to something that was planned or intended but that did not happen.
(b) We **are supposed to have made up** the exam by next week.	We use a present tense form of *be supposed to have* when we expect something to be completed in the future.
(c) I **was to have graduated** in June, but I need to take two more courses for my degree.	*Be to have* expresses similar meanings as *be supposed to have. Be to have* is more common in formal English. Like *be supposed to have, be to have* refers to a past event that did not occur when *be* is past tense. It refers to a future expectation when *be* is present tense.
(d) Governor Carroll **is to have submitted** his resignation by next Friday.	

EXERCISE 5

Complete the sentences below to express obligations or expectations. The first has been done as an example.

Example: I was supposed to have <u>transferred to another college</u> this year, but <u>I needed more financial aid than I was offered.</u>

1. I was supposed to have _____ this year, but _____.

2. In my _____ class, I was supposed to have _____ by (put in a day or date here) _____, but _____.

3. I was to have _____ last (insert time phrase: weekend/month, etc.) _____, but _____.

4. My family was _____.

EXERCISE 6

Interview a classmate to find out three things that she or he was supposed to have done during the last few months but didn't do. Report at least one of them to the class.

Example: *Fan was supposed to have gone to the mountains last weekend, but her car broke down before she even got out of town.*

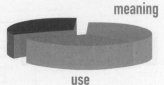

meaning

use

<table>
<tr><td>

FOCUS 4
</td><td>

Inferring/Making Deductions from Past Evidence: *Must (Not) Have, Can't Have, Should (Not) Have, Would (Not) Have*
</td></tr>
</table>

Modal perfect verbs can express two kinds of past inference: We may infer that something (1) almost certainly did or did not happen or (2) probably did or did not happen.

EXAMPLES	EXPLANATIONS
	Inferring Near Certainty
(a) **Myla:** Our chemistry experiment failed. We **must have followed** the procedures incorrectly. (We **must not have done** it the right way.)	We use *must have* when we infer that something almost certainly happened.
(b) **Alberto:** We **can't have done** them incorrectly! I read every step carefully before the experiment and checked each one afterwards, too.	*Can't have* is the opposite of *must have*. We use it to express a belief that something is almost impossible or unbelievable.
(c) If the test tubes aren't here, Brian **must have taken** them.	These examples express strong inferences, not facts. Since both (a) and (b) refer to the same event, one of them must be wrong. Unlike *must have, should have* does not express an inference that something almost certainly happened.
(d) **NOT:** If the test tubes aren't here, Brian **should have taken** them.	
	Inferring Probability
(e) Let's check on our second experiment. The powder **should have dissolved** by now.	We use *should have* to express an expectation about a past event. We may infer that something happened, but we don't know for sure.
(f) We **should have gotten** a chemical reaction when we heated the solution, but nothing happened. I wonder what went wrong.	Sometimes we use *should have* to express an expectation about a past event that we know did not occur.
(g) If our observations are correct, the burglary **would have occurred** shortly after midnight.	*Would have* may also express an inference that something probably happened. We use it to speculate about what happened if we accept a certain theory or if we assume certain conditions. Sometimes the condition is stated in an *if*-clause as in (g).
(h) About one hundred seconds after the big bang, the temperatures **would have fallen** to one thousand million degrees.	The condition may be implied rather than directly stated. In (h), the implied condition is: if we accept the big bang theory as a model of how the universe began. The writer uses *would have fallen* instead of *fell* because the big bang theory is hypothetical.

EXERCISE 7

According to one model of how the universe began, between ten and twenty thousand million years ago the density of the universe and the curvature of space-time became infinite; this point in space-time was termed the "big bang." The following passage describes what some physicists believe probably happened after the big bang. Underline or write down the modal perfect verbs that express probability. Why does the author use these forms instead of simple past tense?

(1) Within only a few hours of the big bang, the production of helium and other elements would have stopped. (2) And after that, for the next million years or so, the universe would have just continued expanding, without anything much happening. (3) Eventually, once the temperature had dropped to a few thousand degrees, and electrons and nuclei no longer had enough energy to overcome the electromagnetic attraction between them, they would have started combining to form atoms. (4) The universe as a whole would have continued expanding and cooling, but in regions that were slightly denser than average, the expansion would have been slowed down by the extra gravitational attraction. (5) This would eventually stop expansion in some regions and cause them to start to recollapse.

EXERCISE 8

The following sentences express some hypothetical statements about how native languages are learned. Fill in the blanks, using *must have, can't have,* or *should have* and the correct form of the verb in parentheses.

Example: *Researchers believe children* <u>can't have</u> *learned their first languages just by memorizing words.*

1. The number of possible sentences in any language is infinite. For this reason, we (learn) _____ our native languages by simply storing all the sentences we heard in a "mental dictionary." That would be impossible!

2. Children (develop) _____ their ability to speak their native languages by learning rules from adults because adults are not conscious of all grammar, pronunciation, and meaning rules either.

3. A child (acquire) _____ his or her native language by the age of 5; if not, we suspect that something is physically or psychologically wrong.

4. When a native English-speaking child says words like *ringed* and *doed*, this shows that he or she (apply) _____ a familiar rule for the past tense.

5. Similarly, if a child says words like *tooths* and *childs,* we speculate that he or she (overgeneralize) _____ the rule for regular plurals.

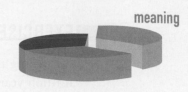

FOCUS 5 | **Expressing Guesses About Past Situations:** *May Have, Might Have, Could Have, Can Have*

We use certain modal perfects to make statements about the past when the speaker is not sure what happened.

EXAMPLES	EXPLANATIONS
(a) The movie **may have** already **started**. There are only a few people in the lobby. (b) I **might have gotten** an A on the test. I think I knew most of the answers.	*May have* and *might have* indicate that the speaker doesn't know if an event has occurred but has reason to believe that it has.
(c) I **may have met** him a long time ago. Both his name and face are very familiar. (d) I **might have met** him a long time ago, but I doubt it. He doesn't look at all familiar.	From the speaker's viewpoint, *might have* sometimes expresses less possibility of a past event having occurred than *may have* does.
(e) I don't think insects killed our strawberry plants. We **could have used** the wrong kind of soil. Or maybe we didn't fertilize them enough.	*Could have* often expresses one possible explanation among others. The speaker may imply that other explanations are possible.
(f) **Might** Carol **have been** the one who told you that? (g) **Could** too much water **have killed** the plants? (h) **Can** that **have been** Tomás on the phone? I didn't expect him to call back so soon.	*Might have, could have, can have* (but not *may have*) are also used in questions. *Might have* and *could have* in questions express guesses about a past event. We use *can have* only in questions. Usually a form of *be* is the main verb. The first sentence of (h) can be paraphrased: *Is it possible that Tomás was on the phone?*

EXERCISE 9

Each numbered group of statements below expresses certainty about the cause of a situation. For each, give an alternate explanation, using a perfective modal that expresses possibility. Can you think of any others?

Example: Look! The trunk of my car is open! Someone must have broken into it!

Alternate explanation: *You may have forgotten to shut it hard and it just popped open.*

1. Rebecca made a lot of mistakes on her economics assignment. She must not have studied the material very carefully.

   Alternate explanations: _____

   _____

2. Our English teacher didn't give us back our homework today. He must have been watching TV last night instead of reading it.

   Alternate explanations: _____

   _____

3. We invited Nora and Jack to our party but they didn't come. They must have found something better to do.

   Alternate explanations: _____

   _____

4. There was so much food left over from the party. Our guests must not have liked what we served.

   Alternate explanations: _____

   _____

5. Carlos usually gets off of work at five and is home by six. It's now eight and he's still not home. He can't have left work at five.

   Alternate explanations: _____

   _____

6. The crowd was laughing at the politician's speech last night. They must have thought she was really funny.

   Alternate explanations: _____

   _____

EXERCISE 10

To review the uses of perfect modals so far, return to the letters at the beginning of this chapter. Which of the letters in the Opening Task on pages 240 and 241 has a modal expressing advisability? Which has an inference modal? Which one includes a modal expressing possibility? Identify the perfective modals the letter writers used. Did you use these same modals in your answers? If you did, share some of your answers with the class. If not, give a one-sentence answer to each, now using these modals in perfective forms.

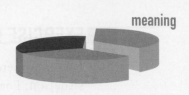

FOCUS 6	Expressing Results of Unreal Conditions: *Would Have, Could Have, Might Have*

EXAMPLES	EXPLANATIONS
Unreal Condition **Hypothetical Result** (a) If Bruno had arrived before noon, he would have seen us. **Actual Condition** **Actual Result** (b) Bruno arrived after noon, so he missed seeing us.	*Would have, could have,* and *might have* express hypothetical results of conditions that did not happen (unreal conditions).
(c) If I had been at that intersection ten minutes earlier, **I would have seen** the accident. (d) If the car had stopped for the light, the accident **could have been avoided.** (e) If Grace had been wearing her seat belt, she **might have escaped** injury.	The following modals express different degrees of probability of the results: • high probability • capable of happening • a chance of happening

We also use these modals in statements that only **imply** the condition rather than state it directly. These statements may express a missed opportunity or a rejection of one option for another.

EXAMPLES	IMPLIED UNREAL CONDITION	IMPLIED FACT
(f) Tim **would have been** a great father.	if he had been a father	He was not a father.
(g) I **could have gone** to medical school.	if I had wanted to go to medical school	I did not go to medical school.
(h) Fiona **might have made** the debate team.	if she had tried out for the debate team	She did not try out for the debate team.

EXERCISE 11

Modal perfect verbs in the sentences that follow express unreal conditions. Identify each modal perfect verb. Then decide whether each of these modal perfects is the result of a stated condition or the result of an implied condition. If the condition is implied, state what you think a possible condition might be.

Example: I could have driven you to your doctor's appointment.   *Implied condition*
Possible condition: *If I had known you needed a ride, . . .*

1. Seth would have turned in your assignment for you yesterday if you had let him know you wouldn't be able to attend class.

2. I'm sorry you got stuck in traffic. You could have gotten off the freeway and taken street routes to get here.

3. If I had known the grammar class would be offered in the spring, I might have waited to take it then.

4. I could have told you that the swimming pool was closed today.

5. If that lecture had gone on any longer, I might have fallen asleep.

6. We could have gone out of town for our vacation, but we decided to stay home and remodel the kitchen instead.

7. I think my sister would have been a good math teacher.

8. That car accident might have been worse than it was.

EXERCISE 12

For each sentence, give two result modals (*would have*, *could have*, or *might have*) that would be appropriate, using the verb in parentheses as the main verb. For each, explain the difference in meaning and/or use between the two modals you choose.

Examples: If the weather had been nicer, they (stay) _____ longer at the beach.
(1) *would have stayed*
(*They definitely wouldn't have left so early; they had intended to be there longer.*)
(2) *could have stayed*
(*It would have been possible to stay longer; this form might be used if cold or rainy weather forced them to leave.*)

1. If Sam had been prepared for the interview, he (get) _____ the job.

2. If you had let me know you needed transportation, I (drive) _____ you to your appointment.

3. If we had been more careful about our environment, we (prevent) _____ damage to the ozone layer.

4. The chairperson (call off) _____ the meeting if she had known so many committee members would not be here today.

EXERCISE 13

Choose three of the five conditions below. Make up three hypothetical results to follow each condition. Use *would have, could have,* and *might have.* Explain your choices of modal based on the degree of probability of each result.

Example: If I had lived in the nineteenth century, *I would have owned a horse instead of a car. I could have learned how to make ice cream instead of buying it from the supermarket. I might have wanted to be a farmer instead of going into business.*

Explanation: *It is quite likely that I would have owned a horse rather than a car. It is somewhat probable that I would have learned to make ice cream. It's possible, but not very likely, that I would have wanted to be a farmer.*

1. If I could have picked any city to grow up in,
2. If I had been the leader of my country during the last decade,
3. If I could have been present at one historical event before I was born,
4. If I had been born in another country,
5. If I had been able to solve one world problem of this past century,

EXERCISE 14

What might be an implied condition for each of the following hypothetical statements? Write down a few of your answers for each sentence. Share your responses with your classmates.

Example: I could have won the race.
Possible implied conditions:
If I had just run a little faster at the beginning, I could have won the race.
I could have won the race if I had trained harder.

1. This could have been a much better year for me.
2. My parents might have been even more proud of me than they are.
3. My financial situation would have been improved.
4. I could have been a more fluent speaker of (*state a language here*).
5. I might have considered being a (*state a career or profession here*).

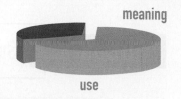

FOCUS 7 — Predicting the Completion of a Future Event: *Will Have, Shall Have*

Will have and *shall have* are future perfect modal forms. They express the completion of a future event before another future time.

EXAMPLES	EXPLANATIONS
(a) By the time you get this postcard, I **will have left** Portugal.	Possible meaning: You will get this postcard in a week or so. I'm leaving Portugal tomorrow.
(b) At the end of this week, **I'll have been** in Athens for four months.	In spoken English, *will* is often contracted.
(c) By this date next year, we **shall have reduced** our air pollution by 30 percent.	*Shall have* has the same meaning as *will have*. American English speakers rarely use this form in everyday English. Some types of formal English, such as speeches or legal documents, use *shall have*.

EXERCISE 15

The following predictions have been posted to the Long Bets Foundation Web site, which provides a forum for bets, debates, and discussions about the future. Rewrite the information in the chart below as predictions with future perfect modal verbs. You can use the verb in parentheses to create your sentence or some other verb. Make other sentence structure changes as needed. If time permits, discuss which predictions, if any, you think will come true. An example has been provided for the first one.

Example: *By 2020, technology will have been developed that allows people to "fax" (teleport) objects such as books, clothing, and jewelry.*

Event or condition:	Predicted to happen by:
1. technology allows people to "fax," or teleport, objects such as books, clothing, and jewelry (develop)	2020
2. technology for tracking and identification is inside the bodies of at least 50 percent of U.S. citizens (embed)	2025
3. computers instead of surgeons administer and monitor all surgical anesthesia (replace)	2030
4. intelligent signals from outside our solar system (received)	2050
5. governments of the world legally permit global mobility: people may live anywhere on earth if they obey local laws (legalize)	2103
6. mandatory classes in defending against robot attacks in over 50 percent of schools in the USA or Europe (require)	2150

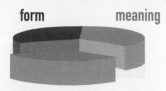
FOCUS 8   Summary of Modal Perfect Verbs

EXAMPLES	MODAL PERFECT VERBS	IMPLIED FACT	MEANING/USE
(a) You **should have** told me.	*should have* *could have* *might have*	You didn't tell me.	Judgment of past situation
(b) We **were supposed to have left** before Thursday.	*be supposed to have* *be to have*	We didn't leave.	Expectation, obligation
(c) Our professor **must have cancelled** class today.	*must have* *can't have*	—	Inferring near certainty about past situations
(d) The film I dropped off **should have been developed** yesterday.	*should have* *would have*	—	Inferring probability about past situations
(e) She **may have missed** the bus. I don't see her anywhere.	*may have* *might have* *could have* *can have*	—	Expressing guesses about past situations
(f) He **would have written** if he had known you wanted him to.	*would have* *could have* *might have*	He didn't write.	Result of stated unreal condition
(g) You **could have stayed** with us.	*would have* *could have* *might have*	You didn't stay with us.	Result of implied real condition
(h) By next month, they **will have finished** the first stage of the project.	*will have* *shall have*	—	Predicting completion of a future event.

EXERCISE 16

Edit the following sentences to correct any errors in modal perfect verb form or use.

Example: I think I might met you at Diane's party last month.
Correction: *I think I might have met you . . .*

1. In my presentation to the class on learning strategies, I should have emphasize more the need to try out different strategies and then to evaluate them.

2. I am glad that my grandmother was able to get out of New Orleans before the hurricanes. That might of been a very frightening experience for her.

3. Our advisor would have being very proud of us if he had known we won the award for the best poster at the engineering poster session, but he was away for a conference.

4. That movie was interesting, but it was so long! I think it could been edited to make it about a half hour shorter.

5. We were suppose to have turned in our projects at the beginning of class last Friday.

6. If the prize for the Biology Department raffle had been something I really wanted, I would buy a ticket.

7. You lost your sweater? Well, let's go back to our English classroom to see if you might've leave it there.

8. My brother and my sister-in-law got married in 2005. So if they stay married, by 2055, they will be married 50 years!

Use Your English

CD Tracks
18, 19

Listen to the audio. You will hear two telephone conversations. The first is between friends; the second is a business conversation. Each conversation elicits some type of advice or judgment from one of the speakers.

■ **STEP 1** Listen to the two conversations once to get the meaning.

■ **STEP 2** Listen to each conversation a second time. At the end of each one, take the role of the person who offers advice or makes a judgment. Provide an appropriate response to the person asking for your advice or opinion. Use a perfect modal verb. Write down your responses; then compare them with those of some of your classmates.

ACTIVITY **2** writing

Write three brief scenarios that describe thoughtless, rude, or somehow inappropriate behavior. Exchange scenarios with a classmate and write at least one judgment about each of the situations your classmate has written, using *could have, might have,* or *should have.* Use a variety of modals in responding. Afterwards, if time permits, share a few of your situations and responses with the class.

Example: *You were riding a subway train to school. You were standing up because it was very crowded, and suddenly the train stopped. A woman next to you spilled her diet soda all over your new jacket.*

Judgments:
She shouldn't have been drinking a soda on the train.
She could at least have offered to pay for dry cleaning the jacket.

ACTIVITY 3 writing

Write five sentences stating situations that would (could, might) have happened in the past if circumstances had been different. Choose one of your sentences to explain in more detail. Write a paragraph based on the sentence you selected.

Example: *If my family had not moved to the United States, I might not have learned English . . .*

ACTIVITY 4 research on the web

In Unit 14, Exercise 7, page 270, some of the current effects of global warming are described. Read the descriptions in that exercise. Then, using a search engine such as Google® or Yahoo®, research the topic of global warming on the Internet to find some specific claims about changes that will have occurred by a particular time period. Write down four or five of the predictions you find using perfect modal verbs, citing the source for your information.

Example: *According to the National Resources Defense Council, scientists project that if the current rates of ice cap melting continue, by 2100, the sea level <u>will have risen</u> by 3 feet.*

ACTIVITY 5 reflection

In trying to develop proficiency in a language other than our native language, almost all of us have had some second thoughts—or "coulda, shoulda, woulda's," as the expression goes—about what we might have done differently. In many cases, our second thoughts involve ideas about what we could have or should have done both inside and outside the classroom. Reflect on your experiences learning English or another language. Write down at least three things you think you could have, should have, or, given your feelings now, would have done to make the most of opportunities for language learning. One example is given here:

In revising my last paper, I could have paid more attention to the vocabulary suggestions that my teacher made.

DISCOURSE ORGANIZERS

UNIT GOALS

- Know how discourse organizers help listeners and readers understand information

- Use appropriate connectors to introduce, organize, and summarize topics

- Use *there + be* appropriately to introduce topics

- Use rhetorical questions to introduce and change topics and to focus on main points

OPENING TASK

Analyzing Issues

What global, national, or local issues interest you most?

■ STEP 1

With a partner, choose one of the following topics. Each of you will be writing a paragraph about some aspect of the topic.

- pollution
- the homeless
- illiteracy
- global warming
- an important health issue (e.g., smoking, obesity)
- censorship on the Internet

- immigration policies
- a social or political problem in the area where you live
- something that needs to be changed at your school or campus (course requirements, needed facilities, methods of teaching, etc.)

■ STEP 2

With your partner, explore the topic by writing four or five questions about it. Here is an example for the topic of overpopulation:

1. Is overpopulation becoming a more serious problem?
2. How should the problem of overpopulation be dealt with in developing countries?
3. Does anyone have the right to tell others how many children they should have?
4. What are the religious, cultural, and individual factors we need to consider in addressing the population problem?
5. Can we ever solve the problem of overpopulation?

■ STEP 3

Each of you should select one of the questions you wrote in Step 2 to answer in one paragraph. Save the questions and the paragraphs you wrote for exercises later in this unit.

form

use

This unit presents structures that speakers and writers use to signal or emphasize the organization of discourse. These structures help the listener or reader follow the discourse, focus on main points, and understand how parts are related. The following are uses of the discourse organizers covered in this unit.

EXAMPLES	EXPLANATIONS
(a) **First,** we need to examine the root causes of crime in our city, such as lack of education. (b) **After that,** the existing laws and programs should be evaluated. (c) **Finally,** we need to determine who will pay for new programs.	**Form:** sequential connectors **Use:** to show the sequence of topics or main point
(d) **There are** many reasons why crime is increasing in our cities.	**Form:** *there + be,* **Use:** to introduce topics
(e) **Is crime really increasing as much as everyone thinks it is?** The answer to this question may surprise you.	**Form:** rhetorical questions **Use:** to introduce topics
(f) **So far,** we have considered the positive side of general education requirements. **Next,** let's look at some of their drawbacks. (g) Lack of education may be one cause of crime. **But what about parental responsibilities in cases of juvenile crime?**	**Forms:** sequential connectors, rhetorical questions **Use:** to signal topic shifts
(h) **To summarize,** the statistics just presented indicate that air quality has been steadily improving during the last decade. (i) This paper examines the contributions of recent immigrants to the state economy. **Overall,** my research will show that immigrants have played a significant role in economic development.	**Form:** summary connectors **Use:** to introduce or make a summary of what has been or will be discussed
(j) **Should we be paying more tuition when we cannot even get the courses we need to graduate on time?**	**Form:** rhetorical questions **Use:** to emphasize key points, especially in argumentative discourse

EXERCISE 1

Match each of the sentences containing discourse organizers in the first column with topics in the second column. Then identify the form of discourse organizer in each and its apparent use. More than one use might be possible. The first has been done as an example.

Example: 1. i. (kinship systems); Form: *there + be*; Use: *to introduce a topic*

<u>i</u> 1. There are two types of family relatives I will discuss today: those involving blood relations and those resulting from marriage.

_____ 2. What does your clothing reveal about your identity?

_____ 3. To summarize, I have described several types of behavior that are typically regarded as masculine.

_____ 4. So far I have discussed the benefits of regular exercise. But what about people who become obsessed with workouts and spend half their lives at the sports club?

_____ 5. Lastly, I will talk about adrenaline, which is produced by the adrenal gland and raises blood pressure in stress situations.

_____ 6. Is there any reason why women and minorities should earn less than white males in comparable jobs?

_____ 7. To start with, we will describe one of the most widely used services, known as e-mail. After that, we will discuss news bulletin boards.

_____ 8. Thirdly, let's consider programs that feature real-life police on patrols dealing with violent criminals.

_____ 9. There are two main types of theories that can categorize most of modern cosmology: evolutionary theories and continuous creation theories.

_____ 10. In summary, my presentation today will provide several compelling reasons why our campus needs more space for cars.

a. How the universe was created and evolved

b. Basics of the Internet

c. Violence on television

d. Parking problems on campus

e. Gender roles

f. How people express themselves through their style of dress

g. Major hormones in the human body

h. Starting a physical fitness program

i. Kinship systems in anthropology

j. Job equality

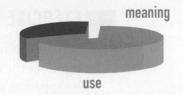

FOCUS 2 — Sequential Connectors: Chronological and Logical

EXAMPLES	EXPLANATIONS
	Sequential connectors may be chronological, logical, or both.
(a) **At first,** the lake seemed very cold. **Later,** after we had been swimming for a while, it seemed warmer.	Chronological connectors signal the sequence of events in time, such as the events of a story or the steps of a procedure.
(b) I have several items of business to share with you at this meeting. **First,** I will report on our latest expenditures. **Then,** I will present a proposal for our next ad campaign. **Lastly,** I will tell you about holiday party plans.	Logical connectors organize the sequence of events in a text, such as the parts of a speech or an essay. They are especially common in formal spoken English contexts, such as presentations and academic lectures.

Chronological

EXAMPLES	CONNECTORS	USES
(c) **At first,** Frederick didn't like his new neighbor.	*at first*	beginning continuation
(d) Eva was running slowly in the race at first. **Eventually** she pulled ahead, though.	*eventually*	
(e) Our first destination was Seoul, Korea. **Subsequently** we went to Bangkok, Thailand.	*subsequently*	
(f) **At last** they reached Vancouver, where they planned to spend the night.	*at last*	conclusion
(g) **In the end,** both our hero and his adversary die.	*in the end*	

Chronological or Logical

CHRONOLOGICAL	LOGICAL	CONNECTORS	USES
(h) **First,** turn on the ignition.	(i) **First,** let's consider the main issues.	*first*	beginning
(j) **First of all,** check the gas level.	(k) **First of all,** I will discuss the arguments against building the new subdivision.	*first of all*	
(l) **To start with,** open a new file and save it.	(m) **To start with,** the developers have not done an environmental impact study.	*to start with*	beginning
(n) **To begin with,** Matt went to Costa Rica.	(o) **To begin with,** let's look at the effects of air pollution in the valley.	*to begin with*	
(p) **Next,** he flew to Venezuela.	(q) **Next,** I will explain my opponent's stand on this issue.	*next*	continuation
(r) **Then,** he traveled to Brazil.	(s) **Then,** I will summarize the main points of the debate.	*then*	
(t) **After that,** he visited a friend in Argentina.	(u) **After that,** I will evaluate the various arguments.	*after that*	
(v) **Finally,** he spent a few weeks in Chile.	(w) **Finally,** I will present the implications of my position.	*finally*	conclusion
(x) **Lastly,** check the oil level.	(y) **Lastly,** new jobs are needed.	*lastly*	

Logical

EXAMPLES	CONNECTORS	USES
(z) **The first type of pollution** I'd like to discuss is that caused by automobiles.	*the first* + noun	beginning
(aa) **One cause of prejudice** is ignorance.	*one* + noun	
(bb) **In the first place,** we need to get more legislation to help the disabled.	*in the first place*	
(cc) **Secondly,** we also have a problem with noise pollution.	*secondly*	continuation
(dd) **The second point** concerns the issue of whether . . .	*the/a second*	
(ee) **A second question we might ask** is who should take responsibility for the homeless?	*(third, fourth, etc.)* + noun	
(ff) **In the second place,** we need to change our attitudes.	*in the second place*	
(gg) **The last reason** is one I am sure everyone is aware of.	*the last* + noun	conclusion
(hh) **A final question** might be how we will fund our project.	*a final* + noun	
(ii) **To conclude,** pollution is obviously getting worse in our city.	*to conclude*	
(jj) **In conclusion,** parents must take a more active role in schools.	*in conclusion*	

■ EXERCISE 2

Make up a sentence with a beginning sequential connector that could follow each of the sentences below. Try to use a variety of connectors.

Example: *My family is very special.* **In the first place,** *my father and mother have worked very hard to provide all of us an education.*

1. My family is very special.

2. Making a plane reservation on the World Wide Web is easy.

3. I appreciate many of the things my friends do for me.

4. Smoking can cause a lot of health problems.

5. We need to start taking major steps to save our planet.

6. When I started learning English, I encountered many difficulties.

7. A person who has really had an influence on my life is (*put person's name here*).

EXERCISE 3

For five of the sentences below, list ideas that could follow, using beginning, continuation, and concluding sequential connectors in your list. Try to use a variety of connectors.

Example: I can think of several things I don't have that I'd like to have. *To start with, I'd like to have a really good camera. Next, I wouldn't mind having a new car. Lastly, I'd love to have my own house.*

1. There are several things I'd like to do on my next vacation.
2. Our school could use a few improvements.
3. I have a few gripes about _____. (*You pick the topic.*)
4. I think I have made progress in several respects during the past few years.
5. My home (apartment/room) is a comfortable place for several reasons.
6. Several world problems seem especially critical to me right now.
7. I have several goals for my future.

EXERCISE 4

Exchange the paragraph you wrote for the Opening Task with either your partner for that task or another classmate. Did your classmate use any sequential connectors in the paragraph? If so, which ones? If not, would any of the connectors in the Focus 2 charts on pages 264–266 be appropriate to organize ideas in the paragraph? Discuss your analysis with your classmate.

FOCUS 3   *There + Be* as a Topic Introducer

There + be often introduces a topic that the speaker or writer has classified into different parts.

EXAMPLES	EXPLANATIONS
(a) **There are** three ways to get to the freeway from campus. (b) **There were** four principal causes for the recession. (c) **There could be** several explanations for this child's behavior.	The *be* verb can be any tense and can follow a modal verb such as *can, could,* or *may.*
(d) There are { three / a few / several / many / a number of } { aspects / causes / effects / factors / methods / principles / reasons / rules / stages / steps / strengths / theories / ways } to consider.	Noun phrases that come after the *be* verb often include a number or a quantifier (for example, *four, several*) and an abstract general noun (for example, *aspects, reasons*).
(e) There are **three kinds of** rhetorical questions. (f) There are **several types of** students.	Classifying phrases such as *kinds of* or *types of* often follow *there + be.*
(g) There are many driving rules to keep in mind when you get behind the wheel. **The first** rule of the road is to be courteous to other drivers. (h) There are five stages in this process. **In the first stage,** water is drawn through a tube.	You may use sequential connectors, as shown in Focus 2, to organize topics that follow an introduction with *there + be.* The sequential connectors in this chart are most often used for subtopics after *there + be* introducers.

Beginning	Continuing	Ending
first	*second, third, etc.*	*last*
first of all	*secondly*	*finally*
to start with	*next*	*lastly*
the first + noun	*the second, the third, etc.* + noun	*the last* + noun
one	*a second, a third, etc.*	*the last*
one + noun	*a second* + noun, *etc.*	*a final* + noun
in the first place	*in the second place*	*finally*

Guides to writing often caution writers against overusing *there + be.* This is good advice to avoid wordiness; keep in mind that this is not the only way to introduce a topic.

▪ EXERCISE 5

Fill in the blanks with appropriate words or phrases from the chart on page 268. Use different forms of connectors for each passage. Add commas where needed.

Example: <u>There are</u> two <u>kinds</u> of twins. <u>The first</u> is called identical. <u>The second</u> is called fraternal.

1. (a) _____ three (b) _____ of extrasensory perception, or ESP, that I will be discussing in today's lecture. (c) _____ I will talk about telepathy, perhaps the best known and most researched area. (d) _____ I will explain telekinesis, which concerns the ability to move a distant object through will power alone. (e) _____ I will describe the phenomenon of precognition, which involves knowing ahead of time about an event.

2. If you have pollen allergies, (a) _____ a number of (b) _____ that you might try to avoid pollen. (c) _____ stay in an air-conditioned room. (d) _____ when you drive, keep your windows up and your air-conditioning on. (e) _____ shower as soon as you go inside after being exposed to a lot of pollen. (f) _____ get an air-filter system in your home. (g) _____ if you live in the United States, move to Europe! That continent does not have the ragweed pollen that plagues people in the United States.

3. (a) _____ three main (b) _____ in the process of making rayon, a fabric produced from soft woods and other vegetable materials. (c) _____ the material is pulped. (d) _____ it is treated with caustic soda, nitric acid, and other substances until it turns into a liquid. (e) _____ it is forced through tiny holes in metal, forming liquid filaments which solidify into threads.

4. (a) _____ of pasta, with a great variety of shapes. (b) _____ is macaroni, which is a curved tube. (c) _____ is fettuccine, which looks like a thin ribbon. Capelletti is (d) _____; it is shaped like a hat. (e) _____ is ravioli; it is square-shaped or round-shaped and stuffed with cheese or meat. (f) _____ is rotelle, which has a corkscrew shape. And these are only a few of them!

EXERCISE 6

Write a sentence with *there + be* to introduce a classification for each topic below. Then write at least two or three sentences that could develop the topic.

Example: Topic: Three grammar points

There are three grammar points to study this week. One is relative clauses. A second is correlative conjunctions. The last is generic articles.

1. Types of books you like the best

2. Things that you think make a good movie or TV program

3. Topics that you are covering in a particular class for a specific amount of time (a week, a quarter, a semester)

4. Steps for performing a procedure that you know how to do (replacing a printer cartridge, solving a math problem, studying for an exam, parallel parking)

5. Professions or careers that would be good for someone who likes people

6. A topic of your choice

EXERCISE 7

The paragraph below has too many uses of *there + be* verb. Rewrite the paragraph, eliminating some of these forms to improve the information flow of the paragraph.

There is increasing evidence that our oceans have been warming up because of human activity. There are a number of serious ecological problems that have already resulted from an increase in ocean temperatures. For example, in Alaska's Bering Sea, there is a decrease in the population of some coldwater fish. In addition, the sea ice that polar bears live on near Hudson's Bay has been melting earlier, which has decreased their hunting season on the ice. There have also been negative effects on the ecology of the tropics. For instance, there were many coral reefs severely damaged by El Niño conditions in the late 1990s. Scientists believe that the upper regions of oceans are becoming more acidic from all of the CO_2 humans have put into the atmosphere, much of which ends up in the oceans. There are many organisms, including corals, that have difficulty growing shells with this increased acidity. Scientists worry that there will only be an increase in these disruptive effects of global warming on our planet's ecology.

EXERCISE 8

Look again at the paragraph you wrote for the Opening Task on page 261. Did you use a *there + be* introductory phrase? If so, read your sentence to the class. If not, make up a sentence that might be used to develop one of your questions, using *there + be* as an introducer.

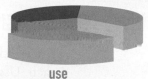

use

FOCUS 4 — Summary Connectors

Summary connectors also help to organize discourse. Some of these connectors signal that the ideas expressed summarize what has been said before.

EXAMPLES	CONNECTORS	USE
(a) **In summary,** drug abuse is a major problem today.	*in summary*	general summary
(b) **To summarize,** we should all exercise our right to vote.	*to summarize*	
(c) **As has been previously stated,** many people did not consider AIDS a serious problem at first.	*as (has been) previously stated/ mentioned*	review of main idea

Some summary connectors can be used either for introductions—summarizing what is to be presented—or for conclusions, summarizing what has already been stated.

LINK TO FOLLOWING DISCOURSE (INTRODUCTION)	LINK TO PRECEDING DISCOURSE (CONCLUSION)	CONNECTORS	USE
(d) I have been asked to report on our recent experiments. **All in all,** they have been very successful.	(e) From the presentation I have just given, I hope you will agree that, **all in all,** our experiments have been successful.	*all in all*	summary of points
(f) **Overall,** the quality of television appears to be declining. For example, the news is becoming more and more like entertainment.	(g) From the evidence I have presented in this essay, it appears, **overall,** the quality of television is declining.	*overall*	
(h) **Briefly,** the arguments for gun control can be summed up so far in the following way.	(i) **Briefly,** so far I have discussed three of the arguments for gun control.	*briefly*	condensation of points
(j) **In short,** the arguments against euthanasia, which I will discuss next, are mostly religious ones.	(k) **In short,** as I have shown, the arguments against euthanasia are mostly religious ones.	*in short*	

Choose three of the sentences or brief passages below. Write a summary statement for each. Use the summary connector indicated in parentheses. In small groups, compare the summary statements you wrote with those of your classmates.

Example: My paper will discuss the problem of overpopulation. (briefly)
Summary statement: *Briefly, overpopulation is a serious threat to the survival of all life on earth.*

1. Today, I'd like to talk about something I know every one of you is concerned about. (briefly)

2. By hooking a computer into a national electronic system, you can communicate and get information in a number of ways. For example, you can send and receive messages from others who have subscribed to the system or get the weather report for the day. You can take courses or play computer games. You can make travel reservations or look up information in an encyclopedia. (all in all)

3. Without iron, the body wouldn't have hemoglobin, which is an essential protein. Hemoglobin, found in red blood cells, carries oxygen to the rest of the body. A deficiency of iron can cause headaches and fatigue. (in short)

4. Good friendships do not develop easily; they require effort. You need to make time for your friends. You should be prepared to work out problems as they arise, since things will not always go smoothly. You shouldn't expect perfection from your friends. (in summary)

5. So far I have discussed several of the causes and effects of divorce. (as has been previously mentioned)

6. There are several things to keep in mind if you want to train a dog to obey you. First, you need a lot of patience. Secondly, you should not punish your dog for misbehaving but rather correct the inappropriate behavior. You should never hit a dog unless it is threatening to bite someone. Finally, remember to praise your dog for behaving properly. (all in all)

7. Fellow classmates: We have finally reached this proud moment, when we will receive our diplomas as testimony of our many achievements. In my speech to you this afternoon, I would like to stress what I believe is one of the most important purposes of education. (briefly)

8. In many American cities, it's difficult to get much real news from the local television news programs. For example, the local news on a typical hot summer day might feature interviews with people who are complaining about the weather and perhaps take a look at this season's swimwear fashions. You may find out how much money a blockbuster movie made at the box office over the weekend. Another "news" segment might tell you about some new product that you can buy. (overall)

FOCUS 5 — Rhetorical Questions to Introduce and Shift Topics

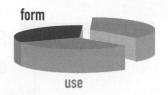

form

use

Rhetorical questions, unlike other questions, are not used to ask for information. In discourse, rhetorical questions are used to introduce topics and to shift from one topic to a new one.

EXAMPLES	EXPLANATIONS
(a) How does nitrogen circulate? (b) What are the most common causes of fatigue? (c) Is aggression a part of human nature? (d) Can Congress save the budget?	The form of a rhetorical question may be either a *Wh*-question (*who, what, when, where, why*) or a *yes/no* question.
(e) "What Is a University?" by John Henry Newman (f) "Are Women Human?" by Dorothy Sayers (g) "Were Dinosaurs Dumb?" by Stephen Jay Gould	Titles of books, articles, and speeches also use rhetorical questions to introduce topics.
(h) Remember the great health care debate?*	Rhetorical questions may introduce background information about a topic.
(i) So far, we have looked at some of the causes of teenage gangs. But what are the effects on the communities in which they live?	We also use rhetorical questions to signal a shift from one subtopic to another.

* Note that this question leaves off the first two words, "*Do you,*" of the full question form for an informal, conversational tone.

■ EXERCISE 10

The excerpts below use rhetorical questions to introduce topics. For each, predict what the topic is about.

1. What do we know about the universe, and how do we know it? Where did the universe come from, and where is it going? Did the universe have a beginning, and if so, what happened before then? What is the nature of time? Will it ever come to an end?

2. Have you ever heard the sound a duck makes as it dies a slow and painful death? In other words, have you ever heard a sixth grader with no musical experience try to play the oboe?

3. Do you believe that the more you diet, the harder it is to lose weight because your body adapts and turns down your rate of burning calories—your metabolism?

Rhetorical Questions to Focus on Main Points

use

Another kind of rhetorical question focuses the listener/reader on the main points of a topic and emphasizes the speaker/writer's viewpoint. It is sometimes called a "leading question."

EXAMPLES	SPEAKER/WRITER VIEWPOINT	EXPLANATIONS
(a) Haven't we had enough wars?	We have.	Leading rhetorical questions seek agreement from the listener or reader. They imply a *yes* answer. In other words, from the writer's or speaker's viewpoint, a negative answer is not possible.
(b) Don't divorced fathers as well as mothers have rights?	They do.	
(c) Isn't English hard enough to learn without all those different article usage rules?	It is.	
(d) We've had enough wars, haven't we?	We have.	Leading questions have the same meaning as negative tag* questions that seek agreement (falling tone in spoken English).
(e) What kind of solution is that to the rising cost of medical care?	It is a bad solution.	Another type of rhetorical question that focuses on main points implies a response in the negative. In other words, the speaker/writer will not take *yes* for an answer. Note that examples (e), (f), and (g) are all *wh*-questions.
(f) How much longer can we ignore the signs of global warming?	We can't ignore them any longer.	
(g) Who was more committed to nonviolence than Gandhi?	No one was more committed.	

*Note: **A tag question** is a short question that is added at the end of a statement seeking either agreement or confirmation. (e.g., *That's not right, is it? That's right, isn't it?*) When the speaker seeks agreement, he or she ends the sentence with falling intonation.

EXERCISE 11

Write a leading rhetorical question to express each of the following opinions. More than one form is possible, and some ideas need to be rephrased, not just transformed into a question. State the positive implication of each in parentheses.

Example: We've gone far enough in the space race.
Possible questions and implications:

Isn't it time to stop the space race? (It is.)
Haven't we gone far enough in the space race? (We have.)
Shouldn't we consider stopping the space race? (We should.)

1. Our senior citizens deserve more respect.

   _____

2. We need to start thinking more globally.

   _____

3. Our school already has too many required courses.

   _____

4. Women deserve the same job opportunities as men.

   _____

5. All people should have a place to live.

   _____

6. (Your choice: Write your own rhetorical question about a topic.)

   _____

EXERCISE 12

State the writer's viewpoint for the rhetorical questions in each of the following excerpts. Then state what you think is the thesis (the main point) of each text. Discuss which of the questions you find most effective in making their points.

Example: How many Americans can afford an $80,000 Mercedes-Benz? Should auto safety be reserved only for the wealthy?

Writer's viewpoint: *Not many Americans can afford a Mercedes and auto safety should not be reserved for only the wealthy.* Thesis: *Auto safety devices should be put on all cars, not just expensive cars.*

1. Fair-minded people have to be against bigotry. How, then, can fair-minded people ignore, condone, or promote discrimination against divorced fathers—100 percent of whom are men—and make believe it isn't discrimination?

2. I am, I hope, a reasonably intelligent and sensitive man who tries to think clearly about what he does. And what I do is hunt, and sometimes kill. . . . Does the power that orchestrates the universe give a deer more importance than a fly quivering in a strip of sticky tape?

3. One of the more popular comic book characters is Wolverine, a psychopath with retractable metal claws embedded in his hands and a set of killer instincts that makes him a threat to friend and foe alike. This is a proper role model for children?

4. I will not lie: sometimes I doubt why I stay in orchestra. I question my devotion each time I get politely yelled at by my orchestra teacher. I especially regret my choice on those days when I seem to create my own horrifying pitch. Wouldn't my GPA, the school, and the world be better off without my violin screeching? Wouldn't my parents get a better night's sleep? Wouldn't I?

5. My hands are restless. They drum on the top of the desk. It seems my hands have something to say. If my hands could talk, you'd have trouble getting them to stop. They would apologize to my grandma, because what kind of Chinese hands can't figure out how to use chopsticks?!

EXERCISE 13

The following excerpts from an essay by Isaac Asimov use six rhetorical questions to develop an argument about the need for population control. Identify the rhetorical questions. Then discuss how the author uses them to develop his ideas. What is the overall effect of the questions? Discuss which ones you think are most effective in emphasizing key points and introducing subtopics.

Let's Suppose . . .

1 Suppose the whole world became industrialized
2 and that industry and science worked very
3 carefully and very well. How many people could
4 such a world support? Different limits have been
5 suggested, but the highest figure I have seen is
6 twenty billion. How long will it take before the
7 world contains so many people?

8   For the sake of argument, and to keep things
9 simple, let's suppose the demographic growth rate
10 will stay as it is, at two percent per annum. . . .
11 At the present growth rate our planet will contain
12 all the people that an industrialized world may
13 be able to support by about 2060 A.D. . . .

14   Suppose we decide to hope for the best. Let us suppose that a change *will* take
15 place in the next seventy years and that there will be a new age in which population
16 can continue rising to a far higher level than we think it can now. . . . Let's suppose
17 that this sort of thing can just keep on going forever.

18   Is there any way of setting a limit past which nothing can raise the human
19 population no matter how many changes take place?

20   Suppose we try to invent a real limit; something so huge that no one can imagine
21 a population rising past it. Suppose we imagine that there are so many men and
22 women and children in the world, that altogether they weigh as much as the whole
23 planet does. Surely you can't expect there can be more people than that.

24   Let us suppose that the average human being weighs sixty kilograms. If that's the
25 case then 100,000,000,000,000,000,000 people would weigh as much as the whole
26 Earth does. That number of people is 30,000,000,000,000 times as many people as
27 there are living now.

28   . . . Let us suppose that the population growth-rate stays at 2.0 percent so that the
29 number of people in the world continues to double every thirty-five years. How long,
30 then, will it take for the world's population to weigh as much as the entire planet?

31   The answer is—not quite 1600 years. This means that by 3550 A.D., the human
32 population would weigh as much as the entire Earth. Nor is 1600 years a long time.
33 It is considerably less time than has passed since the days of Julius Caesar.

34   Do you suppose that perhaps in the course of the next 1600 years, it will be
35 possible to colonize the moon and Mars, and the other planets of the solar system?
36 Do you think that we might get many millions of people into the other world in the
37 next 1600 years and thus lower the population of the Earth itself?

38   Even if that were possible, it wouldn't give us much time. If the growth-rate
39 stays at 2.0 percent, then in a little over 2200 years—say by 4220 A.D.—the human
40 population would weigh as much as the entire Solar system, including the Sun.

Use Your English

CD Track 20

You may at times have wished you had a photographic memory—that is, one that remembers everything it receives as input—especially when you need to study for an exam. However, not being able to forget anything can be detrimental, as case histories in abnormal psychology have shown. Listen to the audio. You will hear a brief psychology lecture on the benefits of forgetting. Listen for the discourse organizers (sequential connectors, *there + be*, summary connectors, rhetorical questions) that the speaker uses as cues to introduce topics and focus on the main points. Take notes on the main ideas of the lecture on a separate sheet of paper. Then, listen to the audio one more time and write down the discourse organizers the speaker used to organize the lecture. Compare your notes and the list of discourse organizers with several classmates.

ACTIVITY **2** reading/writing

Are you familiar with the saying "It's as American as baseball, motherhood, and apple pie"? The apple pie reference probably means eating it rather than making it, but here's a chance to test your knowledge of American cooking. The recipe below explains how to make an apple pie. The directions, however, are not in the proper sequence. In small groups or with a partner, rewrite the steps of the recipe. Add sequential connectors to some of the sentences to help organize the text.

APPLE PIE

- Stir the mixed ingredients with the apples until the apples are well coated.
- Dot the top of the pie with 1/2 tablespoon of butter before putting on the top crust.
- Line a 9-inch pie pan with a pie crust; put aside while you prepare the apple filling.
- Cover the pie with a top crust and bake it in a 450-degree oven for 30 minutes.
- Peel, core, and cut 5 to 6 cups of apples into very thin pieces.
- Place the coated apples in layers in the pie shell.
- When the pie comes out of the oven, sprinkle 1 cup of grated cheese on top and put it under a broiler to melt the cheese.
- Combine and sift over the apple slices 1/2 cup of brown sugar, 1/8 teaspoon of salt, 1 tablespoon of cornstarch, and 1/4 teaspoon of cinnamon.

ACTIVITY 3 · writing

Choose one of the topics from the Opening Task on page 261 or another issue that interests you. Write a persuasive essay in which you express an opinion on the topic. Try to convince your readers of the validity of your viewpoint. Use appropriate discourse organizers in developing your essay.

ACTIVITY 4 · research on the web

A recent trend in international travel has been greater attention on the part of tourists to ethical issues such as respecting and enhancing the environment and promoting the welfare of the people who live in the places visited. These trends are known by such names as ecotourism and geotourism.

Find an article about the topic of ecotourism or geotourism on *InfoTrac®College Edition*. Write a summary of the article, using a variety of discourse organizers.

Example: *To start with, the author describes different kinds of "ethical tourism" and gives examples of questions tourists may ask about places they plan to visit.*

ACTIVITY 5 · reflection

One of the ways to improve your comprehension of academic lectures is to pay attention to the kinds of discourse organizers that speakers use to introduce topics and to change topics. Speakers use these organizers to signal or "signpost" the structure of a lecture. Often professors will also give a preview of the lecture to students beforehand, such as handing out an outline of topics to be covered in the next lecture. Listen carefully to a lecture for one of your classes or download one of the many lectures available from Web sites, and note the kinds of discourse organizers that are used. Write them down and report on your findings to your class.

CONDITIONALS
If, Only If, Unless, Even Though, Even If

UNIT GOALS

- Know the different kinds of conditional sentences in English

- Use *if, only if, unless, not unless,* and *if not* correctly to express conditions

- Know the difference between *even though* and *even if* and use them correctly

- Use conditional forms to give advice

OPENING TASK
When They Were Young

"When I was growing up, we went out to eat only if it was a special occasion."

"When I was a child, our parents wouldn't let us stay up late even if we begged them!"

"When I was your age, we couldn't leave the dinner table unless we asked permission."

Do these comments sound familiar? Part of the process of growing up is listening to your parents, grandparents, or other older relatives or adults tell you how things were different "back then" or "when we were your age."

■ STEP 1

In many societies, life in the past was more difficult than it is now, and children had less freedom than they do today. Consider what your older relatives (parents, aunts and uncles, grandparents, etc.) have told you about the way life was for them when they were younger. List some of the rules, restrictions, and hardships they have described.

■ STEP 2

In small groups, discuss and write down some of the things your older relatives *could not do* or *had to do* as a result of family customs, cultural rules, or simply the lifestyle of past generations.

Examples: *Lucy's mother couldn't drive a car even after she got her license unless one of her parents went with her.*

Antonio's great-aunt could go out on dates only if one of her older brothers went along.

To help out his family, Hyung's grandfather started working full-time when he was 16 even though he had wanted to finish high school.

■ STEP 3

Report some of your group's most interesting descriptions to the rest of the class.

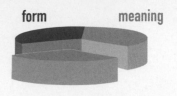

FOCUS 1   Review of Conditional Sentences with *If*

EXAMPLES	EXPLANATIONS
General Truth (a) If you **are** 65 or older, you **qualify** for senior citizen discounts.	**Factual Conditionals** One common type of factual conditional describes general truths. This type of conditional is often used in the sciences to describe physical laws.
Habitual Present (b) If my great-grandmother **comes** over, we usually **go** to the park.	Another common type of factual conditional refers to habitual events. The event may be present or past.
Habitual Past (c) When my mother was young, if relatives **visited** on Sunday, they **stayed** all day. **Inference: Explicit** (d) If that **was** grandmother on the phone, she **must have missed** the train. **Inference: Implicit** (e) If that **is** grandmother on the phone, she **is** still in Connecticut.	A third type of factual conditional infers something. The inference may be explicit or implicit. In explicit inference, the main-clause verb includes the modal *must* or *should*.
(f) If my great-grandmother **comes** tomorrow, we **may go** to a restaurant.	**Future Conditionals** These conditionals describe future events.
Present Hypothetical (g) If we **lived** closer to our grandparents, **we would see** them more often. (We don't live close to our grandparents; we don't see them as often as we would like to.) (h) If my great-grandmother **were** alive today, she **might** not **approve** of the tattoos that many young people have. **Past Hypothetical** (i) If my great-aunt **had been born** about 50 years later, she **might have been** a doctor instead of a nurse.	**Hypothetical Conditionals** The present hypothetical conditional describes conditions that are untrue or hypothetical. Past hypothetical conditionals describe conditions and results that were unreal or untrue in the past.

TYPE OF CONDITIONAL	IF-CLAUSE	MAIN CLAUSE
Factual: general truth	simple present	simple present
Factual: habitual	simple present	simple present
	simple past	simple past
Factual: inferential	simple present	various tenses
	simple past	
	will } + base verb	
	be going to	
Future	simple present	*will* }
		could
		may } + base verb
		might
		be going to
Hypothetical: Present	simple past or subjunctive	*would* }
	were	*could* } + base verb
		might
Hypothetical: Past	past perfect	*would have* }
	(*had* + past participle)	*could have* } + past participle
		might have

EXERCISE 1

To review verb tenses for conditional tenses, complete each of the blanks by writing the appropriate form of the verb in parentheses. The first has been done as an example.

1. If my aunts and uncles (go) _____*go*_____ out for dinner, they always (eat) _____*eat*_____ at the same Italian restaurant.

2. My mother has two older sisters. She told me that she was glad that she was the youngest child because if she (be) _____ the oldest, her parents (expect) _____ her to do much of the housework.

3. If my brother (come) _____ for a visit from Ecuador next summer, he (bring) _____ his entire family, including two dogs and a parrot.

4. I (telephone) _____ my family this weekend if I (stay) _____ on campus.

(*Continued on next page*)

5. My parents said that if they (have) _____ the time, they (like) _____ to organize a big family reunion, but for the time being they are just too busy with their jobs.

6. If the man in this photo (be) _____ my great-grandfather, that (must, be) _____ my great-aunt next to him.

7. If family members (disagree) _____ about values, they (should, remember) _____ that it is natural for different generations to think differently.

8. Gretchen (spend) _____ the whole year with her grandfather in Berlin if she (finish) _____ her senior project before June.

9. Could you see who's at the door? If that (be) _____ my sister, she (have) _____ the charcoal for the barbecue.

10. We're not going on vacation until next month. If we (go) _____ now, we (miss) _____ seeing my cousins, who are touring the east coast this summer.

■ EXERCISE 2

With a partner, take turns asking and answering the following questions about the school or schools you have attended. Answer each question with a complete conditional statement. If necessary, think of a particular class in a school you attended.

Examples: What happened if a student got into a fight at your school?

Possible answers:

In my elementary school, if a student got into a fight, the principal called up the parents.

If a student got into a fight in my high school, he or she was suspended for a few days.

What happened in one of your classes in elementary, middle, or high school if:

1. a student walked in 20 minutes late to class?

2. a student didn't turn in the homework assignment?

3. a student cheated on an exam?

4. a student constantly interrupted the teacher?

5. a student broke a classroom rule such as not to chew gum, not to forget textbooks, etc.?

EXERCISE 3

Complete each of the following past conditional statements. First complete the conditional statement with any other information you want to add; then express a hypothetical past result.

Examples: If my elementary school had . . .

If my elementary school had offered English classes, I would have learned English more easily.

If my elementary school had been less strict, I would have enjoyed it more.

1. If I had had a chance to . . .
2. If my parents (or mother or father) had lived . . .
3. If my grandparents had been able . . .
4. If my family had been . . .
5. If my English teacher had given . . .

EXERCISE 4

Add a condition to each of these past hypothetical statements.

Example: I would have studied more

If I had known I was going to get a C in my biology course last quarter, I would have studied more.

1. I would have worked harder
2. I would have been happier
3. the last year in school would have been easier for me
4. my parents would have been upset with me
5. my life would have been less complicated

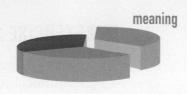

FOCUS 2 — Exclusive Conditions: *Only If* and *Unless*

We use both *only if* and *unless* to express the only condition under which an event will or should take place.

EXAMPLES	EXPLANATIONS
Main Clause: Affirmative (a) As a girl, my grandmother went shopping **Condition** **only if** she had finished her assigned chores.*	Use *only if* when the main clause is affirmative. It means "only on the condition that."
Main Clause: Negative (b) As a girl, my grandmother didn't go **Condition** shopping **unless** she had finished her assigned chores.	Use *unless* when the main clause is negative. It means "except on the condition that."
Main Clause: Affirmative (c) As a girl, my grandmother visited cousins **Condition** on Saturday **unless** her mother needed her to help at home.	You can also use *unless* when the main clause is affirmative. The implication, however, is negative. In (c), the implication is that Grandmother didn't visit cousins on Saturday if her mother needed her.
(d) Nowadays, my grandmother would spend the day shopping **only if** she **were** bored.	For hypothetical present, use the subjunctive form *were* in formal written English, just as with other hypothetical conditionals.

*In spoken English, native speakers often separate *only if,* placing *only* before the main verb and *if* after it: As a girl, my grandmother *only* went shopping *if* she had finished her chores; she would *only* spend the day shopping now *if* she were bored.

Decide whether *if, only if,* or *unless* should be used in each blank. The first one has been done for you.

In the Old Days . . .

As each generation matures, it tends to judge the younger generations as somehow not quite measuring up to those of the past: the new generation may be regarded as a bit lazier, less disciplined, or less imaginative. My family was no exception.

"Drive to school!" my father would exclaim to my siblings and me. "Why, when we were your age, we walked everywhere (1) _____ unless _____ there was a severe snowstorm. And if we couldn't walk, we went by car (2) _____ the buses weren't running." The meal options were generally fewer for my parents' generation also: (3) "_____ we didn't like what was served for dinner," my mother would remind us, "we had to eat it anyway." According to my parents, entertainment was more active before television watching became the main leisure activity, and obligations were more strictly enforced. As children, they usually played games outside (4) _____ the weather was terrible. And outdoor play was allowed (5) _____ all homework had been completed. When my mother was in high school, her parents wouldn't let her go out on dates (6) _____ her school grades were acceptable, and then (7) _____ her mother and father had a chance to meet the potential date.

Perhaps people shouldn't talk about the past (8) _____ they promise not to gripe about how easy the younger generation has it today!

EXERCISE 6

Make each of the following a negative condition by using *unless* instead of *only if* and making other changes as necessary.

Example: When I was your age, we went to the movies only if it was a holiday.
*When I was your age, we **didn't go** to the movies **unless** it was a holiday.*

1. Back in the old days, we only locked our houses if we were going on a vacation.

   _____

2. We could have ice cream for dessert only if it was a special occasion.

   _____

3. We could only go out after dinner if we had cleaned up the kitchen.

   _____

4. In high school, we were permitted to stay overnight at our friends' houses only if all the parents had met each other.

   _____

5. We were allowed to go to house parties only if they were chaperoned by adults.

   _____

form

use

FOCUS 3 — Fronted* *Only If* and *Not Unless* Clauses

EXAMPLES	EXPLANATIONS
(a) **Only if** our parents approved Verb Subject Verb | | | could we go out on a date.	You can use *only if* or *not unless* at the beginning of a sentence to emphasize a condition. Invert the subject and the first verb in the main clause.
(b) **Not unless** a party was chaperoned Verb Subject Verb | | | did my parents allow me to attend.	The first verb may be an auxiliary (*be, have, do*), a modal verb (*will, could, may*, etc.), or main verb *be*.
(c) **Unless** he finishes his chemistry project, Subject Verb | | he is not **going** on the weekend trip.	Do not invert the subject and first verb when you begin a sentence with *unless*. Separate the condition from the main clause with a comma.

* *Fronting* refers to putting words or structures that typically occur in other positions in sentences at the beginning of a sentence. Structures are often fronted for emphasis.

EXERCISE 7

Add an *only if* or *not unless* conditional clause to the beginning of each of the following statements to emphasize a condition. Make other changes as needed.

Example: It's fun to do calculus problems.
> *Only if you love mathematics is it* fun to do calculus problems.

1. Learning the conditional forms in English is easy.
2. Going bungee jumping is fun.
3. Spiders make great pets.
4. I'll help you with your English homework.
5. I will get up at 4 A.M. tomorrow.
6. I'll quit (name a "bad habit" you have).

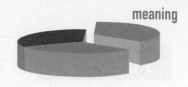

FOCUS 4   If . . . *Not* versus *Unless*

EXAMPLES	EXPLANATIONS
Future Main Clause (a) Juana will take the computer science course . . . **Future Conditional Clause** . . . if it does not conflict with her work schedule. . . . unless it conflicts with her work schedule. **Future Main Clause** (b) She won't take a writing course . . . **Future Conditional Clause** . . . **if** it does **not** satisfy a requirement. . . . **unless** it satisfies a requirement.	**Future or Hypothetical Conditions** In statements that express future or hypothetical events, subordinators *if . . . not* and *unless* have roughly the same meaning. They describe the negative conditions under which something will or may happen.
Main Clause: Contrary to Fact (c) Violeta couldn't have passed her Latin exam . . . **Condition: Contrary to Fact** . . . **if** she had**n't** had a tutor. **Main Clause** (d) Violeta couldn't have passed her Latin exam . . . **Condition** . . . **unless** she'd had a tutor.	**Past Conditions** In statements that express past conditions, use *if . . . not* to express a condition that is contrary to fact when the main clause is also contrary to fact. The meaning of (c) is that Violeta **did** pass the exam and she **did** have a tutor. Two meanings are possible when we use *unless* to state the condition. In (d) the most probable meaning is the same as example (c): Violeta **did** have a tutor; she **did** pass the exam. However, another possible meaning is that Violeta **did not** pass the exam and that only tutoring might have kept her from failing.
(e) Wen wouldn't have so much homework **if** he were **not** taking calculus. (f) **NOT:** Wen wouldn't have so much homework **unless** he were taking calculus. (g) Thanks for helping me get my new job. **If it weren't for** you, I would still be working at that horrible place. (h) **If it hadn't been for** the encouragement of her English-speaking friends, Pham wouldn't be so fluent in English. (i) **NOT: Unless** it were for you . . . (j) **NOT: Unless** it had been for the encouragement of her English-speaking friends . . .	**Present: Contrary to Fact Main Clause** To express a statement that is contrary to present fact, use *if . . . not* to state the condition. In (e), Wen is taking calculus, so he **does** have a lot of homework. We do not use *unless* for this meaning. We also use the expressions *if it weren't for* + noun and *if it hadn't been for* + noun to express conditions with main clauses that are contrary to present fact. In (g), the speaker is not working at the horrible place; in (h), Pham is fluent in English. The conditions have made these present facts possible. We do not use *unless* as shown in (i) and (j) when the main clause expresses a present result.

EXERCISE 8

For each situation below, choose the best paraphrase among the statements that follow.

1. Esther has made tentative plans to go to Greece for a vacation next summer. The only thing that might prevent her from doing so is if her mother needs to go away on business. In that case Esther would need to stay home to take care of her brother.
   a. Esther will go to Greece next summer if her mother takes a business trip.
   b. Unless her mother stays home, Esther will go to Greece next summer.
   c. Esther will go to Greece next summer unless her mother has to take a business trip.

2. The pioneers who settled the frontiers of North America confronted many dangers traveling to their new homelands, including fierce animals, terrible storms, and rivers they had to cross. Without great courage, they probably would have turned back.
   a. The pioneers would probably have turned back if they had not possessed great courage.
   b. The pioneers could not have reached their new homelands if they had possessed great courage.
   c. The pioneers could not have possessed great courage unless they had reached their new homelands.

3. My family went to my grandmother's house for dinner last night. We all ate so much pasta that no one could eat dessert. The only way we could have had room for dessert would have been to wait for three hours, but since we had tickets for a concert that evening, we had to leave shortly after we finished the main course.
   a. We couldn't have eaten dessert if we had not waited for 3 hours after our meal.
   b. We couldn't have eaten dessert unless we had waited for 3 hours after our meal.
   c. We could have eaten dessert unless we had waited for 3 hours after our meal.

4. David is on the college tennis team and has won all of his matches so far this year. He credits his high school coach for his success and says he wouldn't have even made the team without the excellent training his coach provided.
   a. David says he wouldn't be on the tennis team unless it had been for his coach's training.
   b. David says if it weren't for his coach's training, he wouldn't be on the tennis team.
   c. David says if it had been for his coach's training, he wouldn't be on the tennis team.

EXERCISE 9

Complete the following sentences with statements about yourself.

Example: If it hadn't been for my parents, *I might not have gone to college.*

1. If it hadn't been for my parents,

2. If it weren't for my friends,

3. If it weren't for (name)'s good advice,

4. If it hadn't been for my knowledge of (subject),

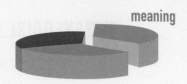

FOCUS 5 — *Even Though* and *Even If*

Both *even though* and *even if* emphasize conditions. However, their meanings are different.

EXAMPLES	EXPLANATIONS
(a) My uncle walked to work **even though** **Actual Condition** his job was five miles away. (His job was five miles away; nevertheless, he walked to work.)	*Even though* is an emphatic form of *although*. It means "despite the fact that." The condition after *even though* expresses a reality.
(b) My uncle will walk to work **even if** **Real or Not Real Condition** it is raining. (He walks when it rains as well as when it doesn't rain.)	*Even if* is an emphatic form of *if*. It means "whether or not." The condition after *even if* may or may not be a reality.
(c) My uncle { walks / used to walk } to work **even if it** { rains. / was raining. }	*Even if* can mean "even when" with habitual present conditions and past tense conditions. We can paraphrase (c): He walks to work even when it rains; he used to walk to work when it was raining.
(d) **Even if** I have to stay up all night, I will finish this paper. (e) **NOT: Even** I have to stay up all night, I'll finish this paper. (f) **Even though** it was late, we stayed up to find out who had won the election. (g) **NOT: Even** it was late, we stayed up to find out who had won the election.	**Even versus *Even If* and *Even Though*** *Even* cannot be used as a substitute for *even though* or *even if*. *Even* is not a subordinator. In your writing, you should check any uses of *even* to make sure that you don't mean *even if* or *even though*.

EXERCISE 10

Choose the correct form, *even though* or *even if*, for each blank.

Example: The children bought their mother a special gift last Mother's Day
_____even though_____ they didn't have much money.

1. Fran's mother was never without a car. However, she would often walk three miles to the market _____ she could have driven if she had wanted to.

2. _____ Duane's grandfather had a daytime job, he also worked every evening for many years.

3. Our family had a rule for dinner: We had to eat at least a few bites of each kind of food. _____ the food was something we had tried before and didn't like, we still had to eat a mouthful.

4. Last Christmas Eve, _____ the temperature dropped to below zero, my father insisted we take our traditional stroll through the neighborhood singing Christmas carols.

5. We'd love for you to spend the holidays with us. It would be wonderful if you could stay at least a week. But _____ it's only for a day or so, we hope you'll plan to come.

EXERCISE 11

Choose five of the following quotations and write a brief explanation or paraphrase of what you think each means.

Example: Even if you do learn to speak correct English, whom are you going to speak it to? (Clarence Darrow)

Explanation: *Darrow jokingly implies that many people do not speak "correct English," which he seems to equate with formal English. He uses the word whom, which people rarely use in conversational English.*

1. A house is no home unless it contains food and fire for the mind as well as the body. (Margaret Fuller)

2. Make a decision, even if it's wrong. (Jarvis Klem)

3. We rarely think people have good sense unless they agree with us. (François de la Rochefoucald)

4. A loud voice cannot compete with a clear voice, even if it's a whisper. (Barry Neil Kaufman)

5. It is impossible to enjoy idling unless there is plenty of work to do. (Jerome K. Jerome)

6. The trouble with the rat race is that even if you win, you're still a rat. (Lily Tomlin)

7. Don't make use of another's mouth unless it has been lent to you. (Belgian proverb)

8. Even if you're on the right track, you'll get run over if you just sit there. (Will Rogers)

FOCUS 6 Giving Advice

EXAMPLES	EXPLANATIONS
(a) Don't make reservations at the Four Seasons restaurant **unless** you're prepared to spend a lot of money. (b) Take a foreign language course **only if** you're willing to do homework faithfully every day. (c) You should pay your taxes on time **even if** you have to borrow the money. (d) Be sure to take a trip to the waterfall **even though** it's a long drive on a dirt road. It's well worth the trouble!	We often use connectors such as *unless, only if, even if,* and *even though* in statements that offer advice to specify conditions under which the advice holds.
(e) Don't go to see the movie *Last Alien in Orlando* **unless** you need a nap. (Implication: The movie is really boring!) (f) Take English 4 **only if** you have nothing to do on the weekends. (Implication: The class is difficult; you'll have a lot of homework.)	We sometimes use humorous conditions with advice statements to make a point indirectly. The advice in (e) and (f) has an ironic tone; the conditions are not meant to be taken literally.

EXERCISE 12

Make advice statements by combining information in the Condition and Advice columns on the next page. First match each condition with an appropriate piece of advice. Then make a full statement, using an appropriate conjunction: *if, only if, unless, even if, even though*. Make any changes necessary. The Conditions statements can either begin or end your sentences.

Examples:

Condition	Advice
you have plenty of water	take a hike in Death Valley

Unless you have plenty of water, don't take a hike in Death Valley.

Take a hike in Death Valley only if you have plenty of water.

Condition	Advice
1. you don't have a wetsuit to keep you warm	a. order the Jamaican spice chicken
2. you are taking a vacation in South Carolina	b. take a riverboat cruise on the Mississippi River
3. you don't mind huge crowds	c. try walking to the top of the cathedral in Seville, Spain
4. you love spicy food	d. visit the Grand Canyon in July
5. you are flying across time zones	e. treat yourself to a good meal in Paris
6. you like slow-moving leisurely travel	f. don't go swimming off the Oregon coast in winter
7. you don't mind climbing a lot of stairs	g. be sure to visit one of the old southern plantations
8. your budget is limited	h. be sure to set your watch accordingly if you have to change planes during travel

EXERCISE 13

Working with a partner, make up sentences that offer advice for at least five of the following situations using an *only if* or a *not unless* clause.

Example: What to do or not to do in the city where you live
Don't plan to go out for dinner at a restaurant in my hometown unless you can get there before 10 P.M.

1. How not to get lost at a particular place (your campus, a shopping mall, a city)

2. What to wear or what not to wear for a night on the town where you live

3. How to be culturally appropriate on a trip to a particular country

4. A place someone shouldn't shop at because of high prices or poor quality

5. A course or subject not to take at your school

6. A movie someone should not waste time to see

7. A book someone should not bother to read

EXERCISE 14

The paragraph below has five errors involving the conditionals focused on in this unit. Identify and correct them.

How to Evaluate Health News

(1) These days we are constantly hearing and reading about biomedical studies concerned with factors that affect our health. (2) Even these studies often present results as general "facts," the conclusions are not always true. (3) Only if multiple studies have been done it is wise to generalize results to a larger population. (4) Furthermore, you shouldn't be too quick to believe a study unless the number of subjects involved isn't large, because generalizations cannot be made from a small sample size. (5) Even the sample size is big enough, the results may not be statistically significant. (6) In other words, a statistical difference between two factors may be important only the difference could not happen by chance.

Use Your English

ACTIVITY **1** listening

CD Tracks 21, 22

Listen to the audio. You will hear two brief passages providing advice about health and safety issues. After each one you will hear three statements. Only one is a correct paraphrase of an idea in the passage. Circle the letter of the correct paraphrase below. Compare your answers with those of your classmates.

1. a b c   2. a b c

ACTIVITY **2** writing/speaking

Consider some of the family or school rules that you, your siblings, and your friends had to follow when you were younger. Create a list of rules that could be expressed with *if, unless,* or *only if* conditions. Use the categories below for ideas. In small groups, compare your lists. If possible, form groups that include different cultural backgrounds and discuss some of the cultural similarities and differences revealed by your lists.

- Mealtime etiquette
- Eating snacks
- Watching television or playing computer games
- Having friends over or staying at friends' houses

- Dating
- Going out with friends at night
- Making long distance phone calls
- Classroom rules
- School cafeteria rules

Examples: *In my elementary school in Taiwan, we were allowed to speak in class only if we raised our hand and the teacher gave us permission.*

When I was in high school, I couldn't have any of my friends over to visit unless one of my parents was home.

ACTIVITY 3 writing/speaking

Most of us have some strong opinions or beliefs about things that we would never do or that we would be very unlikely to do. For example, a person might believe that she would never accept a job that she hated or would never live in a very cold climate.

■ **STEP 1** Make a list of five things that you believe you would be very unlikely to do. For each item on your list, imagine a circumstance under which you might change your mind or be forced to behave differently, and write it down as a possible exception. Use either *unless* or *only if*.

Example: *I wouldn't live in a very large city.*

Exception: *I would do it only if I could be chauffeured wherever I wanted to go.*

■ **STEP 2** Compare your responses with those of your classmates.

ACTIVITY 4 writing

Here's a chance to share your knowledge. Either individually or as a collaborative project with some of your classmates, create a brief guide for one of the following topics. Your guide could be intended as a Web page for the Internet or a poster.

- A guide that informs students which courses at your school to avoid or which to take only under certain conditions
- Advice about what to do or not to do in your hometown or country
- A travel guide to some place you've been to that you like
- A guide for what to wear and how to behave at a formal occasion such as a wedding
- A guide for women on understanding men
- A guide for men on understanding women
- A guide of your choice

For as many items as possible, use condition statements with *only if, unless, even if,* or *even though.* Your conditions could be humorous or serious.

ACTIVITY 5 writing

Imagine that you could be in charge of your school or city for a year. You could make any rules or laws you wish, and everyone would have to obey them. Make a list of the regulations you would enforce, using conditional statements where they might be needed.

ACTIVITY 6 research on the web

Use an Internet search engine such as Google® or Yahoo® or other Web source to learn more about the way people in the United States or Canada lived during some period in the past. Try to find out some of the hardships they endured and the ways in which their lives differed from our lives today. Enter keywords such as a decade (e.g., 1830's), the country's name and your area of interest (e.g., lifestyle). Write a brief report on your findings, using conditional sentences to express some of the information you found.

Example: *Even though the pioneers were afraid of thieves coming into their houses, they had no way to lock their houses when everyone was away. They could only latch the door from within.*

ACTIVITY 7 reflection

Accomplishing the goals we set for ourselves usually involves some sacrifice. No pain, no gain, as the saying goes! Think of three things that you have accomplished in your learning even though these were not easy for you, and another three things that you will try to accomplish even if you need to make sacrifices to do so. Write a sentence for each, using *even though* and *even if* conditions to express what you have done or will do to achieve your goals.

Examples: *Even though I don't like studying grammar, I memorized most of the irregular verb forms in English. I will try to read one book every month even if I have to give up some of my TV watching time.*

REDUCING ADVERBIAL CLAUSES

UNIT GOALS

- Know how to reduce adverbial clauses of time and cause

- Position and punctuate reduced adverbial clauses

- Reduce adverbial clauses with emotive verbs

- Avoid dangling participles in writing

OPENING TASK

The Lone Traveler

On one of your hiking trips to Mills Landing, you found an old diary with a few notes scrawled in it. Apparently, a lone traveler had kept a record of his travels about one hundred years ago.

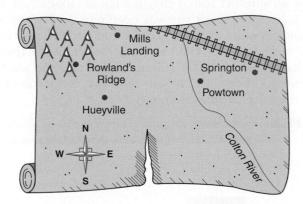

Jan. 30: Discouraged by poor crops. No cash. Left Springton by wagon in search of work.

Feb 4: Today searched for job in Powtown. No luck. All jobs require skills I don't have.

March 15: Crossed the Colton River but raft turned over. Lost everything except diary and watch. Walked to Hueyville.

March 18: No work in Hueyville. Met kind woman there. Told me about vacant house abandoned by miners near Rowland's Ridge.

March 21: Sold my watch for supplies. Hiked to Rowland's Ridge. Found shack and moved in.

> March 27: Days and days of rainy weather. Decided to fix up place. Borrowed tools to fix roof, walls, and floors.
>
> March 29: Hammering floorboards. Saw red bag. Opened it. Eureka! A bag full of money. I am rich.
>
> April 8: Guilty conscience. Worry about possible owner. Hiked to Mills Landing and asked Sheriff what to do. Says the money is mine because money left long ago. No one will ever claim.

■ STEP 1

Using the map, trace the traveler's steps with a partner.

■ STEP 2

With your partner, write a brief article for the local newspaper about the lone traveler's story. Describe the traveler's route and what occurred along the way.

Example:

100-Year-Old Diary of Traveler Found

Yesterday a diary was found that tells the story of a former resident of the area. Apparently, one hundred years ago, a lone traveler, discouraged by poor crops and having no cash, had left Springton in order to find work. Searching for a job in Powtown, the traveler . . .

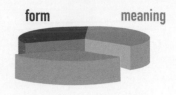

FOCUS 1   Reducing Adverbial Clauses of Time

We can reduce adverbial clauses of time that contain the words *before, after, while, when,* and *since.* To do this, the subject of the main clause and the adverbial clause must be the same. These reduced clauses are called participle phrases and use verb + *-ing.*

FULL ADVERBIAL CLAUSE	REDUCED ADVERBIAL CLAUSE*	TIME MEANING
(a) **While we are hiking/were hiking/hiked,** we admire/admired the scenery around us. *are/were* V + *-ing* ⟶	(b) **(While) hiking,** we admire/admired the scenery around us. V + *-ing*	A time happening at the same time as the time expressed in the main clause.
(c) **Since he has/had been living in Paris,** he has/had learned to speak French quite well. *has/had been* V + *-ing* ⟶	(d) **(Since) living in Paris,** he has/had learned to speak French quite well. V + *-ing*	A time occurring before and up to the point of the time expressed in the main clause.
(e) **After we have/had hiked around the canyon,** we are/were exhausted. *have/had* V + *-ed* ⟶	(f) **(After) having hiked around the canyon,** we are/were exhausted. *having* + V + *-ed*	A time occurring before the time expressed in the main clause.
(g) **While they are/were being searched,** they feel/felt nervous. *are/were + being* + V + *-ed* ⟶	(h) **(While) being searched,** they feel/felt nervous. *being* + V + *-ed*	A time occurring at the same time or immediately after the time expressed in the main clause.
(i) **When Sam gets tired,** we will leave.	(j) **NOT:** Getting tired, we will leave.	The subject of the main clause and the subject of the adverbial clause are not the same. The adverbial clause cannot be reduced.

*For some of these reduced adverbial clauses, you can either keep or leave out the adverbial (in parentheses), as in (b), (d), (f), and (h) above.

EXERCISE 1

Complete the following sentences about the out-of-doors. Give advice, using *should* or *shouldn't*.

Example: After getting lost in the woods, <u>you should look for familiar landmarks such as hills or trees</u>.

1. While walking along a narrow ridge, _____.
2. When hiking in an area with poisonous snakes, _____.
3. After having fallen into icy water, _____.
4. Before entering a meadow filled with deer, _____.
5. When washing dishes in the wilderness, _____.
6. Before lighting a fire in the woods, _____.
7. Before being attacked by mosquitoes, _____.
8. After having spotted a bear, _____.

EXERCISE 2

Read the following story. Reduce the full adverbial clauses of time where possible. The first one has been done for you.

           graduating
(1) Since ~~he graduated~~ from high school, Juan has been working and studying very hard. (2) While he attends classes at a community college, he works part-time at a bank. (3) After he graduates from the community college, he would like to attend a four-year university in order to become an architect. (4) Some day Juan would like to get married and have a family. (5) However, before he gets married, he is planning to take a trip to Europe. (6) When he is traveling through Europe, he hopes to see the great architecture of France, Spain, and Italy. (7) After he returns, he will begin looking more seriously for a partner.

EXERCISE 3

Reflect on your last month of activities and write at least five sentences containing reduced adverbial clauses of time like those shown in in the chart on page 302.

Example: *After having taken my biology exam, I had to study for my history exam.*

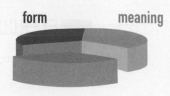

form   meaning

FOCUS 2 Reducing Adverbial Clauses That Show Cause

We can also reduce adverbial clauses containing *because, since,* and *as* to *-ing* phrases. Again, the subject in the main clause must be the same as the subject in the adverbial clause.

FULL ADVERBIAL CLAUSE	REDUCED ADVERBIAL CLAUSE*	CAUSAL MEANING
(a) **Because we take/took/are taking/were taking the bus,** we save/saved a lot of money.	(b) **Taking the bus,** we save/saved a lot of money.	The participle phrase contains the cause or reason. The main clause contains the result. The participle phrase can refer to present and past time as was shown in Focus 1.
(c) **Since I have/had been rehearsing every day,** I am/was ready to perform.	(d) **Rehearsing every day,** I am/was ready to perform.	
(e) **As I have/had never gone skiing,** I want/wanted to take lessons.	(f) **Never having gone skiing,** I want/wanted to take lessons.	In the reduced form, a negative word like *never* or *not* can precede the auxiliary verb. This means that the action did not occur.
(g) **Because he is/was not being watched by the police,** he is/was free to move.	(h) **Not being watched by the police,** he is/was free to move.	

*These reduced clauses do not include the adverbial. That is, it is not possible to say "Because taking the bus, we saved a lot of money."

EXERCISE 4

Tony and Maria have had several mishaps on their camping trip. Suggest a cause for each mishap by adding a reduced adverbial clause to each sentence below. Compare your completed sentences with a partner.

Example: They got lost on their hike.
Not having brought a map, they got lost on their hike.

1. Tony was bitten by mosquitoes.
2. They were very thirsty.
3. They were very hungry.

4. Maria jumped in fright.
5. Maria was shivering.
6. Tony developed a blister.

EXERCISE 5

Imagine that you have received a letter from a friend who is having a difficult time adjusting to life at a university in the United States. She is making excuses for several of her actions. Write a piece of advice for each problem, using a reduced causal adverbial clause.

Example: Because I arrived at my first class late, I waited outside the room and missed the entire lecture.

Having arrived to the class late, you should have quietly entered the room and sat down.

1. Because I have no computer, I do not type my papers.

2. Watching too much TV, you should have had more self-control and turned it off so that you could concentrate on your homework.

3. As I have not understood my instructor, I have stopped going to class.

4. Because I do not know anyone, I sit alone in my room for hours.

5. Since I hate the food on campus, I go out for dinner every night and now I'm almost broke.

6. As I am embarrassed by my accent, I do not speak to many people.

7. As I am very shy, I do not ask questions about my assignments in class.

8. As I got a D on my last test, I am planning to drop my class.

9. Because I made expensive long distance calls to my family every other night, I ran up a huge phone bill.

10. Since I did not have enough time to write my research paper, I copied most of the information from an encyclopedia.

11. Because I was put on academic probation, I have felt very depressed.

12. Since I do not speak English very well, I speak my native language with friends from my native country.

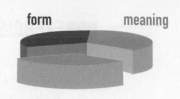
FOCUS 3	Position and Punctuation of Reduced Adverbial Clauses

EXAMPLES	EXPLANATIONS
(a) **Hiking alone in the mountains,** Diane always carries water and a compass.	Reduced adverbial clauses (participle phrases) may appear at the beginning, middle, or end of a sentence.
(b) The doe, **having been frightened by the noise,** disappeared from the clearing.	
(c) The trackers waded across the river, **holding tightly to the reins of their horses.**	
(d) The trackers waded across the river **while holding tightly to the reins of their horses.**	Commas are needed in all positions, except the sentence-final position with the adverbial included, as in (d).

EXERCISE 6

Insert commas where needed in the following story.

(1) Tiffany was a very lucky girl. (2) Being born into a very wealthy family she always got everything she wanted. (3) She was given a pony before celebrating her eighth birthday. (4) After turning 10 she had a tutor to teach her anything she wanted to learn. (5) Enjoying sports she learned how to sail, ski, and scuba dive. (6) Turning 12 her interests changed to travel. (7) Enjoying traveling she decided to have her sixteenth birthday on a ship. (8) For a whole weekend, she and her friends were eating, playing games, and dancing while cruising to Mexico.

(9) Tiffany's luck began to change, however, on her eighteenth birthday. (10) Her parents promised her a shiny red sports car, but they told her that she would have to pay for the registration and the insurance herself. (11) She paid for the first installment of her insurance, but not having a well-paying job she avoided paying for the second installment of the insurance and drove her car anyway. (12) One night, speeding along a winding road she saw another car coming towards her. (13) She beeped loudly, but the car did not move over. (14) She swerved her car to the right barely missing the other car as it drove by. (15) Her car hit a tree, but she was not hurt. (16) Arriving on the scene a police officer asked to see her driver's license and her up-to-date insurance identification. (17) Lucky Tiffany's luck ran out when she told him that her insurance had expired. (18) Unfortunately, her license was revoked and she had to pay for the damages to the car out of her own pocket not having adhered to her parents' agreement.

Match the following main clauses and participle phrases. Try placing the participle phrases in different positions, using commas as necessary.

Example: *Returning to Europe, Christopher Columbus brought cocoa beans from the new world.* (7-f)

Christopher Columbus, returning to Europe, brought cocoa beans from the new world. (7-f)

Participle Phrases	Main Clauses
1. Having healed numerous individuals from malaria	a. agriculture and industry have ruined tropical lands.
2. Conquering American tropical lands	b. bananas are available in every season.
3. Sold either as fresh fruit or made into juice	c. the natives sucked on the tender green shoots.
4. Upsetting the natural order of climate and ecology	d. pineapple has been an important cash crop.
5. Prompting explorers to leave on long voyages	e. pepper was a prized commodity in the Middle Ages.
6. Grown almost year-round	f. Christopher Columbus brought cocoa beans from the new world.
7. Returning to Europe	g. the Spaniards were introduced to cocoa and chocolate.
8. Extracting the sweet juice from the sugarcane	h. quinine is a very useful medicinal plant.
9. Dried	i. cinnamon rolls up into small sandy-brown cigarette shapes.

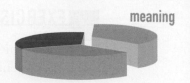

FOCUS 4 — Reduced Adverbial Clauses with Emotive Verbs

EXAMPLES	EXPLANATIONS
Emotive Verbs: amuse confuse frustrate please annoy embarrass interest puzzle bewilder excite intrigue shock bore frighten irritate surprise captivate	Reduced adverbial clauses often contain emotive verbs (verbs that express feelings or emotions).
(a) **Amused** by the movie, Tony laughed out loud. (b) **Frightened** (by the noise), Donna left to investigate.	If we use the *-ed* participle, the focus is on the person experiencing the emotion.
(c) The clown stood on his head, **amusing** the spectators. (d) Two students whispered in the back of the room, **annoying** the teacher.	If we use the *-ing* participle, the focus is on the person or thing causing the emotion.

EXERCISE 8

Circle the correct option.

Example: Nick jumped, ——————————— by the lighting.
     (a.) frightened   b. frightening

1. The hikers, ——————, gazed at the lovely waterfall.
   a. surprised and bewildered   b. surprising and bewildering

2. —————— by mosquitoes, Miko could not sleep.
   a. Bothered   b. Bothering

3. The movie, while —————— and sensational, was inappropriate for children.
   a. intrigued   b. intriguing

4. —————— that the bears had invaded the camp, the family left.
   a. Irritated   b. Irritating

5. —————— by the lecture, many students fell asleep.
   a. Bored   b. Boring

6. —————— in Indian artifacts, Martin collected arrowheads.
   a. Interested   b. Interesting

7. They walked on their hands, —————————— all of the bystanders.
   a. shocked   b. shocking

8. The play, while —————————— and funny, did not keep us awake.
   a. amused   b. amusing

meaning

FOCUS 5   Avoiding Dangling Participles

Writers often use reduced adverbial clauses in their sentences. If the subject in the reduced clause is different from the subject in the main clause, the reduced clause is called a "dangling participle" and may result in a miscommunication. To avoid this error, writers need to make sure that the performer of the action in the main clause is the same as the performer of the action in the reduced clause. To correct this error, the subject of the main clause should be changed to match the subject in the reduced clause. Or the reduced clause should be expanded to a full adverbial clause.

DANGLING PARTICIPLES	MEANING AS WORDED
(a) The path was more visible **carrying a flashlight.**	Miscommunication: The path was carrying a flashlight. Reworded: Carrying a flashlight, I could see the path more visibly. OR The path was more visible when I was carrying a flashlight.
(b) **Using binoculars,** the pond was clearly defined.	Miscommunication: The pond was using binoculars. Reworded: Using binoculars, I could see the pond clearly defined. OR While I was using binoculars, the pond was clearly defined.
(c) **Enclosed in a waterproof can,** the hikers kept the matches safe.	Miscommunication: The hikers were enclosed in a waterproof can. Reworded: Enclosed in a waterproof can, the matches were kept safe by the hikers. OR Because the matches were enclosed in a waterproof can, the hikers kept the matches safe.
(d) **After carefully reading it over,** the diary should be revised for gaps and inconsistencies.	Miscommunication: The diary is reading itself over. Reworded: After you carefully read it over, the diary should be revised for gaps and inconsistencies. OR After carefully reading it over, you should revise the diary for gaps and inconsistencies. OR After carefully reading it over, revise the diary for gaps and inconsistencies.
(e) **When keeping a diary,** dates and places should be carefully recorded.	Miscommunication: Dates and places are keeping the diary. Reworded: When you are keeping a diary, dates and places should be carefully recorded. OR When keeping a diary, people should carefully record dates and places. OR When keeping a diary, it is important to carefully record dates and places.**

Note: Because the subject of the reduced adverbial clause is the same as the imperative "you" in the main clause, the reduced clause is not a dangling participle.

**When the adverbial clause contains a nonreferential "it," which is assumed to be the same subject as the generic people who keep diaries, the rule for the same subject in both clauses is relaxed.

EXERCISE 9

While hiking in the woods in some parts of the world, a person may encounter a skunk and be unexpectedly sprayed. The following sentences relate to Jane's experience with this, but some of them contain dangling participles. Identify which sentences are incorrect, explain why they are humorous as they are presently stated, and reword the main clause to make each sentence correct.

Example: Hiking in the woods, a skunk crossed Jane's path. *This sentence is humorous because it suggests that the skunk, not Jane, was hiking in the woods. The appropriate form would be "While Jane was hiking in the woods, a skunk crossed her path."*

1. Having been sprayed by a skunk, she screamed loudly.
2. Frightened and humiliated, we walked Jane back to the campground.
3. Having returned to the campground, we looked for some catsup.
4. Applying a thick coat of catsup all over her body, the skunk smell was neutralized.
5. Soaking her clothing for 30 minutes in vinegar and water, the smell diminished.
6. Having been victimized by a skunk, we were informed by Jane that she will think twice about hiking in the woods again.
7. It is wise to bring catsup and vinegar when camping in skunk country.

EXERCISE 10

Rewrite these sentences to correct the participle errors. There may be several ways to correct a sentence.

Example: After having been bitten by mosquitoes, the ointment felt soothing to her skin.
After having been bitten by mosquitoes, she rubbed a soothing ointment onto her skin.

1. James pet the dog, while barking.
2. While having a bath, water leaked over the sides of the tub.
3. The hurricane terrified people, being driven from their homes.
4. When amused by their children's naughty pranks, a straight face is always a good solution for parents.
5. Slithering along the path, I spied a snake.
6. Nearly suffocated by the heat, the room was packed with people.
7. The canned fruits and jams helped the family survive, having prepared for the winter.
8. Sobbing and wailing, the search party was able to locate many survivors.
9. Sitting on the beach, the waves seemed huge to Martin.
10. After carefully reading it over, the diary should be revised for gaps and inconsistencies.

Use Your English

CD Track 23

STEP 1   Relax, close your eyes, and listen attentively to the audio for five descriptions. Each one is unfinished. Use your imagination to create a mental image that completes each piece. Listen to each description a second time. Stop the audio after each one. What do you see? Write your ideas in complete sentences. Try to use as many participle phrases as you can.

Example: *Looking ahead, I see high jagged peaks. Each one is covered with snow. Dotting the landscape below, hundreds of lakes are nestled among groves of trees.*

STEP 2   Now listen again and write down any *-ed* or *-ing* participle phrases that you hear.

Example: *The propeller turning and the engine roaring, the plane is ready for takeoff. Ascending higher and higher, you see nothing but white fog in every direction.*

ACTIVITY 2 writing

We often use reduced adverbial clauses to give directions for carrying out some procedure. Consider something you know how to do very well that requires several motions (for example, making beef jerky, changing a tire, operating a video camera). Then, write the directions to do this activity, using at least two reduced adverbial clauses.

Example: *Before making beef jerky, purchase three pounds of lean beef. Cut strips of the beef about one-half-inch thick. Then, hang these strips on a wood framework about four to six feet off the ground. After building a smoke fire, allow the meat to dry in the sun and wind.*

ACTIVITY 3 listening/speaking

Check out a book recorded on audiotape or CD novel (for example, Charles Dickens's *A Tale of Two Cities*, Mark Twain's *Huckleberry Finn*, Willa Cather's *O, Pioneers!*) from your local library or video store. Listen to the audio and identify one or two descriptive passages. Within these passages, listen for examples of reduced adverbial clauses. Share these examples with your classmates.

ACTIVITY 4 research on the web

 Go to the Internet and use an Internet search engine such as Google® or Yahoo® to research the topic "California Gold Rush." Read and take notes on several articles to familiarize yourself with when it happened, who was involved, what challenges were encountered, what successes were achieved, etc. Then, write a short fictional piece about a miner's life during that time.

Example: *Living near the town of Coloma, California, Peter Jacobson, one of the many California gold miners at the time of the Gold Rush experienced many hardships . . .*

ACTIVITY 5 reflection

Review an essay that you wrote previously. Analyze it sentence by sentence and reduce adverbial clauses appropriately. See the example on page 313.

Examples:

> Many people have been moving to Southern California from colder regions of the United States. <u>When people have been living in Southern California for a while</u>, they assume new habits and lifestyles. It does not take long for them to begin wearing shorts and sandals. <u>While they were living in Minnesota or New York</u>, they got used to winters where they bundled up from head to toe. <u>Since they arrived to the west coast</u>, they wear shorts and sandals all year round. In the past, they often watched Hollywood movies on TV in their living room. Now, <u>because they are living near the entertainment industry</u>, they can drive to see movie premieres or even live filming of TV dramas.

■ **STEP 1**   Underline time or causal adverbial clauses.

Examples:

TIME:
<u>*When people have been living in southern California for a while*</u>, *they assume new habits and lifestyles.*
<u>Living in southern California for a while</u>, they assume new habits and lifestyles.

CAUSAL:
Now, <u>*because they are living near the entertainment industry*</u>, *they can drive to see movie premiers or even live filming of TV dramas.*
Now, <u>living near the entertainment industry</u>, they can drive to see movie premiers or even live filming of TV dramas.

■ **STEP 2**   Label each type of clause and determine whether or not one or more clauses can be reduced or reordered. Revise the sentences for greater conciseness and clarity.

■ **STEP 3**   Submit your revised paper to your instructor for feedback.

UNIT GOALS

- Use verbs with the correct preposition clusters

- Use adjectives with the correct preposition clusters

- Use common multiword preposition clusters

- Use preposition clusters to introduce a topic or identify a source

OPENING TASK

■ STEP 1

Look at the following pictures and captions describing immigrants and refugees from around the world.

Guatemalans fleeing to Mexico during civil war

Turks displaced to Europe after earthquake

STEP 2

Now think about one group of refugees or immigrants that has recently settled in your native country or in a country you are familiar with. Think about the circumstances surrounding the group's departure from their homeland and present living conditions in the new country. Jot down notes about these circumstances in the chart below.

Immigrant or Refugee Group _____	
1. Why they departed from their country	
2. What they hope for in their new country	
3. What group (if any) they are at odds with in the new country	
4. What aspects of life they are unaccustomed to in the new country	
5. Who they associate with in the new country	
6. What geographical areas they are attracted to in the new country	
7. How their contributions result in a richer cultural heritage for the new country	

STEP 3

Discuss the results of your brainstorming with your classmates.

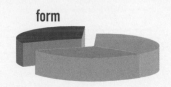

FOCUS 1 | Verb + Preposition Clusters

Preposition clusters are prepositions that follow and are closely associated with verbs and adjectives or prepositions that appear in common phrases.

EXAMPLES	EXPLANATION
(a) Refugees **differ from** immigrants in that they have not left their homelands by choice.	These verb + preposition clusters must be followed by noun phrases (a) or gerunds (b).
(b) Refugees usually **plan on** returning to their homeland as soon as the hostilities are over.	(Gerunds will be covered more fully in Unit 18.)

Other examples of verb + preposition clusters are:

consist of	count on
hope for	deal with

EXERCISE 1

There are four verb + preposition clusters in the chart prompts in the Opening Task. Can you identify them? Now, use your notes from the chart and write four sentences about the immigrant or refugee group you described, using verb and preposition clusters.

Example: *The Vietnamese departed from Vietnam in order to find better economic and political conditions.*

EXERCISE 2

The following incomplete sentences contain verb + preposition clusters. Complete them in two ways, with a noun phrase and with a gerund.

Example: The new parents marveled at

the beauty of their child. (noun phrase)

seeing their son for the first time. (gerund)

1. A healthy diet consists of _____.

_____.

2. The plan called for _____.

_____.

3. Does anyone object to { _____ _____?
                             _____?

4. Ever since I was a child, I have counted on { _____.
                                                   _____.

5. As it is very late, you can dispense with { _____.
                                                 _____.

6. After the accident, Jaime withdrew from { _____.
                                               _____.

7. Will the president succeed in { _____?
                                     _____?

8. The protesters were demonstrating against { _____.
                                                 _____.

9. Why can't she distinguish between { _____?
                                         _____?

10. I don't agree with the politician who believes in { _____.
                                                          _____.

FOCUS 2 — Verb + *With* Clusters

EXAMPLES	EXPLANATION
(a) The laborers **consulted with** their union. (b) They decided not to **cooperate with** management.	Verb + *with* clusters show association between or among people.

Other examples of verb + *with* clusters are:

associate with	join with	unite with
deal with	side with	

EXERCISE 3

Ask and answer *should* questions with a partner. Use the subject in the first column and then make sentences with the verb + preposition clusters and the objects in the second and third columns

Example: Q: Should homeowners deal with realtors to sell their homes?

A: No, they shouldn't deal with realtors; they should try to sell the houses themselves.

Subject	Verb + Preposition	Object
1. homeowners	associate with	their children
2. criminals	cooperate with	students
3. the rich	consult with	ophthalmologists
4. parents	deal with	the police
5. patients	join with	realtors
6. young people	side with	gangs
7. teachers	unite with	the poor

FOCUS 3 Verb + *From* Clusters

EXAMPLES	EXPLANATION
(a) The garage was **detached from** the house. (b) Rice pudding **differs from** bread pudding.	Verb + *from* clusters imply separation.

Other examples of verb + *from* clusters are:

| abstain
desist
deviate
dissent | } from | emerge
escape
flee
migrate | } from | prevent
prohibit
recede
recoil | } from | retire
separate
shrink
withdraw | } from |

EXERCISE 4

Fill in one of the verbs + *from*, using the examples above, in each blank below. You may need to change the verb form in some examples.

1. Certain groups follow restrictive dietary laws. For example, Orthodox Jews (a) _____ pork and shellfish. Sometimes these and other groups who (b) _____ the status quo or (c) _____ the norm are considered strange by outsiders but extremely religious by those from within the same community.

2. Refugees come to a foreign country to live for many different reasons. They want to (a) _____ persecution, war, disaster, or epidemics. Certain Southeast Asians have (b) _____ tragic conditions in their native lands but have become successful in their new homes around the world.

3. Some newcomers to a country go through culture shock. This phenomenon makes some people (a) _____ social relationships. Because of depression, they also sometimes (b) _____ responsibilities. They may even (c) _____ psychological help because they are not used to dealing with doctors for psychological problems.

4. Mr. Johnson is getting older. His hair (a) _____ his forehead. Next year he plans to (b) _____ his job.

FOCUS 4   Verb + *For* Clusters

EXAMPLES	EXPLANATION
(a) I **long for** a cigarette every morning. (b) I **pray for** the strength to stop smoking.	Several verb + *for* clusters relate to desire or need.

Other examples of verb + *for* clusters are:

ask for	thirst for	hope for	yearn for	wish for

EXERCISE 5

Use several of the verb + preposition clusters above to describe desires for yourself or someone you love.

Example: I hope for better health for my whole family.

EXERCISE 6

Select one or two of the groups of preposition clusters below. Create one to two short paragraphs for each group of verb + preposition clusters and then share the results with your class.

Example: rebel at, shudder at, jeer at

*The people held up their fists and **jeered at** the tanks as they moved into the city. They had been **rebelling at** following the central government for the past 25 years. They **shuddered at** the thought of military rule in their own quiet neighborhoods.*

1. talk of, think of, disapprove of
2. listen to, object to, reply to
3. plan on, embark on, live on

4. believe in, persist in, result in
5. look at, laugh at, point at

EXERCISE 7

Study the chart on the next page about immigration movements to the United States. Use different verbs + *for* to describe why the different groups came to the United States.

Example: Cubans   *The Cubans longed for freedom in a non-Communist country.*

1. Irish
2. Germans
3. Norwegians
4. Poles
5. Jews

6. Austrians
7. Italians
8. Mexicans
9. Haitians
10. Vietnamese

What other immigrant groups are coming to the United States today? Why?

MAJOR IMMIGRATION MOVEMENTS TO THE UNITED STATES

Group	When	Number	Why
Irish	1840s and 1850s	About 1½ million	Famine resulting from potato crop failure
Germans	1840s to 1880s	About 4 million	Severe economic depression and unemployment; political unrest, and failure of liberal revolutionary movement
Danes, Norwegians, Swedes	1870s to 1900s	About 1½ million	Poverty; shortage of farmland
Poles	1880s to 1920s	About 1 million	Poverty; political repression; cholera epidemics
Jews from Eastern Europe	1880s to 1920s	About 2½ million	Religious persecution
Austrians, Czechs, Hungarians, Slovaks	1880s to 1920s	About 4 million	Poverty; overpopulation
Italians	1880s to 1920s	About 4½ million	Poverty; overpopulation
Mexicans	1910 to 1920s	About 700,000	Mexican Revolution of 1920; low wages and unemployment
	1950s to present	About 2 million	Poverty; unemployment
Cubans	1960s to present	About 700,000	Communist takeover in 1959
Dominicans, Haitians, Jamaicans	1970s and 1990s	About 900,000	Poverty; unemployment
Vietnamese	1970s and 1990s	About 500,000	Vietnam War 1957 to 1975; Communist takeover
Iranians	1980s to 2000s	About 200,000	Political unrest; religious persecution
Chinese	1990s to 2000s	About 600,000	Poverty; Communist takeover of Hong Kong

Adapted from U.S. Immigration and Naturalization Service and Bureau of U.S. Citizenship and Immigration Service sources.

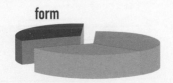

form

FOCUS 5 Adjective + Preposition Clusters

EXAMPLES	EXPLANATION
(a) The house stands **adjacent to** the river. (b) The town is **dependent on** fishing.	Adjective + preposition clusters
(c) We **are burdened with** high taxes. (d) Miwa **is accustomed to** eating three meals a day.	*Be* + adjective (*-ed*) + preposition clusters

Other examples of adjective + preposition clusters are:

free ⎫
immune ⎬ from
safe ⎭

eager ⎫
homesick ⎬ for
sorry ⎭

compatible ⎫
unfamiliar ⎬ with
content ⎭

expert ⎫
good ⎬ at
swift ⎭

proficient ⎫
rich ⎬ in
successful ⎭

careless ⎫
happy ⎬ about
enthusiastic ⎭

ignorant ⎫
afraid ⎬ of
proud ⎭

EXERCISE 7

Create your own questions for the following answers, using two different adjective + preposition phrases from the chart above.

Examples: A healthy mathematician *Who is **free from** disease and **good at** math?*

A sloppy executive *Who is **careless about** his appearance and **successful in** his job?*

1. A calm athlete

   _____

   _____

2. A claustrophobic politician

   _____

   _____

3. An anxious addict

   _____

   _____

4. A clean mechanic

_____

_____

5. A weary worrier

_____

_____

6. A joyful seamstress

_____

_____

7. A repentant runner

_____

_____

8. (Your suggestion)

_____

_____

EXERCISE 8

Discuss what the following organizations are *interested in, concerned about, accustomed to, committed to, dedicated to*, and/or *preoccupied with.* Also, come up with another organization to discuss.

Example: The World Bank

   The World Bank is interested in aiding the world's poor.

1. Greenpeace
2. European Community
3. The Peace Corps
4. The United Nations
5. The Red Cross
6. The Red Crescent
7. UNICEF
8. The Fulbright Program
9. Amnesty International
10. (Your suggestion)

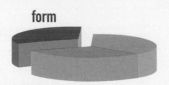

FOCUS 6 | Multiword Preposition Clusters

Some preposition clusters consist of three or more words.

EXAMPLES	EXPLANATIONS
(a) Some refugee groups are **at odds with** immigrants from other countries. (b) **In case of** an emergency, please call campus security.	Multiword preposition clusters follow this pattern: *preposition + (article) noun + preposition.* Many clusters use *in* or *on* as the first preposition and *of* as the second preposition.

Common multiword clusters:

in + noun + *of*	*on* + noun + *of*	*in* + *the* + noun + *of*	*on* + *the* + noun + *of*
in case of	on account of	in the course of	on the advice of
in charge of	on behalf of	in the event of	on the basis of
in place of	on top of	in the habit of	on the part of
in lieu of	on grounds of	in the name of	on the strength of
in favor of		in the process of	on the face of

Less regular combinations:

by means of	in return for	at odds with	with the exception of
with respect to	in addition to	for the sake of	

▮ EXERCISE 9

Write *in (the)* or *on (the)* in the following blanks; the first one has been done for you.

Example: ___On the___ basis of the evidence, the defendant was acquitted.

1. _____ case of an emergency, duck under your desks and cover your heads.

2. _____ account of his great skill, he completed the task with ease.

3. _____ advice of my physician, I must take these pills and get plenty of rest.

4. I have decided to buy the warehouse _____ strength of expert opinion.

5. _____ event of an earthquake, do not panic.

6. She wants a divorce _____ grounds of mental cruelty.

7. He will pay the bail _____ lieu of staying in jail.

8. She is _____ habit of joking when she should be serious.

9. _____ behalf of the committee, I would like to thank you for all of your work.

10. _____ course of the evening, everyone laughed and had a good time.

Working with a partner, fill in the following blanks with the expressions below. Compare your answers with those of your classmates.

in the habit of	with reference to	for the sake of
as a consequence of	with the purpose of	in lieu of
for lack of	with an eye to	for fear of
on account of	in addition to	

Example: __With reference to__ your question, many Afghans are living in Pakistan and Iran.

1. The United States is _____ turning back many Mexicans from its southern border.

2. Bulgarians of Turkish descent are emigrating from Bulgaria _____ reuniting with their families in Turkey.

3. European Jews and North American Jews have inhabited Israel _____ recreating a Jewish homeland.

4. _____ economic incentives, many British have been lured to move to New Zealand.

5. Indonesians live in tents and makeshift huts _____ funds to rebuild their homes after the tsunami.

6. Salvadoreans do not want to return to El Salvador from the United States _____ encountering dangerous gangs and sexual discrimination.

7. After 1975 many Cambodians escaped into Thailand _____ humane treatment.

8. _____ Moroccans and Tunisians, Senegalese have immigrated to Italy to find work.

9. _____ starvation, Nigerians, Ugandans, Sudanese, and Chadian have fled to other African countries.

10. _____ staying in Romania, many Romanians of Hungarian descent are moving to Hungary.

Preposition Clusters: Introducing a Topic/Identifying a Source

use

EXAMPLES	EXPLANATIONS
(a) **Pertaining/Relating to** immigrant quotas, the United States has tightened its restrictions in recent years.	Some preposition clusters can introduce a topic.
(b) **Speaking about/of** persecution, certain immigrant groups have endured more than others.	
(c) **With respect/reference to** culture shock, most immigrant groups experience it in one form or another.	
(d) **Based on/upon** immigration statistics, more men than women emigrate from their native countries.	Other preposition clusters can identify a source.
(e) **According to** Professor Herbert, many immigrants decide to return to their native countries after a few years.	

EXERCISE 11

Complete the following sentences.

Example: Based on the weather report, <u>hurricane conditions will prevail for this week</u>.

1. According to scientists, _____.

2. With respect to our solar system, _____.

3. With reference to recent political events, _____.

4. Speaking about discrimination, _____.

5. Relating to my last conversation with my family, _____.

6. Based upon my own observations, _____.

7. According to the dictionary, _____.

8. Pertaining to the death penalty, _____.

9. With respect to the students in this class, _____.

10. Speaking of good movies, _____.

EXERCISE 12

Supply the appropriate prepositions for the blanks in the following passage.

People have migrated (1) _____from_____ one country to another throughout time. The first humans emerged (2) _____ Africa and spread throughout the globe. A momentous movement of "barbarians" (consisting (3) _____ such groups as the Huns, Goths, Visigoths, and Vandals) departed (4) _____ Central Asia and were successful (5) _____ toppling the Roman Empire. The Islamic Moors crossed over (6) _____ Arabia into Europe, Central Asia, and the Balkans. The Vikings migrated (7) _____ Norway and Sweden into Russia.

    Recent migrations include a large number of Europeans and Africans moving (8) _____ North and South America, Indians moving (9) _____ all parts of the former British Empire, Chinese settling (10) _____ Southeast Asia, and Mexicans crossing (11) _____ to the United States.

    Why do people migrate (12) _____ one region (13) _____ another? They may flee (14) _____ serious environmental conditions like earthquakes and floods or dangerous political situations like wars and rebellions. They may be in search (15) _____ better economic conditions. Or on the advice (16) _____ family or friends, they decide that a new location will be better for raising a family or for retirement.

    According (17) _____ experts, several barriers limit migration. People may be ignorant (18) _____ what exists in other places. They may be accustomed (19) _____ their own homes and find it too difficult to leave. They may be unfamiliar (20) _____ foreign immigration policies. In addition (21) _____ these factors, there are other personal characteristics which limit migration, including age, gender, and education. For example, a well-educated young male differs (22) _____ a poor uneducated female in his ability and willingness to move (23) _____ one country to another.

Use Your English

Listen to the audio and take notes about the administration of President John F. Kennedy, one of the most famous U.S. presidents of the twentieth century. After listening to the audio, answer the following questions, using preposition clusters in each response.

CD Track 24   **Example:** What is one positive cause that JFK contributed to?
He contributed to the establishment of the Peace Corps.

1. What was Kennedy's administration known for?
2. How did he unite with Americans of all colors and religions?
3. What were the elderly happy about?
4. Speaking about school segregation, what did Kennedy do?
5. Who cooperated with local technicians to build roads in Tanganyika, Africa?
6. Who did the United States join with to form the Organization for Economic Cooperation and Development?
7. What were the Latin Americans enthusiastic about in 1962?
8. Why did the United States and Russia consult with each other?

> Give me your tired, your poor
> Your huddled masses yearning to breathe free,
> The wretched refuse of your teeming shore.
> Send them, the homeless, tempest-tossed to me,
> I lift my lamp beside the golden door!

Do you believe it is possible for countries such as the United States to have an open-door policy? How has the open-door immigration policy of the United States changed over the last few decades? Do you agree or disagree with the changes? Write a short composition on this topic, incorporating at least five preposition clusters you have learned in this unit.

ACTIVITY 3 listening/writing

Watch 15 minutes of a nature TV show or video that describes the life cycles, migration patterns, communication habits, etc. of an animal (for example, polar bear, bumblebee, salmon, jackrabbit, Canada goose). Jot down examples of preposition clusters that you hear.

Example: *Canada geese depart from their homes in the north and fly south for the winter.*

ACTIVITY 4 research on the web

The following terms relate to intercultural contact or movement from, to, or within a country. Find definitions of the following terms on the Internet, using a search engine. Give definitions of these terms while citing your specific sources, using the expression *according to,* for example, *"**According to** the Internet, a **refugee** is any uprooted person who has a well-founded fear of persecution for reasons of race, religion, nationality, membership in a particular social group, or political opinion."*

1. refugee
2. emigrant
3. guest worker
4. brain drain
5. multiculturalism
6. political correctness
7. melting pot
8. xenophobia

ACTIVITY 5 reflection

Knowing vocabulary means knowing how different words collocate or group together. With a partner, consider words you encounter in your academic texts and brainstorm:

a. What words depend on this word as a root?

Example: migrate   *migration, migratory, immigration, immigrant*

b. What other words are associated with or co-occur with this word?

Example: migrate   *migrate to, migrate away from*

c. What words are similar to and/or different from this word? Does the word have a synonym or antonym?

Example: migrate   *similar: immigrate, move   different: remain stationary*

GERUNDS AND INFINITIVES

UNIT GOALS

- Identify the functions of gerunds and infinitives in a sentence

- Use a variety of gerund and infinitive structures correctly

- Distinguish gerunds from infinitives

- Use *for* with infinitives and *'s* with gerunds

- Use gerunds as objects of prepositions and phrasal verbs

OPENING TASK

Skills and Qualifications

You and a partner have been asked to consider the strengths and weaknesses of the following ten applicants described on the next page for "Altacreat," an artistic community in the northwestern United States designed to provide artistic space for ten artists in residence for periods of up to three months. Specially designed studios inspire "cutting-edge" artistic creations and common eating, and conversation spaces provide contexts for global intellectual exchange after the day's work is done.

Altacreat has individual apartments and studios for each artist, all room and board paid for by scholarships, a library, a computer center, and communications facilities for all artists, the capability to receive international newspapers, mail, and television broadcasts, 24-hour computer access, and interactions with the public through on-site visits by local schools and businesses.

STEP 1

In pairs, jot down ideas about why you think each person in the chart that follows might like to be a candidate. Think about why he or she would want to be part of the center and what positive skills or characteristics he or she could bring. The first one has been done as an example.

CANDIDATE	RATIONALE
Composer: Female, wife of architect, Korean, 25 years old Specialization: classical piano	Playing the piano could entertain and inspire the other artists to design better creations. She might also want to co-design with her husband (if he is also selected) modern piano studios for home and commercial use.
Architect: Male, husband of piano composer, Japanese, 35 years old Specialization: modern styles mixed with very traditional	
Novelist: Female, Hungarian, 40 years old, married, expects to have a baby in one month Specialization: novels about gypsies in Europe	
Opera Singer: Female, Russian, 32 years old, single Specialization: dramatic, passionate roles in Italian operas	
Screenplay Writer: Female, wife of filmmaker, 39 years old, American (U.S.) Specialization: detective mysteries	
Filmmaker: Male, husband of screenplay writer, 60 years old, Mexican Specialization: love stories	
Poet: Male, 28 years old, Vietnamese, widowed Specialization: effects of technology on everyday life	
Landscape Architect: Female, 23 years old, Brazilian, single Specialization: sunken gardens	
Artist: Female, 36 years old, Turkish, married Specialization: geometric mosaics	
Digital Artist: Female, 28 years old, Chinese, single Specialization: collecting photos from Webcams and arranging them in displays	

STEP 2

Share the results of your brainstorming with your classmates.

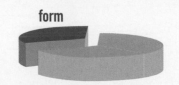

FOCUS 1 — Overview of Gerunds and Infinitives

EXAMPLES	EXPLANATIONS
	Infinitives (*to* + verb) or gerunds (verb + *-ing*) can have various functions in a sentence:
(a) **Speaking English** is fun.	**Subject:** Gerunds and infinitives can function as subjects. However, it is more common for infinitives that are subjects to move to the end of the sentence with *it* as the new subject.
(b) **To compose a sonata** would take months.	
(c) It would take months **to compose a sonata.**	
(d) His dream was **to direct the ultimate Mexican love story.**	**Subject Complement:** A subject complement follows *be* and refers back to the subject of the sentence.
(e) Her hobby is **weaving baskets.**	
(f) I don't understand the need **to take a ten-minute break.**	**Noun Complement:** Noun complements explain the nouns that they refer to. The infinitive can be a complement to certain abstract nouns (for example, *advice, decision, desire, fact, opportunity, order, plan, possibility, proposal, request, refusal, requirement, suggestion, way, wish*). (See Unit 21, Focus 1, for a more extensive list of abstract nouns.)
(g) The instruction **to wear safety goggles** has saved many people's eyes.	

EXAMPLES	EXPLANATIONS
(h) I am sorry **to inform you of the delay.**	**Adjective Complement:** Certain adjectives can be followed by infinitives. These include:
(i) They were pleased **to meet you.**	

afraid	*disappointed*	*pleased*
amazed	*eager*	*proud*
anxious	*eligible*	*ready*
apt	*(un)fit*	*reluctant*
ashamed	*fortunate*	*sad*
bound	*glad*	*shocked*
careful	*happy*	*sorry*
certain	*hesitant*	*sure*
content	*liable*	*surprised*
delighted	*likely*	*upset*
determined		

EXAMPLES	EXPLANATIONS
(j) Paco hopes **to see the play.**	**Direct Object:** A direct object follows a verb. Depending upon the verb and accompanying meaning, the object may be an infinitive or a gerund.
(k) Carol remembered **mailing the package.**	
(l) **By studying hard,** you can enter a good school.	**Object of Preposition:** Gerunds, not infinitives, are objects of prepositions.
(m) Thank you **for helping me.**	
(n) **NOT:** He lost the deal because of wait too long.	

Read the following text and underline all gerunds and infinitives. Then identify the function of each one (subject, subject complement, noun complement, adjective complement, direct object, or object of preposition).

(1) Alan Loy McGinnis in his book *Bringing Out the Best in People* (Augsburg Publishing House, Minneapolis, 1985) describes 12 important principles or rules for helping people to perform to the best of their ability. (2) The first rule is to expect the best from the people you lead. (3) A true leader needs to drop the role of "watch-dog" and to display a positive attitude toward everyone who works under him or her. (4) The second principle is to make a thorough study of the other person's needs. (5) Walking a mile in another person's shoes will allow a leader to truly understand someone he or she is working with. (6) The third rule is to establish high standards of excellence. (7) Many people have never learned the pleasure of setting high standards and living up to them. (8) The fourth rule is to create an environment where failure is not fatal. (9) People who expect to succeed all of the time often cannot rise from a failure. (10) An effective motivator needs to know how to help people deal with their failure.

(11) "Climbing on other people's bandwagons" is the fifth principle that McGinnis suggests. (12) A good leader needs to identify the beliefs and causes of the people that he or she works with. (13) By using these good ideas, he or she can encourage them to pursue as many of these goals as possible. (14) Employing models to encourage success is the sixth rule. (15) Everyone loves hearing about true success stories of others to build confidence and motivation. Recognizing and applauding achievement is the seventh rule. (16) A good leader tries to look for strengths in people and catch them "doing something right" so that he or she can compliment them.

(17) The eighth rule is to employ a mixture of positive and negative reinforcement. (18) Using praise is only one of many methods used to motivate. (19) Sometimes a person does his or her best because he or she is afraid to be punished. (20) The ninth and tenth rules relate to appealing sparingly to the competitive urge and placing a premium on collaboration. (21) Some competition is good; however, the decision to work with other people creates good morale and allows the job to be completed more efficiently.

(22) The eleventh principle is to learn how to deal with troublemakers in a group. (23) A leader who does not learn how to handle a problematic person will never learn how to stay in difficult situations and solve them. (24) Finally, the twelfth rule is to find ways to keep the motivation of the leader, himself or herself, high. (25) Renewing oneself through sports, reading, going to a restful spot, etc. are all necessary for the good leader to become energized and to successfully perform the other eleven principles.

Which functions of gerunds and infinitives are most common in this selection? Is the "*to*-verb" structure always a complement? What other meaning can it have? (Hint: Review sentences 15 and 18.)

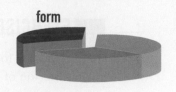

form

FOCUS 2	Infinitives and Gerunds in Perfective, Progressive, and Passive

EXAMPLES	EXPLANATIONS
(a) Eva's plan has always been **to return** to her homeland.	simple infinitive (*to* + verb)
(b) She hoped **to have earned** an Olympic gold medal by the time she was 20.	perfective infinitive (*to* + *have* + past participle)
(c) Their goal is **to be working** by March.	progressive infinitive (*to* + *be* + present participle)
(d) We wanted **to have been swimming** by now.	perfective progressive infinitive (*to* + *have* + *been* + present participle)
(e) The suggestion **to be seen** by a surgeon was never followed.	passive infinitive (*to* + *be* + past participle)
(f) They were happy **to have been chosen** for the award.	perfective passive infinitive (*to* + *have* + *been* + past participle)
(g) Part of the problem **is** not **knowing** enough.	simple gerund (verb + *-ing*)
(h) She was excited about **having watched** the race from start to finish.	perfective gerund (*having* + past participle)
(i) **Being appointed** to the board of directors is a great responsibility.	passive gerund (*being* + past participle)
(j) **Having been selected** for the experiment gave her career a boost.	perfective passive gerund (*having been* + past participle)

EXERCISE 2

With a partner, discuss the following topics using infinitives and gerunds. Use the appropriate simple, perfective, progressive, or passive form and give reasons for your response for each item.

Example: a movie you enjoyed seeing
I enjoyed seeing "Star Wars I" because I like science fiction.

1. a holiday food you like to eat

2. a present you would like to be surprised with

3. a sport you enjoy playing

4. a place you are excited about having seen

5. another name you would like to have been named

6. a job you would like to be doing right now

7. a famous person in history you would like to have met

8. a topic you would like to have been studying by now

9. a story you liked being told as a child

10. a feeling you had after having been recognized for something

EXERCISE 3

A woman received a $1000 prize for winning a short-story writing contest. Her acceptance speech appears below. Fill in the appropriate gerund or infinitive. In some cases, more than one answer may be correct.

It is a great honor (award) _to be awarded_ this generous prize tonight.
(1) _____ (present) an award for something that I enjoy doing anyway thrills me. (2) _____ (say) that I am indebted to my parents would be an understatement. (3) _____ (have) parents who were trained as teachers gave me an important start. From the time I was very young, (4) _____ (study) four hours every day after school was required. It was a frequent sight (5) _____ (see) my siblings discussing main points and rehearsing the answers to problems. (6) _____ (scold) by our parents for not paying enough attention to our work would have been the greatest shame.

   Besides doing my homework for school, (7) _____ (read) fiction and nonfiction books took up much of my leisure time. (8) _____ (read) so many types of books by the time I got to college proved to be a marvelous advantage. (9) _____ (see) so many good written models allowed me to creatively and effortlessly produce my own work for my university English classes.

   Today, it requires more discipline for me (10) _____ (be) a good writer. (11) _____ (marry) with three children leaves less time to write. It requires initiative (12) _____ (arise) every day at 5:00 A.M. to write. (13) _____ (write) in this manner is the only way that I have been able to produce several short stories and a few poems. (14) _____ (not receive) very good marks on my essay pieces in college, I have left essay writing to some other writer! Well, I can see that my time is up. It has been an honor (15) _____ (select) as the winner of this contest and I thank my parents, family, and all of you for your recognition today.

EXERCISE 4

Fill in the following blanks with appropriate infinitives. More than one answer may be possible.

Example: The requirement _to wear_ a spacesuit is an essential rule for the astronaut to follow.

1. Few people have made the decision ＿＿＿＿＿＿＿＿ an astronaut.

2. The proposal ＿＿＿＿＿＿＿＿ expendable rockets with rockets that could return to Earth saved a great deal of money for the taxpayer.

3. The space program strictly heeded the advice ＿＿＿＿＿＿＿＿ the astronauts for 18 days after their flight to the Moon in order to assure their good health.

4. The suggestion ＿＿＿＿＿＿＿＿ a "moon base" would allow much useful scientific research.

5. A precaution ＿＿＿＿＿＿＿＿ after every spaceflight includes isolating lunar samples until the scientific team is satisfied that no risk of contamination remains.

6. The decision ＿＿＿＿＿＿＿＿ space-walks occurred in 1964 with Project Mercury.

7. The first words ＿＿＿＿＿＿＿＿ by Neil Armstrong as he stepped on to the surface of the moon were "That's one small step for a man; a giant leap for mankind."

8. The next challenge ＿＿＿＿＿＿＿＿ is a mission to Mars.

EXERCISE 5

With a partner, take turns asking and answering the following questions. Use an adjective complement in each of your responses.

Example: What are you bound to do after you finish your schooling?
I am bound to get a job as a computer technician.

1. What type of food are you hesitant to eat?

2. What are you apt to do in the next few weeks?

3. Which clubs here or in your native country are you eligible to join?

4. What sport are you reluctant to try?

5. What movie are you likely to see in the next few weeks?

6. Which country would you be delighted to visit?

7. Which student in your class is most liable to be successful?

8. What are you sure to do after your class today?

9. Which friend are you most happy to know?

10. What movie star or musical star would you be ready to meet?

meaning

FOCUS 3 Gerunds versus Infinitives

Certain types of verbs (verbs of emotion, verbs of completion/incompletion, and verbs of remembering) can be affected by the choice of infinitive or gerund.

EXAMPLES	EXPLANATIONS
(a) **To eat** too much sugar is not healthy. (b) **Eating** too much sugar is not healthy.	Infinitive and gerunds as objects and subjects sometimes have equivalent meanings.
(c) ACTUAL: For the time being, **I prefer being** a housewife. (d) POTENTIAL: When my children are grown, I would **prefer** *to get* a job outside the home. (e) ACTUAL: **Playing** golf every day is boring. (f) POTENTIAL: **To play** golf every day would be my idea of a happy retirement.	In other cases, we choose an infinitive or gerund by the meaning of an action. We often use gerunds to describe an actual, vivid, or fulfilled action. We often use infinitives to describe potential, hypothetical, or future events.

(Continued on next page)

Verbs of Emotion

ACTUAL EVENT	POTENTIAL EVENT
(g) Did you **like** *dancing* that night? You seemed to be having a good time.	(h) Do you **like** *to dance?* I know a good nightclub.
(i) Tim **hates** *quarreling* with his wife over every little thing.	(j) Tim **hates** *to quarrel* with his wife. It would be the last thing he would want to do.
(k) **I preferred** *studying* astronomy over physics.	(l) **I prefer** *to study* physics next year.

Verbs of Completion/Incompletion

ACTUAL EVENT	POTENTIAL EVENT
(m) I **started** *doing* my homework. Question #1 is especially hard.	(n) Did you **start** *to do* your homework?
(o) Did you **continue** *watching* the program yesterday after I left?	(p) Will you **continue** *to watch* the program after I leave?
(q) He **began** *speaking* with a hoarse voice that no one could understand.	(r) He **began** *to speak*, but was interrupted by the lawyer.
(s) She **stopped** *listening* whenever she was bored.	(t) She **stopped** *to listen* to the bird that was singing. (Note: *to* means "in order to.")
(u) They **finished** *reading* the book.	(v) I will **finish** *reading* this book before I go shopping. (Note: *Finish* always requires a gerund.)
	(w) **NOT:** I will finish to read the book.

Verbs of Remembering

EXAMPLES	TIME SEQUENCE	EXPLANATION
(x) Tom **remembered** *closing* the door.	First: Tom closed the door. Then: Tom remembered that he did so.	Besides the real event and potential event meanings, *remember, forget,* and *regret* signal different time sequence meanings when we use a gerund or an infinitive.
(y) Tom **remembered** *to close* the door.	First: Tom remembered that he needed to close the door. Then: Tom closed the door.	

EXERCISE 6

In the Opening Task on pages 330 and 331, you and your classmates considered the candidates for Altcreat. At the last minute, the media released new information about the candidates based on several confidential interviews. Read and select the correct verb in each of the quotes that follow. In some cases, both verbs may be correct. Explain why one verb or both verbs are correct.

Example: **Composer:** I would like (to go/going) only if my husband could go.
*(**To go** is preferred because the situation is hypothetical.)*

1. **Composer:** (To work/working) at Altacreat without my husband would be dreadful.

2. **Poet:** I love (to smoke/smoking). As a matter of fact, I smoke three packs of cigarettes a day.

3. **Artist:** (To paint/painting) in silence is impossible. I cannot get anything done unless two or three people are talking around me.

4. **Novelist:** I mean (to stay/staying) at Altacreat only until my baby is born.

5. **Landscape Architect:** I hated (to work/working) in cold weather when I went to school in Wisconsin. That's why I transferred to another university where the climate was warmer.

6. **Architect:** (To pass/passing) the Architectural Boards Exam this fall is my intention. Unfortunately, I have already failed it twice.

7. **Opera Singer:** I would not like (to fly/flying) to Altacreat in the United States because I have acrophobia.

8. **Digital Artist:** I regret (to inform/informing) the committee in my application that I was a digital artist because I actually have limited knowledge of computers.

9. **Filmmaker:** I will continue (to benefit/benefiting) from this experience even after I return to Mexico.

10. **Screenplay Writer:** Did I remember (to tell/telling) you that funding for future Altacreat projects will be one of my major publicity campaigns once my three-month project is finished?

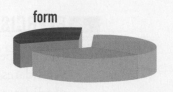

FOCUS 4

Gerunds and Infinitives as Direct Objects

EXAMPLES	EXPLANATIONS
	Another way to predict the form of a direct object complement (either gerund or infinitive) is by the choice of verb in the base sentence.
(a) Scientists **appear** to be getting close to an explanation.	• An infinitive must follow *want, need, hope, promise,* and *appear* (and other verbs in List A on page A-8). Notice here that many of these verbs (although not all) signal potential events, a meaning of infinitives discussed in Focus 3.
(b) **NOT:** Scientists appear being getting close to an explanation.	
(c) Juan **hates** (for) **Grace** to worry.	• Some verbs from List A (*desire, hate, like, love,* and *prefer*) may optionally include *for* with the infinitive complement when the infinitive has an explicit subject.
(d) Einstein **convinced other scientists** to reject Newtonian physics.	• *Advise, convince, invite,* and *warn* (and other verbs in List B on page A-9) are followed by infinitive complements with explicit subjects.
(e) **NOT:** Einstein convinced to reject Newtonian physics.	
(f) **NOT:** Einstein convinced other scientists rejecting Newtonian physics.	
(g) Einstein **risked** introducing a new theory to the world.	• *Appreciate, enjoy, postpone, risk,* and *quit* (and other verbs in List C on pages A-9 and A-10) take only gerunds. Notice that many of these verbs (although not all) signal actual events, a meaning of gerunds discussed in Focus 3.
(h) **NOT:** Einstein risked to introduce a new theory to the world.	

Read the following text. Underline all direct object infinitives, and circle all direct object gerunds. (Not every sentence may have one.)

Then, make a list of the verb + infinitive or gerund combinations that you find.

Example:

Verb	+	Infinitive		Verb	+	Gerund
learn		*to speak*		*prefer*		*saying*

Einstein's Early Education

(1) Albert Einstein was born in Ulm, Germany, in 1879. (2) Because he learned <u>to speak</u> at a late age, his parents feared that he was retarded. (3) Modern observers prefer (saying) that he was a daydreamer. (4) When he was 5 years old, Einstein began to attend a Catholic school. (5) One instructor was especially critical of his abilities and told his parents that it did not matter what field young Albert chose because he would not succeed in it. (6) In 1889, Einstein transferred to a very strict German school called the Luitpold Gymnasium. (7) The rigid structure forced Einstein to distrust authority and become skeptical.

(8) At age 12, Einstein picked up a mathematics textbook and began teaching himself geometry. (9) By 1894, Einstein's father's business had failed to prosper, and the family moved to Italy. (10) Einstein, however, remained behind and began feeling lonely and unhappy. (11) Consequently, he paid less attention to his studies and was finally asked by one of the teachers to leave. (12) He joined his family in Italy but was not able to matriculate at a university because he did not have a diploma. (13) When he heard that a diploma was not necessary to enter at the Swiss Polytechnique Institute in Zurich, he decided to apply.

(14) Einstein traveled to Switzerland but did not pass the entrance examination. (15) He was not prepared well enough in biology and languages, so he enrolled in the Gymnasium at Aarau to prepare himself in his weaker subjects. (16) Albert enjoyed studying in Aarau more than at the Luitpold Gymnasium because the teachers wanted to teach students how to think. (17) He took the exam again and was finally permitted to matriculate into a four-year program. (18) Einstein did not excel during these years at the Institute. (19) In fact, he rarely attended the lectures. (20) He read his books at home and borrowed his classmates' notes to pass tests.

(21) When Einstein graduated in 1900, he failed to obtain a position at the Institute. (22) His professors did not intend to reward Einstein's lackadaisical attitude toward classes with a position. (23) Because he did not get an academic appointment, he worked at the Swiss Patent Office. (24) He worked there for several years until he was offered an appointment as Associate Professor of Physics at the University of Zurich. (25) It was there that Einstein's revolutionary theories of space-time began to take hold and threatened to destroy the reputations of other colleagues who had built their careers on Newton's ideas of a clockwork universe.

What meaning does the "*to*-verb" structure have in sentences 15 and 20?

EXERCISE 8

Complete the following sentences based on the passage in Exercise 7. Use an infinitive or gerund. The first one has been done for you.

Example: As a baby, Einstein appeared <u>to be</u> retarded.

1. As a young child, he failed _____ his teachers.

2. At age twelve, Einstein decided _____ himself geometry.

3. Einstein neglected _____ his homework.

4. When Einstein's family left for Italy, he quit _____.

5. Because of this, one teacher advised him _____ school.

6. Without his family, he couldn't help _____ lonely.

7. He didn't mind _____ his family in Italy.

8. Unfortunately, he couldn't begin _____ at a university without a diploma.

9. He tried _____ the Swiss Polytechnique but could not pass the entrance exam.

10. He regretted _____ the entrance exam the first time.

11. Professors at the Polytechnique declined _____ Einstein a position because of his lackadaisical academic performance.

12. As a clerk at the Swiss Patent Office, he continued _____ about physics.

13. The University of Zurich invited Einstein _____ a faculty member.

14. Many professors couldn't help _____ Einstein's unusual ideas.

15. Soon he began _____ well-established professors with his revolutionary theories.

EXERCISE 9

Look back at the notes you made for the Opening Task on page 331 and additional information you learned in Exercise 6. Assume that only five of the applicants can be chosen for the three-month project at Altacreat.

STEP 1   In pairs, rank order the applicants from 1 (= most desirable) to 10 (= least desirable). Consider what might be the appropriate mix of males and females, whether married couples or singles are preferable, what skills and abilities are most essential for global exchange, what compatibility factors should be considered, etc.

STEP 2   As a class, come to a consensus about which five applicants would be most desirable.

STEP 3   After this discussion, answer the following questions.

1. Who has the class chosen to be the top five finalists?
2. Was there any candidate that you personally regretted eliminating?
3. Did any of your classmates persuade you to select someone that you had not originally selected?

FOCUS 5   *For* with Infinitives and *'s* with Gerunds

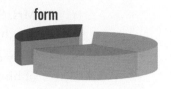

form

EXAMPLES	EXPLANATIONS
(a) (**For people**) to see is a wonderful gift. (b) (**Your**) neglecting your teeth will cause an earlier return to your dentist.	The subject of an infinitive or a gerund is often not stated but can be implied from context. It will either have a general reference or a specific one that can be determined from other references in the sentence or paragraph.
(c) **For a Russian** to be the first man in space was commendable. (d) Her desire was **for them** to take a trip around the world.	When an infinitive functions as a subject or a subject complement, any stated subject of the infinitive should be preceded by *for*. If a pronoun follows *for*, it must be in object form.
(e) They hoped **for her** to be able to attend the concert. (f) I expected (**for**) **him** to be there when I finished. (g) We advised **the couple** to postpone their marriage.	When the infinitive functions as a direct object, its stated subject should take object form if it is a pronoun and may or may not be preceded by *for*. Three options are possible depending on the verb. (See Focus 4.)
(h) **Their denying the allegation** was understandable. (i) I didn't like **the dog's barking** all night.	When the subject of a gerund is stated, it takes the possessive form.

EXERCISE 10

Read the descriptions of problem situations. Following each description is a statement about the problem. Fill in the blank with *for* + *noun/pronoun* or a possessive construction to complete each sentence.

Example: Sue went to a party. Ralph did not speak to her all evening. Sue disliked
Ralph's ignoring her at the party.

1. Burt did not get enough sleep last night. He ended up yelling at Mrs. Gonzalez, his boss. _____ yelling at his boss was a big mistake.

2. Mrs. Sutherland warned students to do their own work during the test. Sue got caught cheating. _____ to get caught cheating was shameful.

3. Tony did not watch where he was going and ran into the rear end of the car in front of him. The driver of the car resented _____ hitting her car.

4. Nina always goes to bed at 9:00 P.M. Her friend, Nathan, forgot and called her house at 11:00 P.M. Nina was very angry. Nina expected _____ to call at an earlier hour the next time.

5. Bill's grandmother mailed him a birthday package, which arrived a week before his birthday. Bill couldn't wait and opened the package early. Bill's mother was upset about _____ opening the present before his birthday.

6. Ursula left the house when it was still dark. When she got to school, she noticed that she was wearing one black shoe and one brown shoe. _____ to leave the house without checking her shoes was very silly.

7. Mrs. Lu has several children who make a lot of noise everywhere they go. All of her neighbors are very upset. _____ to let her children run wild angers the neighbors.

8. Michelle has asked Than to go to the movies several times. Than always tells her that he can't because he has to watch a TV show, do his homework, call his mother, etc. Michelle is tired of _____ making excuses.

EXERCISE 11

Read the following sentences. Write *C* beside correct sentences and *I* beside the incorrect sentences and make all necessary corrections. Be sure to refer to Focuses 3, 4, and 5 to review the rules.

Example: ⊥ He agrees speak at the convention.

1. _____ I expected him to see me from the balcony, but he didn't.
2. _____ They intended interviewing the ambassador the last week in November.
3. _____ I regretted to tell her that she had not been sent an invitation to the party.
4. _____ Patty has chosen attending the University of Michigan in the fall.
5. _____ Have you forgotten to fasten your seat belt again?
6. _____ Terry getting married surprises me.
7. _____ Would you please stop to talk? I cannot hear the presenter.
8. _____ Did he suggest us go to a Japanese restaurant?
9. _____ She can't stand to do her homework with the radio turned on.
10. _____ Mr. and Mrs. Hunter forced their daughter's joining the social club against her will.
11. _____ For they to be traveling in Sweden is a great pleasure.
12. _____ Please remember working harder.
13. _____ Mary tends to exaggerate when she tells a story.
14. _____ I don't mind Tai to arrive a little late to the meeting.
15. _____ Would you care have a drink before we eat dinner?
16. _____ John avoided go to the dentist for three years.
17. _____ They can't afford taking a trip to the Caribbean this year.
18. _____ She coming late to the appointment was a disappointment.
19. _____ Some schools decide participating every year.
20. _____ They ceased to comply with the rules.
21. _____ Has he not offered resign?
22. _____ There complaining about discrimination is understandable.
23. _____ You starting a fight will have a negative end.
24. _____ My hope is for my children earn a good living.
25. _____ I disliked Tom repetitive questions all through the meeting.

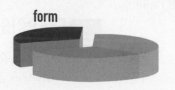

form

| FOCUS 6 | Gerunds as Objects of Prepositions and Phrasal Verbs |

EXAMPLES	EXPLANATIONS
(a) The Altacreat's selection committee could not **agree to** the poet's **being** on the list of finalists. (b) The members **argued about keeping** the novelist and the opera singer as well.	Gerunds generally follow verbs + prepositions, such as *agree to, look at, worry about,* etc.
(c) The teacher **asked for the committee to make** a decision within 20 minutes. (d) She **hoped for them to make** their announcement by 4:00.	An exception to this is when the preposition is *for* with such prepositional verbs as *ask for, ache for, care for, hope for, long for,* etc. In this case, use an infinitive with a "subject."
(e) The artists will be able to **depend on eating** gourmet meals at regular times. (f) They can **cut down on** disturbing distractions. (g) They will not **look forward to** returning to their routine lives after they leave Altacreat.	Phrasal verbs and phrasal verbs followed by prepositions (*put up with, cut down on, stand up for,* etc.) always take the gerund (not the infinitive) form. Note that the first *to* is not an infinitive marker in (g) but is a part of the phrasal verb + preposition *look forward to.*
(h) The artists are **accustomed to creating** things on their own. (i) They are **suspicious of relying** on others' intuitions.	We also use gerunds following adjective + preposition combinations such as *content with, surprised at, annoyed by.*

EXERCISE 12

Since the beginning of time, human beings have tried to understand who they were and where they came from through religious beliefs, theories, and rituals. Write general statements about these ideas, using the prompts below. Include a gerund or infinitive in each response.

Example: people believe in   (human beings evolved from apes)
Some people believe in human beings' having evolved from apes.

1. religions   insist on   (God has created living things)

_____

2. cultures   call for   (people have dietary restrictions)

_____

3.	cultures	think about	(their ancestors are pleased or displeased with them)
4.	people	hope for	(relatives are reunited in an afterlife)
5.	members	wait for	(God returns to the chosen people)
6.	believers	complain about	(other people don't believe)
7.	religions	argue about	(priests have proper authority)
8.	members	agree to	(their children are baptized)

EXERCISE 13

Read the following notes about important figures in scientific history. Write sentences about each person, using one of the following expressions: *celebrated for, famous for, good at, proficient in, renowned for, skillful in,* or *successful in.*

Examples: Aristotle, Greek philosopher, laws of motion

Aristotle was a Greek philosopher who was famous for developing theories about motion.

1. Ptolemy, Egyptian philosopher and astronomer, made charts and tables from an observatory near Alexandria, Egypt

2. Descartes, French philosopher, developed a theory of knowledge by doubting, believed intuition was the key to understanding

3. Copernicus, Polish astronomer, concluded that the sun was at the center of the universe

4. Kepler, German astronomer and mathematician, realized that planets travel in ellipses rather than circles

5. Galileo, Italian astronomer and physicist, improved the telescope; wrote *The Starry Messenger*, which refuted the prevailing theory of an earth-centered universe

6. Newton, English mathematician, determined general laws of motion and the laws of gravity

7. Einstein, German physicist, published the Special Theory of Relativity and the General Theory of Relativity, introduced the concepts of gravitational fields and curved space

Fill in the following blanks with a gerund or infinitive.

After taking off on the last Mercury mission, Gordon Cooper settled in for a good night's sleep halfway through his journey. Compared with most of the duties of spaceflight, it seemed (1) _____ to be _____ (be) an easy enough undertaking. But Cooper ended up (2) _____ (have to wedge) his hands beneath his safety harness to keep his arms from (3) _____ (float around) and (4) _____ (strike) switches on the instrument panel.

Since Cooper's flight, (5) _____ (sleep) in space has become a routine matter—maybe too routine. When carrying out an especially boring or tiring task, some astronauts have nodded off—only they didn't really nod: they simply closed their eyes and stopped (6) _____ (move). There are none of the waking mechanisms that we would expect (7) _____ (have) on earth—one's head (8) _____ (fall) to one side or a pencil (9) _____ (drop) to the floor.

Space crews have also found that they don't need handholds and ladders to get around; they quickly learn (10) _____ (push off) with one hand and float directly to their destinations. (11) _____ (eat), use a computer, or do some other stationary task, astronauts now slip their stockinged feet into loops or wedges attached to the floor. Similarly, a single Velcro head strap suffices (12) _____ (keep) sleeping astronauts from (13) _____ (drift out) toward the ventilation ducts.

A favorite recreation in space is (14) _____ (play) with one's food. Instead of carrying food all the way to their mouths with a utensil, some experienced astronauts like (15) _____ (catapult) food from spoons. Although (16) _____ (drink) coffee seems like the most natural thing on Earth, in space it won't work. If you tried (17) _____ (tip) the cup back to take a drink, the weightless coffee would not roll out. One astronaut offers the following advisory: "Don't let your curiosity tempt you into (18) _____ (explore) a larger clump of liquid than you're prepared (19) _____ (drink) later." If you don't start (20) _____ (drink) your blob with a straw, it eventually attaches itself to the nearest wall or window.

Although spaceflight has its irritations, these are necessary if astronauts are to soar. The whole idea of airborne testing is to make (21) _____ (live) and (22) _____ (work) in weightlessness easy and unremarkable for ordinary folk.

Adapted from: D. Stewart, "The Floating World at Zero G," *Air and Space* (August/September 1991): 38.

Use Your English

ACTIVITY 1 listening

Listen to the audio, a story about a famous unsolved mystery. Use information from the audio to complete each sentence below. Use a phrase containing an infinitive or a gerund based on what you have heard.

Example: *Cullen was not good at* ____conversing____.

1. _____ describes Priscilla's fashion tastes.

2. Cullen finished _____.

3. _____ was one indication of Cullen's violence.

4. Priscilla and Cullen decided _____.

5. Priscilla allowed various characters _____.

6. Cullen probably resented Priscilla's _____.

7. Beverly Bass and her friend "Bubba" Gavel tried _____.

8. Soon after the crime, the police succeeded in _____.

9. _____ was "Racehorse" Haynes's best talent.

10. "Racehorse" Haynes convinced the jury _____.

11. The prosecutors failed _____.

12. The jurors admitted _____.

ACTIVITY 2 writing

You are a news reporter called to interview a visitor from another planet. Although this creature looks very much like a human being and speaks English, you find that she has some very different characteristics. Describe what you learned from the alien as a result of your interviews. You might include some information about what the alien is accustomed to, annoyed at, capable of, concerned about, desirous of, incapable of, interested in, suited for, susceptible to, sympathetic toward, and weary of. Use at least five gerund complements in your report.

Example: *The alien has a very unusual diet. She is used to eating tree bark and grass.*

ACTIVITY **3**   research on the web

Go to the Internet to read facts about the life of one of your favorite artists, musicians, architects, or writers, using a search engine such as Google® or Yahoo®, or another source you may know. Write a short composition in which you use at least two gerund complements and four infinitive complements in your writing.

Example: Leonardo Da Vinci

Leonardo Da Vinci was a famous painter, sculptor, architect, and musician who began displaying his artistic abilities early in life. In Florence, he loved to associate with gifted artists such as Botticeli . . .

ACTIVITY **4**   reflection

Review the following learning strategies and indicate with a check (✓) the ones you enjoy doing, don't mind doing, can't stand doing, or simply forget to do. Share your chart with a partner, and discuss ways that you might improve your learning strategies.

	ENJOY DOING	DON'T MIND DOING	CAN'T STAND DOING	FORGET TO DO
Preview main ideas by skimming reading material before actually reading it.				
Check the accuracy of your oral production while you are speaking.				
Judge how well you have done a learning activity after you have completed it.				

	ENJOY DOING	DON'T MIND DOING	CAN'T STAND DOING	FORGET TO DO
Use reference materials such as dictionaries and encyclopedias to assist with learning.				
Write down key words and concepts during a listening or reading activity.				
Make a mental or written summary of information gained through listening or reading.				
Play back in your mind the sound of a word, phrase, or fact in order to assist comprehension.				
Use information in a reading text to guess meanings of new items, predict outcomes, or complete missing parts.				
Elicit from a teacher or peer additional explanations or examples.				
Work together with others to solve a problem.				
Reduce anxiety by using mental techniques to reduce stress.				

PERFECTIVE INFINITIVES

- Use the correct forms of perfective infinitives

- Use perfective infinitives to express ideas and opinions about past events

- Use perfective infinitives to express emotions and attitudes

- Use perfective infinitives to express obligations, intentions, and future plans

- Use perfective infinitives with *enough* and *too*

OPENING TASK

Time Travel to the Past

Have you ever wished you could go back in time and meet famous people from past eras, see things that no longer exist in the world, or participate in exciting historical events?

Confucius

Queen Cleopatra

Mount Fuji

STEP 1

Which of the following statements reflect things you'd like to have seen, heard, or done? Which sound less appealing to you? Rank the statements from 1 through 8, with 1 representing your first preference and 8, your last.

- observe dinosaurs when they roamed the earth _____
- speak with Confucius, the great Chinese philosopher _____
- live in an ancient Mayan city _____
- take a cruise on the Nile River in Queen Cleopatra's barge _____
- see the Japanese volcano Mount Fuji when it erupted in 1707 _____
- listen to Beethoven play his Fifth Symphony for the first time in Vienna in 1808 _____
- accompany Orville Wright on the first airplane flight in 1903 _____
- attend a performance by the famous twentieth-century American blues singer, Billie Holiday _____

STEP 2

Compare your ratings with those of a few of your classmates. Briefly explain the reasons for your top one or two choices.

Example: *I would like to have attended a performance by Billie Holiday because I've heard some of her songs, and I saw a movie about her life.*

STEP 3

Write two more statements expressing things that you would like to have seen, heard, or done.

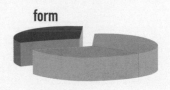

form

FOCUS 1 — Review of Perfective Infinitive Structures

Perfective infinitives (*to* + *have* + past participle) express events that are past in relation to a present, past, or future moment of focus.

EXAMPLES	EXPLANATIONS
Perfective Infinitive (a) I'd like **to have been** at the first Olympic games in Greece. (b) Many people claim **to have seen** UFOs. (c) I expect **to have finished** my term paper by tomorrow night.	**Forming the Perfective Infinitive** Perfective infinitives have the form *to* + *have* + past participle (*-ed* or irregular verb form).
	Types of Perfective Infinitive Clauses Like other infinitives, perfective infinitives occur in a number of clause types in sentences:
(d) **To have won** the Boston Marathon was a dream come true for her.	• subject
(e) It is helpful **to have reviewed** the chapter assignment before you attend the class lecture.	• postponed subject after introductory *it*
(f) I would love **to have seen** my friend's face when he opened his gift from all of us.	• object
(g) The question **to have been** debated at last week's meeting was whether our school needed a new swimming pool, but the meeting got postponed.	• adjective
(h) Research writing is a good course **to have taken**.	
(i) My sister was too young **to have known** she shouldn't have picked the flowers in the park.	• degree complement
(j) Those pants were big enough **to have fit** a giant!	

■ EXERCISE 1

In the following passage, Ted Turner, a well-known American businessman, talks with interviewer Studs Terkel about some of the things he would like to have done. Underline the perfective infinitives he uses. The first one has been done as an example.

(1) I would like <u>to have lived</u> a whole bunch of lives. (2) I would like to have gone to West Point or Annapolis and had a military career, I would like to have been a fireman, I would like to have been a state trooper, I would like to have been an explorer, I would like to have been a concert pianist, an Ernest Hemingway, an F. Scott Fitzgerald, a movie star, a big league ballplayer, Joe Namath. (3) I like it all.

(4) I would like to have been a fighter pilot, a mountain climber, go to the Olympics and run the marathon, a general on a white horse. (5) A sea captain, back in the days of sailing ships, sailed with Horatio Nelson. (6) I would like to have gone with Captain Cook to find the Spice Islands, with Columbus, with Sir Francis Drake. (7) I would like to have been a pilot, a privateer, a knight in shining armor, gone on the Crusades. (8) Wouldn't you? (9) I'd like to have gone looking for Dr. Livingston, right? (10) In the heart of darkest Africa. (11) I would like to have discovered the headwaters of the Nile and the Amazon River.

EXERCISE 2

Write three statements about things you would like to have done, using perfective infinitive clauses. Exchange the three statements you wrote with another classmate. Report one or more of your classmate's statements to the rest of the class or a small group, using a *that*-clause with a modal perfect verb.

Example: Statement: *I would like to have discovered the North Pole.*
Paraphrase: *Olivia wishes that she could have discovered the North Pole.*

Note that in the paraphrase, *could* is used as the modal with *wish* as the main clause verb.

EXERCISE 3

Complete the blanks with perfective infinitives. Use the verb in parentheses.

Example: She was happy (break) __to have broken__ the record for the one-hundred-meter dash.

1. (a) The elderly gentleman next door considers himself (be) _____ quite a romantic fellow in his younger days. (b) He claims (write) _____ passionate love letters to more than a dozen women. (c) Not all of his letters got the responses he had hoped for, but in his opinion, as the saying goes, it was better (love) _____ and lost than never (love) _____ at all.

2. **David:** (a) It was really nice of Hector (give) _____ us his car for our trip to the Grand Canyon. We had a great time.
   Alana: (b) Oh, he was happy (be able to) _____ help you out. (c) I'd really like (go) _____ with you on your trip, but my cousins were visiting that weekend.

3. (a) Jeanne is too smart (believe) _____ the story Russ told her the other day. (b) His story was outlandish enough (convince) _____ her that it was far from the truth.

4. (a) Dear Fran: Accepting that job offer was a wise decision for you (make) _____. (b) We're glad (have) _____ you as our office mate for the past three years. (c) Good luck! With your talent, we expect you (receive) _____ a big promotion before long.

FOCUS 2 Expressing Past Events

EXAMPLES	EXPLANATIONS
(a) Jamie is happy **to have finished** her report last night so she can go to the soccer game with us today.	**Past in Relation to the Present** Perfective infinitives signal an event or condition in the past. The event or condition may continue to the present.
(b) Ben considers Phillipe **to have been** his best friend ever since they started college three years ago. (Ben still considers him to be his best friend.)	
(c) Dr. Yamada wanted **to have completed** her research before last August. However, her funds for the project ran out.	**Past in Relation to the Past** The event expressed by the infinitive clause may be unfulfilled.
(d) The driver claimed **to have stopped** for the traffic light before the accident occurred.	With verbs that express beliefs or attitudes, such as *claim* or *consider*, the event in the infinitive clause may or may not have actually happened.
(e) Winona expects **to have made** all of her plane reservations by next week.	**Past in Relation to the Future** The event expressed by the infinitive clause may be a future event that takes place before another time in the future.
(f) Winona expects **to make** all of her plane reservations by next week.	We also commonly use infinitives that are not perfective (*to* + verb) to carry the same meaning for future events.
Perfective: Past (g) It **was** nice of you **to have done** that. **Nonperfective: Past** (h) It **was** nice of you **to do** that.	**Past Tense vs. Present Tense Main Clauses** When the main clause is past tense, speakers often use nonperfective infinitives to express the same meanings as perfective ones.
Perfective: Past (i) It **is** nice of you **to have done** that. (You did something in the past.) **Nonperfective: Present, Future** (j) It **is** nice of you **to do** that. (You are doing something right now or will do something in the future.)	When the main clause is present tense, use: *Infinitive* *To Express* perfective past meaning nonperfective present or future meaning

EXERCISE 4

Complete each blank with a perfective infinitive, using the verb in parentheses. Then state which type of meaning each one expresses: past relative to the present, to the past, or to the future.

Example: I would like (accompany) <u>to have accompanied</u> the Castenada family on their travels across the country.

1. The Castenada family has been traveling in the United States all summer and has only two weeks left of their trip; by the end of August, the family plans (tour) _____ most of the East Coast.

2. The Castanedas intended (visit) _____ all of their West Coast relatives before the end of June, but they couldn't because of car trouble.

3. Eight-year-old Ruby Castenada says that she would like (spend) _____ the entire summer at Disneyland.

4. So far, Mr. and Mrs. Castenada consider the highlight of their vacation (be) _____ their camping trip in Michigan.

5. At the beginning of the trip, Javier, their teenage son, was upset (leave) _____ all his friends for the whole summer.

6. However, now Javier admits that he would like (see) _____ even more of the country and hopes to travel again soon.

7. The Castenadas' goal is (visit) _____ all of the continental United States before Javier goes away to college.

EXERCISE 5

Restate the infinitives in the following quotations as perfective infinitives. If you had to choose one of them for a maxim to live by, which one would you select? Can you think of any other sayings that use perfective infinitives?

Example: To win one's joy through struggle is better than to yield to melancholy.
(Andre Gide, French author)
To have won one's joy through struggle is better than *to have yielded* to melancholy.

1. What a lovely surprise to finally discover how unlonely being alone can be. (Ellen Burstyn, American actress)

2. To endure what is unendurable is true endurance. (Japanese proverb)

3. I would prefer even to fail with honor than to win by cheating. (Sophocles, Greek dramatist)

4. To teach is to learn twice over. (Joseph Joubert, *Pensées*)

5. It is better to be happy for a moment and burned up with beauty than to live a long time and be bored all the while. (Don Marquis, "the lesson of the moth," *Archy and Mehitabel*)

6. Youth is the time to study wisdom; old age is the time to practice it. (Rousseau, *Reveries of a Solitary Walker*)

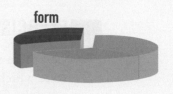

form

FOCUS 3 | Progressive and Passive Forms of Perfective Infinitives

EXAMPLES	EXPLANATIONS
	Progressive Form
(a) I'd like **to have been watching** when Bart received his award for bravery.	*to* + *have* + *been* + verb + *-ing*
(b) Mr. Ford believed the police **to have been guarding** his store when the robbery occurred.	
	Passive Form
(c) Bart would like me **to have been sent** a ticket to the ceremony.	*to* + *have* + *been* + past participle
(d) Mr. Ford believed his wife **to have been given** false information by the police.	

EXERCISE 6

Rewrite each of the following clauses as a perfective infinitive clause. The clauses begin with *that*, Ø-*that* (*that* has been deleted), or *when*. Make any word changes that are necessary.

Examples: Ø-*that* clause: Josef wishes he could have discovered the Cape of Good Hope with Bartolomeu Dias in 1488.

infinitive clause: *Josef would like to have discovered the Cape of Good Hope with Bartolomeu Dias in 1488.*

that-clause: Veronica believes that she was shortchanged.

infinitive clause: *Veronica believes herself to have been shortchanged.*

1. Our English teacher expects that we will finish our oral reports on our favorite celebrities by the end of next week.

2. Josh would prefer that he be the last one to present, but unfortunately for him, he is scheduled to be first.

3. Isela believes she was greatly misinformed by one of her interview subjects.

4. We wish we could have heard more about Shaun's talk with Beyonce. (Change *wish* to *would like.*)

5. Jocelyn hoped she would be given a chance to interview her favorite author, but the interview didn't work out.

6. Gerard claims that he was sent an autograph from a "major motion picture star," whose identity he is keeping a secret.

7. Sandra reported that Angelina Jolie, her favorite actress, had been sitting in front of her at a Carnegie Hall concert.

8. Ty thinks that he has gotten the most interesting interview with a celebrity. (Use *consider* for the main verb.)

9. Berta wishes that she had been eating dinner at the Hollywood restaurant last Friday night because someone told her that her favorite basketball player was there.

10. I will be relieved when I have presented my report since getting up in front of others makes me anxious.

FOCUS 4 — Negative Forms of Perfective Infinitives

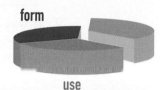

form

use

EXAMPLES	EXPLANATIONS
	Formal English
(a) The three nations were wise **not to have signed** the agreement until they could discuss it further.	In formal written English, put negative forms (*not, never*, etc.) before the infinitive verbs.
(b) **Not to have been contacted** for a job interview was a big disappointment for Daniel.	
(c) Senator Bolan appears **never to have voted** in favor of extra funding for child care.	A paraphrase of (c) would be the following: *It appears that Senator Bolan has never voted in favor of extra funding for child care.* Note that in example (c), the person's name replaces the subject *it* when the perfective infinitive follows *appears*.
	Informal English
(d) **To have not been invited** to the party made her really upset.	In less formal English, speakers sometimes put negative forms after *have*.
(e) I seem **to have not brought** the book I meant to give you today.	
(f) That woman claims **to have never seen** the money that turned up in her purse.	

In the following summary of a murder case, French Detective Henri Armand investigates the activities of a suspect, Dr. Moreau. Rewrite the underlined part of each of the following sentences so that it contains a negative perfective infinitive clause. Use the pattern for formal written English.

Example: It seemed that Dr. Moreau had not told the truth.
  Dr. Moreau seemed <u>not to have told</u> the truth.

1. Contrary to what Dr. Moreau claimed, <u>it appeared he had not been out of town the last weekend in April</u>.

   _____

2. It was quite strange, Detective Armand thought, <u>that Dr. Moreau had not told his housekeeper he would be away the weekend the murder occurred</u>. (Replace *that* with *for.*)

   _____

3. Furthermore, the doctor did not seem to remember much about the inn he claimed <u>he had stayed in</u> that weekend. How very odd!

   _____

4. Also, the doctor claimed <u>that he had not known the victim, Horace Bix</u>; yet Bix's name was found in Dr. Moreau's appointment book.

   _____

5. All in all, Detective Armand believed <u>that Dr. Moreau had not given the police truthful answers to most of their questions.</u>

   _____

Expressing Likes, Preferences, and Dislikes Contrary to Past Fact

use

	EXAMPLES	EXPLANATIONS
Would + verb		
would like	(a) **I would like to have spent** the class period reviewing for the exam. (I would have liked to spend the class period reviewing for the exam.)	Use *would* + verbs with perfective infinitives to express likes, dislikes, and preferences about things that did not happen.
would love	(b) My parents **would love to have joined** us for dinner. (My parents would have loved to join us for dinner.)	Alternative forms of these sentences are given in parentheses. The alternative form has a perfective main clause verb and a nonperfective infinitive.
would prefer	(c) **I would prefer not to have had** an early morning class. (I would have preferred not to have an early morning class.)	
would hate	(d) **Wouldn't you hate to have been** in that crowded room? (Wouldn't you have hated to be in that crowded room?)	
	(e) We **would have liked to have spent** the class period reviewing for the exam. (incorrect)	Native English speakers sometimes use perfective forms for both clauses in speech. Although this pattern would sound fine to many native English speakers, it is not considered standard for written English.
	(f) We **would like to have spent** the class period reviewing for the exam. (correct)	

EXERCISE 8

Choose any five of the following topics. For each topic, write a statement expressing a past wish. With a classmate, explain the reasons for one or two of your statements.

Example: An experience while traveling
I would prefer to have flown from England to France instead of going by boat across the channel.
Reason: *The sea was very rough that day and I got seasick.*

1. The way you spent your last vacation
2. Your participation in a sports event
3. A course you had to take
4. A paper you had to write
5. A meal you had recently
6. An experience you had at a party
7. (A topic of your choice)

Use the cues below to make sentences expressing a past wish that did not materialize or an unpleasant event that was avoided. Use the standard English pattern of *would like*, *would love*, *would prefer*, *would not like*, *would hate* followed by a perfective infinitive. Make any changes that are necessary, including any needed verb tense changes.

Example: be asked to present my report first
I would like to have been asked to present my report first.

1. take all of my final exams on one day instead of on several days

2. forget the answers to the vocabulary test questions

3. go to the movies instead of just staying home Saturday night

4. be the only one in our math class without the assignment done

5. be given true-false questions for the entire test rather than essay questions

6. study geology instead of biochemistry last semester

7. walk into the English classroom and find out the teacher was absent

---

| **FOCUS 6** | **Expressing Other Emotions and Attitudes with Perfective Infinitives** |

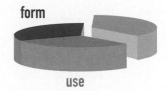

form

use

EXAMPLES	**EXPLANATIONS**
(a) I **am sorry** to have missed your graduation party.	• *be* + adjective
(b) They **were shocked** to have been treated so rudely by the waiter.	
(c) **It was really generous of you** to have lent us your bicycles.	• *it* + *be* + adjective (+ *of* + noun)
(d) **It is annoying** to have been waiting so long to buy a ticket.	
(e) **It is such a pleasure** to have met you after reading many of your books.	• *it* + *be* + noun phrase
(f) **It was a miracle** to have found the contact lens in the swimming pool.	
(g) **It was fortunate for us** to have discovered the mistake so quickly.	• (*it* + *be* + adjective) *for* + noun/objective pronoun
(h) **For them** to have had three plane delays in one day was very unlucky.	
(i) It **must** be exciting to have lived in so many countries!	You may also use modal verbs before *be* with many of the expressions.
(j) It **would** be disappointing to have missed the parade. I'm glad we made it on time!	

EXERCISE 10

Choose five of the numbered items below. Make sentences with perfective infinitive clauses, using the cues. Use a variety of structures and add descriptive words or phrases to expand the cues into sentences. *Note:* For some phrases, either personal or impersonal, *it* could be the subject for a sentence, but some phrases allow only one choice.

Examples: Be foolish . . . think

John must be foolish to have thought that no one would notice he had taken the dangerous chemicals from the lab.

It was foolish of us to have thought no one would notice we were missing from class.

1. Be happy . . . find out
2. Be surprising . . . hear
3. Be unwise . . . build
4. Be kind . . . donate

5. Be so annoying . . . get
6. Be really thrilling . . . find out
7. Be a tragedy . . . lose
8. Be sad . . . learn

EXERCISE 11

Use an expression from Exercise 10, or a similar one, to make up a brief response for each of the situations below. Use a perfective infinitive in your response.

Example: You have recently spent three days at the beach house of your parents' friends while they were not there. You are writing them a thank-you note.

It was very generous of you to have let me stay in your beach house during my trip to the coast. I really appreciate your kindness. Thank you!

1. You have just remembered that today is the birthday of one of your friends who lives in another city, and you forgot to send her a birthday card. You buy a card and want to write a note to tell her you're sorry.

2. A friend helped you move to an apartment. You want to send him a thank-you note.

3. You are having a conversation at a party with someone you have just met. She has been telling you about her trip to see the Summer Olympics.

4. You recently went shopping. When you tried to purchase something, the salesman kept you waiting for several minutes while he chatted with a friend on the phone. You are writing a letter of complaint to the manager of the store.

5. You are writing a letter to a friend. You want to tell her how fortunate you were recently. You just heard that you were awarded two scholarships to attend school next year.

6. You call up the mother of a friend to thank her for having given a going-away party for you before you move to another city.

7. A friend did not show up for a class three sessions in a row. This strikes you as strange because he has never missed a class before. Another friend asks you if you know where he has been, but you don't.

8. A friend just wrote you an e-mail telling you that she enrolled a few weeks ago in a Web design class. You think she made a smart decision and want to let her know.

use

EXAMPLES	EXPLANATIONS
(a) I **seem to have forgotten** my homework assignment. Oh wait, here it is in my notebook!	After the verbs *seem* and *appear*, perfective infinitives express uncertainty about past events based on present evidence.
(b) This assignment **appears to have been written** rather hastily.	Sometimes the "uncertainty" is actually a way to avoid directly accusing or criticizing someone.
(c) Hmmm . . . someone **seems to have eaten** all the ice cream. I wonder who did that!	Note on informal English: When speakers use perfective infinitive in fast speech, *to have* tends to sound like "*to-uv.*"
(d) An increase in the medication **seems to have lowered** the patient's blood pressure.	*Appear* and *seem* followed by perfective infinitives are often used as "hedges" in formal speech and writing, such as medical reports, news reports, and academic writing, both to express uncertainty and to avoid direct criticism.
(e) The election results **appear to have been influenced** by voters' opposition to the war.	
(f) There **appears to have been** a storm during the time we were gone.	When *there* is the grammatical subject of *seem* or *appear* + perfective infinitive, the logical subject follows the verb if it is active.
(g) There **appear to have been** some conclusions **made** without evidence to support them.	If the verb is passive, as in (g), the logical subject comes between the auxiliaries and the main verb. In (g), the logical subject is *conclusions*.

EXERCISE 12

Match each of the questions in the Questions column with a response from the Responses column to make conversational exchanges. With a partner, compare your answers and then read the exchanges out loud with appropriate expression.

Questions	Responses
1. Gee, it's already 8 o'clock. I guess I'd better get up! Have you looked to see what the weather is like this morning?	a. Uh-huh, it seems to have gone sour. You should ask the waiter to get you another glass.
2. Hmm . . . you know, that t-shirt looks kind of tight on you. Are you sure it's a medium? Maybe you should check with the sales clerk.	b. Well, there appears to have been a robbery there last night, so it's not going to open until the police have investigated.
3. Does this milk taste a little funny to you?	c. Yeah, I did just a few minutes ago. It appears to have stopped raining, at least for the time being,
4. Wow! I can't believe we've been sitting in this traffic for half an hour. What do you think is going on?	d. Oh, she seems to have found out we were awarded that big project for next month. So I guess she thinks we deserve it!
5. Hey, I just heard that the boss said we could all leave the office at noon today. What brought that on?	e. You're right. It seems to have been mismarked. I think it's actually a small.
6. How come the video store is closed? Shouldn't it have opened an hour ago?	f. I'm not sure, but from what I can see, there appears to have been some sort of accident up ahead.

EXERCISE 13

Rewrite each of the following statements with hedges, using an appropriate form of *appear* or *seem* followed by a perfective infinitive. (In some cases, either present or past tense of *appear* or *seem* may be used.)

Example: In this study, several of the formulas were miscalculated.
Rewrite: *In this study, several of the formulas appear to have been miscalculated.*

1. The train accident involved the conductor's error in judging the amount of time needed to clear the railroad tracks.

2. During the riots last night, bystanders stole goods from a number of stores on State Street.

3. Dr. Rushmore misdiagnosed the patient and treated him with an inappropriate medication.

4. The patient contracted malaria several weeks ago but ignored the symptoms.

5. The vases recently found by the archeologists were made during the 4th century BC.

6. Dogs evolved from wolves, differing only 1% in their mitochondrial DNA.

7. The migration of ancient animals thousands of miles from their original homes resulted from factors related to continental drift.

8. What caused the suspension bridge to collapse after the earthquake? According to preliminary investigations, it was not constructed according to engineering codes.

EXERCISE 14

Make up a sentence with *appear* or *seem* followed by a perfective infinitive for each of the following situations.

1. You go for a job interview. The interviewer asks to see your application form. You realize you must have left it at home. Respond to the question.

2. You are a teacher. One of your students looks as if she is on the verge of falling asleep. Make a comment to her.

3. As you are getting ready to leave the classroom, you discover that you no longer have your notebook, which was with you when you entered the room. Make a comment to your classmates as they are walking out.

4. You have just stopped reading a novel that is one of worst ones you have ever read. Make a comment to a friend about the author of the book.

5. When your teacher starts going over a homework assignment, you realize that you did the wrong one. The teacher calls on you for an answer. Give an appropriate response.

Expressing Obligations, Intentions, and Future Plans

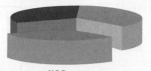

use

EXAMPLES	EXPLANATIONS
(a) You **needed to have submitted** a petition by last Friday to drop your composition course. (b) You **will need to have completed** one more English course by the end of this year in order to graduate.	After *need to*, perfective infinitives can express past obligations not fulfilled or future obligations depending on the tense of the main verb. Note that a time *by-phrase* is often used.
(c) You **will want to have started** applying for jobs in early spring.	*Will want to* + perfective infinitive can also express future obligation.
(d) The engineers **were supposed to have checked** all the controls before the shuttle was launched. (e) Caroline **was to have spent** the entire summer sculpting, but she ended up working at a bank for a month.	Perfective infinitives may follow phrasal modals *be supposed to, be to*. With past forms of the main verbs, they express past obligations or plans that were or might not have been fulfilled.
(f) Do you **plan to have written** your report before Sunday? (g) The weatherman **expects** the rains **to have ended** by next weekend.	With verbs such as *plan, intend, hope*, and *expect*, perfective infinitives express a future time before another future time.

EXERCISE 15

Complete the following sentences with information about yourself; use a perfective infinitive clause in each.

Example: By tomorrow, I intend <u>to have bought my sister a birthday present</u>.

1. By next week, I plan _____.

2. I intend _____ within the next five years.

3. I was supposed _____ but I didn't because

   _____.

4. By the end of the year, I will need _____.

5. I expect _____ before _____.

6. By _____ I hope _____.

FOCUS 9 — Perfective Infinitives with *Enough* and *Too*

EXAMPLES	EXPLANATIONS
adjective + *enough* (a) The earthquake was **powerful enough** to have destroyed a whole city. (The earthquake could have destroyed a whole city.) ***enough* + noun** (b) I got **enough homework** on Friday to have kept me busy for a week. (The homework could have kept me busy for a week.)	***Enough*** Following *enough*, perfective infinitives often express an event that could have happened but did not necessarily happen. In other words, they express past possibilities.
***too* + adjective** (c) We were **too tired** to have gone anywhere last night. (We didn't go anywhere last night because we were too tired.) ***too* + many/much + noun** (d) She has **too much intelligence** to have done so poorly on the exam. (She did poorly, but I am surprised because she is so intelligent.)	***Too*** Following *too*, perfective infinitives may express events that did not occur. The main clause gives a reason. The perfective infinitive after *too* may also express the speaker's disbelief that something did not occur.

◼ EXERCISE 16

Use the phrases below to create sentences about past possibilities using perfective infinitives.

Example: poison . . . strong enough
The poison that the child accidentally swallowed was strong enough to have killed her, but fortunately she recovered completely.

1. music at the concert . . . loud enough
2. they made enough money . . .
3. fireworks . . . bright enough
4. wind . . . strong enough
5. the weather in (your hometown) . . . hot/cold enough

EXERCISE 17

The following sentences express disbelief about an event or explain why something didn't happen. Combine the ideas in each pair of sentences into one sentence, using a perfective infinitive clause. (*Hint:* Start with the sentence that has a *too* + adjective phrase, changing pronoun subjects if needed.)

Example: Rachel couldn't have done well in the marathon last fall. She had sustained too many minor injuries.

Combined: *Rachel had sustained too many minor injuries to have done well in the marathon last fall.*

1. My brother couldn't have cheated on a test. He is too honest.
2. You couldn't have stopped taking piano lessons! You have too much talent.
3. Stan couldn't have bought that wild tie himself. He is too conservative.
4. Charmaine didn't stay at that low-level job. She has too much ambition.
5. They couldn't have taken on any more debts. They have too many already.

Use Your English

CD Tracks
26–29

Imagine that you have just returned from a two-week vacation. The dates of your vacation were July 14 through the 28th. Listen to the audio. You will hear four messages that have been left on your telephone answering machine.

■ **STEP 1**   Take notes as you listen to each message.

■ **STEP 2**   Use your notes to create responses that you could leave on the answering machines of the people who called. Use at least one perfective infinitive form in each response.

■ **STEP 3**   Share your favorite responses with a small group of classmates.

ACTIVITY **2** research/speaking/writing

Interview five people about regrets—either their greatest regrets or most recent ones. Then write the results of your interviews using statements with perfective infinitives. Share the results with your classmates. Here are some examples of paraphrases:

Examples: Jack's regret: that he quit his job
Paraphrase: *Jack is sorry to have quit his job.*

Risa's regret: that she didn't go to Vienna for her vacation
Paraphrase: *Risa is sorry not to have gone to Vienna for her vacation.*

Blanca's regret: that she never learned Spanish from her mother
Paraphrase: *Blanca is sorry never to have learned Spanish from her mother.*

ACTIVITY 3 — writing/speaking

STEP 1 Consider a procedure from your major field of study or one of the following topics for which you can list a number of things that need to have been done in preparation. Possible topics: studying abroad, studying for a particular kind of exam (e.g., math, English), going out on a date, getting married, going fishing, playing a team sport.

STEP 2 Create a list of 4–5 items using *will need* or *will want* + perfective infinitives. A few examples are given below.

Example: Taking a trip abroad
The travelers will need to have gotten a passport.
They will want to have checked to see if they need immunizations.

STEP 3 When you have finished, share your information in small groups and answer any questions your classmates may have about your list.

ACTIVITY 4 — research on the web

Using *InfoTrac® College Edition* or other Web-based resources, research the life of a famous composer such as Beethoven, Mozart, Tchaikovsky, or Gershwin. With your classmates, take turns reporting on some of the information you learned, using perfective infinitives to express your emotional reaction toward it.

Examples: *I was surprised to have found out that Beethoven was mathematically illiterate.*
I was sad to have read how lonely Beethoven was.

ACTIVITY 5 — reflection

Consider what you would like to have accomplished this year in English studies or any of your academic subjects. Make a list of at least five things you expect or hope to have achieved by next year at this time.

Example: *I hope to have improved my ability to use verb tenses correctly in writing essays.*

ADJECTIVE COMPLEMENTS IN SUBJECT AND PREDICATE POSITION

UNIT GOALS

- Use three types of adjective complement structures

- Use adjective complements in subject and predicate position

- Choose among infinitives, gerunds, and *that* clauses

- Order *that*-clauses and infinitives to introduce new information or to refer to known information in discourse

OPENING TASK

Human Beings' Relationship to Animals

STEP 1

Some things that further human progress, comfort, or enjoyment may have negative effects on animals. As you look over the following list, think about the positive and negative associations each term has.

■ STEP 2

Discuss five of the terms with a partner and jot down your ideas in the chart below.

TERM	POSITIVE	NEGATIVE
1. animal research	provides a way to test the safety of drugs and cosmetics	animals dissected, injected, and killed in experiments
2. fur coat		
3. zoo		
4. oil tanker		
5. veal		
6. ivory		
7. pesticide		
8. campground		
9. bullfight		
10. hunting		
11. highway construction		

■ STEP 3

After your discussion, write down statements about several of the terms, including both positive and negative associations. Here are some sample statements about the first term, *animal research*:

It is unethical for researchers to use animals like gorillas and chimpanzees in medical studies. That this research tests the safety of drugs and cosmetics is undeniable. But researchers' blindly generalizing the findings from these experiments to human beings does not make sense. In addition, injecting and killing these animals during experiments is inhumane.

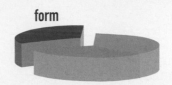

FOCUS 1 — Overview of Adjective Complements

EXAMPLES	EXPLANATIONS
adjective complement + *be* + adjective (a) **Killing these animals** is inhumane.	Adjective complements can appear in subject position in front of linking verbs (such as *appear, be, become, look, remain, seem*) followed by adjectives.
(b) **That the blue whale is becoming extinct** seems sad. (c) **For campers to pollute streams** is irresponsible. (d) **Bulls' being killed** in bullfights appears brutal.	Adjective complements are of three types: • *that*-clause (consisting of *that* + clause) • infinitive (consisting of *for* + noun phrase + *to* + base verb) • gerund (consisting of *'s* + verb + *-ing*)
(e) The captain appears ready **for the media to interview** him about the shipping accident. (f) The senator is eager **for investigators to determine** the cause of the oil spill.	The adjectives that precede adjective complements and follow animate subjects generally show positive expectation (e.g., *ready, anxious, happy, eager, glad*, etc.).
(g) The senator is eager to win the next election. (h) **NOT:** The senator is eager for himself to win the next election.	If the main subject and the complement subject are alike, we delete the *for* phrase.

EXERCISE 1

Read the following text. Underline examples of adjective complements.

Recently, the topic of animal research has become quite controversial. Animal rights activists believe that animal experimentation for medical purposes is not necessary because sophisticated computer modeling can accomplish the same result. Researchers disagree and claim that animal research should precede human research when serious health risks are involved. That 90% or more of the genes linked to diseases are the same in animals and humans is a convincing reminder that animal experimentation with rats, mice, pigs, and monkeys can successfully lead to medical advances and cures. That animals in research should be carefully guarded against disease and suffering is obvious. However, researchers' discontinuing the use of animals in experiments which could lead to cures for cancer and AIDS would be very unfortunate.

In the past few years, animal rights activists from organizations like ALF (Animal Liberation Front) have targeted research labs across the United States. Last year, protesters broke into a university lab to release hundreds of research animals. They destroyed computers containing research data and painted slogans on the walls such as "Mice Have Feelings Too" and "Free the Animals." Others sent hate mail and made threats to families of university researchers.

That individuals feel strongly about a cause is commendable. For them to trespass, destroy property, and harass researchers' family members is not. Animal rights activists have now become one of the top U.S. domestic terrorism threats. Several universities have been forced to investigate the backgrounds of their graduate student researchers, change keys to electronic security cards, and set up cameras to record who is entering or leaving the research facilities. It is unfortunate that this level of security has become necessary. It is tragic that many medical advances will be thwarted or slowed because of the activities of a few overzealous individuals.

EXERCISE 2

In the following short texts about animals and their unusual habits, complete the adjective complements with *that*-clauses, *for/to* infinitives, or gerunds.

Example: Elizabeth Mann Borghese, who was the daughter of the writer Thomas Mann, taught her dog to take dictation on a special typewriter. Her dog's _taking dictation_ is hard to believe.

1. Once a woman was thrown off a yacht and three dolphins rescued her and led her to a marker in the sea. Another time, several fishermen were lost in a dense fog, and four dolphins nudged their boat to safety. Dolphins' _____ is well-documented.

2. Mrs. Betsy Marcus's dog Benjy was known to sing "Raindrops Keep Fallin' on My Head." For a dog _____ is incredible.

3. At one time, passenger pigeons were very numerous. Now there are none because of massive hunting and the destruction of their natural forest home. That hunters _____ is sad.

4. Jaco, an African gray parrot, could speak German. When his master left the house alone, he said, "God be with you." When his master left with other people, he said, "God be with you all." Jaco's _____ is fascinating.

5. The dwarf lemur and the mountain pygmy possum were considered extinct. However, in recent years, these animals have reappeared. For seemingly extinct animals _____ is inspiring.

6. Washoe, a female chimpanzee, was taught sign language. She was able to make up words like *drink-fruit* for watermelon and *water-bird* for swan. That Washoe _____ is intriguing.

EXERCISE 3

STEP 1 Imagine that you are an animal. What would make you happy if you were one of the following pets? Write your answers in first person and use one of the adjectives: *anxious, eager, glad, happy,* or *ready.*

> **Example:** cat *I would be **eager** for my owner to feed me a tuna casserole.*
> *I would be **happy** to lie around in the sun.*

1. horse   3. dog   5. goldfish
2. parrot   4. mouse   6. snake

STEP 2 Write 3 more sentences like Step 1 and have the class guess which additional animals might express these thoughts.

FOCUS 2   **Adjective Complements in Subject and Predicate Position**

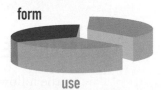

form

use

EXAMPLES	EXPLANATIONS
(a) I am sorry to say that certain businesses that sell sculptured ivory objects have hired poachers to kill elephants for their tusks. Known Information **For poachers to take the tusks from live elephants** is alarming. Known Information **That they sell them is** abominable. Known Information Worst of all, **elephants' becoming an endangered species because of this** is criminal.	In subject position, adjective complements usually contain a known idea, either previously mentioned or assumed through context.
It + linking verb + adjective + adjective complement (b) It is interesting **that medical researchers have made important medical discoveries through animal research.** They need to continue this work. (c) It is necessary **for protesters to call for a moratorium on animal testing.** Animals have rights too!	When *that*-clauses and infinitives contain new information, they will more commonly appear in predicate position preceded by *It* + linking verb + adjective.
(d) **NOT:** It is abominable poachers' killing elephants.	Gerunds do not normally occur with *it* constructions.

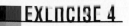

Fill in the blanks with a variety of appropriate linking verbs and adjectives from the following lists. More than one answer may be correct.

Linking Verbs	Adjectives		
appear	*apparent*	*improper*	*obvious*
be	*bad*	*inappropriate*	*odd*
become	*compulsory*	*irrational*	*sad*
look	*depressing*	*irritating*	*surprising*
remain	*disappointing*	*likely*	*true*
seem	*impossible*	*necessary*	*unfortunate*

Example: From all of the evidence, it _____was obvious_____ that the defendant was guilty.

1. Crime is rampant in many parts of the world. That teenagers commit many of these crimes _____.

2. It _____ for children to attend elementary and secondary school in the United States.

3. It was a long, hard winter. Felicia's being shut inside every day _____.

4. It _____ that the president will be reelected if the economy continues to recover.

5. The young man stayed out until 3:00 A.M. For him not to listen to his parents _____.

6. All of the other men had been rehired by the company. John's still being unemployed _____.

7. It _____ for two wrongs to make a right.

8. Everyone knew that President Rabin had been shot. That he had been shot by one of his own people _____.

9. The fashion designer's clothes this season are very extreme. For vinyl to be mixed with fur _____.

10. I have stopped going to the theater on Saturday afternoons. Children's whispering and throwing popcorn in the air _____.

EXERCISE 5

What do you think about the following activities or ideas? Use adjective complements in your answer.

Examples: (you) saving a little money every month

It's wise (for me) to save because I might need some extra money some day.
OR *My saving money has become essential to my future.*

1. (you) studying English grammar
2. (you) slipping on a puddle of water in front of your friends
3. (your friend) copying someone else's paper
4. (your relative) riding a motorcycle without a helmet
5. (a single person) joining an online dating service
6. (a poor person) winning the lottery
7. (cities) banning smoking in all public places
8. (teachers) creating schools for profit rather than teaching in public schools
9. (elderly people) skydiving (= jumping from a plane with a parachute on)
10. (the government) making alcohol illegal

EXERCISE 6

Comment on the following facts found in the *Book of Lists 2* using a *that*-clause in subject position.

Example: Tigers do not usually hunt humans unless they are old or injured. However, a tigress, the Champawat man-eater, killed 438 people in the Himalayas in Nepal between 1903 and 1911.
That so many people were killed in Nepal by a tiger is tragic.

1. Black bears do not usually hurt humans unless they are hungry. When the Alaskan blueberry crop was poor in 1963, black bears attacked at least four people, one of whom they killed, because no other food was available.

2. In the central provinces of India, leopards have been known to enter huts and kill humans. One famous leopard, the Panawar man-eater, is reputed to have killed four hundred people.

3. On March 25, 1941, the British ship *Britannia* sank in the Atlantic Ocean. While the 12 survivors sat in a lifeboat, a giant squid reached its arm around the body of one of them and pulled him into the ocean.

4. In South America, people have reported losing fingers, toes, or pieces of flesh while bathing in piranha-infested waters.

5. In 1916, four people were killed as they were swimming along a 60-mile stretch of the New Jersey coast. The attacker was a great white shark.

Consider your responses during the Opening Task on page 373 and what you know about environmental issues to create dialogues with facts about animals, using a *that*-clause and the adjective provided.

Example: shocking   Q: What's so shocking?
                  A: **It's shocking** that the oil from the grounded oil tanker killed thousands of innocent animals.

1. irresponsible   4. important
2. encouraging   5. outrageous
3. sad   6. fortunate

meaning

FOCUS 3   Infinitives, Gerund, and *That*-Clauses

EXAMPLES	EXPLANATIONS
(a) Many zoos have instituted stricter laws regarding the care of their animals. **That zoos protect their animals is important.** (b) **Zoos' protecting their animals** is important.	Infinitive, gerund, and *that*-clauses have different meanings. *That*-clauses and gerunds refer to actual or fulfilled events. In (a) and (b), the adjective complements refer to the fact that zoos actually do already protect their animals.
(c) Many zoos have reported higher numbers of animals dying in captivity. **For zoos to protect their animals is important.**	Infinitives refer to future ideas or potential events. In (c), zoos potentially can protect their animals (but they don't necessarily do so).

EXERCISE 8

Circle the best option and explain your decision.

Example: 1. ⓐ It is heartening that the Beauty Cosmetics Company of London has refused to test its products on animals since its establishment.

     b. It would be heartening for the Beauty Cosmetics Company of London to refuse to test its products on animals.

*(The Beauty Cosmetics Company has actually refused already, so answer **a** with the **that**-clause is correct.)*

1. a. It is shocking that commercial whalers have almost exterminated the blue whale.
   b. It would be shocking for commercial whalers to almost exterminate the blue whale.

2. a. It is sad that dolphins catch diseases from humans at dolphin recreational swim centers.
   b. It would be sad for dolphins to catch diseases from humans at dolphin recreational swim centers.

3. a. After an oil spill, it will be important that animals are rescued.
   b. After an oil spill, it will be important for animals to be rescued.

4. a. Companies' cutting down the Amazonian rain forests will lead to ecological disaster.
   b. For companies to cut down the Amazonian rain forests would lead to ecological disaster.

5. a. For healthcare workers to stop the AIDS crisis in Africa would be inspiring.
   b. That healthcare workers' stopped the AIDS crisis in Africa is inspiring.

EXERCISE 9

What would be out of the ordinary for the following types of people to do or to have done? Comment on their activities using the following *-ly* adverb + adjective clusters: *wholly unexpected, particularly odd, really surprising, extremely unusual, virtually impossible, incredibly strange, terribly funny*.

Example: Inuits   *Inuits' living in grass huts would be incredibly strange.*

1. dictators
2. busybodies
3. bus drivers
4. procrastinators
5. professional athletes
6. English teachers
7. Hollywood stars
8. your mother
9. your friend's father
10. our class

Use Your English

ACTIVITY **1** listening

CD Tracks
30–34

Listen to the audio and circle the appropriate comment that would follow from what you have heard. Here is an example of the type of exchange you might hear.

Example: Tonya: Did you hear the good news?

Francisco: No, what?

Tonya: Rosa's parents just bought her a car for her birthday.

(a.) That Rosa got a new car for her birthday is amazing.

b. For Rosa to get a new car will be amazing.

1. a. It's annoying that such a smart aleck like Tom should have such luck!
   b. For Harvard to give such an expensive scholarship is annoying.
2. a. It is essential for human beings to revere animals for their intelligence and strength.
   b. It is true that many human beings have killed animals in order to obtain food and clothing.
3. a. That citizens care so much about the needy in Los Angeles is encouraging.
   b. Citizens' neglecting the needy in Los Angeles will lead to serious consequences.
4. a. Scientists working in the Gobi Desert is extraordinary.
   b. That we now know something about dinosaur parental care is astonishing.
5. a. It's great that she got a new computer.
   b. It's great for her to get a new computer.

ACTIVITY **2** research/writing

Research several animals that are in danger of becoming extinct. Find out how they are dying or being killed. Then, write a short paragraph, giving your feelings and opinions about **one** of these animals. Several suggestions are given below.

California condor   spotted owl   blue whale

Arabian oryx   orangutan of Borneo   giant Panda

ACTIVITY 3   reading/speaking

Comment upon a current problem in your community, your country, or the world. Indicate how certain or impossible a solution will be in the near future using one of the following adjectives: *certain, likely, probable, possible, unlikely,* or *impossible.*

Example: *For the past few years the European Union has discussed a common constitution. It now appears likely that the majority will ratify the constitution in the near future.*

ACTIVITY 4   writing

Rosary beads, piano keys, and dice are all made of ivory, sometimes illegally obtained. Hunters cut the tusks from elephants with chainsaws and then sell the tusks to businesspeople who smuggle them out of the country. Often political officials collaborate in the crime by issuing false import permits.

Imagine that you have bought an ivory figure for $1000 and later learned that the ivory had been illegally obtained. Write a letter of complaint to the company from which you bought the figure. Use statements such as, "I have just learned that the figure I bought from you was made of illegally obtained ivory. Your selling me such an item is outrageous."

ACTIVITY 5   writing

Michael W. Fox, in his book *Inhuman Society: The American Way of Exploiting Animals,* has expressed his opinion on modern zoos in the following way:

Today's zoos and wildlife safari parks are radically different from the early iron and concrete zoos. It takes money to run a modern zoo, and zoo directors realize that they must compete with a wide variety of leisure-time activities. Concession stands, miniature railroads, and other carnival amusements, as well as dubious circuslike shows with performing chimps or big cats, lure many visitors to some of our large zoos and wildlife parks. What tricks and obedience the animals display are more a reflection of the power of human control than of the animals' natural behavior. Performing apes, elephants, bears, big cats, dolphins, and "killer" whales especially draw the crowds. Man's mastery over the powerful beast and willful control over its wild instincts is a parody of the repression and sublimation of human nature and personal freedom.

Individually, write a short paragraph explaining whether or not you agree with Fox. What statements are true? What are questionable? (Use at least three adjective complements in your writing.)

Using an Internet search engine such as Yahoo® or Google®, or another Web site or source you may know of, search the Internet to find out how animals have been used in research of one of the following diseases: polio, diphtheria, mumps, hepatitis, diabetes, arthritis, high blood pressure, AIDS, or cancer. As a result of your research, express your opinions in a short oral report on the use of animals in furthering medical progress. Do you feel that it is important or unnecessary?

Example: *It is important for researchers to use animals in their research . . .*

ACTIVITY 7 reflection

Students have to develop good study habits in order to get assignments finished and to pass their exams. With a classmate, discuss your opinions about the following activities. Give the reason why these are or are not suitable study options. In your discussion, use several adjective complements in subject or predicate position.

Example: Cramming for tests

Students' cramming for tests is not consistent with the type of regular, frequent study needed to learn a subject.

It's not good <u>to cram for tests</u> because it is difficult to retain material after the test is over.

1. Going to bed at 2:00 A.M. on weeknights

2. Designating particular times each day to devote to your studies

3. Staying out late every Saturday night

4. Surveying materials before you read them

5. Looking up every unknown word in a dictionary

6. Rehearsing learned material with a friend

7. Asking questions of your teacher if you do not understand something

8. Going to a movie instead of going to class

9. Getting involved in many extracurricular activities

10. Studying at a cafeteria

NOUN COMPLEMENTS TAKING *THAT* CLAUSES

UNIT GOALS

- Use noun complements to explain abstract nouns

- Distinguish *that* clause noun complements from restrictive relative clauses

- Use *that* clause noun complements in subject position to signal known or implied information

- Use *the fact* + *that* noun complements appropriately

- Appropriately use *that* clause noun complements after transitive adjectives and phrasal verbs

OPENING TASK
Explaining Natural Phenomena

How good are you at explaining natural phenomena? Would you be able to explain why the North American and South American eastern coastlines and the Eurasian and African western coastlines appear to be mirror images of each other? One account for this phenomenon is the theory that all of these continents once formed a single continent and subsequently moved apart.

STEP 1

Discuss at least five of the following questions with your classmates. Try to write down the facts that could explain these intriguing natural events.

1. What explains the observation that in some parts of the world leaves change color and fall from the trees each year?
2. What explains the observation that shooting stars speed across the sky?
3. What explains the fact that there are oases in desert environments?
4. What accounts for the fact that some rainbows are partial and some are full?
5. What could illustrate the idea that physical activity is difficult at high altitudes?
6. What could illustrate the law that heat flows from a warm place to a cooler place?
7. What fact could explain the reason for the sun and moon to appear larger near the horizon?
8. What fact could account for the reason for a person's reflection appearing upside down in a spoon?

STEP 2

Now add a few questions of your own concerning other intriguing natural events that you are curious about. Once you have written your questions, see if your classmates know the facts that explain them.

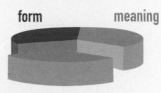

FOCUS 1   Overview of Noun Complements

Noun complements explain or provide the complete content of certain nouns.

EXAMPLES	EXPLANATIONS
(a) The theory **that water expands when it is frozen** is testable. (b) The requirement **for workers to wear safety glasses** is important.	Noun complements are of two types: *that* clauses and infinitives. • The *that* clause is a way of explaining the noun. • The *for-to* infinitive also explains the noun. • Both types of complements follow abstract nouns. Many abstract nouns have verb counterparts (*requirement/require, advice/advise, reminder/remind*, etc.).

Abstract Nouns (+ *That* Clause):			With the abstract nouns listed here, we use a *that* clause to form noun complements.
answer	*news*	*reply*	
appeal	*notion*	*request*	
axiom	*possibility*	*statement*	
fact	*proposal*	*suggestion*	
hypothesis	*reason*	*theory*	
idea	*reminder*	*thesis*	

Abstract Nouns (+ Infinitives):			Another group of abstract nouns takes infinitives.
advice	*permission*	*request*	
appeal	*plan*	*requirement*	
command	*preparation*	*suggestion*	
instruction	*proposal*	*tendency*	
motivation	*recommendation*		
order	*reminder*		

EXAMPLES	EXPLANATIONS
(c) Most people understand the recommendation **that citizens should pay higher taxes.** (d) Most people understand the recommendation **for citizens to pay higher taxes.**	Some nouns, such as *request, recommendation,* and *suggestion* may take either a *that* clause or an infinitive as a complement.
(e) The fact **that the parties were able to meet** indicates the commitment of everyone to cooperate. (f) Does he understand the need **for leaders to establish some guidelines?**	Noun complements may appear with nouns either in subject or object position.

EXERCISE 1

Underline each noun complement. Circle the abstract noun that precedes it.

Example: Early scientists believed (the notion) that matter could be divided into four basic elements: earth, water, air, and fire.

1. The tendency for liquids to turn into gases is well known.

2. Moisture in the air provides the catalyst for industrial fumes to react and form acid rain.

3. Galileo proposed the hypothesis that all falling bodies drop at the same constant speed.

4. The possibility for scientists to intercept messages from space is increased by using radio telescopes.

5. The idea that songbirds may hear their own songs while they sleep is confirmed by a University of Chicago study.

6. The fact that overhead cables sag on a hot day proves that solids expand when heated.

EXERCISE 2

Summarize the information from the text by completing the statements that follow.

> ### SOLAR RAYS AND OUR SKIN
>
> The increase of hydrofluorocarbons in the atmosphere is dangerously depleting the earth's ozone layer. The effect of this is that people are having greater exposure to ultraviolet light rays. Can these solar rays increase the chances of skin cancer? Yes, in fact, they increase the cases of malignant melanoma—the deadliest type.
>
> According to The American Cancer Society, hundreds of thousands of new cases of skin cancer will be diagnosed in the United States each year. About 5 percent of these will be malignant melanoma. To prevent more cases, many doctors say that people should stay out of the sun altogether. This is especially true for redheads and blondes with freckled skin who have less natural protection against the sun's rays. At the very least, a person should cover up and wear a sunscreen with a high sun-protection factor (15, 25, or 30) during the periods of the day when ultraviolet rays are strongest.
>
> A good example of an anti-skin-cancer campaign comes from Australia. Life-guards in the state of Victoria wear T-shirts with the slogan "SLIP! SLOP! SLAP!"—which means slip on a shirt, slop on some sunscreen, and slap on a hat. Although these hints may not please all sunbathers on beaches around the world, they might very well save their lives.

Example: The news that <u>hydrofluorocarbons are depleting the ozone layer</u> is alarming.

1. The fact that _____ indicates why there has been an increase in cases of malignant melanoma.

2. The fact that _____ explains why blondes and redheads burn easily.

3. The fact that _____ is evidence that ultraviolet rays can cause skin cancer.

4. The doctors' recommendation for _____ is not very popular.

5. The amusing reminder for _____ has changed the sunbathing habits of people in Australia.

EXERCISE 3

Reread the questions in the Opening Task on page 385, Step 1, and answer at least five of them, using a *that* clause in subject position.

Example: What explains the observation that "shooting stars" speed across the sky?

The observation that "shooting stars" speed across the sky can be explained by meteorites' burning up as they hit the earth's atmosphere.

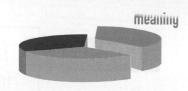

FOCUS 2	*That* Clause Noun Complements versus Restrictive Relative Clauses

EXAMPLES	EXPLANATIONS
(a) The story that she opened a restaurant is untrue. (b) The requirement that criminals serve 85 percent of their time is strictly reinforced.	A *that* clause noun complement defines an idea. In (a), *opened a restaurant* is "the story." The sentence still makes sense even if *the story* is deleted. In this sentence, *which* cannot replace *that*. Likewise in (b), the main idea of the sentence is kept even if *the requirement* is omitted.
(c) The story that/which she told was untrue. (d) The requirement that/which most annoys criminals in prison is the "lights out" curfew.	A restrictive relative clause limits an idea. *The story* in (c) relates to a particular story, the one that she told. The sentence will not make sense if *the story* is deleted. In this sentence, *which* can replace *that*. The same is true in (d), where the sentence will not make sense if *the requirement* is deleted.

EXERCISE 4

Which sentence in each of the following pairs contains a noun complement? Circle your choice.

Example: (a.) The idea that they didn't question the witnesses was shocking.
b. The idea that he had was exciting.

1. a. Many people dispute the fact that human beings evolved from apes.
   b. Many people accept the fact that he just mentioned.

2. a. The suggestion that she included in the letter will never be followed.
   b. The suggestion that a person should warm up before jogging is important.

3. a. The reply that she did not need help came as a surprise.
   b. The reply that contained important information was received too late.

4. a. I believe the theory that opposites attract.
   b. I believe the theory that my uncle proposed.

5. a. The students will select the answer that they think is correct.
   b. The students will select the answer that one oxygen and two hydrogen molecules constitute water.

6. a. They discussed the possibility that there may be additional concerns.
   b. They discussed the possibility that was predicted earlier.

7. a. I understand the statement that was made by the Turkish ambassador.
   b. I understand the statement that "two wrongs don't make a right."

FOCUS 3 · *That* Clause Noun Complements in Subject Position

EXAMPLES	EXPLANATIONS
(a) Harry had to write many papers in college. He never learned how to type. **The idea that Harry graduated from college without knowing how to type** astonishes me.	*That* clause noun complements in subject position contain known or implied information. The predicate comments upon the facts or ideas contained in *that* clauses following *the fact/idea/news,* etc.).
(b) When Teresa was diagnosed with cancer, everyone thought that she would not survive. Then, after several months of chemotherapy, the doctor said he could see no trace of the disease. **The fact that she was cured** is a miracle.	

EXERCISE 5

The following paragraphs describe amazing facts about famous people. Make observations about each set of facts using a *that* clause following *the fact/idea/news*, etc.

Example: When Beethoven was 28 years old, he became deaf. In spite of this, he was still able to compose music.

The fact that Beethoven composed music while he was deaf is amazing.

1. Marie Antoinette and Louis XVI ate very well, while their Parisian subjects could not afford bread. When hearing of this, the unsympathetic queen is reported to have said, "Why, then, let them eat cake."

2. United States President Richard Nixon resigned from office in 1974 after a very serious governmental scandal. Republican associates who were interested in having him re-elected had installed wiretaps at the headquarters of the Democratic National Committee at the Watergate Hotel. Rather than being honest, Nixon tried to cover up the scandal, and this led to his downfall.

3. In 1919, Rudolph Valentino, a famous American movie star, married Jean Acker. In his silent films, he played the part of the great lover. But, on the wedding day, Acker ran away and Valentino never consummated his marriage with her.

4. For years, athletes did the high jump by jumping sideways or straddling over the bar. Then, Dick Fosbury discovered that he could break world records by going over head first, flat on his back. The technique is now called the Fosbury Flop.

5. The Japanese had long revered their emperor as divine. However, Emperor Hirohito destroyed this image by announcing to his people in 1946 that it was a false conception that he was descended from God. In fact, even at the early age of 14, Hirohito had doubted his own divinity.

FOCUS 4 — *The Fact That . . .*

use

EXAMPLES	EXPLANATIONS
(a) **Less formal:** The fact that she refused the money showed her sense of pride. (b) **Formal:** That she refused the money showed her sense of pride. (c) **Less formal:** People generally acknowledge the fact that Japan must find alternate ways to use its space. (d) **Formal:** People generally acknowledge that Japan must find alternate ways to use its space.	*The fact* + *that* clause noun complements in (a) and (c) are similar in meaning to the *that* clauses in (b) and (d); however, we generally consider them less formal.
(e) **Wordy:** He believed the fact that his daughter had been kidnapped, and he understood the fact that he would need to pay a ransom. (f) **Concise:** He believed that his daughter had been kidnapped, and he understood that he would need to pay a ransom.	In writing, overuse of *that* clauses in object position with *the fact* can lead to wordiness. In most cases, it is better to use the simple *that* clause.
(g) The detectives concealed **the fact that** they had searched the room. (h) The soldiers accepted **the fact that** they had been defeated. (i) The police officers disregarded **the fact that** they needed a search warrant. (j) NOT: The police officers disregarded that they needed a search warrant.	Certain verbs (such as *accept, conceal, discuss, dispute, disregard, hide, overlook, support*) require the use of *the fact that* clauses in object position, however.

EXERCISE 6

Read the following passage and write a short paragraph explaining the facts about ice. Exchange your paragraph with a classmate and check each other's paragraphs for excessive use of *the fact + that* clauses.

Example: Several facts about ice can be explained quite easily. For example, ~~the fact~~ that skaters appear to glide as they skate as if they are on water can be accounted for by ice melting underneath a skater's blade. . . .

National Geographic World, Dec 1998 i280 p4(1)

Why in the world? Scientific Facts About the Properties of Ice by *Judith E. Rinard.*

Abstract: Ice has certain properties that make it ideal for sports such as ice skating. Icebergs usually have the larger part submerged and leaving the smaller peak visible. The International Iceberg Patrol leaves warning signs for the safety of ships in polar waters.

Full Text: COPYRIGHT 1998 National Geographic Society

Brrrr! These ICY questions may make you shiver.

WHY DO ICE SKATES GLIDE?
Ice-skaters seem to slide along in a fluid motion. In fact they really do slide on fluid! The fluid is water. Under pressure, ice melts. A skater's whole body weight is concentrated on the blades. The pressure of the blades melts the ice. This forms a thick film of water. Once the skater moves on, the ice immediately refreezes.

WHY DOES ICE STICK TO ME?
When the warm, moist surface of your wet hand meets the freezing cold surface of an ice cube, heat gets transferred. The warmth of your hand heats the ice enough to melt the outside. But the ice quickly cools your skin. The surface of your skin may get so cold that the melted ice freezes again and—ouch! You're stuck. Only ice that's in or just removed from the freezer is cold enough to stick to you. A word of advice: Don't pop an ice cube straight from the freezer into your mouth.

WHY ARE ICEBERGS DANGEROUS?
The R.M.S. *Titanic* is a good example of how a collision with an iceberg can quickly sink a ship. Icebergs are huge chunks of ice floating in the sea. The most dangerous thing about them is that most of their bulk is hidden underwater, and only the tip of an iceberg may be visible. People on a ship may not spot the berg until the ship has slammed into the submerged part. The sharp, deadly ice can rip a hole in a ship. Today the International Iceberg Patrol provides ships with early warnings of icebergs.

WHY SHOULDN'T I TOUCH DRY ICE?
Most ice is frozen water. But dry ice is solid carbon dioxide and much colder than ordinary ice. When heated, it doesn't melt into a liquid. It turns into a smoky-looking gas. Handling dry ice is dangerous because of its super-cold temperature—lower than minus 100 [degrees] F. Touching it can cause frostbite in the fingers. For safety, people wear heavy gloves when handling dry ice.

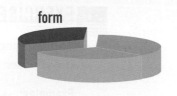

FOCUS 5 — *That* Clause Noun Complements Following Transitive Adjectives and Phrasal Verbs

EXAMPLES

(a) He is tired of **the fact that she refuses to see him.**

(b) NOT: He is tired of that she refuses to see him.

(c) He played down **the news that his team won.**

(d) NOT: He played down that his team won.

EXPLANATION

When *that* clause noun complements follow transitive adjectives (adjective taking a preposition + a noun phrase) or phrasal verbs (verb + preposition), they must be *that* clauses using *the fact/news/idea/theory*, etc. rather than simple *that* clauses.

Examples of Transitive Adjectives	Examples of Phrasal Verbs
disappointed in	*play down*
worried about	*make up*
proud of	*give in*
sick of	*face up to*
tired of	*put up with*

EXERCISE 7

Imagine that a very wealthy entrepreneur has just lost his fortune. Comment upon the circumstances of his condition using the words below and *the fact/idea/news, etc. that* clauses.

Examples: businessman (face up to)
> *The businessman had to face up to the fact that he had lost his millions.*

1. his mother (worried about)
2. his dynamic personality (not make up)
3. his creditors (wary of)
4. his employees (indignant at)
5. his wife (put up with)
6. the lawyers (proud of)

EXERCISE 8

Suppose you saw people doing the following strange actions. What facts would you bring up in order to help clear up their confusion? Write a sentence about what you would say.

Examples: reading a book upside down
I would bring up the fact that it is easier to read a book right side up.

1. washing the dishes with laundry detergent
2. making lasagna without cheese
3. playing soccer with a baseball
4. going to the beach without sunglasses
5. having the radio on with the sound turned all the way down
6. writing the word *fake* with *ph* before *a* instead of *f*.

EXERCISE 9

The following sentences review the structures learned in this unit. Correct those that contain errors or are too wordy according to formal writing rules. Write OK next to those that are correct.

Examples: The teacher overlooked the fact that Hung had not done his homework. OK
The fact that she made a confession ^was untrue.

1. Tom believes the fact that light travels faster than sound.
2. The request for her to stop smoking was ignored.
3. The fact that the automobile increased the distance a person could travel made it possible for a person to live and work in different places.
4. She is tired of that she always has to wash the dishes.
5. We are concerned about that there will be no more food.
6. I am grateful for the fact that the doctor assisted me in my decision.
7. Did the glasses help to conceal the fact that he had a scar on his left eyelid?
8. The fact that Mary finished her homework.
9. The fact that twenty million Russians died during World War II is tragic.
10. The request that we ignore the crime was considered unacceptable.
11. Do you agree the statement that blondes have more fun?
12. That Jerome passed the bar examination made it possible for him to practice law.

EXERCISE 10

What world changes will occur during the rest of the third millennium? In a book called *Megatrends 2000* (New York: Morrow, 1990) John Naisbett and Patricia Aburdene describe what they believe will transform the world, or, in some cases, American culture over the next 1000 years. Here are some of their predictions:

1. The English language will become the world's first truly universal language.

2. Nations, especially the "superpower" countries, will regard war as an obsolete way of solving problems.

3. Even as peoples of the world communicate more closely, individual cultures will increasingly find their unique qualities important and seek to preserve racial, linguistic, national, and religious traditions.

4. The arts will replace sports as American society's dominant leisure activity; Americans will consider alternatives to attending sports events such as football and baseball.

5. The trend of the future in the global economy is "downsizing": producing and using smaller, lighter, and more sophisticated products (for example, smaller computers, lighter building materials, electronic impulses used for financial transactions instead of paper).

6. In the first decade of the third millennium, we will think it quaint that women in the late twentieth century were excluded from the top levels of business and politics.

7. The world's nations will increasingly cooperate to address global environmental problems.

Which of these hypotheses do you consider almost a certainty by the end of the twenty-first century? Which do you think probable? Which do you find unlikely developments? Fill in the following blanks with your opinions.

Examples: I agree with the idea that <u>the arts will become popular, but I do not believe that Americans will lose their love of football</u>.
The prediction that <u>English will be the world's universal language is already true</u>.

1. I am skeptical of the notion that _____.
2. The tendency for _____.
3. I believe the statement that _____.
4. The suggestion that _____.
5. I doubt the possibility that _____.

Use Your English

 **ACTIVITY 1 listening/speaking**

CD Track 35

■ **STEP 1** Listen to the audio. It is a recording of an interview between a university admissions officer and several interested high school seniors. Take note of any interesting facts you hear.

■ **STEP 2** Describe the interesting facts you learned to a classmate. Use as many noun complements as you can.

Example: *The fact that the admissions officer mainly looks at GPA and college entrance examination scores surprises me.*

ACTIVITY 2 reading/writing

Have you ever wondered what causes static electricity? Or why geese fly in a "V"? Or why the ocean is blue? Research one of these questions or one of the issues mentioned in the Opening Task (meteorites, rainbows, oases, etc.). Write a short report explaining what facts give natural phenomena their unusual properties. Use at least three noun complements in your report.

Example: *Some people say that lightning never strikes the same place twice. However, the fact that we cannot scientifically predict when or where lightning will strike makes it difficult to refute this idea . . . .*

ACTIVITY 3 reading/writing

Editorials and opinion essays can be found in newspapers, magazines, and online. Read several editorials or opinion essays. Then write your own view of the ideas in the essays by using noun complements.

Example: *The idea that terrorist cells will ever be abolished completely seems unlikely.*

ACTIVITY 4   listening/speaking

■ **STEP 1**   Watch a mystery or detective program on TV or at the movies with your classmates. Discuss why the central characters were not able to solve the mystery or crime sooner than they did. What facts were concealed, disregarded, or overlooked? What facts finally led to the solution of the mystery?

Example: *The mother concealed the fact that Tony had a twin brother. The fact that Tony had a twin brother made the police finally realize that it was Tony's twin, Jimmy, who had stolen the valuable painting.*

■ **STEP 2**   Watch a sports event such as soccer or baseball on TV. Discuss the facts that explain causes or effects of key events during the game.

Example: *The fact that the Giants hit three home runs in the first inning of the game gave them a clear advantage against the Dodgers. The news that Keiji Omura had sprained his ankle while sliding into third base didn't help the situation.*

ACTIVITY 5   research on the web

On the Internet, research an environmental problem such as pollution of cities, extinction of animals, or toxic waste. Then, discuss with your classmates the specific reasons behind the problem.

Example: *The fact that people have continued to drive gasoline engines has created a huge pollution problem in cities.*

ACTIVITY 6   reflection

Reflect on the oral or written presentations of your classmates from the past week. What theories, axioms, facts, hypotheses, ideas, proposals, statements, or theses were presented? Summarize your classmates' ideas and then make judgments about them using a *that* clause noun complement.

Example: *My classmate made a presentation on the theory that aliens from outer space visited the earth in 1955. I don't agree with the idea that extraterrestrial beings have ever visited the earth.*

SUBJECTIVE VERBS IN *THAT* CLAUSES

UNIT GOALS

- Use subjunctive verbs in *that* clause complements with verbs of advice and urging

- Use subjunctive verbs in noun complements that refer to nouns of advice or urging

- Use subjunctive verbs in adjective complements

OPENING TASK
Solving Problems

It is not uncommon for two different people or groups of people to disagree about the rightness of an issue or the solution to a problem. Often another person who does not favor either side will be called in to serve as an *arbitrator*.

For this task, one or more classmates should role-play each side of one or more of the following issues. One other person, as the arbitrator, should listen, ask questions, and give recommendations to the two parties (for example, *I suggest that _____; I recommend that _____; I propose that _____*).

CASE 1

A young woman would like to attend an all-male college. The president of the advisory board of the college wants to maintain the one-hundred-year tradition of an all-male campus.

CASE 2

A man was in a serious car accident one year ago. He has been in a coma ever since and is not expected to recover. The man's parents want to keep him alive. The man's wife sees that there is no hope for his recovery and would like to remove him from the life-support system.

CASE 3

A father keeps his children at home rather than sending them to school because he feels children are being taught ideas against his religion. The school board feels it is unlawful to prevent children from getting a well-rounded education.

CASE 4

A supervisor fires a worker because the supervisor believes she is often late, undependable, and disrespectful. The worker denies these charges and claims that she is overworked and called names by her supervisor.

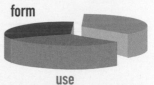

form

use

FOCUS 1 | Subjunctive Verbs in *That* Clauses

EXAMPLES	EXPLANATIONS
(a) The arbitrator recommends that Susan not **be** fired. (b) It was stipulated that he **abandon** the plans.	*That* clause complements of verbs of advice and urging must contain a present subjunctive verb.
(c) Her father demanded that they **be** back by 12:00. (d) The committee stipulated that Mary **follow** all of the instructions.	The subjunctive verb is the base form of the verb: *be, go, take,* etc. We use the base form for all singular and plural subjects.
(e) **Formal:** The president insisted that the meeting **begin** on time. (f) **Informal:** Jody suggested that we **should eat** at 6:00.	For a similar yet less formal effect, use *should* + base form instead of the subjunctive.

Verbs of advice and urging that require subjunctive verbs in *that* clauses:

advise	*insist*	*prefer*	*stipulate*
beg	*move*	*propose*	*suggest*
command	*order*	*recommend*	
demand	*pledge*	*request*	
determine	*pray*	*require*	

EXERCISE 1

Use the following sentence model to make comments about each of the numbered items. Fill in the first blank with the correct form of the verb in parentheses and the second blank with a subjunctive verb or *should* + base form, whichever is more appropriate.

Base sentence: She (or he) _____ that he (or she) _____.

Example: A boss to her employee (recommend)
She <u>recommends</u> that he <u>call her tomorrow</u>.

1. A friend who wants to give another friend some information (insist)

2. An actor to a director who may offer him a part in a play (suggest)

3. A doctor to a patient who might have a deadly disease (require)

4. A neighbor to another neighbor who is too busy to talk (propose)

5. A father to an unsuitable companion for his daughter (forbid)

6. A salesperson to a customer (advise)

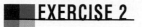

EXERCISE 2

During the role-play portion of the Opening Task on pages 398 and 399, what were some of the recommendations that the arbitrator made to the conflicting parties?

Example: *He suggested that the president of the advisory board reconsider the all-male policy.*

form

FOCUS 2	**Subjunctive Verbs in Noun Complements**

EXAMPLES	**EXPLANATIONS**
(a) *Suggest*: **The suggestion that he be fired** was met with resistance. (b) *Request*: She didn't listen to **his request that she file a complaint.** (c) *Advise*: **His advice that the criminals be set free** was premature.	Nouns that come from verbs of advice and urging may also take a *that* clause with a subjunctive verb. Some of these nouns are *advice, command, decision, demand, order, pronouncement, recommendation, request,* and *suggestion.*

EXERCISE 3

Imagine that you live in an apartment complex surrounded by some very disagreeable neighbors in apartments 4A through 4F. Answer the following questions, using the prompts provided and a subjunctive verb in a noun complement.

Example: What did the man in 4A do when you told him his music was too loud?
ignore/suggestion.
He ignored my suggestion that he turn down the stereo.

1. What did the person in 4B do when you asked her to return your watering can? (not heed/proposal)

2. What did the man in 4C do when you wanted him to stop being a Peeping Tom? (laugh at/demand)

3. What did the woman in 4D do when you told her to stop stomping around? (not listen to/demand)

Imagine that an arbitrator listened to two sides of a case and made the following decisions. What is your opinion of the arbitrator's advice?

Example: Mr. Jones built a work shed that interfered with his neighbor's, Mr. Rodriguez's, view of the city. Mr. Jones provided the city maps that showed the shed was built on his property. The arbitrator demanded that Mr. Jones tear the shed down. *The demand that Mr. Jones tear down his shed is unfair considering he had legally built the shed on his own property.*

1. Ms. Nguyen went to an emergency room to deliver her baby. The hospital stated that Ms. Nguyen was not insured and would have to pay for the delivery. The arbitrator decided that the hospital would have to cover the costs of the delivery.

2. Celia Velez was going to get married in December but now she has changed her mind. She had bought a wedding dress at a sale for $3000. She tried to return the dress three days later but the salesperson in the store told her that all sale items were final. The arbitrator recommended that the store take back the dress and charge a 10 percent stocking fee but return the remainder of the money to Celia.

3. Todd Simpson got a poor grade in a class. He claimed that the professor was absent during five weeks of the semester and did not properly mark his assignments. The arbitrator demanded that Todd be given a passing grade because it was determined that he had been given a lower grade than deserved.

4. Mr. and Mrs. Scott paid $5000 for a luxury cruise to the Greek Isles. Mrs. Scott's sister got deathly ill and so Mr. and Mrs. Scott cancelled their cruise in order to assist her. Ms. Nakamura, the cruise line sales manager, refused to refund their ticket because the cancellation had taken place too late. The arbitrator requested that the Scotts be given a full-price ticket on a future cruise.

5. Mr. Liu's dog barks all night long. Mr. Hesterman asked Mr. Liu to quiet his dog on three separate occasions but then called the police to remedy the situation. The police confiscated the dog and charged Mr. Liu a $500 fine for disturbing the peace. The arbitrator ordered that Mr. Liu pay the fine and get rid of the dog.

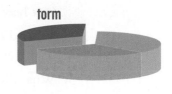

form

FOCUS 3   Subjunctive Verbs in Adjective Complements

EXAMPLES	EXPLANATIONS
(a) **That he type** is essential.	Adjective complements sometimes take subjunctive verbs. This is true when advice adjectives like *advisable, desirable, essential, imperative, important, mandatory, necessary, urgent,* and *vital* are in the main clause.
(b) It is essential **that he type.**	
(c) **That she be punctual** is important.	
(d) It is important **that she be punctual.**	

EXERCISE 5

STEP 1 Using the information from the following job advertisements, fill in the following statements with *that* clauses containing subjunctive verbs.

> **Example:** It is important <u>that the accounting applicant be bilingual in Chinese and English.</u> (accountant)

1. _____ is essential. (chemist)
2. It is mandatory _____. (shuttle driver)
3. _____ is desirable. (file clerk)
4. It is imperative _____. (manager)
5. It is necessary _____. (nurse)

STEP 2 Create five more of your own sentences with information from the ads.

---

236 Employment

Accountant ★
Accounting firm seeks individual w/ min 2 yr exp. Good communication skills & ability to assist clients. Biling Chinese required. Previous exp in CPA firm a plus. Call Mr. Tang 213-555-1409

Accountant Executive
Local firm has a fabulous opportunity for a tax accountant. Two + years tax or accounting experience, a strong client service mentality, and a team oriented approach required. Position can be full time. Send in resume 555 East King, Big City, PA 34543

Chemist ★
Stable, fast-growing company seeks chemist for formulation of industrial products. Must have BS degree chemistry & min. 5 yrs. exp. Nonsmoker preferred. Excellent benefits. Redex Co. 714-555-2221

Customer Service lot of work full-time. Fax resume to 234-555-4567

236 Employment

Customer Service
30 Jobs Temp to Perm
WANTED!
People with good Customer Service skills that can work 3:30pm to 12am 5pm-9pm. If you can, we need you ASAP Call! 458-555-6666

Drivers-Shuttle ★
AIRWAY Shuttle needs outstanding drivers for day and eve shifts. Must be clean-cut, highly ethical, energetic. Great benefits and friendly environment.
AIRWAY 818-555-8156

Education:
Elementary Principal Twelve month position available on or before January 1, 2001. Elementary teaching experience and elementary certification required. Knowledge certification required.

236 Employment

File Clerk
Min. 1 yr exp in law file rm. Knowledge of ofc equipment. Ability to work without supervision. Good command of English for switchboard relief. Mrs. Jacobsen 310-555-6662

Grocery
Fox's market has immediate! openings for part-time or full-time meat cutters. Vacation, Life insurance, Medical insurance, Profit sharing. Call 333-555-4444

Manager ★
10 new Asst. Managers for marketing & sales needed. No exp. necessary. We will train. Must be 18 & older. Must have car. Work in a wild & crazy office.
Super's 818-555-8234

Nurse ★
Opportunity for career-minded RN. Participate in clinical trials & oversee needs for patients on daily basis. Need good track record of exp. be able to learn fast, self-starter. If interested, call Westside Hospital 213-555-6210

Use Your English

ACTIVITY 1 listening/writing

CD Track 36

Listen to the audio of a radio broadcaster who gives people advice about relationships.

■ **STEP 1** Jot down notes about each of the problems and the advice given.

	Problem	Advice
a. Female Caller:		
b. Male Caller:		

■ **STEP 2** Now write a short paragraph summarizing your opinion of the broadcaster's advice to these two callers. Use at least two subjunctive complements in your writing.

ACTIVITY 2 reading/writing

Read at least five advice letters and responses in the newspaper from advice columnists such as "Ann Landers," "Dear Abby," or "Miss Manners." Summarize the problems and the advice given to persons requesting the advice.

Example: *A man had attempted many times to quit smoking. Counseling, nicotine chewing gum, and "cold turkey" were all ineffective. Abby suggested that he try acupuncture.*

ACTIVITY 3 — research on the web

Select a political, environmental, or civic problem and research the problem on the Internet using a search engine such as Google® or Yahoo®, or a Web site you may know of. Then write a letter to the editor of a newspaper. Include the following parts in your letter and at least two subjunctive complements.

- summary of the issue
- statement of your own opinion
- list solutions to the problem or suggestions for improvement

ACTIVITY 4 — reflection

Imagine that your favorite relative or a good friend is having difficulty getting good grades in school. What is some advice that you could give him/her to improve his/her time management, study skills, interaction with professors, etc.?

Example: *I would suggest that he make a schedule with class time, study time, and meal time clearly delineated.*

UNIT GOALS

- Use emphatic *do* to add emphasis to a sentence

- Choose *no* versus *not* to emphasize a negative statement

OPENING TASK
Looking at Consumer Needs

Advertising agencies spend a lot of time and money finding out what consumers like and dislike. VALS™ (Values and Lifestyles) typology* is a system for describing different types of consumers. Imagine that you work for an advertising agency and that you are trying to identify the likes and dislikes of potential consumers. Use the VALS™ typology to help you make your decision.

■ STEP 1

Read the VALS™ (for Values and Lifestyles) descriptions. List items or services that you think the eight groups of consumers would and would not want to purchase.

*VALS™ typology, originally developed by SRI International, is now owned by SRI Consulting Business Intelligence (SRIC-BI). Source: SRI Consulting Business Intelligence (SRIC-BI); www.sric-bi.com/VALS (retrieved on February 12, 2007)

VALS™ TYPOLOGY CONSUMER TYPES	CONSUMER ITEMS OR SERVICES THAT WOULD OR WOULD NOT APPEAL TO GROUP
1. **Survivors:** Have few resources, think the past is better than the future, try to meet basic needs rather than fulfill desires, live lives with a narrow focus. Cautious consumers who may purchase favorite brands at a discount.	NEED: good medical care DON'T NEED: luxuries (expensive fur coats, etc.)
2. **Makers:** Motivated by self-expression, doers, practical, self-sufficient, suspicious of new ideas, resent government intrusion on individual rights, live within context of family, practical work, and physical recreation. Practical consumers who buy basic products at a good value.	
3. **Strivers:** Trendy, fun-loving, stylish, have jobs but not serious careers, desire more money to meet needs. Active consumers who sometimes make impulsive purchases to demonstrate their ability to buy.	
4. **Believers:** Conservative, conventional, traditional values established by family, religion, community and the nation, follow established routines. Predictable consumers who buy familiar products and established brands but sometimes feel victimized.	
5. **Experiencers:** motivated by self-expression, young, enthusiastic, impulsive, seek variety, excitement, risk. Avid consumers of products relating to fashion, entertainment, and social life.	
6. **Achievers:** motivated by achievement, goal-oriented, deep commitment to career and family, politically conservative, respect authority, value predictability and stability. Image-conscious consumers who want many products and services to demonstrate prestige to peers.	
7. **Thinkers:** motivated by ideals, conservative, mature, wealthy, well educated, active decision-makers, well informed about the world, open to new ideas. Conservative consumers who value durability, functionality, and good value.	
8. **Innovators:** receptive to new ideas, high self-esteem, sophisticated, wealthy, image is important for self-expression rather than power, leaders, lives are varied. Active consumers with upscale tastes.	

▪ STEP 2

Conduct a mock advertising agency meeting where you convince members of your team of the needs of each type of consumer.

Example: *Survivors really do need medical care!*   *Survivors will have no money for luxuries.*

*Survivors won't buy any expensive fur coats, but they **will** buy practical warm woolen ones!*

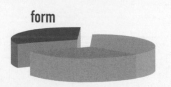

FOCUS 1 Emphatic Structures

EXAMPLES	EXPLANATIONS
(a) I **will** write you a letter as soon as I arrive. (b) He **is** going to Mexico during the winter break. (c) Sally **has** finished her homework. (d) Todd **is** a world-class swimmer.	We can add emphasis to a sentence by orally stressing the auxiliary verb or the *be* verb.
(e) I **do** believe in miracles. (f) Professor Dean **did** get her conference paper accepted.	In sentences where there is no auxiliary or *be* verb, we can add *do* and stress it for emphasis.
(g) Juan **really does** know the answer to the question. (h) They **certainly did** see us at the exposition.	We often add extra emphasis with an emphatic adverb like *really* or *certainly* and a strongly stressed *do*.

EXERCISE 1

Imagine that you are a salesperson. What will you say to each type of consumer listed in the Opening Task in order to persuade them to buy a product? On a separate piece of paper, write two sentences per item using a variety of emphatic structures. Underline each emphatic structure.

Example: Survivor: *I <u>do</u> understand that you need to be careful with your money. But you really <u>must</u> buy this basic black dress for all occasions.*

1. Survivor
2. Maker
3. Striver
4. Believer
5. Experiencer
6. Achiever
7. Thinker
8. Innovator

use

EXAMPLES	EXPLANATIONS
	Emphatic *do* can:
(a) **A:** You have a good thesis. **B:** Really? **A:** Yes, you really **do** have a good thesis.	• add emphasis to a whole sentence.
(b) **Do** come in! (c) **Please do** give him my best regards!	• add emphasis to an imperative. This use of emphatic *do* softens a command and shows polite encouragement.
(d) **A:** You didn't lock the back door. **B:** You're wrong. I **did** lock it.	• contradict a negative statement. This use of emphatic *do* is very common in arguments. In such situations, the *do* verb generally refers back to a previous statement.
(e) **A:** Bob didn't cheat on the test. **B:** Then, what **did** happen? OR Who **did** cheat? OR What **did** he cheat on?	• be used to ask a clarification question about a previously mentioned negative statement.
(f) It was no surprise to me. He seldom **did** complete his homework. (g) To make a long story short, she always **does** get her own way.	• add emphasis to a verb used in connection with an adverb of frequency such as *never, rarely, seldom, often,* or *always.*
(h) I'm relieved that he **does** have his credit card (because I thought he might have forgotten it).	• emphasize a positive result regarding something that had been unknown or in doubt.
(i) Even though I do not usually enjoy fiction, I **did** enjoy John King's latest novel.	• indicate strong concession bordering on contrast.

EXERCISE 2

Circulate around the room and give at least ten compliments to other students using the auxiliary, *be,* or emphatic *do* verbs.

Examples: *You **have** done your hair very nicely.*
*You certainly **are** wearing a beautiful necklace.*
*That certainly **is** a nice shirt.*
*I really **do** like your loafers.*

EXERCISE 3

Use *do* structures to make the following invitations, requests, or suggestions.

Example: suggestion to sit down
Do sit down.

1. invitation to put a friend's bags in your room
2. request to come early to the party
3. suggestion to tell the children to quiet down
4. invitation to have some more punch
5. request to put the money in a safe place
6. suggestion to turn off the lights when you leave the conference room
7. invitation to have a bite to eat
8. request to let relatives know you'll be late for your visit

EXERCISE 4

Bruce and Gary are brothers, but they often have arguments. Read the following argument and cross through all the places where you think it is possible to use emphatic *do*. Rewrite those sentences with an appropriate form of the *do* verb. The first one has been done for you.

Bruce: Did you take my flashlight? I can't find it anywhere.

Gary: Well, I haven't got it. I always return the stuff I borrow.

Bruce: No, you don't.

Gary: That's not true! ~~I return the things I borrow!~~ *I do return the things I borrow!* It's probably on your desk. I bet you didn't look for it there.

Bruce: No, I looked on my desk, and it's not there.

Gary: Well, don't blame me. You can't find it because you never clean your room.

Bruce: I clean my room!

Gary: Oh, no you don't!

Bruce: I certainly clean it up! I cleaned it up last night as a matter of fact.

Gary: You didn't.

Bruce: I really cleaned it up last night. Hey, there's my flashlight under your bed.

Gary: Well, I didn't put it here.

Bruce: I bet you put it there. Anyhow, that proves it: You take my stuff and you don't return it.

Gary: I told you before: I return everything I borrow. You just don't look after your things properly.

Bruce: I look after my things. Anyway, from now on, I'm going to lock my door and keep you out.

Gary: You can't. That door doesn't have a key.

Bruce: That's where you're wrong. It has a key and I'm going to lock you out!

Gary: Oh, be quiet!

Bruce: Do you know something? You make me sick. You really make me sick.

Gary: You make me sick too!

Get together with another student and take the parts of Gary and Bruce. Read the dialogue, paying particular attention to the stress patterns of emphatic *do*. If possible, record yourselves and listen to how emphatic you sound.

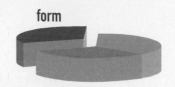

form

FOCUS 3 — *Not* versus *No*

EXAMPLES	EXPLANATIONS
(a) They do not have any suggestions for the project. They have **no** suggestions for the project. (b) Norwegian tourists did not come to Miami this year. **No** Norwegian tourists came to Miami this year.	To emphasize a negative statement, we can use *no* + noun in place of *not/-n't* + verb.
(c) I have **no** fear of flying. (d) She is taking the bus because she has **no** car today. (e) He has **no** chairs in his apartment.	We use *no* with noncount nouns, singular count nouns, and plural count nouns.
(f) They are indebted to **no one**. (g) I saw **nobody** by the river. (h) He managed **nothing** well. (i) That business decision led him **nowhere**.	We can combine *no* with other words to make compounds. *no + one = no one* *no + body = nobody* *no + thing = nothing* *no + where = nowhere*
(j) Mike doesn't have **any** money. (k) We haven't seen **any** pelicans all day. (l) NOT: She won't earn no money.	In standard English, a negative sentence (with *not* after the first auxiliary verb or *be*) with a second negative component uses *not . . . any*.

STEP 1   Fiona went to a party last night. To fill in what happened after that, match the first part of the sentence in column A with something from column B that makes sense and is grammatical. The first one has been done for you.

A	B
1. She had hoped to make some new friends, but she didn't meet	a. any food left.
2. She had to drive home, so she didn't drink	b. anyone to dance with.
3. She was very hungry, but when she arrived there wasn't	c. any more parties.
4. She talked to a few people, but she didn't have	d. anyone interesting.
5. Some people were dancing, but Fiona didn't have	e. any fun!"
6. She wanted to sit down, but there weren't	f. any alcohol.
7. Finally, she said to herself: "This party isn't	g. anything to say to them
8. So she went home early and decided not to go to	h. any chairs.

STEP 2   Rewrite each sentence of Step 1 using *no* or an appropriate *no* + compound. Change the verbs as necessary. The first one has been done for you.

> *She had hoped to make some new friends, but she met nobody interesting.*

EXERCISE 6

Edit the following speech for errors with negative constructions. When you are finished, read it aloud to a partner and see if there are any more changes you want to make. The first sentence has been edited as an example.

(1) The year 2025 ~~no is~~ is not as far away as it might seem. (2) Today we don't have no direction. (3) If we don't get any direction, our dream for our nation is sure to explode. (4) No children will have the things we had. (5) There isn't nobody who cannot benefit from the few principles I will share with you today. (6) Please listen carefully. (7) If you don't listen to anything I say, the consequences will be fatal.

(Continued on next page)

(8) First, it isn't good for nobody to feel that they deserve everything when they don't put any sweat and struggle in getting it. (9) Even more, this nation can't tell nobody nowhere that it is entitled to world leadership just because they had it in the past. (10) You can never take nothing for granted in this country. (11) I hope you will work hard to achieve your dream.

(12) Next, I believe that no people should set goals and then do anything not to achieve them. (13) If you set a goal, work hard and humbly to accomplish it. (14) Even if you don't get no credit, it is important to keep trying because you and your maker know what you accomplished.

(15) Another important piece of advice is not to work just for money. (16) Money alone can't strengthen nobody's family nor help nobody sleep at night. (17) Don't let nobody tell you that wealth or fame is the same as character. (18) It is not O.K. to use drugs even if everyone is doing it. (19) It is not O.K. to cheat or lie even if every public official does.

(20) Finally, no person should be afraid of taking no risks. (21) No anybody should be afraid of failing. (22) It shouldn't matter to nobody anywhere how many times you fall down. (23) What matters is how many times you get up.

(24) Let's not spend no more time talking. We are all responsible for building a decent nation to live in! Let's not let no more minutes pass.

FOCUS 4 — When to Use *No* for Emphasis

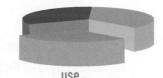

use

EXAMPLES	EXPLANATIONS
(a) I didn't have any friends when I was a child. (b) I had **no** friends when I was a child.	Statements using *no* as the negative word instead of *not* emphasize what is missing or lacking. In speaking, we often stress the word *no* for extra emphasis.
(c) **Neutral:** I didn't meet anybody interesting at the party. (d) **Emphatic:** I met **nobody** interesting at the party. (e) **Neutral:** I didn't learn anything new at the conference. (f) **Emphatic:** I learned **nothing** new at the conference.	*No* + compound also emphasizes what is missing or lacking. Sentence (c) sounds neutral, a statement of fact. Sentence (d) sounds more emotional, emphasizing the lack of interesting people.

EXERCISE 7

Fiona is describing the party (in Exercise 5) to her best friend and is telling her what a miserable time she had. Imagine you are Fiona and try describing the party from her point of view, emphasizing all the negative aspects of the evening. If possible, record yourself and listen to see how emphatic you sound.

EXERCISE 8

Emphatic language is very common in public speeches. Read aloud the extracts from speeches below and notice the different ways each speaker uses language to emphasize his message. Underline any examples that you can find of the emphatic language discussed in this unit. Do you notice any other techniques the speakers use to get their points across?

1. Jesse Jackson: Speech to the Democratic National Convention, July 20, 1988

When I was born late one afternoon, October 8, in Greenville, South Carolina, no writers asked my mother her name. Nobody chose to write down our address. My mama was not supposed to make it. You see, I was born to a teenage mother who was born to a teenage mother. I understand. I know abandonment and people being mean to you, and saying you're nothing and nobody, and can never be anything. I understand . . . I understand when nobody knows your name. I understand when you have no name . . . I really do understand.

2. Donald Kagan: Address to the Class of 1994 of Yale College, September 1, 1990

We now have the mechanisms that do permit the storage of data in staggering amounts and their retrieval upon demand. And one of the by-products is the approaching end of the age of specialization. The doom of the specialist draws closer every time someone punches the keys on a word processor. Of course, we will still need doctors, lawyers, plumbers, and electricians. But will there still be a brisk market for all the specialties we have fostered in the economic and social fields? I doubt it. The future will belong to those who know how to handle the combinations of information that come out of the computer, what we used to call the "generalist." The day of the generalist is just over the horizon and we had better be ready for it.

Use Your English

CD Track 37

ACTIVITY 1 listening/writing/speaking

■ **STEP 1** Listen to the audio, a lecture on how to create a good advertisement. Take notes and pay special attention to the suggestions given.

■ **STEP 2** Summarize the speaker's advice in a short paragraph.

Example: *A good ad should have three main ingredients.*
The ad should include information about the product and its unique advantage. . . .

■ **STEP 3** Now revise your paragraph so that it sounds more emphatic. Use some of the techniques you have learned in this chapter.

■ **STEP 4** Now read your paragraph aloud to a classmate, stressing words appropriately.

ACTIVITY 2 writing/speaking/listening

■ **STEP 1** Organize a political campaign in class. Divide into groups. Each group represents a new political party. With your group, create a name and draw up a list of all the things you stand for and all the things you will do if you are elected.

■ **STEP 2** Make a poster representing your beliefs and prepare a short speech to persuade people to vote for you. Each member of your group should be prepared to speak on a different aspect of your party's platform.

■ **STEP 3** Give your speeches to the rest of the class and decide who has the most persuasive approach. If possible, record your speech and afterward listen to what you said, taking note of any emphatic structures you used and how you said them.

ACTIVITY 3   research on the web/writing/speaking

■ **STEP 1**   Think of someone famous whom you truly admire because of his or her ideas. This person could be an important figure in any field, such as:

Communications	Katie Couric, Rush Limbaugh, Oprah Winfrey
Politics	Hillary Clinton, Kofi Annan, Hugo Chavez
Business	Bill Gates, Martha Stewart, Rupert Murdoch
Entertainment	Tom Cruise, Angelina Jolie, Stephen Spielberg
Sports	Sanmy Sosa, Lance Armstrong, Anna Kournikova

■ **STEP 2**   Go on to *InfoTrac® College Edition* or the Internet to do research about the person you have selected.

■ **STEP 3**   Write a short essay describing what traits, activities, or ideas of this person impress you the most.

■ **STEP 4**   Give a speech to your classmates convincing them of the admirable traits, activities, ideas, or accomplishments of this person. Use as many emphatic structures from this unit as you can.

Examples: *Even though some people think Rush Limbaugh is an egotistical talk show host, his commentaries do contain some informative news.*

Despite Martha Stewart being a convicted felon, she does continue to be a powerful businesswoman influencing style and homekeeping trends.

There is no Hollywood movie star as controversial as Angelina Jolie.

ACTIVITY 4   reflection

Students often find themselves distracted from their studies. A little grocery shopping or a quick trip to the mall may be a good way for a change of pace. However, certain individuals sometimes end up wasting a lot of time or, even worse, a lot of money shopping when they should be studying. Look at the consumer types in the Opening Task on page 407 and select the type of consumer you are. Then, write a short paragraph describing the shopping temptations you might have at college and how you might overcome these temptations so that you can complete your academic goals. Finally, discuss these ideas with a partner, using emphatic structures from the unit.

Example: *I am an Experiencer. Because of this, I really **might** have the temptation to overspend while I am at college. For this reason, I **do** need to create a budget. . . .*

FRONTING STRUCTURES FOR EMPHASIS AND FOCUS

UNIT GOALS

- **Know what kinds of structures can be moved to the front of sentences for emphasis**

- **Know when to change the subject/verb order for fronted structures**

- **Use fronted negative forms for emphasis**

- **Use fronted structures to point out contrasts and focus on unexpected information**

OPENING TASK

Film Scenarios

When someone mentions the film industry, we usually think first of actors and directors. When film awards are handed out, however, we are reminded that behind all good movies stand creative scriptwriters.

■ STEP 1

Form groups or teams of scriptwriters. Imagine that you are being considered for a film company contract based on your imaginative ideas.

■ STEP 2

Choose one of the following film scenarios, and complete the last line of dialogue or description. Then add a few sentences to further the plot or the description.

■ STEP 3

When the groups have finished, take turns reading the scenarios along with the completions.

Film 1: Science Fiction

SCENARIO: For weeks the townspeople of Spooner, a small lake resort town, have observed signs that something dreadful has invaded their community. Trees, shrubs, and even the flowers have begun to die. Dogs howl at night and cats are afraid to go out. One sultry summer Saturday night, many of the townsfolk are, as usual, celebrating the end of the week at the local dance hall. Suddenly, they become aware of an eerie, green glow outside. They peek out of the windows to see what it is. In front of them, moving slowly toward them across a field . . .

Film 2: Ghost Story

SCENARIO: Ten men and women have agreed to spend a week in a large and very old mansion on the edge of town. Strange sounds and sights have been observed in this house over the past few years, and the people assembled this evening want to find out if there is truth to rumors that the house has been cursed. They are all seated at the dining room table, with their leader, Madame Montague, at the head.

Madame Montague: *My friends, you all know why we are here. Before we spend another hour in this house, there is one thing that I must demand of all of you. Under no circumstances . . .*

Film 3: Romance

SCENARIO: Brad and Lindsay met about a month ago in a city park when Brad was walking his faithful terrier, Sam, and Lindsay was with her golden retriever, Stella. Ever since then, they have run into each other frequently in the park during their dog walks and have carried on long conversations, but only as friends. Brad, however, is interested in a relationship beyond just a friendship. He wants to let Lindsay know how he feels. One evening, they are sitting on the grass while Sam and Stella romp with each other. Brad looks longingly at Lindsay, and says . . .

Film 4: Mystery

SCENARIO: Detective Hendershot has been asked to investigate the disappearance of Daisy O'Connor, a very wealthy elderly woman, who was last seen at home when one of her friends came for tea. Hendershot has wandered through the house, making numerous observations in his notebook but sees nothing that would give him any leads. Finally, he makes his way out to the garage, which is separated from the house by a narrow walkway. With a key he has found in the kitchen, he slowly opens the garage door. There on the floor of the garage . . .

Film 5: Adventure Story

SCENARIO: After three days of wandering aimlessly in the heart of the Brazilian rain forest, a group of scientists have to admit that they are hopelessly lost. The head of the expedition, Professor Winbigler, feels it is time to warn the others of a great danger to them that she has encountered while separated from the group.

Professor Winbigler: *My fellow scientists, I didn't want to tell you this, but now that I fear we may not get out of here for a while, I believe you should be alerted. Far more threatening to our survival than the poisonous snakes and spiders . . .*

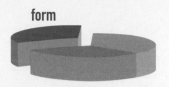

FOCUS 1

Fronted Structures

EXAMPLES		EXPLANATIONS
Not Fronted	**Fronted**	In English, you can place special emphasis on some ideas by moving words or phrases from their usual place in a sentence to the front of the sentence. This process is called "fronting," and the resulting structures are known as "fronted structures."
(a) The townspeople went outside **because they were curious.**	(b) **Because they were curious,** the townspeople went outside.	
(c) I would **not** leave this town **for anything.**	(d) **Not for anything** would I leave this town.	
(e) **The storm was** so terrible that many people lost their homes.	(f) So terrible **was the storm** that many people lost their homes.	**Subject-Verb and Subject-Auxiliary Order** When you front some structures, the word order in the rest of the sentence changes. The order of the subject and verb or the subject and the auxiliary is reversed (inverted). The verb or the auxiliary comes before the subject instead of after it. These structures will be shown in Focus 3 and Focus 4.

 EXERCISE 1

In the dialogue script on the next page, five friends who have just been backpacking in the mountains are telling some of their classmates about their trip. Each numbered clause contains a fronted structure. For these sentences, underline the subject and circle the main verb and any auxiliaries. If the subject and the verb (or the subject and an auxiliary) have been inverted, write "I" at the end of each sentence.

Example: Not once (did) we (see) a wild animal. I

Judy: Well, to begin with, we had to hike straight uphill for six miles. I couldn't believe how steep it was! Let me tell you, (1) never have I been so tired in my whole life!

Toshi: Really! Listen, next time all the food will be freeze-dried. (2) Not for anything would I carry a 20-pound pack uphill again!

Phan: (3) At dusk we finally got up to our campsite; it was gorgeous! We were on the shores of a pristine mountain lake, surrounded by pine trees. (4) Nowhere could we see a single person—other than ourselves, that is.

Kent: (5) However, no sooner had we dropped all our stuff on the ground than the storm clouds rolled in. (6) So, in a big hurry we unpacked everything we had.

Mario: (7) Yeah, and not until then did I discover that I hadn't packed my rain poncho.

Judy: (8) Neither had the rest of us.

Toshi: We tried to pitch the tents as fast as we could but it wasn't fast enough. (9) With every stake we pounded in, it seemed to rain harder. (10) Not only did we get soaked, but some of our food got wet too.

Phan: But fortunately the storm ended almost as quickly as it had started. (11) And on the other side of the lake the most beautiful rainbow suddenly appeared.

Mario: All in all, even though it was a hard climb getting there, it was worth it. (12) You know, seldom do you realize how peaceful life can be until you get away from civilization!

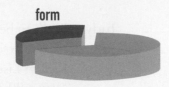
form

| FOCUS 2 | Order of Subjects and Auxiliaries |

Chart 1: Fronted Structures That Do Not Require Inversion

When some types of adverbials are fronted, the order of the subject and the verb or the subject and the first auxiliary do not change.

ADVERBIAL NOT FRONTED	FRONTED ADVERBIAL	TYPE OF ADVERBIAL
(a) Lindsay sometimes walks her dog **during the evenings.**	(b) **During the evenings** Lindsay sometimes walks her dog.	Time
(c) Detective Hendershot sorted the evidence **with great care.**	(d) **With great care,** Detective Hendershot sorted the evidence.	Manner
(e) Something strange must be happening **if the dogs are howling.**	(f) **If the dogs are howling,** something strange must be happening.	Condition
(g) Brad showered Lindsay with compliments **in order to win her heart.**	(h) **In order to win her heart,** Brad showered Lindsay with compliments.	Purpose
(i) The townspeople left **because they were afraid.**	(j) **Because they were afraid,** the townspeople left.	Reason
(k) The group would meet in the living room of the old mansion **every night.**	(l) **Every night** the group would meet in the living room of the old mansion.	Frequency (after verbs)

Chart 2: Fronted Structures That Require Inversion

In other types of adverbial fronting, the verb or the first auxiliary must come before the subject.

NOT FRONTED	FRONTED WITH INVERSION	STRUCTURE
(a) The townspeople *were* so **afraid** that they hardly ventured out of their neighborhoods.	(b) **So afraid** *were* the townspeople that they hardly ventured out of their neighborhoods.	Adverbials of extent or degree (*so* + adjective/adverb + *that*)
(c) A small boy *was* in the **library.**	(d) **In the library** *was* a small boy.	Adverbials of position when the main verb is *be*
(e) We *have* **never** *seen* such a strange sight.	(f) **Never** *have we seen* such a strange sight.	Negative adverbials of frequency that come before the main verb (*never, rarely, seldom*)
(g) Brad *would* **not** leave Lindsay **for anything.**	(h) **Not for anything** *would* Brad *leave* Lindsay.	Other negated structures
(i) A beam of light *was* **moving toward them.**	(j) **Moving toward them** *was* a beam of light.	Present participle + modifiers
(k) A note *was* **stuck in a branch of the willow tree.**	(l) **Stuck in a branch of the willow tree** *was* a note.	Past participles + modifiers
(m) The cinematography of this movie *is* **more interesting than** the plot.	(n) **More interesting than** the plot of this movie is the cinematography.[*]	Comparative structures
(o) (Paraphrase: The soldiers *did not know* that the enemy was just over the hill.)	(p) **Little** *did* the soldiers *know* that the enemy was just over the hill.	Implied negation (Because the negation is implied rather than explicit, there is no nonfronted form with *little*.)

[*]Note in (n) that the phrase *of this movie* has also been moved to the front to give the reader more information at the beginning of the sentence.

Chart 3: Optional Inversion with Fronted Structures

ADVERBIAL NOT FRONTED	FRONTED ADVERBIAL	TYPE OF ADVERBIAL
(a) A leopard appeared **from the western hills.**	(b) **From the western hills** a leopard *appeared*. (No inversion) (c) **From the western hills** *appeared* a leopard. (Optional inversion)	Direction
(d) An old woman sits **on the park bench.**	(e) **On the park bench** an old woman *sits*. (No inversion) (f) **On the park bench** *sits* an old woman. (Optional inversion)	Position, when the main verb is not *be*.

■ EXERCISE 2

Use the cues in parentheses to add adverbial phrases or clauses to the end of each sentence. Then to emphasize the description you added, move it to the front of a new sentence. You will need to write two sentences for part a. and two for part b. If you wish, you can add other descriptive words or phrases. Be creative; try to use new vocabulary!

Examples: The odd creatures were standing in front of them. (a. manner b. time)

    a. *The odd creatures were standing in front of them with hungry looks on their angular faces.*

    Fronted: *With hungry looks on their angular faces, the odd creatures were standing boldly in front of them.*

    b. *The odd creatures were standing in front of them shortly before midnight.*

    Fronted: *Shortly before midnight, the odd creatures were standing in front of them.*

1. The townspeople were absolutely terrified. (a. time b. frequency)

2. Detective Hendershot will find out what happened to the elderly woman. (a. condition b. manner)

3. The group explored the nooks and crannies of the old house. (a. time b. purpose)

4. The scientists wandered. (a. direction b. purpose)

5. Professor Winbigler faithfully writes in her journal. (a. position b. condition)

Use an appropriate word or phrase from the list below to complete the blanks with fronted structures.

little did I know	peeking out from under a snowdrift
not for anything	stuffed into the toe
never	so embarrassed
sitting at the bottom of the hill	worse than the beginning of my excursion
coming toward me from the right	

I'm not sure if I ever want to go skiing again. (1) _____ have I felt so frustrated trying to have fun! First, I had trouble just getting on the boots and skis I had rented. One of the boots wouldn't fit; then I discovered that (2) _____ was an old sock. I was so nervous that I hadn't realized what it was. Next I discovered that getting to the top of the hill on the chair lift was no small feat. (3) _____ that one could fall numerous times before even getting started. Once I made it to the top, I couldn't believe how small everything looked down below. (4) _____ was a tiny building that I recognized as the chalet. My first thought was: (5) _____ am I going to go down this slope. As it turned out, my first thought was probably better than my second, which was to give it a try. (6) _____ was the end of it. As I raced uncontrollably down the slope terrified, I suddenly saw that (7) _____ was another skier. We collided just seconds later. (8) _____, I muttered an apology. That was it for me for the day. (9) _____ did I feel that I spent the rest of the afternoon finding out how to enroll in a beginning ski class.

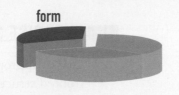

FOCUS 3 — Patterns of Inversion with Fronted Structures

EXAMPLES		EXPLANATIONS

Not Fronted	**Fronted**	**Pattern 1: Simple Verbs**
(a) I never **said** such a thing!	(b) Never **did I say** such a thing!	When you front a structure requiring inversion and the sentence has only a simple verb, add *do* except when the main verb is a form of *be*.
(c) **He searched** the house so carefully that it it took him two hours to complete the task.	(d) So carefully **did he search** the house that it took him two hours to complete the task.	

		Pattern 2: Complex Verbs
(e) **The group could** never have guessed what was in the mansion.	(f) Never **could the group** have guessed what was in the mansion.	Complex verbs have a main verb and one or more auxiliaries. In sentences with complex verbs, invert the first auxiliary and the subject.
(g) **They would** not stay in that house for anything.	(h) Not for anything **would they** stay in that house.	

		Pattern 3: *Be* Verbs
(i) **The director is** seldom here on time.	(j) Seldom **is the director** here on time.	When the verb is *be* with no auxiliaries, invert the subject and *be*.
(k) **The speaker was** so boring that many in the audience fell asleep.	(l) So boring **was the speaker** that many in the audience fell asleep.	

		Pattern 4: *Be* + Auxiliary Verbs
(m) **There has** never been been so much excitement in this town.	(n) Never in this town **has there** been so much excitement.	In sentences with fronted adverbials, invert the first auxiliary and the subject.
(o) **The dust has been** more annoying than the noise during the remodeling of the library.	(p) More annoying than the noise **has been the dust** during the remodeling of the library.	In sentences with fronted comparatives, put both the auxiliary and *be* before the subject.

EXERCISE 4

After each of the following phrases, add a main clause that expresses your opinions or provides information. If the fronted part is a position adverbial, use a *be* verb to follow it.

Examples: Near the school
Near the school is a small coffee shop.
So puzzling . . . that
So puzzling was the homework assignment that most of us didn't finish it.

1. Seldom during the past few years
2. More fascinating than my English class
3. Rarely during my lifetime
4. In my bedroom
5. More important to me than anything
6. Seldom in the history of the world
7. More of a world problem than air pollution
8. So interesting . . . that
9. Stored in my memory, never to be forgotten,
10. Waiting for me in the future
11. In the front of my English textbook
12. Better than ice cream for dessert
13. Loved and respected by many admirers
14. So terrible . . . that

EXERCISE 5

Make up a sentence in response to each of the following. Use a fronted structure for emphasis.

Example: Describe what is in some area of your classroom.
In the back of our classroom are posters of many countries of the world and a large map of the world.

1. State how exciting something is to you by comparing it in degree to something else. (Start with "More exciting . . .")
2. Tell how infrequently you have done something.
3. Describe how angry you were in a certain circumstance. (Start with "So angry . . .")
4. Describe how happy you were in another circumstance.

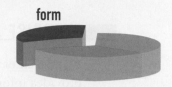

form

FOCUS 4   Fronted Negative Forms: Adverbials

For all of these fronted negative adverbials below, you must invert the subject and auxiliary or the subject and the simple verb.

Adverbs and Adverb Phrases

WORD/PHRASE	NOT FRONTED	FRONTED
never	(a) The townspeople had **never** witnessed such a strange sight.	(b) **Never** had the townspeople witnessed such a strange sight.
not once	(c) I have **not** missed my Portuguese class **once** this semester.	(d) **Not once** have I missed my Portuguese class this semester.
not for + (noun)	(e) I would **not** commute four hours a day **for all the money in the world!**	(f) **Not for all the money in the world** would I commute four hours a day!
not until + (noun)	(g) She did **not** realize the ring was missing **until the morning.**	(h) **Not until the morning** did she realize the ring was missing.
not since + (noun)	(i) We have **not** had so much rain **since April.**	(j) **Not since April** have we had so much rain.
under no circumstances	(k) You will **not** be allowed to leave **under any circumstances.**	(l) **Under no circumstances** will you be allowed to leave. *(not any → no)**
in no case	(m) We can **not** make an exception **in any case.**	(n) **In no case** can we make an exception.
in no way	(o) This will **not** affect your grade **in any way.**	(p) **In no way** will this affect your grade.
no way (informal)	(q) I am **not** going to miss that concert **for any reason!**	(r) **No way** am I going to miss that concert.
nowhere	(s) I have **not** been **anywhere** that is as peaceful as this place.	(t) **Nowhere** have I been that is as peaceful as this place.

* Note: Refer to Unit 23, Focus 3 page 412 for a review of double negatives.

Adverb Time Clauses

CLAUSE	NOT FRONTED	FRONTED
not until + clause	(u) I will **not** believe it **until I see it!**	(v) **Not until I see it** will I believe it!
not since + clause	(w) I have **not** had so much spare time **since I started high school.**	(x) **Not since I started high school** have I had so much spare time.

EXERCISE 6

Add the negative fronted structure in parentheses to the following sentences for emphasis. Make any other changes that are necessary.

Example: I hadn't ever been so upset. (never)
Never had I been so upset.

1. We can't let you retake the examination. (under no circumstances)

2. I haven't missed an episode of my favorite program. (not once)

3. My parents won't miss graduation. (not for anything)

4. This didn't change my attitude about you. (in no way)

5. I won't tell you my secret. (not until + a time phrase)

6. She hasn't allowed any changes in the procedures. (in no case)

7. You may not have access to the files. (under no conditions)

8. I wouldn't trade places with him. (not for a million dollars)

EXERCISE 7

Complete the following with a statement based on your experience or opinions.

1. Not since I was a child . . .

2. Not until I am old and gray . . .

3. Not until many years from now . . .

4. Not since I started . . .

5. Nowhere . . .

6. Not for anything . . .

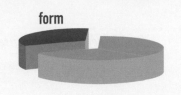

FOCUS 5 Fronted Negative Forms: Objects and Conjunctions

As with the negative adverbials in Focus 4, these fronted structures require subject-auxiliary or subject-verb inversion.

Noun Phrase Objects

PHRASE	NOT FRONTED	FRONTED
not + singular noun*	(a) The sky was brilliant; he could **not see one cloud** in any direction.	(b) The sky was brilliant; **not one cloud** could he see in any direction.
	(c) We will **not** spend **another penny** on repairing our DVD player.	(d) **Not another penny** will we spend on repairing our DVD player.

*A plural form is possible with *no* (*no clouds could he see*), but the emphasis would not be as strong as with the singular form.

Conjunctions

WORD/PHRASE	NOT FRONTED	FRONTED
neither, nor	(e) I had no idea how the mystery would end.	
	(f) My mother **didn't either.**	(g) **Neither** did my mother.
	(h) My sister **didn't either.**	(i) **Nor** did my sister.
	(j) **No one** else did **either.**	(k) **Neither** did anyone else.
not only (. . . but also)	(l) That movie does **not only** have amazing visual effects, **but** it **also** has a great soundtrack.	(m) **Not only** does that movie have amazing visual effects, **but** it **also** has a great soundtrack.
no sooner (. . . than)	(n) The movie had **no sooner** started **than** the power went out.	(o) **No sooner** had the movie started **than** the power went out.

After each of the following statements, add a sentence using the fronted negative in parentheses.

Example: The German swimmers did not win any medals at the Olympics. (Nor)
   Nor did any swimmers from France or the United States.

1. I tried to do the homework but I couldn't understand the assignment. (neither)
2. I've been working on this math assignment almost the entire night. (not one more minute)
3. The main star of the film could not get along with the director. (nor)
4. I just love to visit big cities. (not only)
5. Look how skinny that model is! (not one ounce of fat)
6. We do not want to buy products from companies who use dishonest advertising. (not another dollar)
7. Leon was sorry he had decided to go sailing yesterday. (no sooner)
8. Our art history professor will not accept late papers. (neither)
9. Learning Greek could help you in several ways. (not only)
10. That new romantic comedy was a little disappointing. It did not have a very original plot. (nor)

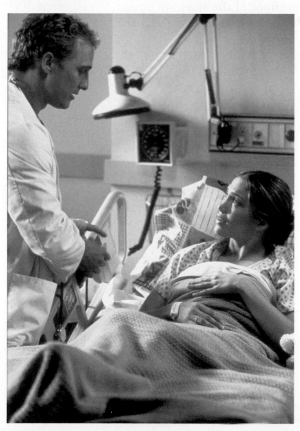

FOCUS 6 — Fronted Structures: Emphasizing, Contrasting, and Focusing on Unexpected Information

use

EXAMPLES	EXPLANATIONS
	Adverb Phrases Reasons for fronting: • to emphasize information • to point out contrasts
Emphasis (a) **In the evenings** she writes. It is a time when the house is quiet and peaceful and she can concentrate.	
Contrast (b) **In the evenings** she writes. **The mornings** are devoted to gardening and **the afternoons** to her job at a publishing company.	For adverbials of time, place, or frequency, the context determines whether contrast or some other kind of emphasis is intended.
Emphasis (c) **On the first floor of the store** are men's clothes. This floor also has luggage.	The fronting of contrast phrases emphasizes parallel structures. Parallelism of this kind is a stylistic device used to stress ideas and create rhythm.
Contrast (d) **On the first floor of the store** are men's clothes. **On the second floor** are women's clothes and linens.	

EXAMPLES	EXPLANATIONS
(e) Who could be at Sara's door at this late hour? Sara squinted through the peephole to see who the mystery caller was. **Participle** **Focus on Subject** **Staring back at her** was her long-lost brother. **Comparative** (f) **More important to me than anything** **Focus on Subject** **else** is my family.	**Participle Phrases and Comparatives** Reason for fronting: • to emphasize a subject that contains new or unexpected information by moving it to the end of the sentence.
(g) **Never** have I seen such a display of bravery! (h) **Not until the last votes were counted** would the senator admit defeat. (i) **Under no circumstances** may you enter this building after midnight. (j) **Not a single promise** did he make that wasn't eventually broken.	**Negative Structures** Reasons for fronting:* • to emphasize unusual or unexpected actions or events. • to stress particular aspects of events or actions. • to create strong commands that prohibit actions. • to emphasize the "negativeness" of things, events, or actions.

*These uses often overlap; a fronted negative may emphasize in several different ways.

State what you think is the main reason for fronting each of the underlined structures. Do you think it is primarily for (1) emphasis of the fronted structure, (2) contrast of the structure, or (3) focus on a delayed subject that contains new or unexpected information? More than one reason may apply. Be prepared to explain your choice.

1. <u>Only when Marta drives</u> does she get nervous. At other times she's quite calm.

2. The phone rang. Howard was sure it was his best friend Miguel calling. Picking up the phone, he shouted, "Yo!" <u>Responding to his greeting</u> was his biology professor.

3. <u>Not since I was in elementary school</u> have I been to the circus. Believe me, that was a long time ago!

4. Welcome to the Little River Inn. We hope you will enjoy your stay here. <u>To your right</u> is a cooler with ice and the soft-drink machines. <u>To your left and around the corner</u> is the swimming pool and jacuzzi.

5. <u>To start this lawnmower</u>, you need to pull the cord very hard and quickly. To keep it going, you should set the lever in the middle.

6. Minh heard a noise coming from underneath his parked car. Getting down on his knees, he looked under the front of it. <u>There, crouched on the right front tire</u> was a tiny kitten.

7. <u>Not until I hear from you</u> will I leave. I promise I'll stay here until then.

8. <u>During the long winters</u> Bonnie does a lot of reading. She loves to lounge by the fire with a good book.

9. The crowd was waiting excitedly to see who would win this year's Boston marathon. <u>A few minutes later, across the finish line</u> came a runner from Kenya.

10. <u>Had I known the movie was so long</u>, I doubt I would have gone to see it. I had no idea that it would last for five hours!

Fronted Structures: Creating Cohesion in Discourse

use

EXAMPLES	EXPLANATIONS
	Fronted structures are also used to create cohesion with ideas that have been previously expressed, especially in written English and more formal spoken English. Such structures often express comparisons between ideas across sentences.
(a) *Star Wars* was one of the most successful films ever in terms of box office sales. **Even more successful** was *Titanic,* the highest grossing film of the twentieth century.	In (a), *even more successful* implies *"than Star Wars."* Thus it creates a cohesive link to the previous sentence. Note that we could not understand the second sentence without reference to the first one.
(b) When you write a film script, it is essential that you tell your story so that the reader can "see" it. **Equally important** is making your directing descriptions concise.	In (b), *equally important* is also a comparison, implying *"as important as telling your story so that the reader can see it."*

EXERCISE 10

The following passage offers information and advice about how to be a scriptwriter for films. Underline each fronted structure that is used to create cohesion. The first has been done as an example.

(1) A film script is a document that outlines all of the elements needed to tell a story in a film. (2) Included in these elements are the setting and character descriptions, dialogue, behavioral cues, and sound. (3) It is crucial to keep in mind that since film is a visual medium, you must *show,* not tell your audience what is going on. (4) Equally critical is to be passionate about the characters you create so your audience will share your feelings about them. (5) And certainly as important as creating characters that the audience will care about is developing an engaging conflict or obstacle that the characters have to deal with. (6) The conflict could be something personal, such as a romantic obstacle, or for the good of all people, such as the freedom of a country. (7) Not only do you need to develop some kind of obstacle or conflict but you need a good "hook," that is, an interesting plot idea with an original twist that will captivate your audience and make them want to read on. (8) By creating a hook, you will set your script apart from the many others that agents receive. (9) Finally, be sure to read up on all of the conventions and formatting for scriptwriting so that you meet the expectations of your audience. (10) So important is this last point that if you ignore it and decide to do things your own way, your script will probably end up in the wastebasket.

EXERCISE 11

Correct the errors in word order in the following sentences.

1. So great the visual effects were in *The Matrix Reloaded* that I saw the movie twice.

2. Why some people didn't like the sequels to *The Matrix* never I could understand.

3. When putting together a film script to send to an agent, you should not create a fancy title page but keep the page simple. Neither you should put in any illustrations in your script, no matter how nice you think they may be.

4. For any media script you write, be sure to proofread very carefully when you are done. Under no circumstances your script should have any misspellings or grammar mistakes.

Use Your English

ACTIVITY **1** listening

CD Tracks
38, 39

In a recent survey, a number of well-known Americans, including authors, media specialists, politicians, and artists, were asked to name movies that they felt defined the American character. Listen to the audio; you will hear descriptions of two of these films. After you have listened to each description, choose the statement which accurately paraphrases an idea in the description.

Pollyanna

a. Americans have never hated or envied the rich.

b. Americans have never hated the rich, just envied them.

Mr. Smith Goes to Washington

a. Political corruption in Washington continues until an innocent man from a small town arrives.

b. Political corruption in Washington stops before an innocent man from a small town arrives.

ACTIVITY **2** writing/speaking

Make a list of some things you believe you would **never** do under any circumstances. Then share your list with one or more classmates to see if they also would never do the things on your list, and have them discuss their lists with you. Finally, write a summary of your discussion, pointing out your similarities and differences.

Examples: *Under no circumstances would I take an advanced course in physics.*
No way would I ever eat squid. (informal usage)

ACTIVITY 3 · writing/speaking

Advertisements and commercials often use strong claims to sell products. Team up with a classmate and imagine you are copywriters for an ad agency. With your partner, choose a product (one that already exists or make one up) to sell; write an advertisement for either print media (magazine, newspaper), radio, or television. Present your ad/commercial to the class, and give them a chance to discuss your claims.

ACTIVITY 4 · writing

Write a paragraph in which you describe one of the following:

- the contents of a room as someone might see the room upon entering it.
- a machine or appliance with a number of parts.

Examples: *As you come into the living room, there is a large chintz sofa. In front of the sofa is a maple coffee table. To the left of it is an end table that matches the coffee table, and to the right stands a bookcase. On top of the bookcase sits my favorite vase. It's a deep turquoise blue.*

The parts of my computer include the monitor, the printer, the computer itself, and the control panel. On the control panel are four switches. To the far left is the switch for the computer. Next to it is the switch for the monitor. To the right of the monitor switch is the one for the printer.

ACTIVITY 5 speaking

With a partner or in a small group, describe an event that affected you strongly; for example, a time when you were especially happy, excited, angry, frightened, surprised, etc.

ACTIVITY 6 research on the web

Look up some film reviews of movies you have seen or would like to see on one of the many Web sites dedicated to this purpose (for example, http://www.mrqe.com/lookup has thousands of reviews). Skim the reviews and try to find four to five examples of fronted structures.

Example: *With her crested gray mane, laser glare and perfectly modulated stealth missile sarcasm, Miranda Priestly, the editor-in-chief of the fictional Vogue clone,* Runway, *is still a monster.* (Carina Chocano, *LA Times,* June 30, 2006).

Then write your own review of a movie or television show that you especially liked or disliked.

ACTIVITY 7 reflection

Think of three things you currently do to improve your writing. Write three statements that represent ways you will try to take each of these things one step beyond what you are currently doing.

Example: *Activity: Proofreading my papers when I have finished writing them*
Not only will I try to be more careful in proofreading my papers in general, but I will check especially for my two most common errors, which are subject-verb agreement and the -s plural on nouns.

FOCUSING AND EMPHASIZING STRUCTURES
It-Clefts and *Wh*-Clefts

- Use *it*-cleft sentences to put special emphasis on information

- Know what parts of a sentence can be used for focus in *it*-clefts

- Know how to use other kinds of cleft sentences for questions and statements

- Use *wh*-clefts to put focus on information at the end of sentences

OPENING TASK

Does Birth Order Influence Personality?

You may have at times judged someone's behavior according to that individual's position in a family as the oldest, youngest, middle, or only child. For example, you might have considered a friend's "take charge" attitude as characteristic of an oldest child. As for youngest children in a family, people often assume they are the ones who will be the most pampered and spoiled. If you are an only child, you may have heard the generalization that only children are very confident. While controversy continues about whether birth order actually affects adult personalities, it remains a very popular topic in psychology and issues about parenting.

■ STEP 1

On the next page, read the observations about personality traits that have commonly been associated with particular birth orders: oldest, middle, youngest, and only child.

PERSONALITY TRAITS ASSOCIATED WITH BIRTH ORDER

a. tends to be a high achiever and goal-oriented

b. is often the most secretive

c. is usually very comfortable with older people

d. tends to be skilled at defending himself or herself

e. often acts as a negotiator or mediator

f. may find it harder than other children to learn to share

g. often feels most obligated to follow the parents' rules

h. are often creative and open to exploring new ideas

i. tends to be the most conservative

j. is typically self-sufficient

k. may be confused about self-image as a result of being both welcomed and at the same time disliked by siblings

l. tends to be independent because of greatest freedom from parental attention

■ STEP 2

Based on your knowledge of your family members' personalities (including yours) or the personalities of friends whose birth order you know, guess which order each trait characterizes: the only child, the oldest child, the middle child, or the youngest child. Here are answers to *a* and *b*:

a. *It's the oldest child who tends to be a high achiever.*

b. *It's the middle child who is the most secretive.*

■ STEP 3

After you have guessed a birth order for each trait, briefly discuss your choices in small groups.

■ STEP 4

Check the answers to this task on page A-16. Comment on ones that surprised you the most.

Example: *What surprised me the most is that the middle child is often secretive. My brother's girlfriend is a middle child, and she tells everyone about everything!*

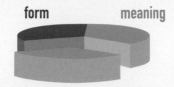

FOCUS 1   Structure of *It*-Cleft Sentences

EXAMPLES	EXPLANATION
(a) **No Special Emphasis**: My brother is conservative, not me.	"Cleft" means to divide. *It*-cleft sentences put special emphasis on one part of a sentence.
(b) **Emphasis: It is my brother** who is conservative, not me!	The part that is emphasized is introduced by *it* and a form of *be*.

	Focus Element	**Clause**	
(c)	It is the youngest child	who is often both a rebel and a charmer.	The cleft sentence divides a sentence into two parts: (1) a focus element and (2) a clause beginning with *that, who, when,* or *where*.
	Singular Plural		
(d)	It **is** oldest children and only children	who tend to be the most assertive.	The verb is singular even when the focus element is plural.
	Future		
(e)	It **will be** on a Saturday	that we leave, not a Sunday.	The *be* verb is usually present tense. However, we also use other tenses.
	Past		
(f)	It **used to be** my mother	who did all the cooking, but now we all help.	
(g)	It **must** be red wine	that stained this carpet.	We can use modal verbs in cleft sentences to express degrees of probability.
(h)	It **can't** be the youngest child	who is the most conservative.	

▮ EXERCISE 1

Complete each blank below with a word or phrase that fits the context. Use a singular or plural form of noun as appropriate for agreement. The first has been done as an example.

1. It couldn't be ___only children___ who are confused about self-image because they don't have any siblings.

2. I think it must be _____ who often has the self-image problem because the older ones might have mixed feelings about the baby of the family.

3. It might be _____ who is generally self-sufficient because as a child he or she might have had to do a lot of things alone.

4. Some psychologists claim that, of all birth order positions, _____ the middle child who is apt to be the most popular among other people.

5. It is _____ who may be fearless and have a strong sense of exploration because that child often feels protected by older siblings.

6. Experts on parenting have observed that _____ who tend to have difficulty dealing with interruptions from others because they did not have brothers or sisters who interrupted them.

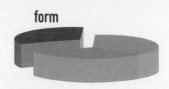

FOCUS 2 | Focus Elements in Cleft Sentences

We can focus on various parts of a sentence in the focus element of cleft sentences.

ORIGINAL SENTENCE	CLEFT SENTENCE	FOCUS
The students are organizing an English book club.	(a) It is **the students who** are organizing an English book club.	Subject
	(b) It is **an English book club that** the students are organizing.	Direct object
We wish to speak to the President of the university about this issue.	(c) It is **the President of the university** to whom we wish to speak about this issue. (formal)	Object of preposition
	(d) It is **the President of the university** who we want to speak to about this issue. (less formal)	
They painted the dormitory recreation room an awful shade of yellow.	(e) It was **an awful shade of yellow** that they painted the dormitory recreation room.	Complement (noun)
They painted it greenish yellow.	(f) It was **greenish yellow** that they painted it.	Complement (adjective)
The President resigned due to illness.	(g) It was **due to illness** that the President resigned.	Prepositional phrase
The baby boom began in the United States after World War II ended.	(h) It was **after World War II ended** that the baby boom began in the United States.	Dependent clause
An amendment to the U.S. Constitution was passed in 1920 to ensure the right of women to vote.	(i) It was **to ensure the right of women to vote** that an amendment to the U.S. Constitution was passed in 1920.	Infinitive or Infinitive clause

Restate the following sentences about the United States civil rights movement of the 1950s and 1960s to emphasize the information indicated in parentheses. Change any other wording as necessary and check to make sure the *be* verb tense is appropriate for the meaning.

Example: Americans honor the famous civil rights leader Martin Luther King Jr. with a national holiday in January. (Emphasize the month).

It is in January that Americans honor the famous civil rights leader Martin Luther King Jr. with a national holiday.

1. Rosa Parks is known as "the mother of the civil rights movement" in the United States. (Emphasize the person's name.)

2. Parks challenged the South's policy of segregating races on buses in 1955 by refusing to get up and give her bus seat to a white passenger. (Emphasize the date.)

3. White and black civil rights workers sat together in "white only" sections of restaurants and other public places in 1960 to protest segregation in the South. (Emphasize the purpose.)

4. In 1962, President John Kennedy sent United States marshals to protect James H. Meredith, the first black student at the University of Mississippi. (Emphasize the place.)

5. The civil rights movement reached a climax in 1963 with the march on Washington. (Emphasize the event.)

6. Martin Luther King Jr. delivered his famous "I Have a Dream" speech during the march on Washington. (Emphasize the speech.)

7. King led civil rights marches in Selma, Alabama, and Montgomery, Mississippi, in 1965. (Emphasize the places.)

EXERCISE 3

Imagine that each of the situations below is true. Provide an explanation, either serious or humorous, emphasizing the reason.

Example: You were late to class yesterday.

It was because the bus didn't come that I was late to class.

1. You didn't have an assignment done that was due.

2. You missed a medical appointment.

3. You forgot a relative's birthday. (You choose the relative.)

4. You didn't eat anything for two days.

5. You fell asleep in your one of your classes.

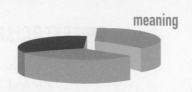

FOCUS 3 **/t-Clefts in Spoken and Written Communication**

EXAMPLES	EXPLANATIONS
(a) **It is the middle child** who is most secretive. (The middle child is distinguished from the eldest and youngest children.) (b) **It is only love** that can bring world peace. (Love is the only thing that can bring world peace.) (c) **It is only my best friend** who can cheer me up when I'm down. (My best friend is the only person who can cheer me up.)	**Distinguish Member of a Group** *It*-cleft sentences can distinguish one member of a group as having certain qualities. In some cases the "group" may include all other things or people. We use *only* before the focus element to convey this meaning.
(d) **A:** I think the youngest child is the one who tends to be secretive. **B:** I don't agree. **It's the middle child,** I think, who is most secretive. (e) What color paint is this? **It was** *blue* that I ordered, not green!	**Express Contrast** We sometimes use cleft sentences to point out a contrast or to note something that is commonly believed but not true. In spoken English, the contrasting word or phrase receives extra stress. In (e), *blue* is stressed because it contrasts with *green*.
(f) **It was out of concern** that we called our neighbor to see if she was all right. (g) **It was for a general education requirement** that I took art history.	**Emphasize Purpose or Cause** *It*-clefts can also emphasize the purpose or cause of something. These often include prepositional phrases beginning with *out of* or *for*.

EXERCISE 4

Which person in your family or circle of friends best matches the following descriptions? In your response, use a cleft sentence beginning with *it is* (or *it's*). Also, try to paraphrase (put in your own words) each description instead of just repeating it, as shown in the example.

Example: would be most likely to complain about young people's behavior

It's my grandmother who would be most likely to say that young people don't act the way they should.

1. tends to watch the most TV
2. has the best sense of humor
3. would be most likely to park a car and forget where it was
4. has the most trouble getting up in the morning
5. is the most artistic
6. would be most likely to stop and help if he or she saw someone in trouble
7. most often tries to get out of doing housework
8. most enjoys shopping

EXERCISE 5

Complete each blank by choosing a word from the list below for a focus element and creating a cleft sentence. The first has been done as an example.

anger	faith	pride
curiosity	music	a sense of humor

1. ____It was anger____ that made God banish Adam and Eve from the Garden of Eden, according to the Judeo-Christian Bible.
2. _____ that often keeps us from admitting our mistakes.
3. _____ that caused Pandora's downfall in the Greek myth; she had to find out what was in the box.
4. _____ that has been called the language of the soul.
5. _____ that keeps most of us from taking ourselves too seriously and helps us to deal with the ups and downs of life.
6. _____ that has helped many people withstand religious persecution.

■ EXERCISE 6

Imagine you have been asked to edit a reference book for errors. Each of the facts below has one incorrect part. Identify the incorrect part. Then write a sentence indicating what needs to be corrected, using a cleft sentence to highlight that element.

Example: Shakespeare wrote *Hamster*, one of his most famous plays, at the beginning of the seventeenth century.

Correction: *It was **Hamlet** that Shakespeare wrote.*

1. Mexico borders the United States to the north.
2. The 2004 Olympics were held in Athens, Italy.
3. One of the most famous tragedies of all time, *Romeo and Juliet,* was written by Molière in 1595.
4. Christopher Columbus sailed to India in 1492.
5. United States astronauts first landed on Mars in 1969.
6. In 1260 Kublai Khan founded the Yuan dynasty in Japan.
7. Leonardo da Vinci painted the famous *Moaning Lisa* around 1500.
8. The brain, the spinal cord, and the nerves are parts of the body's digestive system.
9. Nefertiti ruled India along with her husband King Akhenaton during the fourteenth century BC.

■ EXERCISE 7

STEP 1   Make lists of your four favorite foods, your four favorite movies (or TV programs), and your four favorite school subjects.

STEP 2   To indicate which item ranks highest in each of the three lists, fill in the blanks of the sentences below. Share one of your responses with classmates.

1. I love to eat _____, _____, and _____. But it is _____ that I would choose if I had to eat only one food for a week.

2. I could watch _____, _____, and _____ quite a few times, but it is _____ that _____.

3. I enjoy _____, I like to study _____, and I also like _____. However, if _____, it is _____ that I would choose.

STEP 3   Make up another list of four favorite things of some other category (e.g., books, sports). Then write a sentence using the pattern in Step 2.

FOCUS 4 — *It*-Clefts: Emphasizing Time, Place, and Characters

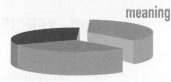

EXAMPLES	EXPLANATION
(a) It was **in the early spring** that Sylvia finally felt well enough to make the trip to Budapest.	In narratives such as stories or historical accounts, we may use cleft sentences to emphasize the time, place, characters (or real people) in the narrative.
(b) It was **on a cold day in February, 1860,** that Abraham Lincoln delivered his eloquent Cooper Union speech against slavery.	
(c) It was **in Barbizon** that Rousseau founded the modern school of French landscape painting.	
(d) It was **Shakespeare** who inspired Beethoven's creation of his String Quartet opus 18, number 1.	

Choose one feature to highlight in the following historical facts and write an introductory sentence for a historical narrative about each.

Examples: *It was Cheops who started building the pyramids in Egypt around 2700 BC.*
(Emphasizes person)

It was around 2700 BC that Cheops began building the pyramids in Egypt.
(Emphasizes date)

PERSON	DATE	PLACE	EVENT
Cheops (king)	around 2700 BC	Egypt	started building the Pyramids
Machiavelli (statesman)	1513	Florence, Italy	accused of conspiracy
Chikamatsu Monzaemon (playwright)	1703	Kyoto, Japan	wrote *The Love Suicides at Sonezaki*
John James Audubon (artist)	April 26, 1785	Cayes, Santo Domingo	born
Joaquium Machado de Assis (writer)	1869	Rio de Janeiro, Brazil	married Portuguese aristocrat, Carolina de Novaes
Jean Sibelius (composer)	1892	Helsinki, Finland	wrote the symphonic poem "Kullervo"
Aung San Suu Kyi	1991	Myanmar	received word that she had won the Nobel Prize

EXERCISE 9

Write five autobiographical sentences about yourself, using introductory *it*-cleft structures to highlight places, dates, or events, as in Exercise 8.

Examples: *It was in the spring of 1985 that I was born.*
It was learning to play the piano that made me want to become a musician.

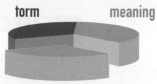
form   meaning

| FOCUS 5 | Other Forms of Cleft Sentences |

EXAMPLES	EXPLANATIONS
(a) **Who was it** that gave you that information?	**Wh-Cleft Question** In *Wh*-questions, it and *be* are inverted, changing the order to *be* + *it* after the question word (question word + *be* + *it*). In examples (b) and (c), *that* is in parentheses because it is optional.
(b) **Why was it** (that) they decided to move?	
(c) **When was it** (that) you left Shanghai?	
(d) **Was it out of pity** (that) he let the old man move into his house?	**Yes-No Cleft Questions** We must also invert *it* and *be* in *yes-no* questions.
(e) **Is it Spanish 3** (that) you're taking this quarter?	
(f) **What a nice essay it was** (that) you wrote about your father!	**What a + Noun Phrase** This type of cleft sentence *(What a + noun phrase + it + be)* expresses wonder, delight, admiration, or surprise.
(g) I told you before **(that) it was Marsha who called you**, not Marianne.	**That Clauses** As you have seen in some exercises in this unit, focus elements may be *that* clauses in reported speech.
(h) The President announced **(that) it was because he was ill that he would not be seeking re-election.**	

Make up a cleft sentence or question for each situation that follows to emphasize some piece of information.

Example: You told a friend that *The Lord of the Rings* was going to be on TV on Monday night. He thought you said Tuesday and missed seeing it. Tell him what you said.

I told you it was on Monday night that it was going to be on, not Tuesday!

1. You're not sure why a customer service representative at a bank wanted to know your place of birth for a checking account application you were filling out. Ask him.

2. You want to compliment a classmate on a great speech that she gave in class the day before.

3. You've been listening to a history lecture about China and missed hearing the date when the Chinese revolution ended the Manchu dynasty. Politely ask your instructor to tell you the date again.

4. You and your family are watching the news. The newscaster has just announced the cause of a major plane crash to have been an engine failure. A member of your family was distracted and didn't hear this information. Tell him or her what the newscaster said.

5. You have been trying to call a close friend for three hours, but the line has been busy. You wonder who she could be on the line with. When you finally get through, you ask her.

use

EXAMPLES	EXPLANATIONS
(a) What the world needs **is peace and justice.** (b) What we want **is a woman in the White House.**	Unlike *it*-clefts, *wh*-clefts put focus on information at the end of the sentence.

	Starting Point	Be Focus	
(c)	**Where** he goes	**is a mystery to me.**	
(d)	**What** Fay Tomas offers	**is honesty and compassion.**	
(e)	What she is **is a brilliant politician.**		

The starting point (what we already know or understand) is introduced by a *wh*-word. The focus adds new information. A form of *be* links the two parts of the sentence.

When the sentence has two *be* verbs, the second *be* links the two parts. In spoken English, the first *be* verb would be stressed and followed by a pause. (What she *is* is . . .)

EXERCISE 11

Match the phrases in column A with the appropriate word or phrase from column B. Write the letter on the line. Connect them with an appropriate form of *be* and write complete sentences. The first has been done as an example.

Example: 1. *What a lepidopterist specializes in* **is** *the study of moths and butterflies.*

A	B
_____ 1. What a lepidopterist specializes in	a. turkey
_____ 2. What Florida produces	b. Seoul
_____ 3. What Alexander Graham Bell invented	c. Portuguese
_____ 4. What Martin Luther King Jr. believed in	d. the study of moths and butterflies
_____ 5. Where the United States President lives	e. in Egypt
_____ 6. Where the capital of South Korea is	f. the 42nd President
_____ 7. What "mph" means	g. racial equality
_____ 8. Where the Pyramids are located	h. in the White House
_____ 9. What Brazilians speak	i. citrus fruit
_____ 10. What most Americans eat at Thanksgiving	j. the telephone
_____ 11. What Bill Clinton was	k. miles per hour

Using *Wh*-Clefts for Emphasis

use

EXAMPLES	EXPLANATION
(a) **A:** How much money does the director earn? **B: What she earns** is none of your business! (b) **A:** Mozart wrote plays. **B:** Actually, **what Mozart wrote** was music. Perhaps you mean Moliere.	*Wh*-clefts are more common in spoken English than in written English. The *Wh*-phrase often refers to a statement or idea that has been previously expessed.

EXERCISE 12

Rewrite the underlined words using a *Wh*-cleft. Then act out the conversations with a partner, using appropriate emphasis. The first has been done as an example, with the emphasis in bold italics.

1. **Matt:** Henry drives a Porsche.
   David: Are you kidding? <u>He drives a Ford</u>.
   Matt: Really? He told me it was a Porsche.

   Example: *What he drives is a **Ford**.*

2. **Frank:** Margo tells me you're a painter.
   Duane: That's right.
   Frank: Do you sell many of your paintings?
   Duane: Well, actually, <u>I paint houses</u>.

3. **Nick:** I'm tired. I think I'm going to take a nap.
   Lisa: Nick, <u>you need some exercise</u>. That will make you feel much better than a nap, I think.

4. **Teacher:** Do you have any suggestions about how we can improve this class?
   Fusako: <u>We'd like less homework</u>.
   Ricardo: And <u>we'd prefer a test every week</u>.
   Soraya: And <u>I need more grammar to pass my writing exam</u>.
   Bernadine: And <u>I'd like a different textbook</u>. This one isn't very challenging.

5. **Howard:** Do you know Barry? He writes novels.
   Tessa: I don't think that's true. <u>He writes instruction manuals for computer programs</u>.

6. **Lia:** What are you getting Carol and Bart for their wedding?
   Shelley: <u>They'd really like a microwave</u>, but I can't afford it, so I'm getting them a coffee grinder.

Use Your English

ACTIVITY **1** listening/speaking

CD Track 40

Divide into two or three teams for a quiz show competition. Listen to the audio. You will hear questions followed by a choice of three answers. After each question and possible answers, the teacher will stop the audio. Teams will take turns giving answers, which must be in the form of a cleft sentence. For each correct answer, a team will receive two points. Both the answer and the form must be correct to be awarded the points.

Example: Who was president before Bill Clinton?
a. Jimmy Carter b. George Bush c. Ronald Reagan
Correct answer: *It was George Bush who was president before Clinton.*

What does a baseball player get when he or she hits a ball out of the park?
a. an out b. a triple c. a home run
Correct answer: *What the player gets is a home run.*

ACTIVITY **2** writing/speaking

Make up five descriptions that could be used for members of your class. Write your descriptions as verb phrases, similar to Exercise 1. (Be careful not to write any descriptions that would offend anyone or hurt someone's feelings!) Write down who you think best fits the description. Take turns reading your descriptions and have classmates say whom they think matches each, using a cleft sentence. Then tell them whether you agree or disagree. Here is an example to get you started.

Example: A: *tells the funniest stories*
B: *I think it's Josef who does that.*
A: *I agree.*

 **ACTIVITY 3** speaking

What makes you happy? Sad? Angry? Annoyed? Puzzled or confused? With a partner, interview each other to find out the answers to these questions. If you wish, make up additional ones. Report a few of your findings to the class.

Examples: *What really makes Julie annoyed is when people throw litter on the beach.*

What makes John happy is having lots of time to pursue his hobby of photography.

 **ACTIVITY 4** research on the web

 Find out more about how people believe birth order influences personality. Using the keywords "birth order" and "personality" on an Internet search engine such as Google® or Yahoo®, find two or three articles on the topic. Summarize your findings by writing a list of the characteristics you find in addition to ones given in this unit. Use *it*-cleft structures to introduce your statements as was done in the Opening Task.

ACTIVITY 5 reflection

Reflect on five goals that you have for any area of your life. Then state what you have either done or plan to do in the future for the purpose of achieving these goals. In the chart below, state the goal in the left-hand column. State what you are doing or will do to achieve the goal in the right-hand column, using an *it*-cleft structure expression that emphasizes cause or purpose. Two examples are given.

Goal	Activity to Attain Goal
I want to go to law school after graduation.	*It is for this reason* that I am majoring in history.
I would like to improve my tennis game.	*It is for this purpose* that I plan to run at least two miles three times a week.

APPENDICES

Appendix 1A   Present Time Frame

FORM	EXAMPLE	USE	MEANING
SIMPLE PRESENT base form of verb or base form of verb + -s	Many plants **require** a lot of sun to thrive.	timeless truths	now
	Luis **works** every day except Sunday.	habitual actions	
	We **think** you should come with us.	mental perceptions and emotions	
	Veronica **owns** the house she lives in.	possession	
PRESENT PROGRESSIVE *am/is/are* + present participle (verb + *-ing*)	They **are** just **finishing** the race.	actions in progress	in progress now
	She **is picking** straw- berries this morning.	duration	
	Someone **is pounding** nails next door.	repetition	
	My friend **is living** in Nova Scotia for six months.	temporary activities	
	I **am changing** the oil in my car right now.	uncompleted actions	
PRESENT PERFECT *have/has* + past participle (verb + *-ed* or irregular verbs)	She **has attended** the university for four years; she will graduate in June.	situations that began in the past, continue to the present	in the past but related to now in some way
	I **have read** that book too. Did you like it?	actions completed in the past but related to the present	
	The movie **has** just **ended**.	actions recently completed	

(Continued)

Appendix 1A

FORM	EXAMPLE	USE	MEANING
PRESENT PERFECT PROGRESSIVE *have/has* + present participle (verb + *-ing*)	I **have been dialing** the airline's number for hours it seems. I can't believe it's still busy.	repeated or continuous actions that are incomplete	up until and including now
	This weekend Michelle **has been participating** in a job fair which ends on Sunday afternoon.		

Appendix 1B   Past Time Frame

FORM	EXAMPLE	USE	MEANING
SIMPLE PRESENT	So yesterday he **tells** me he just thought of another way to get rich quick.	past event in informal narrative	at a certain time in the past
SIMPLE PAST verb + *-ed* or irregular past form	We **planted** the vegetable garden last weekend.	events that took place at a definite time in the past	at a certain time in the past
	Pei-Mi **taught** for five years in Costa Rica.	events that lasted for a time in the past	
	I **studied** English every year when I was in high school.	habitual or repeated actions in the past	
	We **thought** we were heading in the wrong direction.	past mental perceptions and emotions	
	Jose **had** a piano when he lived in New York.	past possessions	
PAST PROGRESSIVE *was/were* + present participle (verb + *-ing*)	When I talked with him last night, Sam **was getting** ready for a trip.	events in progress at a specific time in the past	in progress at a time in the past

(Continued)

Appendix 1B

FORM	EXAMPLE	USE	MEANING
PAST PERFECT *had* + past participle (verb + *-ed* or irregular form)	My parents **had lived** in Hungary before they moved to France.	actions or states that took place before another time in the past	before a certain time in the past
PAST PERFECT PROGRESSIVE *had* + *been* + present participle (verb + *-ing*)	We **had been hurrying** to get to the top of the mountain when the rain started.	incomplete events taking place before other past events	up until a certain time in the past
	I **had been working** on the last math problem when the teacher instructed us to turn in our exams.	incomplete events interrupted by other past events	

Appendix 1C Future Time Frame

FORM	EXAMPLE	USE	MEANING
SIMPLE PRESENT	Takiko **graduates** next week.	definite future plans or schedules	already planned or expected in the future
	When Guangping **completes** her graduate program, she will look for a research job in Taiwan.	events with future time adverbials (*before, after, when*) in dependent clauses	
PRESENT PROGRESSIVE	I **am finishing** my paper tomorrow night	future intentions	already planned or expected in the future
	Amit **is taking** biochemistry for two quarters next year.	scheduled events that last for a period of time	

(Continued)

Appendix 1C

FORM	MEANING	USE	EXAMPLE
BE GOING TO FUTURE *am/is/are going to +* base verb	The train **is going to arrive** any minute.	probable and immediate future events	at a certain time in the future
	I **am going to succeed** no matter what it takes!	strong intentions	
	Tomorrow you**'re going to be glad** that you are already packed for your trip.	predictions about future situations	
	We **are going to have** a barbecue on Sunday night.	future plans	
SIMPLE FUTURE *will* + base verb	It **will** probably **snow** tomorrow.	probable future events	
	I **will give** you a hand with that package; it looks heavy.	willingness/promises	
	Tomorrow **will be** a better day.	predictions about future situations	
FUTURE PROGRESSIVE *will* + *be* + present participle (verb + *-ing*)	I **will be interviewing** for the bank job in the morning.	events that will be in progress at a time in the future	in progress at a certain time in the future
	Mohammed **will be studying** law for the next three years.	future events that will last for a period of time	
FUTURE PERFECT *will* + *have* + past participle (verb + *-ed* or irregular verb)	He **will have finished** his degree before his sister starts hers in 2001.	before a certain time in the future	future events happening before other future events
FUTURE PERFECT PROGRESSIVE *will* + *have* + *been* + present participle (verb + *-ing*)	By the year 2000, my family **will have been living** in the U.S. for ten years.	up until a certain time in the future	continuous and/or repeated actions continuing into the future

APPENDIX 2   Forms of Passive Verbs

All passive verbs are formed with *be* + or *get* + past participle.

SIMPLE PRESENT *am/is/are* (or *get*) + past participle	That movie **is reviewed** in today's newspaper. The garbage **gets picked up** once a week.
PRESENT PROGRESSIVE *am/is/are* + *being* (or *getting*) + past participle	The possibility of life on Mars **is being explored**. We **are getting asked** to do too much!
SIMPLE PAST *was/were* (or *got*) + past participle	The butterflies **were observed** for five days. Many homes **got destroyed** during the fire.
PAST PROGRESSIVE *was/were* + *being* (or *getting*) + past participle	The Olympics **were being broadcast** worldwide. She **was getting beaten** in the final trials.
PRESENT PERFECT *has/have* + *been* (or *gotten*) + past participle	The information **has been sent**. Did you hear he**'s gotten fired** from his job?
PRESENT PERFECT PROGRESSIVE *has* + *been* + *being* (or *getting*) + past participle	This store **has been being remodeled** for six months now! I wonder if they'll ever finish. It looks as though the tires on my car **have been getting worn** by these bad road conditions.
PAST PERFECT *had* + *been* (or *gotten*) + past participle	The National Anthem **had** already **been sung** when we entered the baseball stadium. He was disappointed to learn that the project **hadn't gotten completed** in his absence.
FUTURE *will* + *be* (or *get*) + past participle *be going to* + past participle	The horse races **will be finished** in an hour. The rest of the corn **will get harvested** this week. The election results **are going to be announced** in a few minutes.
FUTURE PERFECT *will* + *have* + *been* (or *gotten*) + past participle	I bet most of the food **will have been eaten** by the time we get to the party. The unsold magazines **will have gotten sent** back to the publishers by now.
FUTURE PERFECT PROGRESSIVE *will* + *have* + *been* + *being* (or *getting*) + past participle	Our laundry **will have been getting dried** for over an hour by the time we come back. I'm sure it will be ready to take out then. NOTE: The *be* form of this passive tense is quite rare. Even the *get* form is not very common.

(Continued)

PRESENT MODAL VERBS modal (*can*, *may*, *should*, etc.) + be (or *get*) + past participle	A different chemical **could be substituted** in this experiment. Don't stay outside too long. You **may get burned** by the blazing afternoon sun.
PAST MODAL VERBS modal (*can*, *may*, *should*, etc.) + *have* + been (or *gotten*) + past participle	All of our rock specimens **should have been identified** since the lab report is due. The file **might have gotten erased** through a computer error.

APPENDIX 3   Sentence Connectors

MEANING	CONNECTORS

Addition
    Simple addition
    Emphatic addition
    Intensifying addition
	also, in addition, furthermore, moreover, what is more (what's more), as well, besides in fact, as a matter of fact, actually

Alternative	on the other hand, alternatively
Exemplifying	for example, e.g., for instance, especially, in particular, to illustrate, as an example
Identifying	namely, specifically
Clarifying	that is, i.e., in other words, I mean
Similarity	similarly, likewise, in the same way
Contrast	however, in contrast, on the other hand, in fact
Concession	even so, however, nevertheless, nonetheless, despite (+ *noun phrase*), in spite of (+ *noun phrase*), on the other hand
Effects/Results	accordingly, as a result, as a result of (+ *noun phrase*), because of (+ *noun phrase*), due to (+ *noun phrase*), consequently, therefore, thus, hence
Purpose	in order to (+ *verb*), with this in mind, for this purpose

Appendix 4A   Overview of Gerunds and Infinitives

Examples	Explanations
	Infinitives (*to* + verb) or gerunds (verb + *ing*) can have various functions in a sentence:
(a) **To know many languages** would thrill me. (b) **Speaking English** is fun.	• subject
(c) His dream was **to sail around the world.** (d) Her hobby is **weaving baskets.**	• subject complement
(e) Paco hopes **to see the play.** (f) Carol remembered **mailing the package.**	• object
(g) By **studying hard,** you can enter a good school. (h) Thank you for **helping me.**	• object of preposition (gerunds)
(i) I don't understand the need **to take a ten-minute break.** (j) The instruction **to wear safety goggles** has saved many people's eyes.	• noun complement (infinitives)
(k) I am sorry **to inform you of the delay.** (l) They were pleased **to meet you.**	• adjective complement (infinitives following adjectives)

Appendix 4B   Verbs Followed by Infinitives and Gerunds

to + verb

EXAMPLE: Julia hates to be late.

List A

As mentioned in Unit 18, Focus 4, some of the verbs in List A may also take gerund if an actual, vivid or fulfilled action is intended. (Example: Julia hates being late.)

VERBS OF EMOTION

care	loathe
desire	love
hale	regret
like	yearn

VERBS OF CHOICE OR INTENTION

agree	plan
choose	prefer
decide	prepare
deserve	propose
expect	refuse
hope	want
intend	wish
need	

VERBS OF INITIATION, COMPLETION, AND INCOMPLETION

begin	manage
cease	neglect
commence	start
fail	try
get	undertake
hesitate	

VERBS OF REQUEST AND THEIR RESPONSES

demand	swear
offer	threaten
promise	vow

VERBS OF MENTAL ACTIVITY

forget	learn
know how	remember

INTRANSITIVE VERBS

appear	seem
happen	tend

OTHER VERBS

afford (can't afford)	continue
arrange	pretend
claim	wait

List B

object + *to* + verb

EXAMPLE: She reminded us to be quiet.

VERBS OF COMMUNICATION		VERBS OF INSTRUCTION	
advise	permit	encourage	teach
ask*	persuade	help	train
beg*	promise*	instruct	
challenge	remind		
command	require		
convince	tell		
forbid	warn		
invite	urge		
order			

OTHER VERBS		VERBS OF CAUSATION	
expect*	prepare*	allow	get
trust	want*	cause	hire
		force	
* Can follow pattern A also.			

List C

verb + *-ing*

EXAMPLE: Trinh enjoys playing tennis.

Note that when the subject of the gerund is stated, it is in possessive form.

       We enjoyed his telling us about his adventures.

VERBS OF INITIATION, COMPLETION AND INCOMPLETION		VERBS OF COMMUNICATION	
avoid	give up	admit	mention
begin	postpone	advise	recommend
cease	quit	deny	suggest
complete	risk	discuss	urge
delay	start	encourage	
finish	stop		
get through	try		

(*Continued*)

VERBS OF ONGOING ACTIVITY

continue	keep
can't help	keep on
practice	

VERBS OF EMOTION

appreciate	like
dislike	love
enjoy	mind (don't mind)
hate	

VERBS OF MENTAL ACTIVITY

anticipate	recall
consider	remember
forget	see (can't see)
imagine	understand
miss	resent
prefer	resist
regret	tolerate
can't stand	

APPENDIX 5   Preposition Clusters

in + noun + *of*	*on* + noun + *of*	*in* + *the* + noun + *of*	*on* + *the* + noun + *of*
in case of	on account of	in the course of	on the advice of
in charge of	on behalf of	in the event of	on the basis of
in place of	on top of	in the habit of	on the part of
in lieu of	on grounds of	in the name of	on the strength of
in favor of		in the process of	on the face of

Other Combinations

in by means of	in return for	at odds with	with the exception of
with respect to	in addition to	for the sake of	

Appendix 6A   General Types of Relative Clauses

Example:	Noun Phrase in Main Clause	Relative Pronoun in Relative Clause
(a) <u>The contract</u> **that** was signed yesterday is now valid. *(S S)*	Subject	Subject
(b) <u>The contract</u> **that** he signed yesterday is now valid. *(S O)*	Subject	Object
(c) I have not read <u>the contract</u> **that** was signed yesterday. *(O S)*	Object	Subject
(d) I have not read <u>the contract</u> **that** he signed yesterday. *(O O)*	Object	Object

Appendix 6B   Relative Clauses Modifying Subjects

Example:	Types of Noun in Main Clause	Relative Pronouns	Function of Relative Pronoun
(a) A person **who/that** sells houses is a realtor.	person	who/that	subject
(b) The secretary **whom/that** she hired is very experienced.		whom/that	object of verb
(c) The employees **to whom** she denied a pay raise have gone on strike.		whom	object of preposition
(d) Clerks **whose** paychecks were withheld must go to the payroll office.		whose (relative determiner)	possessive determiner
(e) The mansions **that/which** were sold last week were expensive.	thing or animal	that/which	subject
(f) The computer **that/which** they purchased operated very efficiently.		that/which	object of verb
(g) The division **whose** sales reach the million-dollar point will win a bonus.		whose (relative determiner)	possessive determiner

Appendix 6C   Patterns of Relative Adverbial Clauses

RELATIVE ADVERBS WITH HEAD NOUNS

HEAD NOUN	RELATIVE ADVERB	CLAUSE
a place	where	you can relax
a time	when	I can call you
a reason	why	you should attend

RELATIVE ADVERBS WITHOUT HEAD NOUNS

RELATIVE ADVERB	CLAUSE
Where	he lives
When	the term starts
Why	I called
How	she knows

HEAD NOUNS WITHOUT RELATIVE ADVERBS

HEAD NOUN	CLAUSE
the place	we moved to
the time	I start school
the reason	they left
the way	you do this

Appendix 7A   Verb Complements

that	for ... to	's gerund	Type
(a) **That** Tom spent the whole day shopping surprised us.	(b) **For** Tom **to** spend the whole day shopping would surprise us.	(c) Tom's **spending** the whole day shopping surprised us.	SUBJECT basic order
(d) It surprised us **that** Tom spent the whole day shopping.	(e) It would surprise us **for** Tom **to** spend the whole day shopping.	(f) It surprised us— Tom's **spending** the whole day shopping. (When this structure occurs, there is a pause between the main clause and the complement.)	complement after *it* + verb
(g) We hope **that** the children take the bus.	(h) We hope **for** the children **to** take the bus.	OBJECT (i) not applicable	indicative form
(j) Ms. Sanchez suggests **that** he wait in the lobby.	(k) not applicable	(l) not applicable	subjunctive form

Appendix 7B   Adjective Complements

that	for ... to	's gerund	Type
(a) **That** Lisa went to the meeting was important.	(b) **For** Lisa **to** go to the meeting was important.	(c) Lisa's **going** to the meeting was important.	SUBJECT basic order
(d) It was important **that** Lisa went to the meeting.	(e) It was important **for** Lisa **to** go to the meeting.	(f) It was important— Lisa's **going** to the meeting. (When this structure occurs there is a pause between the main clause and the complement.)	complement after *it* + verb

(*Continued*)

Appendix 7B   Adjective Complements

APPENDIX 7   Complement Patterns

that	*for ... to*	*'s gerund*	*Type*
(g) Mr. Walker is happy **that she works** at the company.	(h) Mr. Walker is happy **for** her **to** work at the company. (This structure only occurs with a subset of adjectives like *ready, anxious, happy, eager,* etc.)	(i) not applicable	PREDICATE indicative form
(j) Chong demands **that she be** on time.	(k) not applicable	(l) not applicable	subjunctive form

Base Form	Simple Past	Past Participle	Base Form	Simple Past	Past Participle
arise	arose	arisen	leave	left	left
awake	awoke	awoken	let	let	let
bet	bet	bet	lie	lay	lain
beat	beat	beaten	lose	lost	lost
become	became	become	make	made	made
begin	began	begun	mean	meant	meant
bite	bit	bitten	meet	met	met
bleed	bled	bled	pay	paid	paid
blow	blew	blown	put	put	put
break	broke	broken	read	read	read
bring	brought	brought	ride	rode	ridden
build	built	built	ring	rang	rung
buy	bought	bought	rise	rose	risen
catch	caught	caught	run	ran	run
choose	chose	chosen	say	said	said
come	came	come	see	saw	seen
cost	cost	cost	sell	sold	sold
cut	cut	cut	send	sent	sent
do	did	done	set	set	set
draw	drew	drawn	shake	shook	shaken
dream	dreamt/dreamed	dreamt/dreamed	shine	shone/shined	shone/shined
drink	drank	drunk	shut	shut	shut
drive	drove	driven	sing	sang	sung
eat	ate	eaten	sink	sank	sunk
fall	fell	Fallen	sit	sat	sat
feel	felt	felt	sleep	slept	slept
fight	fought	fought	speak	spoke	spoken
find	found	found	spend	spent	spent
fly	flew	flown	stand	stood	stood
forget	forgot	forgotten	steal	stole	stolen
forgive	forgave	forgiven	strike	struck	struck
freeze	froze	frozen	swing	swung	swung
get	got	gotten	swim	swam	swum
give	gave	given	take	took	taken
go	went	gone	teach	taught	taught
grow	grew	grown	tear	tore	torn
hang	hung	hung	tell	told	told
hear	heard	beard	think	thought	thought
hide	hid	hidden	throw	threw	thrown
hit	hit	hit	understand	understood	understood
hold	held	held	wake	woke	woken
hurt	hurt	hurt	wear	wore	worn
keep	kept	kept	win	won	won
know	knew	known	wind	wound	wound
lay	laid	laid	write	wrote	written
lead	led	led			

ANSWER KEY
(for puzzles and problems only)

UNIT 6

Opening Task Answer Key, page 108

Answers and Explanations

Match each answer with one of the eight statements in Step 1 on page 109.

_____ a. The statement about the extent to which speakers look at their partners is true. Women do look at their partners more than men do. One reason for this may be that women often listen more.

_____ b. This statement is true. Women generally display more animated behavior. Such behavior may include facial expressions, intensity of eye contact and gestures.

_____ c. Most studies indicate that women are more likely to reveal personal information about themselves, so this statement is true . However, in work situations, a subordinate may reveal more information to a superior than the superior reveals to a subordinate; in these situations, the pattern may be reversed.

_____ d. The popular belief that women talk more than men is actually not true, so this statement is false. In classrooms, offices, group discussions and two-person conversations, men talk more than women do. The tendency for men to talk more has been revealed in experimental research studies.

_____ e. This is another false statement as men are more likely than women to answer questions that were not asked of them.

_____ f. The distributions of interruptions are even when women talk with women and when men talk with men. However, when men talk with women, research shows that men tend to interrupt much more than women do, so this claim can be considered true.

_____ g. If you guessed false, you are correct! Research indicates that women are much more likely to smile in many different social situations than men. This does not mean women are happier in such situations, but they return smiles more frequently when people smile at them.

_____ h. Research at a hospital and in manufacturing firms showed that female and male managers did not differ in their friendliness to subordinates. In these contexts, women managers were not more emotionally open, so the statement is false.

UNIT 25

Answers of Opening Task (page 440)

a) oldest, b) middle, c) only, d) youngest, e) middle, f) only, g) oldest, h) youngest, i) oldest, j) only, k) youngest, l) middle

EXERCISES (second parts)

List of Words for Short-Term Memory Experiment (page 61)

book, hand, street, tree, sand, rose, box, face, pencil, nail, pan, dog, door, school, shoe, cloud, watch, lamp, stair, glue, bottle, card, movie, match, hammer, dance, hill, basket, house, river

Definition of the Serial Position Effect (page 61)

If a person is asked to recall a list of words in any order immediately after the list is presented, recall of words at the beginning and end of the list is usually best; words in the middle of a list are not retained as well. This observation is based on a model of learning that assumes the first words are remembered well because they are rehearsed and because short term memory at that point is relatively empty. The last words are remembered well because they are still in the short-term memory' if the person tries to recall immediately.

Opening Task (page 134)

Student B

Guess the Correct Answer:

1. (a) seahorse, (b) boa constrictor, (c) Canadian goose
2. (a) *War and Peace* by Leo Tolstoy, (b) *The Great Gatsby* by F Scott Fitzgerald, (c) *Pride and Prejudice* by Jane Austen
3. (a) Thomas Edison, (b) Richard Nixon, (c) Henry Thoreau
4. (a) mucker, (b) hooker inspector, (c) belly builder

Create a Definition: (* indicates the correct answer)

5. a fly
   It is actually classified as a beetle.
   (a) dragonfly, (b) flycatcher, *(c) firefly
6. a person
   He or she pretends to be someone else.
   (a) cornball, *(b) imposter, (c) daytripper

(Continued)

7. a jar
    Ancient Greeks and Romans used it to carry wine.
    *(a) amphora, (b) amulet, (c) aspartame
8. a piece of clothing
    It is composed of loose trousers gathered about the ankles,
    (a) bodice, (b) causerie, *(c) bloomers

UNIT 8

Opening Task (page 148)

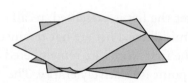

Paper
About A.D. 105

Magnetic Compas
1100s

Television
1920s

Safety Elevator
1853

Typewriter
1867

Laser
1960

Telephone
1876

Gasoline Automobile
1885

Airplane
1903

CREDITS

Photo Credits

page 0: (Top) © Digital Vision/Getty/RF, (Bottom) © David R. Frazier Photolibrary, Inc./Alamy

page 12: © IndexOpen/RF

page 13: © Digital Vision/Getty/RF

page 20: © Photos.com/RF

page 25: © Mike Goldwater/Alamy

page 28: © John Lund/Drew Kelly/Sam Diephuis/Blend Images/Getty

page 34: © IndexOpen/RF

page 38: © Megapress/Alamy

page 41: © Leonora Hamill/Stone/Getty

page 54: © Garry Gay/Alamy

page 60: © E Dygas/Photodisc Red/Getty/RF

page 66: © Photos.com/RF

page 82: © Photos.com/RF

page 87: © Sean Justice/The Image Bank/Getty

page 108: © Bruce Laurance/The Image Bank/Getty

page 120: © Visuals Unlimited/Corbis

page 122: © Photos.com/RF

page 152: © David Glick/Stone/RF

page 158: (Top) © Tom Grill/Iconica/Getty, (Middle Left) © Per Breiehagen/The Image Bank/Getty, (Middle Right) © Juniors Bildarchiv/Alamy/RF, (Bottom Left), © George Disario/CORBIS, (Bottom Right) © Image Source Black/Image Source/Getty/RF

page 173: © Image Source Pink/Image Source/Getty/RF

page 176: © Dennis O'Clair/Stone/Getty

page 177: © Pictorial Press Ltd/Alamy

page 180: © Photos.com/RF

page 181 (Top): © Photos.com/RF

page 181 (Bottom): © Angela Hampton/Alamy

page 185: © Photos.com/RF

page 190: © Photos.com/RF

page 197: © Charlotte Nation/Riser/Getty

page 210: © Photos.com/RF

page 214: © Smart.MAGNA/Alamy

page 229 (Top to Bottom): © Mary Evans Picture Library/Alamy, © Byron Schumaker/Alamy, © Lebrecht Music and Arts Photo Library/Alamy, © Classic Image/Alamy, © Liam White/Alamy, © Bernstein Associates/Getty

page 235: © Photos.com/RF

page 240: © Westend61/Alamy

page 260 (Top): © Paul Glendell/Alamy

page 260 (Bottom): © Chris Hondros/Reportage/Getty

page 267: © Jenny Matthews/Alamy

page 277: © Design Pics Inc./Alamy

page 280 (Top to Bottom): © Hulton-Deutsch Collection/CORBIS, © Fritz Fischer/dpa/Corbis, © Bettmann/CORBIS

page 288: © Gabe Palmer/Alamy

page 289: © Dirk v. Mallinckrodt/Alamy

page 295: (Top Left) © Photos.com/RF, (Top Right) © Photos.com/RF, (Bottom) © Randy Wells/Stone/Getty

page 301: © Nancy G Photography/Alamy

page 310: © Thomas Kitchin & Victoria Hurst/First Light/Getty

page 314: (Top) © AP Photo/Gregory Bull, (Bottom) © AP Photo/Peter Dejong

page 317: © Brand X Pictures/Alamy

page 323: © AP Photo / IMF, Stephen Jaffe, HO

page 330: © Philip Scalia/Alamy

page 341: © POPPERFOTO/Alamy

page 348: © AP photo

page 352 (Top to Bottom): © POPPERFOTO/Alamy, © North Wind Picture Archives/Alamy, © Photo Japan/Alamy

page 360: © John Mottershaw/Alamy

page 369: © Yellow Dog Productions/The Image Bank/Getty

page 372: (Top) © BananaStock/Alamy/RF, (Bottom) © Kevin Schafer/Alamy

page 388: © Andrew Linscott/Alamy

page 390: © Pictorial Press Ltd/Alamy

page 398: © Thinkstock/Alamy/RF

page 406: (Left) © Jennie Hart/Alamy, (Right) © altrendo images/Altrendo/Getty

page 411: © PhotoAlto/Alamy/RF

page 415: © AP Photo/Scott Audette

page 418: (Top) © Hulton Archive/Getty, (Bottom) © RON PHILLIPS/Stringer/AFP/Getty Images

page 421: © Scottish Viewpoint/Alamy

page 431: © Content Mine International/Alamy

page 436: © Pictorial Press Ltd/Alamy

page 440: © Stockdisc Classic/Alamy/RF

page 443: © Christina Kennedy/Alamy

page 449: © Visual Arts Library (London)/Alamy

page 452: © Sarma Ozols/Stone/Getty

Fine Art Credits

Unit 8

page 162: Illustration on page 162, "Eviction" is reprinted by permission of the artist Diedre Luzwick.

Text Credits

Unit 1

page 5: From Studs Terkel (1988). *The Great Divide.* New York: Pantheon Books.

Unit 2

page 12: From Farah Ahmedi with Tamim Ansary (2005). *The Story of My Life: An Afghan Girl on the Other Side of the Sky.* New York: Simon & Schuster.

page 13: From Mike Rose (2005). *Lives on the Boundary.* New York: Penguin Books.

page 16 (top): From James McBride (2006). *The Color of Water: A Black Man's Tribute to His White Mother.* New York: Penguin, 2006, pp. 80–81.

page 16 (below): From Mitch Albom (1997). *Tuesdays with Morrie: An Old Man, A Young Man and Life's Greatest Lesson.* New York: Doubleday, p. 80.

page 19: From Annie Dillard(1974). *Pilgrim at Tinker Creek.* New York: Bantam.

page 22: From James Thurber (1955). *Thurber's Dogs, A Collection of the Master's Dogs, Written and Drawn, Real and Imaginary, Living and Long Ago.* New York: Simon and Schuster.

page 23: Reprinted with permission from J. Michael Kennedy, "It's the Hottest Little Ol' Race in Texas," *Los Angeles Times,* September 2, 1991.

page 30: Reprinted by permission of the U.F.S. Inc.

page 31: From Edith Hamilton, *Mythology.* Copyright 1942 by Edith Hamilton. Copyright renewed 1969 by Dorian Fielding Reid and Doris Fielding Reid. By permission of Little, Brown and Company.

Unit 3

page 39: From *Gallup News Service,* June 3, 2005.

page 43: From *Gallup News Service,* June 3, 2005 and July 21, 1999. www.gallup.com; *The Bookseller,* April 11, 2003 p. 27(3).

page 44: Adapted from Kate Allen and John Ingulsrud, "Manga Literacy: Popular Culture and the Reading Habits of Japanese College Students," *Journal of Adolescent & Adult Literacy,* May 2003, v46, p. 674 (10).

page 52: Information from *Gallup News Service,* June 3, 2005 and July 21, 1999. www.gallup.com.

page 53: Adapted from *Reading At Risk: A Survey of Literary Reading in America.* June 2004. National Endowment for the Arts.

Unit 4

page 67: Reprinted with permission from Rosie Mestel, "Swallowing a Lie May Aid in Weight Loss, Research Suggests," *Los Angeles Times,* August 2, 2005.

page 70: Adapted from Marianne Szedgedy-Maszak, "For True Fulfillment, Seek Satisfaction, Not Happiness," *Los Angeles Times,* September 5, 2005.

page 75: From http://www.guinnessworldrecord.com/ (Accessed June, 15, 2006).

page 77: Adapted from "Decoding of Microbe's Genes Sheds Light on Odd Form of Life," *Los Angeles Times,* August 8, 1996.

Unit 5

page 84: Adapted from P. Master (1996). *Systems in English Grammar.* Englewood Cliffs, New Jersey: Prentice-Hall Regents.

page 95: Adapted from P. Master. "Teahing the English Article System, Part II: Generic Versus Specific." *English Teaching Forum.* July 1988.

page 103 (top): Adapted from J. Mann (1991). "Global AIDS: Revolution, Paradigm, Solidarity." In O. Peterson, (ed.), *Representative American Speeches,* New York: The H.W. Wilson Co.

page 103 (bottom): Adapted from S. Hall (1987). *Invisible Frontiers,* New York: The Atlantic Monthly Press.

page 104: Adapted from "Monterey Pine Struggles to Survive." In *UC MexUS News,* University of California Institute for Mexico and the United States (UC MEXUS), UC Riverside, Number 43, Spring 2006, p. 19.

Unit 6

page 109: Adapted from Gender Communications Quiz, Georgia Department of Education, http://www.glc.k12.ga.us/pandp/guidance/schoices/sc-f20.htm. (Retrieved December 15, 2005)

page 112: From Deborah Tannen (1990). *You Just Don't Understand: Women and Men in Conversation,* Harper Collins Publishers.

page 124: Reprinted by permission. © NAS North America Syndicate.

Unit 7

page 138: From Charles Keller (1979). *The Best of Rube Goldberg.* Rube Goldberg™ and © Rube Goldberg Inc. Distributed by United States.

Unit 9

page 169: The Specialty Travel Index http://www.specialtytravel.com/ (Accessed January 4, 2005).

Unit 12

page 211: Adapted from Maria Leach (1956). *The Beginning: Creation Myths around the World,* New York: Funk & Wagnalls.

page 211: Adapted from "Oceania/Polynesia Creation Myths," *Encyclopedia Mythica,* www.pantheon.org/articles/o/oceania_polynesia_creation_myths.html.

Unit 13

page 245: Adapted from nextstepmag.com, (Retrieved from www.collegeanduniversity.net 6/20/05)

page 245: From John Naisbitt and Patricia Aburdene. Megatrends 2000 Copyright © 1990 By Megatrends LTD.

page 249: From Stephen Hawking (1990). *A Brief History of Time: From the Big Bang to Black Holes,* New York: Bantam.

page 255: From "Long Bets: Accountable Predictions," www.longbets.org (Retrieved June 25, 2006).

page 270: From Colin Woodward (2005). Warming up the seas, Earth Action Network, Inc.

page 276: From Fei Ji (2004). "A Suffering Musician," in Kaplan/*Newsweek* "My Turn" Essay Competition.

page 276: Adapted from Michelle Ng (2004). "My Hands," in Kaplan/*Newsweek* "My Turn" Essay Competition.

pages 276–277: From Isaac Asimov (1974) *Earth: Our Crowded Spaceship,* Greenwich, CT: Fawcett.

Unit 17

page 321: Adapted from U.S. Immigration and Naturalization Service and Bureau of U.S. Citizenship and Immigration Service sources, (2006).

Unit 18

page 348: Adapted from D. Stewart, "The Floating World at Zero G," *Air and Space* (August/September 1991) p. 38.

Unit 20

page 382: From Michael W. Fox (1990). New York: St. Martin's Press, p. 46.

Unit 23

pages 406-407: Reprinted by permission. VALS™ SRI Consulting Business Intelligence (SRIC-BI) http://www.sric-bi.com/VALS (Accessed on June, 22, 2006).

Unit 24

page 436: Adapted from http://www.screenwriting.info/01.php

INDEX

as well as, 42
aspect in verb tense, 2–4
at first/at last, 264
attitudes, perfective infinitives used to express, 363–364

B

be
deleting relative pronouns using, 157–158
emphatic structures and, 408
fronting structures using, inversion of subject-verb in, 423, 426
future perfect progressive verbs and, 33
to have +, in modal perfect verbs, 247, 256
it-clefts using, 442–443
passive gerund using, 334–337
passive verb tenses using, 64, 65
past tense forms of, 40
perfective progressive infinitive using, 334–337
present tense forms of, 40
progressive tense and, 18
reduced relative clauses and, 142–144
supposed to have +, in modal perfect verbs, 247, 256
wh-clefts using, 453
be going to, 32
because, 231
reduced adverbial clause using, 304
subordinating conjunction use of, 213
because of, 231
before
reduced adverbial clause using, 302
subordinating conjunction use of, 213
beliefs (*See* opinions and beliefs)
besides, 215
besides that, 216
body part names, articles used with, 99–100
both/both . . . and
as correlative conjunction, 198–199
subject-verb agreement, 44
briefly, 271
but/but also
coordinating conjunction using, 213
correlative conjunctions using, 198–203
by
Ø used with, 90
passive verbs and, 64–65
stative passive verbs using, 69

C

can, passive verb tenses using, 65
can have/can't have, in modal perfect verbs, 248, 250, 256
cause and effect, reducing adverbial clauses showing, 304–305
character, *it*-clefts to express emphasis on, 449–450
characteristics, stative passive verbs to describe, 69
chronological order expressed using discourse organizers, 264–267
clarification using sentence connectors, 212
clarifying connectors, 222
classification
articles used with, 84–87
nouns for, 98
as reference words, 113
clauses

joining with correlative conjunctions, 200–202
perfect tense in, 21–24
perfective infinitives in, 354–355
relative adverbs used in, 191–192
subject-verb agreement and, 49
such used with, 125
cleft sentences, 440–454 (*See also it*-clefts; *wh*-clefts)
cohesion expressed using fronting structures, 435–436
collective nouns, subject-verb agreement using, 46–48, 51
commas, sentence connectors using, 234
communication means, Ø used with, 90
comparative structures, fronting structures and, 423, 432
completed actions
of future event, expressed using modal perfect verbs, 255
gerunds or infinitives + verbs used to express, 338
complex passive verbs, 72–75
compound prepositions, subject-verb agreement and, 42
concession connectors, 227–230
concrete generic reference using articles, 95–97
condition or state-of-being, subordinating conjunctions expressing, 213
conditionals, 280–296
advice expressed using, 294–296
even though/even if as, 292–293
exclusive conditions expressed using, 286–288
factual conditionals as, 282
fronted *only if/not unless* clauses as, 289
future conditionals as, 282
general truths expressed using, 282
habitual actions expressed using, 282
hypothetical conditionals as, 282
if . . . not vs. unless in, 290–291
if clause used in, 282
inference expressed using, 282
only if as, 286, 289
past perfect tense and, 283
simple past tense and, 283
simple present tense and, 283
subjunctive tense and, 283, 286
unless as, 286, 289
verb tenses used with, 283
conjunctions
correlative, 196–205
fronting structures and, 430–431
consequently, 231
consistency of verb tense usage, 6–7
continuing actions
past progressive tense to express, 29
present perfect tense to express, 27
simple past tense to express, 29
contractions, in modal perfect verbs, 242
contrast
connectors to express, 212, 227
fronting structures used to express, 432–434
subordinating conjunctions expressing, 213
coordinating conjunctions, 213
correlative conjunctions, 196–205
and as, 198–199
both as, 198–199
but also as, 198–203

stative passive verbs using, 69
for example, 212, 221
for instance, 221
for this purpose, 232
for which, relative adverb *vs.* relative pronoun with, 182–183
formal communication, relative clauses used in, 159–160
fractions, subject-verb agreement and, 51–54
from, in preposition cluster, 319
fronted only if/not unless clauses as conditionals, 289
fronting structures, 418–436
    adverb phrases and, 422, 428–429, 432
    adverb phrases and, inversion of subject-verb in, 422–424
    be + auxiliary verbs using, 426
    be verbs and inversion using, 423, 426
    cohesion expressed using, 435–436
    comparative structures and, 423, 432
    complex verbs and inversion using, 426
    conjunctions using, 430–431
    contrast expressed using, 432–434
    emphasis expressed using, 432–434
    focus expressed using, 432–434
    inversion (reversal) of subject-verb order when using, 422–424
    negatives using, 428–431, 433
    neither/nor used in, 430–431
    never used in, 423, 426, 428
    no used in, 428–431
    not used in, 423, 428–431
    noun phrase objects and, 430–431
    participle phrases and, 432
    past participles and, 423
    patterns of inversion for, 426–427
    present participles and, 423
    simple verbs and inversion using, 426
    so + adjective/adverb + *that* in, 423
    subject-auxiliary order for, 420–425
    subject-verb order for, 420–425
furthermore, 215
future conditionals, 282
future event, completion of expressed using modal perfect verb, 255
future perfect progressive tense, 2, 33
    passive verbs used in, 65
future perfect tense, 2
    passive verbs used in, 33, 65
future plans, expressed using perfective infinitives, 365–366
future progressive tense, 2, 32
future tense, 2, 4, 5, 32–34
    passive verbs used in, 65

G

general truths expressed using conditionals, 282
generic nouns, 98–99
generic reference using articles, 92–93
    abstract *vs.* concrete, 95–97
gerund clauses, subject-verb agreement and, 49
gerunds, 330–349
    adjective + preposition combinations using, 346–349
    as adjective complement, 332
    adjective complements used with, 332, 374, 376, 379–380
    as direct object, 332, 340–342

infinitives *vs.,* 337–339
    as noun complement, 332
    as object of preposition, 332, 346–349
    as objects of phrasal verbs, 346–349
    parallelism expressed using correlative conjunctions with, 203
    passive form of, 334–337
    perfective form of, 334–337
    possessives *('s)* used with, 343–345
    progressive form of, 334–337
    simple form of, 334–337
    as subject complement, 332
    as subject of sentence, 332
    using adjective complements, 374, 376, 379–380
get, passive verb tenses using, 64, 65
groups, *the* used with, 93
guesses about past expressed using modal perfect verbs, 250–251

H

habitual actions
    conditionals used to express, 282
    progressive tense to describe, 18
    simple past tense to express, 29
    simple present tense to express, 27
    simple tense verbs to describe, 14
    the used with, 88
have, 21, 25
    deleting relative pronouns and, 157–158
    modal perfect verb use of, 228
    passive verb tenses using, 64, 65
    past perfect tense and, 29
    perfect progressive tense and, 25
    perfect tense and, 21
    perfective infinitive and gerund using, 354
    perfective infinitives using, 354
    present tense forms, 40
    progressive tense and, 25
    reduced relative clauses and, 142–144
have not
    deleting relative pronouns and, 157–158
    reduced relative clauses and, 142–144
have/have been, in modal perfect verbs, 228
head noun identification, subject-verb agreement and, 40, 42–44
hence, 231
how
    relative adverb *vs.* relative pronoun with, 182–183
    relative adverb without head noun and, 189
    relative adverbs modifying nouns using, 191–192
however, 227, 228, 234
hypothetical conditionals, 282

I

I mean, 222
ideas
    added ideas using sentence connectors, 212
    nonrestrictive relative clauses to comment on, 172–173
    simple tense verbs to describe, 14
identification
    articles used with, 84–87
    connectors used for, 221

synonyms, as reference words, 113

T

temporary conditions
    present progressive tense to express, 27
    progressive tense to describe, 18
that and *that* clauses, 42, 49, 451
    adjective complements used in, 374–375, 376, 379–380
    cleft sentences using, 442–443
    complex passives and, 74
    demonstrative pronouns and determiners using, 110
    the fact that phrase used with noun complements, 392–393
    noun complements in subject position and, 386, 390–391
    noun complements using, 384–395
    reduced relative clauses and, 142–144
    as reference word, 110, 113, 118, 119
    relative clauses and, 150
    restrictive clauses *vs.*, in noun clauses, 389
    restrictive relative clause and, 137
    subjunctive verbs in, 400–401
    subordinating conjunction use of, 213
    which vs., in noun complements, 389
that is, 212, 222
the, 84–104
    noun phrases and, 110, 116–117
    plural nouns and, for general reference, 93–94
    as reference word, 110, 113–115, 116, 123–124
    relative adverbs modifying nouns using, 184–187
the fact that phrase used with noun complements, 392–393
the first/the last + noun, 266
the number of, 51, 52
the/a second, 266
them, as reference word, 123–124
then, 265
there
    and *be* as topic introducer in discourse, 262, 268–270
    subject-verb agreement and, 40, 55–56
therefore, 231
these/those
demonstrative pronouns and determiners using, 110
as reference words, 110, 113, 118
they/them, as reference words, 110, 116
this
    demonstrative pronouns and determiners using, 110
    as reference word, 110, 113, 118, 121
though, 213, 227, 234
thoughts (*See* emotions and thoughts; opinions and beliefs)
thus, 231
time
    Ø used with, 90
    chronological order expressed using discourse organizers, 264–267
    completion of future event expressed using modal perfect verbs, 255
    gerunds or infinitives + verbs used to express, 334
    head nouns without relative adverbs in, 189–190
    inferring/deducing from past evidence using modal perfect verbs, 248–249
    it-clefts to express emphasis on, 449–450
    judgment of past expressed using modal perfect verbs, 244–246

perfect tense to describe, 21
progressive tense to describe, 18
reducing adverbial clauses and, 302–303
reference to, 118
relative adverb without head noun and, 188
subordinating conjunctions expressing, 213
time sequences using sentence connectors, 212
time frames, 2–4
    future tense, 32–34
    moment of focus for, 4
    past tense, 29–31
    present tense, 27–28
    shifts in, 7, 8–9
    simple tense verbs to establish, 14
to
    complex passive verbs using, 72
    future tense and, 32
    infinitive use of (*See* infinitives)
    perfective infinitive used with, 334–337
    reduced relative clauses and, 142–144
to begin/start with, 265
to conclude, 266
to illustrate, 221
to summarize, 271
together with, 42
too, 368–369
too, used in perfective infinitives, 368–369
topics
    discourse organizers to signal shifts in/introduce, 262, 273
    preposition clusters to introduce, 326–327
transitive adjectives and noun complements, 393–395
transportation, Ø used with, 90
truths (*See* opinions and beliefs)

U

uncertainty about past events, perfective infinitives to express, 365–366
units of measure, subject-verb agreement and, 48
unless, 213, 294
    as conditional, 286, 289
    if . . . not vs., in conditionals, 290–291
unreal conditions expressed using modal perfect verbs, 252–254
until, subordinating conjunction use of, 213
urging, subjunctive verbs in *that* clauses to express, 400, 401

V

verb phrases, 98
verbs, 12–34
    adjective complements linking, 374–375
    aspect in, 2–4
    consistency of usage in, 6–7
    future perfect progressive tense, 2, 33
    future perfect tense, 2, 33
    future progressive tense, 2, 32
    future tense, 2, 4, 5, 14, 32–34
    gerunds as objects of, 346–349
    infinitives *vs.* gerunds in use of, 337–339
    inversion (reversal) of subject-verb order in fronting structures, 422–424
    irregular forms of, 29